Advance Pr

ANOTHER Fren

"Kevin Barrett is one of the few public intellectuals who understand the pivotal and devastating role being played ongoing today by history's dead-liest deceits: false flag operations. He has edited two must-read books on the highest profile false flags of 2015: *We Are NOT Charlie Hebdo!* and *ANOTHER French False Flag?* Featuring 41 leading public intellectuals, these two volumes contribute significantly to our single most important task: revealing the expansion of Operation Gladio into a global illusion, an integrated false flag blanket fraud called 'the war on terror.' This now is being crystallized into a war on all Muslims. Operation Gladio 2 is com-prised of a series of false flag ops arguably beginning with 9/11 plus all the ones that have followed, including the Madrid train bombings in 2004 and London 7/7, the Bali and Mumbai bombings, and most recently the two 2015 Paris attacks and their sequel in San Bernardino. These ongoing frauds robotize members of the public with such fear that they are in dan-ger of becoming ready to follow a new fuhrer and move 'the West' toward the worst manifestation of fascism: resurgent Nazism. Exposing false flag ops can diminish the false fears they generate and open the way toward a safer and saner planet."

   – Barrie Zwicker, Canadian media critic, filmmaker and author

"We must read and absorb and become the knowledge of the truth. And the best first step is Kevin Barrett's brilliant work contained in these pages. As a career counterterrorism specialist, I discovered this final battle, when I learned that the real terrorists are not the patsies blamed by the media. Be-hind them lurk the hidden operatives of the Deep State. We must work together to expose false flag terror, end the tyrannical reign of the Deep State, and take back our free Republic. Educate yourself by reading, and nourish your souls through praying and fellowship with like-minded souls. Start by reading *Another French False Flag?* — and get ready to help save America."

   – Scott Bennett, former US Army Intelligence Officer, U.S. Special Operations Command, U.S. Central Command, the State Department Coor-dinator for Counterterrorism, and other government agencies.

"This is an important book, an impressive collection by a group of out-standing scholars and researchers. We too often forget the history of terrorism in Europe is a history of false attributions. This refreshingly hon-est examination of the facts is vital for anyone seeking to understand the world around us today."

   – Richard Curtis, Ph.D.

SIFTING & WINNOWING

"WHATEVER MAY BE THE LIMITATIONS WHICH TRAMMEL INQUIRY ELSEWHERE, WE BELIEVE THAT THE GREAT STATE UNIVERSITY OF WISCONSIN SHOULD EVER ENCOURAGE THAT CONTINUAL AND FEARLESS SIFTING AND WINNOWING BY WHICH ALONE THE TRUTH CAN BE FOUND." TAKEN FROM A REPORT OF THE BOARD OF REGENTS IN 1894. MEMORIAL, CLASS OF 1910.

BOOKS

ANOTHER French False Flag?
Bloody Tracks from Paris to San Bernardino

Edited by Kevin Barrett

Library of Congress Cataloging-in-Publication Data
ANOTHER French False Flag? Bloody Tracks
from Paris to San Bernardino
edited by Kevin Barrett
ISBN 978-0-9961430-1-1

1. November 13 Terrorist Attacks, 2015. 2. War on Terrorism—Political aspects. 3. France—Politics and government, 2015. 4. History of
France—Modern—21st Century

Front cover art by David Dees, ddees.com
Back cover and interior art by Anthony Freda, anthonyfreda.com
Cover design by Sandra Taylor, The Graphic Page

CONTENTS

Introduction: ANOTHER French False Flag! Why SHOULDN'T We Jump to Conclusions? *Kevin Barrett* **9**

Part 1: What Really Happened?

1. Paris 11/13/15: The Matrix Extends Its Reach *Paul Craig Roberts* **23**

2. Decoding the Paris Attacks: ISIS Blowback or French-Israeli False Flag? *Brandon Martinez* **37**

3. Paris Again Hit by Fictional Terror *Nick Kollerstrom* **55**

4. Anatomy of a False Flag *Stephen Lendman* **69**

Part 2: False Flags and Deep States: Theory and Practice

5. Deep States: A Threat to Democracy? *Philip Giraldi* **77**

6. Was Paris 11/13 a False Flag Event? A Matrix for Evaluating Possibilities *Robert David Steele* **83**

7. Academic Complicity in the Global War of False Flag Terrorism *Anthony Hall* **91**

8. The War of Terrorism: Drugs, Death Squads, Class Rule and Resistance *Gearóid O Colmáin* **105**

9. Wars: US Militarist Factions in Command *James Petras* **121**

10. The Urgency of Now *Barry Kissin* **137**

11. Why Paris 11/13? *Mujahid Kamran* **145**

Part 3: Who IS ISIS?

12. We Are ISIS *Ken O'Keefe* *161*

13. How We Know ISIS Was "Made in the USA" *Jim Fetzer* *165*

14. All This Has Nothing to Do with Islam *Alain Soral* *169*

15. Calling Takfir on Takfiris and Terrorism *Rasheed al Ḥājj* *177*

16. The Khawarij Phenomenon: A False-Flag War
on the Muslim Ummah *Zaid Hamid* *185*

17. France: The Guinea Pig for War on Russia? *Imran N. Hosein* *203*

18. The Terror Which Could End All Western Democracies
(But Who Killed the French Marianne?) *Catherine Shakdam* *207*

Part 4: Media Lies, Bias, Cover-Ups and Complicity

19. The Role of the Media in Agenda-Driven Coverage
of Terrorist Events *A.K. Dewdney* *219*

20. Covering 11/13: The Stagecraft of "Reliable Sources"
James Tracy *227*

21. The Paris Attacks and the White Lives Matter Movement
Ajamu Baraka *243*

Part 5: False Flags and the New World Order

22. Signs of Satanism: Occult Fingerprints All Over Paris Attacks
Ole Dammegard *249*

23. Cognitive Dissonance: Media Masks Ghastly Truth Behind Terror
Henry Makow *259*

Part 6: Questioning the False Flag Paradigm

24. False Flag? Reflections on Speculation, Certainty, and Resistance
Gilad Atzmon **267**

25: Interpreting Our Long History of 9/11s
Eric Walberg **275**

26: False Flag Paradigm Shift: A Response to Atzmon and Walberg
Kevin Barrett **285**

Part 7: Youth for Truth: A Generational Awakening?

27. Today, Terrorism Is Our Common Worry: A Message from the Leader of the Islamic Republic of Iran to the Youth of Europe and North America *Ayatollah Seyyed Ali Khamenei* **293**

28. US Imperialism and the Wanton Destruction of Cultures: An Open Letter to Iran's Ayatollah Khamenei *Anthony Hall* **299**

Contributors **305**

Notes **313**

INTRODUCTION:
ANOTHER FRENCH FALSE FLAG! WHY **SHOULDN'T** WE JUMP TO CONCLUSIONS?

Kevin Barrett

This book's title poses a question: "ANOTHER French false flag?" It is a question that only you, the reader, can answer.

Next question: Do you think I was being rash, rushing to judgment, overlooking due diligence, or otherwise acting with unreasonable haste when I heard about the 11/13/15 Paris attacks—and immediately assumed, intuited, and felt deep in my gut, even before I began researching the event, that it was in all probability yet another false flag operation?

I did not react that way to the Charlie Hebdo attacks in January. On the contrary, my first reaction had been to accept the official story that angry Muslims shot up the offices of a magazine known for its obscene anti-Islam provocations. It was only when countervailing evidence began to roll in that I changed my mind. The sickening realization that I had been fooled fueled the righteous anger that led me to edit and publish *We Are NOT Charlie Hebdo: Free Thinkers Question the French 9/11*—which came out March 1ˢᵗ 2005, less than three months after the January 7ᵗʰ attacks.

But on November 13ᵗʰ, 2015, I wasn't fooled for a nanosecond. Here is my first-reaction account, published a few hours after the Paris shootings. (I wrote it on the bus home from Chicago after flying in from Paris, having left the City of Light just hours ahead of the initial attack at the Stade de France. The article went viral and passed 100,000 reads within a few days.)

ANOTHER French False Flag?[1]

By Kevin Barrett, Veterans Today Editor

I left Paris Friday at noon. As my plane landed in Chicago at 3:15 p.m. local time (10:15 p.m. Paris time) the media was screaming "Terrorists kill dozens in central Paris; hostages taken." The French military was occupying the City of Lights. It looks like another Charlie Hebdo situation, only bigger and bloodier.

By an eerie coincidence—at least I hope it was a coincidence— I had spent Thursday evening walking around central Paris being interviewed about January's Charlie Hebdo false flag attacks. Little did I suspect that in less than 24 hours an even bigger terror attack would rock the city.

Filmmaker Vincent LaPierre of Egalité et Reconciliation filmed me at the Fontaine St. Michel, in front of the Notre Dame cathedral, and in various Left Bank locations as well as at E&R headquarters with leader Alain Soral. As I pontificated to the camera about false flag terror in general and Charlie Hebdo in particular, passersby looked on with interest; one customer at the outdoor café table next to us told us she loved what she was hearing and appreciated the work we were doing.

Since we now know the Charlie Hebdo attack was a Gladio 2 false flag by the usual suspects (NATO hardliners and Zionists),[2] can we safely make the same assumption about these new Friday the 13th Paris atrocities?

I think we can. Almost every really big, spectacular terror attack turns out, after extensive critical examination, to have been the usual state-sponsored false-flag stuff.[3] There is no reason to think this one will be any different.

The first question, as always, is: Who gains? And the answer, as always, is: Authoritarian insiders. Zionists. Militarists. Islamophobes. New World Order-Out-Of-Chaos freaks.

Speaking of which, the order-out-of-chaos thing is going into overdrive. Between the destruction of several Middle Eastern countries, refugees flooding Europe, preparations for World War III vs. Russia and China, and ongoing false flag terror, it seems the "creative destruction" people are staying busy.

The authorities will surely use these new attacks in the same way they used Charlie Hebdo: As an excuse to shut down critical thinking and dissent. They may even try to prevent me from returning to Paris on December 11th to present a paper exposing the Charlie Hebdo false flag at a mainstream academic conference.[4]

After all, I was already prevented once from entering Canada to give a talk on *We Are NOT Charlie Hebdo: Free Thinkers Question the French 9/11*. France's president Hollande has attacked Charlie Hebdo "conspiracy theorists" in harsh terms, and his think tank, the Jean Jaurés Institute, named me as one of the world's top five "conspiracy intellectuals" to watch out for.[5]

If I were a truly paranoid conspiracy theorist, or conspiracy intellectual, or whatever, I would think somebody staged these new attacks just as I was leaving Paris and planning to return one month later because… well, because they're afraid that my book *We Are NOT Charlie Hebdo* is picking up steam and threatening to expose the state-sponsored crimes of last January. According to this paranoid interpretation, the Charlie Hebdo high perps are "fleeing forward" into even bigger chaos and an even bigger crackdown on freedom…especially the freedom to seek the truth about false flag terror.

This new attack may throw a monkey wrench into my efforts to get *We Are NOT Charlie Hebdo* translated into French—which was one of my items of business in Paris.[6]

It may also impede efforts to save Mohamed Boutiche, a witness to the fact that the Kouachi brothers, the designated Charlie Hebdo patsies, were intelligence assets. I just got word that Boutiche has been jailed and will be audited for trial on November 23rd.[7] The authorities will undoubtedly use the new wave of terror hysteria to try to railroad Boutiche and keep a lid on his Charlie Hebdo revelations.

And let's not forget that the EU just instituted mandatory labeling of products from the Occupied Territories; the Zionists are throwing a gargantuan hissy-fit…just like right before the Charlie Hebdo attacks.[8] Beware of Zionists throwing hissy-fits.

So the least that can be said is that the timing seems extremely suspicious.

Then again, maybe it's all just coincidence. Maybe this is an actual attack by angry Muslims. Maybe there is no state sponsorship. Maybe this time, for once, it actually ISN'T a false flag.

But what would "radical Muslims" gain? It's already being blamed on ISIS; yet that makes no sense, since Russia, not France, is fighting ISIS in Syria. And ISIS, of course, is a fabricated synthetic-terror group, not a real Muslim group, anyway.

To believe the official "Muslims did it" stories of the big terror attacks starting with 9/11, you'd have to think of the ostensible Muslim perps as complete idiots, utterly incapable of strategic thinking, desperate to hand the Zionist neocons exactly the kind of PR they want.

Sure, there are undoubtedly some stupid angry Muslims out there. But they're likely to be patsies, not orchestrators.

So although it's too early to say for sure, I think we can tentatively assume that this Friday the 13th massacre in Paris is just the latest in a long series of false-flag spectacles. And if we let the perps get away with this one, as they've gotten away with all the others, we can expect more of the same.

San Bernardino Sequel: "More of the Same" Comes Sooner Than Expected

While this book was in preparation, an apparent sequel to the 11/13/15 Paris attack occurred in San Bernardino, California. On December 2nd the corporate media informed us that fourteen people had been killed, and more than twenty injured, in a shooting at Inland Regional Center, a facility for disabled people.

How was San Bernardino a sequel to Paris? Laurent Guyénot and Ole Dammegard have shown that the Charlie Hebdo shootings had a prequel (the March 2012 shootings falsely attributed to Mohammed Merah) and a sequel (the February 14th 2015 shootings attributed to Omar Abdel Hamid El-Hussein).[9] This series of three false flag publicity stunts followed the same script and had the same themes. In all three cases, an attack on patriotic national symbols and "freedom" was quickly followed by an apparently unrelated follow-up attack on Jews. The scriptwriters' message was obvious: "They hate our freedoms, and they hate Jews, so we must rally behind Israel in its existential war on Islam and Muslims in general and Palestinians in particular." This is precisely what Netanyahu proclaimed, in so many words, when he barged into Paris and Copenhagen uninvited in the immediate aftermath of those two attacks. To many observers, including Barry Chamish, it looked like Bibi was brazenly taking credit for the barely-veiled false flag attacks he had repeatedly threatened, and which so obviously served his political and geostrategic interests.

With the Paris and San Bernardino false flags, the theme has shifted and the script has changed. The victims are no longer French soldiers and anti-Islam cartoonists; now they are ordinary citizens who have done nothing to offend Muslims. The targets of both late-2015 attacks were selected to evoke sympathy and outrage, and turn key demographic groups against Muslims and Palestinians. In Paris, hip young middle class people at cafés and rock concerts were gunned down for no apparent reason. (As Alain Soral explains in his essay in this book, the Paris victims belonged to the precise social group that has been the backbone of pro-Palestine sentiment in France.) And in San Bernardino, the victims consisted of staff at a facility for disabled people—not exactly the demographic one would expect "radical Muslims" to hate, but a perfect group to target if one's purpose is to brainwash Americans into hating Muslims.

As in the two 2015 Paris attacks, the alleged radical Islamic terrorists in San Bernardino had odd connections to Israel. Syed Raheel Farook, the brother of accused shooter Syed Rizwan Farouk, and alleged accomplice Enrique Marquez were married to a very interesting pair of Russian-Israeli sisters, Tatiana and Mariya Chernykh.[10] As of this writing, speculation about who was manipulating whom on behalf of which intelligence agency remains just that, speculation.

Once again, my first reaction to the news of the shooting was a strong presumption that this would turn out to be another false flag. Sure enough, within a day or two, that conclusion was reinforced by considerable evidence. Here is my initial article about the San Bernardino shooting, written four days after the fact, which quickly garnered more than 300,000 reads:

San Bernardino shooting story shot full of holes by patsies' attorney: Ten questions THEY don't want you to ask

By Kevin Barrett, Veterans Today Editor

As CNN has reported, an attorney in the case, David Chesley, has stated bluntly that the government's account of what happened in San Bernardino "does not add up."[11]

One thing we know for sure: The government is lying. So what really happened? Here are some obvious questions that the mainstream media is afraid to ask.

1) Since the windows of the couple's SUV were found rolled up and blown out, how could the couple have initiated a gun battle with police through rolled-up windows? Nobody is going to fire assault weapons through rolled-up vehicle windows. The logical inference is that the police executed these people in cold blood. There was no "shootout."

2) Both victims were found dead in handcuffs. Are we supposed to believe that they initiated a gun battle with police while wearing handcuffs and shooting through rolled-up windows?! It seems that the two patsies were handcuffed, set in place for execution according to a scripted plan, and summarily shot dead.

3) If the alleged shooters really "had contact with Syrian al Qaeda-affiliated group AND al Shabaab in Somalia"[12] why wouldn't the authorities make every effort to capture them alive so they could be interrogated, and their alleged terror network dismantled? This same question comes up every time the authorities summarily execute terror suspects and/or witnesses —Bin Laden, Mohamed Merah, the Charlie Hebdo patsies, Boston

bombing suspect Tamerlan Tsarnaev and key witness Ibragim Todashev...

4) If the couple was really part of a terrorist network, would the FBI have let the media ransack the crime scene?

5) If this supposed radical Muslim Bonnie-and-Clyde acted alone, who was the third gunman reported by multiple eyewitnesses?[13]

6) Could the five foot tall, under-125-pound woman really have handled: A tactical vest • Body armor • Smith & Wesson M&P .223 Caliber Assault rifle • Magazine re-loading clips • Hand gun • Spare pipe bomb, detonator...and then tweeted her allegiance to Islamic State exactly one minute after the shooting began? "She posted a pledge of allegiance to ISIS leader Abu Bakr al-Baghdadi on Facebook while the shooting was happening, three U.S. officials familiar with the investigation told CNN."

7) Why would Inland Regional Center conduct active shooter drills "every month or so" as reported by the *Los Angeles Times*?[14]

8) Is it just a coincidence that the only center for disabled people in the world that conducts active shooter drills every month (I challenge readers to find another one) happened to be the place where either (a) a huge mass shooting just happened to erupt, or (b) a drill went live?

9) And if it's just a coincidence, were the 46 drills of 9/11[15] also a coincidence, Peter Power's terror drills on 7/7/2005[16] yet another coincidence, the Boston Marathon bomb drills[17] one more coincidence, the multiple-location active shooter exercises in Paris on 11/13 just another coincidence[18] ... and to accept all this "coincidence," do you have to be a batshit-crazy coincidence theorist?

10) If this were really "radical Islamic terrorism," why would the perpetrators target a facility for disabled people, rather than high-level individuals who are responsible for the murder of more than a million Muslims since the 9/11/2001 neocon propaganda stunt?

If we ever hear: "This just in! Radical Muslim terrorists have slaughtered Dick Cheney, George W. Bush, Donald Rumsfeld, Richard Perle, Douglas Feith, Dov Zakheim, and the other architects of the genocidal War on Islam in General and Palestine in Particular launched by the

9/11 inside job," I just might believe it. Until that day, we are safe in assuming that the increasingly ridiculous stories of alleged radical Islamist attacks on random civilians that no Muslim would ever want to harm—like virtually all alleged Islamic terror plots since 9/11, according to Aaronson's detailed investigation[19]—are part of the same Gladio B program[20] launched by the 9/11 neocon coup d'état.

# # #

I followed that up with another article that quickly shot to over 100,000 reads:

BUSTED! San Bernardino shooters were three white men dressed in military attire

My frequent radio guest Martin Hill has discovered another bombshell that blows the official story of the San Bernardino shooting to smithereens. In his new post Martin writes:

> Witness Sally Abdelmageed, who works at the Inland Regional Center and witnessed the shooting in San Bernardino, was interviewed live via telephone by CBS Evening News the day the massacre happened.[21]
>
> The news anchor begins 'She saw the attackers enter the building, and we spoke to her by phone.'
>
> "We saw three men dressed in military attire," she says. "I couldn't see his face, he had a black hat on... black cargo pants on, the kind with zippers on the side... He had a huge assault rifle a lot of ammo..."
>
> She continues, "They opened up the door to building then he starts to, you know, shoot all over into the room – that's the room we have conferences in...
>
> "I called 911 and I just hid under my desk..
>
> "As I was talking to the dispatch, we went into my manager's office and locked the doors ..."
>
> "Mrs. Abdelmageed, can you describe to me in as much details as you can what did the gunman look like?" the CBS anchor asks.
>
> "I couldn't see his face, he had a black hat on. All I could see was a black hat, black long-sleeved shirt... He had extra ammo. He was probably ready for something, to reload – I don't know know...
>
> "I just saw three, dressed exactly the same. They looked like they were athletic in build, and um, they appeared to be tall..."
>
> "You're certain that you saw three men?" the news anchor asks.
>
> "Yeah," she replies, as she continues to describe the THREE WHITE MEN, their muscular build, etc.

After she leaves the line, the anchor insists "and of course we've just learned that one of the suspects was actually a woman."[22]

Now don't get me wrong, folks. I'm a white man myself. And I am proud, not ashamed, of my Irish-Welsh-Scottish-German ancestry. But I'm sick of seeing paramilitary-type white guys committing massacres designed to be blamed on brown-skinned Muslims.

The same thing happened in Paris on November 13th. The shooters at La Belle Equipe restaurant were not brown-skinned Muslims; they were "white, clean shaven ... They looked like soldiers or mercenaries and carried the whole thing out like a military operation."[23]

The killers in the Charlie Hebdo offices last January were also white men with blue eyes—which rules out the brown-skinned brown-eyed patsies, the Kouachi brothers.[24] Likewise, the killers of French soldiers in the 2012 shootings falsely blamed on Mohammed Merah had tattoos worn only by white-power extremists, and therefore were almost certainly white paramilitaries employed by Operation Gladio B.[25] Western governments and their lapdog corporate media, by refusing to investigate, discover and report the truth about these cases, are pumping out racist, Islamophobic hate propaganda in a manner that would shame Dr. Goebbels...

# # #

By now, gentle reader, you may have noticed that the above articles were not written in a tone of soporific scholarly pseudo-objectivity or careful, dispassionate punctiliousness. In these and other *Veterans Today* essays, I am not merely calling attention to discrepancies in the official stories of the Paris and San Bernardino shootings and timidly suggesting that perhaps there ought to be some sort of official investigation. Instead, I prefer to "take the bull by the tail and look the facts in the face," as WC Fields put it. In these and other polemical articles, I offer rough-hewn truth and righteous outrage, in hopes that my readers —a group which, I am told, includes leading figures in the military and intelligence communities—will eventually grow so appalled at the psychopathic behavior of some of their peers that they will finally decide to clean house.

In pursuit of this task, I have made the psychological leap from uncertainty to certainty. And I recommend—but do not insist—that my readers do the same. For me, "Another French False Flag" ends with an exclamation point, not a question mark. For you, perhaps not. You may not have studied these cases as much as I have. Or you may not want to commit yourself to changing yourself and your world, taking big risks in the process. It is much easier to hem and haw like Hamlet, seeking refuge in uncertainty—the best-ever excuse for avoiding action.

I have heard such excuses over and over since I started doing 9/11 truth teach-ins at the University of Wisconsin-Madison in 2004. Virtually all of the many colleagues with whom I discussed the issue wanted to stop short of learning enough to be certain. From professor after professor after professor I heard many versions of essentially the same response: "I'd really rather not look into this, because I'm afraid it might be true." The unspoken corollary: "If I learned enough to know (i.e. feel reasonably certain) that it was true, I would fell morally compelled to do something about it, which would mean risking my personal and professional reputation, my friendships, my family relationships, my job, maybe even my life."

Ordinary people—not just professors and other eggheads—also feel this way. My rusty-pickup-truck-driving, trailer-park-dwelling neighbors have told me: "If I were to accept what you're saying is true, I'd have to pack my gun and head for Washington D.C. right this minute."

Since we all have a powerful, partly-unconscious motivation to remain uncertain, the perpetrators of such big-lie-crimes as 9/11 and its precursor- and successor- false flags attempt to encourage us in our uncertainty so as to continue to enjoy impunity. And they fully expect to succeed. As Karl Rove famously told Ron Suskind:

> The aide (Rove) said that guys like me were "in what we call the reality-based community," which he defined as people who "believe that solutions emerge from your judicious study of discernible reality." ...
> "That's not the way the world really works anymore," he continued. "We're an empire now, and when we act, we create our own reality. And while you're studying that reality—judiciously, as you will— we'll act again, creating other new realities, which you can study too, and that's how things will sort out. We're history's actors...and you, all of you, will be left to just study what we do."[26]

What does Rove mean by "creating reality"? Clearly he is referring to 9/11. On that day, Rove and his colleagues created a new, false reality —a fantasy world in which America was under attack by a powerful and dangerous foe. This paranoid fantasy world was engineered to become the new consensus reality, while actual reality was demoted to the status of "conspiracy theory."

Rove cannot have been talking about relatively minor, non-foundational, non-reality-creating issues—for example, whether the Bush Administration really believed that Saddam Hussein had weapons of mass destruction. Due to the collective emotional reaction to 9/11, and the outrageous and hard-to-believe social engineering project behind it, people who accept the official 9/11 myth are living in a very different world from the (real) world inhabited by those who know the awful truth; whereas those who recognize that Saddam's WMD never existed, however outraged they may be, still inhabit pretty much the same consensus reality as those who haven't figured that out. Rove didn't create a new reality by helping forge the Iraqi WMD myth—which he never could have sold without the foundational, fear-inciting, thought-paralyzing effects of 9/11. So the WMD myth is both ontologically and politically secondary and derivative, while the 9/11 myth is essential and world-changing. In 2003, two years after 9/11, they could have invented virtually any absurd, idiotic excuse to invade Iraq and easily gotten away with it. Before 9/11, no such invasion under any pretext, even a strong one, would have been politically feasible.

Indeed, Rove and such colleagues as public myth specialist Philip Zelikow—who wrote in 1998 that a coming new Pearl Harbor such as the destruction of the World Trade Center, would be a foundational mythic event that would split time into a vaguely-remembered "before" and a whole-new-world "after"—did create a whole new reality with the 9/11 inside job. In that new reality, where five foot tall 100 pound "muscle hijackers" who couldn't fly training Cessnas, armed only with package openers, could conduct the first successful hijackings in decades, somehow preventing pilots from squawking hijack codes, and carry out aeronautically-impossible stunt flights to minimize damage to their most important target, the Pentagon;[27] where giant skyscrapers could explode into powder at free fall acceleration due to relatively small office fires kindled by insignificant amounts of kerosene;[28] and where hundreds of other equally ludicrous contradictions are mindlessly accepted as gospel—in this addled parody of the solipsistic universe of a brain-damaged madman, compliant sheeple would accept any subsequent fear-mongering tale they heard. Or at least enough would accept it to disable serious opposition.

Rove is supremely confident that he and his imperial colleagues will continue to enjoy impunity for their world-creating crimes. Why? The key word he uses is "judiciously." He is sure that those who study 9/11, such as David Ray Griffin and the Architects and Engineers for 9/11 truth, will be so slow and methodical, so tentative and understated in their conclusions, and hence so politically ineffective, that they will remain years if not decades "behind the curve" in developing the degree of certainty required for bold, confident, forthright speech and action.

With due respect to the magnificent achievements of Griffin and Gage, I propose a different (or at least complementary) approach. Based on what we know of other events such as 9/11, I think it's fair to assume these new events are probably false flags, and put the burden of proof on the authorities and mainstream media to prove they aren't. And I think we should hit back as early, as often, and as hard as we can. We should not be pussyfooting around "studying judiciously what they do," but rather engage in an all-out "truth jihad"[29] or infowar against these neocon madmen. As Marx famously said: "Hitherto, philosophers have sought to understand the world; the point, however, is to change it."

On 9/11, Rove, Zelikow and company changed the world for the worse. The point, for us, is to change it back—and then some. How? By exposing 9/11 and the series of false flags around it, and rallying patriots and honest citizens of all political persuasions and outlooks to demand justice "by any means necessary"—and to boil over in so much righteous anger that they will commit themselves entirely and risk everything to attain that goal.

As I write this on the threshold of the 2016 election year, our leaders' last shreds of legitimacy are in tatters. Outsider populist candidates Donald Trump and Bernie Sanders are thriving, even while the media belittles and insults them. Likewise, in France, and the rest of Europe, anti-EU "fringe" candidates such as Marine LePen continue to surge inevitably towards eventual victory despite receiving even harsher media treatment.

The people obviously no longer trust their elites or their media. A revolution is brewing.

I hope this book contributes to that revolution, and helps make it a real revolution rather than a phony, cosmetic one like that "hope and change" thing I warned you about back in 2008.[30]

But I recognize that not all of my readers are there yet. So I also hope to start a conversation with people who are skeptical about my assertions. For that reason, I have invited contributors from a wide variety of outlooks and backgrounds—including some who question my approach to false flags—to be a part of this book. The public intellectuals included in this volume include Jews, Christians, Muslims (Sunni, Shia and Sufi), traditionalists and progressives, Marxists, libertarians, and secular humanists. Represented are professors of economics, sociology, history, physics, biological science and mathematics, journalism and communication, and   globalization studies.

Most contributors, to varying degrees, do share my initial skepticism toward media terror events such as the late-2015 shootings in Paris and San Bernardino, as well as my suspicions about what ISIS really is, what happened on 9/11, and who really created the "war on terror." The two major dissenting voices are ex-Israeli philosopher-musician Gilad Atzmon and geopolitics journalist and author Eric Walberg, both of whom sharply question the approach I have been outlining in this introduction. I hope you will read their essays with care and discernment, employing your critical thinking skills and thoughtfully evaluating their arguments. I worked with both of them (in a somewhat adversarial way) and encouraged them to produce the strongest possible cases for their positions. Please evaluate their essays in light of the material in the rest of the book and try to discern which position(s) seem most credible.

In conclusion, I wish to thank the people who have offered both moral and financial support over the years. Had I remained in the academy, I would have had to lie, or at least tone down my critiques and polemics. But thanks to the generosity of many hundreds of people, who did things like buying me a car, offering me plane tickets and hotel rooms to attend conferences, helping fund the publication and translation of my books, and sending me enough checks and paypal donations to keep me and my family fed and housed, I have been able to work honestly and independently as a public intellectual and person of conscience. So while I lost two million dollars in projected lifetime earnings by conducting research, education and outreach around the 9/11 issue, thereby getting myself chased out of the University of Wisconsin-Madison by a lynch mob of Republican state legislators and Fox News hosts and leaving a trail on the internet that ensures I'll never work in the American academy again, the generosity of hundreds of supporters has allowed me to do better educational work as a freelance gadfly than anything I could have accomplished in a fear-addled, muzzled, self-censored post-9/11 university. I hope this book will stand as a testament to our grandchildren from people who bravely spoke and funded the truth during a time of cowardice and lies. Thank you to all of you—you know who you are—and to the subscribers to my website, TruthJihad.com. This book is for you.

Kevin Barrett
Lone Rock, WI
January 1st, 2016

Part 1: What Really Happened?

PARIS 11/13/15: THE MATRIX EXTENDS ITS REACH

Paul Craig Roberts

Paul Craig Roberts is one of the most courageous and outspoken voices in the truth movement. He has held a long list of prestigious academic, journalistic, and think tank positions at many of America's top universities and media outlets, and has received major public service awards including France's Medal of the Legion of Honor.

Given his world-class resumé—normally a sure ticket to a well-re-munerated establishment position—Dr. Roberts has shown courage far beyond the call of duty by calling attention to the ever-more-outrageous propaganda lies force-fed to the American people since the neoconservative coup of September 11th, 2001. Since he chose to go public with his position on 9/11, Dr. Roberts has dramatically decreased the likelihood that he will ever be hired again by Georgetown University, the Hoover Institution, the Wall Street Journal, or the President of the United States.

Human nature, as economists know, is risk-averse—irrationally so, according to their models. The more one has to lose, the less one wants to risk it. Dr. Roberts, with his impressive list of achievements, has far more to lose than most of the rest of us could ever hope to gain. And yet he chose to speak truth to power, and accept the flurry of scurrilous ad-hominem attacks that he knew would follow. His career as a post-9/11 gadfly, I believe, will one day surpass even his previous high achievements in public memory and the history books. Unfortunately, for the moment, he has to put up with defamatory sniping from third-rate intellects with the ethics of rabid hyenas; and he has to earn his living outside of the established institutions. You can support his work by contributing at PaulCraigRoberts.org.

As passionate as he is erudite, Dr. Roberts is one of the real intellectual heroes of our time. His timely, hard-hitting responses to the two 2015 Paris attacks helped inspire this book and its predecessor, We Are NOT Charlie Hebdo. *Below is a lightly-edited compendium of his columns that followed the Paris events of 11/13/15.*

– Kevin Barrett

Another Paris False Flag Attack?

Paul Craig Roberts – November 13th, 2015

At 7 pm on Friday the 13th we do not have much information about the "terrorist attacks" in Paris other than that Paris is closed down like Boston was after the "Boston Marathon Bombing," also a suspected false flag event.

Possibly believable evidence will be presented that the Paris attacks were real terrorist attacks. However, what do refugees have to gain from making themselves unwelcome with acts of violence committed against the host country, and where do refugees in France obtain automatic weapons and bombs? Indeed, where would the French themselves obtain them?

The millions of refugees from Washington's wars who are overrunning Europe are bringing to the forefront of European politics the anti-EU nationalist parties, such as Pegida in Germany, Nigel Farage's UK Independence Party, and Marine Le Pen's National Front Party in France. These anti-EU political parties are also anti-immigrant political parties.

The latest French poll shows that, as a result of the refugees from Washington's wars, Marine Le Pen has come out on top of the candidates for the next French presidential election. Conclusion: By supporting for 14 years Washington's neoconservative wars for US hegemony over the Middle East, establishment European governments eroded their electoral support. European peoples want to be French, German, Dutch, Italian, Hungarian, Czech, British. They do not want their countries to be a diverse Tower of Babel created by millions of refugees from Washington's wars. To remain a nationality unto themselves is what Pegida, Farage, and Le Pen offer the voters.

Realizing its vulnerability, the French Establishment may have made a decision to protect its hold on power with a false flag attack that would allow the Establishment to close France's borders and thereby deprive Marine Le Pen of her main political issue.

Some people are so naive and stupid as to think that no government would kill its own citizens. But governments do so all the time. There are an endless number of false flag attacks, such as Operation Gladio. Operation Gladio was a CIA/Italian intelligence operation that relentlessly bombed innocent Italians, such as those waiting in a train station, murdering hundreds, and then blaming the violence on the European communist parties in the post-WW II era in order to block the communists from electoral gains.

A president of Italy, Francesco Cossiga, revealed the truth about Operation Gladio, and you can read the sordid details in a number of books and online. The bombings were not done, as was widely reported in the corrupt Western media, by communists. The bombings were done by Italian intelligence aided by the CIA. In one of the Italian investigatory hearings, a member of Italian intelligence said that the sites to be bombed were chosen in order to maximize the deaths of women and children, because these victims were most useful in discrediting the communists.

Considering the Western World's long tradition of false flag orchestrations, the "terrorist attacks" in Paris could be the most recent manifestation.

The Matrix Extends Its Reach

Paul Craig Roberts – November 14th, 2015

NOTE: The remnant of the American left has again fallen in with the official terror story of the Paris attacks, because the official story serves the left-wing's denunciatory needs. I see that the Russians as well are on board with the official story as it serves their posture that we must all unite against terrorism. Amazing. Washington can rely on the world's total blindness.

Within one hour of the Paris attacks and without any evidence, the story was set in stone that the perpetrator was ISIL. This is the way propaganda works.

When the West does it, it always succeeds, because the world is accustomed to following the lead of the West. I was amazed to see, for example, Russian news services helping to spread the official story of the Paris attacks despite Russia herself having suffered so often from planted false stories.

Has the Russian media forgotten MH-17? The minute the story was reported that the Malaysian airliner was hit by a Russian missile over eastern Ukraine in the hands of separatists, the blame was ascribed to Russia. And that is where the blame remains despite the absence of evidence.

Has the Russian media also forgotten the "Russian invasion of Ukraine"? This preposterous story is accepted everywhere in the West as gospel.

Has the Russian media forgotten the book by the German newspaper editor who wrote that every European journalist of consequence was an asset of the CIA?[31]

One would have thought that experience would have taught Russian media sources to be careful about explanations that originate in the West.

So now we have what is likely to be another false story set in stone. Just as a few Saudis with box cutters outwitted the entire US national security state, ISIL managed to acquire unacquirable weapons and outwit French intelligence while organizing a series of attacks in Paris.

Why did ISIL do this? Blowback for France's small role in Washington's Middle East violence?

Why not the US instead?

Or was ISIL's purpose to have the flow of refugees into Europe blocked by closed borders? Does ISIL really want to keep all of its opponents in Syria and Iraq when instead it can drive them out to Europe? Why have to kill or control millions of people by preventing their flight?

Don't expect any explanations or questions from the media about the story that is set in stone.

The threat to the European political establishment is not ISIL. The threats are the rising anti-EU, anti-immigrant political parties: Pegida in Germany, the UK Independence Party, and the National Front in France. The latest poll shows the National Front's Marine Le Pen leading as the likely French president.

Something had to be done about the hordes of refugees from Washington's wars, or the establishment political parties faced defeat at the hands of political parties that are also unfriendly to Europe's subservience to Washington.

EU rules about refugees and immigrants and Germany's acceptance of one million of the refugees, together with heavy criticism of those governments in Eastern Europe that wanted to put up fences to keep out the refugees, made closing borders impossible.

With the Paris terror attacks, what was impossible became possible, and the President of France immediately announced the closing of France's borders. The border closings will spread. The main issue of the rising dissident political parties will be defused. The EU will be safe, and so will Washington's sovereignty over Europe.

Whether or not the Paris attacks were a false flag operation for the purpose of obtaining these results, these results are the consequences of the attacks. These results serve the interests of the European political establishment and Washington.

Is ISIL so unsophisticated not to have realized that? If ISIL is that unsophisticated, how did ISIL so easily deceive French intelligence? Indeed, can French intelligence be intelligent?

Can Western peoples be intelligent to fall for a story set in stone prior to any evidence? In the West, facts are created by self-serving statements from governments. Investigation is not part of the process. When 90 percent of the US media is owned by six mega-corporations, it cannot be any different.

As The Matrix grows in the absurdity of its claims, it nevertheless manages to become even more invulnerable.

French Security Left Blind During Paris Attacks

Paul Craig Roberts – November 15th, 2015

I have received a report from European security that there was a massive cyber attack on French systems 48 hours prior to and during the Paris attacks. Among other things, the attack took down the French mobile data network and blinded police surveillance. The attack was not a straightforward DDOS attack but a sophisticated attack that targeted a weakness in infrastructure hardware.

Such an attack is beyond the capability of most organizations and requires capability that is unlikely to be in ISIL's arsenal. An attack on this scale is difficult to pull off without authorities getting wind of it. The coordination required suggests state involvement.

It is common for people with no experience in government to believe that false flag attacks are not possible, because they think the entire government would have to be involved and not everyone would go along with it. Someone would talk. However, if the report I have received is correct, hardly anyone has to be involved, and security forces are simply disabled.

Remember the reports that during 9/11, a simulation of the actual events that were occuring was being conducted, thus confusing responsible parties about the reality.

I am unable to reveal any further information. If security experts find the information credible, they should direct their inquiries to the French authorities.

Food For Thought: The Found Passport

Paul Craig Roberts – November 15th, 2015

The "found passport" worked for them for 9/11. It worked again for Charlie Hebdo. So now they have used it a third time. They know that Americans are total dumbshits and can be told anything. No matter how preposterous, the dumbshits will believe it. But Americans are not capable of believing truth. They have been brainwashed that truth is "conspiracy theory." A population this stupid has no future.

Remember, on 9/11 an exercise simulating the day's real events was being conducted. Again, we hear the same thing about the Paris attacks. What an unusual coincidence! But the dumbshit Western populations are not capable of noticing. Apparently neither are the Russians.

Reports that French security was blinded by a sophisticated cyber-attack, that CIA Director Brennan met with French Intelligence Chief Bajolet two weeks before the Paris attacks,[32] that "coincidentally" a multi-site active shooter exercise was ongoing on the 13th,[33] and that a fake Syrian passport was planted and trumpeted by the media,[34] taken together, show that there is a lot of room for a lot of suspicion. But blinded eyes cannot see.

"Paris Changes Everything," Say Merkel's German Political Allies

Paul Craig Roberts November 15, 2015

In my recent writings I have explained the many agendas served by the false flag Paris attack. I also predicted that other countries would follow France's lead in closing their borders, thus dispossessing the dissenting political parties of their issue and preserving the political power and control of the European establishment. As predicted, Germany is now moving in the direction of repulsing refugees.[35]

Discussing the situation today with a friend brought to mind another benefit to the establishment of the Paris attack. Donald Trump and Bernie Sanders, who were on the verge of taking the presidential nominations away from the establishment, have had their momentum disrupted by the Paris attack. By the time the Paris attack and all that will come in its wake run their course—new military measures against ISIL, Western intervention without Syrian government approval, PATRIOT Acts for European countries, and possibly a new and more draconian PATRIOT Act for the US, increased association of dissent with ISIL terrorism—Trump and Sanders will no longer command attention. Pushed aside, they will not regain the limelight.

Just as with 9/11, Charlie Hebdo and the Boston Marathon Bombing, the media was scripted with the story and ready to go immediately. There is no investigation, no questioning, just the media moving in lockstep with the scripted official story. Again the perpetrators conveniently leave their ID. Again the attack coincides with an official drill of the attack. No matter how transparent the false flag attack and the agendas served by it, patriotism whipped to a frenzy blinds people to the reality.

Washington Refines Its False Flag Operations

Paul Craig Roberts – November 16, 2015

Washington and its French vassal have refined how they conduct their false flag operations. With the Charlie Hebdo operation, they knew to immediately set the story in stone in order to avoid any questions from the print and TV media and in order to use the set story to take the place of an investigation.

The set story made it unnecessary to explain the mysterious "suicide" of one of the main police investigators while engaged in the investigation of the event. The set story also made it unnecessary to explain why it was necessary to kill rather than capture the alleged perpetrators, or to explain how the French authorities could be so wrong about the alleged get-away-driver but not about the two gunmen. There has been no explanation why the authorities believed there was a get-away-driver, and no such driver has been captured or killed. Indeed, there are many unanswered questions of no interest to any media except the alternative Internet media.

What the US and France learned from the Charlie Hebdo skepticism on the Internet, and in the book *We Are NOT Charlie Hebdo*, is to keep the story flowing. Charlie Hebdo involved two scenes of violence, and the connection between the two acts of terrorism was vague. This time there were several scenes of violence, and they were better connected in the story.

More importantly, the story was followed quickly by more drama, such as the pursuit of a suspected perpetrator into Belgium, a French bombing attack on the Islamic State, a French aircraft carrier sent to the Middle East, a declaration of war by the French President against ISIL, and speculation that Hollande, pressured by Washington, will invoke NATO's Article V, which will pull NATO into an invasion of the Islamic State. By superceding each event with a new one, the public's attention is shifted away from the attack itself and the interests served by the attack. Already the attack itself is old news. The public's attention has been led elsewhere. How soon will NATO have boots on the ground?

The Western media has avoided many interesting aspects of the Paris attacks. For example, what did the directors of the CIA and French intelligence discuss at their meeting a few days prior to the Paris attacks? Why were fake passports used to identify attackers? Why did the attacks occur on the same day as a multi-site simulation of a terrorist attack involving first responders, police, emergency services and medical personnel? Why has there been no media investigation of the report that French police were blinded by a sophisticated cyber attack on their mobile data tracking system? Does anyone really believe that ISIL has such capability?

The Western media serves merely as an amplifier of the government's propaganda. Even the non-Western media follows this pattern because of the titillating effect. It is a good story for the media, and it requires no effort.

Initially even the Russian media served to trumpet the set story that rescues the Western political establishment from political defeat at home and Russian defeat in Syria. But it wasn't too long before some of the Russian media remembered numerous false stories about a Russian invasion of Ukraine, about Assad's use of chemical weapons, about US ABMs being placed on Russia's borders to protect Europe from nonexistent Iranian nuclear ICBMs. And so on.

Russian media began asking questions and received some good answers from Gearoid O Colmain (see his essay in this book, as well as his youtube-sensation RT report from Paris).[36]

To understand the Paris attacks, it helps to begin with the question: "What is ISIL?" Apparently, ISIL is a creation of the CIA or some deep-state organization shielded by the CIA's operations department. ISIL seems to have been used to overthrow Qaddafi in Libya and then was sent to overthrow Assad in Syria. One would think that ISIL would be throughly infiltrated by the CIA, Mossad, British and French intelligence. Perhaps ISIL is discovering that it is an independent power and is substituting an agenda of its own for Washington's, but ISIL still appears to be at least partially dependent on support, active or passive, from Washington.

ISIL is a new group that suddenly appeared, portrayed as barbaric knife-wielding fanatics from medieval times. How did such a group so quickly acquire such extensive global capability as to blow a Russian airliner out of Egyptian skies, conduct bombings in Lebanon and Turkey, outwit French intelligence and conduct successful multi-prong attacks in Paris? How come ISIL never attacks Israel?

The next question is: "How does the Paris attack benefit ISIL?" Is it a benefit to ISIL to have Europe's borders closed, thus halting ISIL's ability to infiltrate Europe as refugees? Does it help ISIL to provoke French bombing of ISIL positions in the Middle East and to bring upon itself a NATO invasion?

Who does benefit? Clearly, the European and American political establishment in so many ways. "Paris changes everything," declares the European establishment, saved from defeat and loss of power. In the US "Paris attacks become focus of 2016 race," declares CNN, benefitting insiders and harming outsider candidates like Trump and Sanders.[37]

Also among the early words from the French president, and without any evidence in support, was Hollande's declaration that the Islamic State had attacked the French nation. Obviously, it is set for Hollande to invoke NATO's Article V, which would send a NATO invasion force into Syria. This would be Washington's way of countering the Russian initiative that has saved the Assad government from defeat by the Islamic State. The NATO invasion would overthrow Assad as part of the war against the Islamic State.

The Russian government did not immediately recognize this threat. The Russian government saw in the Paris attack the opportunity to gain Western cooperation in the fight against ISIL. The Russian line has been that we must all fight ISIL together.

The Russian presence, although highly effective, is small in Syria. What does the Russian government do when its policy in Syria is crowded by a NATO invasion?

The answer to the Roman question, "cui bono," is clear. But don't expect to hear it from the Western media.

More Paris Puzzles

Paul Craig Roberts – November 17th, 2015

Some people who are not inclined to believe the official story of the Paris attack are troubled by the question why Muslim suicide bombers would blow themselves up for a false flag attack. The answer to this question is very simple. But first we should dispose of the question whether suicide bombers did blow themselves up. Is this something that we know, or is it part of the story that we are told? For example, we were told that during 9/11 passengers in hijacked airliners used their cell phones to call relatives, but experts have testified that the technology of the time did not permit cell phone calls from airliners at those altitudes.

To dispose of the question whether we have or do not have any real evidence that suicide bombers blew themselves up, I will assume that they did.

Now turn to the question that troubles some doubters: Why would suicide bombers blow themselves up for the sake of a false flag attack?

As I said, the answer is simple: Why assume that the suicide bombers knew who was organizing the attack? There seems to be abundant evidence that ISIL is a US creation, one that is still dependent on US active or passive support—thus the conflict between Putin and Washington over attacking ISIL. ISIL seems to be what Washington used to overthrow the government in Libya and afterward was sent by Washington to Syria to overthrow Assad. Obviously, Washington has ISIL infiltrated. Washington has long proven is ability to use Islamic extremists. As Washington used them in Afghanistan against the Soviets and in Libya and Syria against independent governments, Washington used them in Paris. By my last count, the FBI on 150 occasions has successfully deceived people into participating into FBI orchestrated "terror plots."

Now let us move to some bigger questions. Why do terrorists attack ordinary innocent people who have neither awareness of "their" government's actions or control over them? The victims of 9/11 were not the neocons and members of the Washington establishment, whose policies in the Middle East justified attacks on their persons. Ditto for the Boston Marathon Bombing, and ditto for the Paris attacks. Innocents were the victims, not those who have taken Muslim lives.

Historically, terror attacks are not on the innocent but on the rulers and those who are guilty. For example, it was the Archduke of Austria/Hungary who was assassinated by the Serbian terrorist, not ordinary people blown up or shot down in a street cafe.

It is interesting that terrorist attacks attributed to Muslims only fall upon ordinary people, not upon the political elites who oppress the Muslims. In past years on several occasions I have remarked in my columns on the total vulnerability of the neoconservatives to assassination. Yet there has been not a single attack by terrorists on a neocon life, and the neocons are the source of the violence that Washington has unleashed on the Muslim world. The neocons walk around without threat free as birds.

How believable is it that Muslim terrorists take their ire out on innocents when the President of France himself, who has sent military forces to murder Muslims, was sitting in the attacked stadium and could easily have been eliminated by a suicide bomber?

Now let us turn to questions of identification of the alleged "Paris terrorists." Is it realistic to suppose that the millions of refugees from Washington and its European vassals' wars in the Middle East have passports? Were these millions of refugees expecting to be driven by White Civilization's Bombs out of their countries and thus had prepared themselves with passports in order to flee?

Did they write on their passport applications that they were going to be visiting Europe?

Was the beleaguered country, their homeland, under full military assault, able to process all these millions of passports?

What sort of dumbshit Western media goes along with the passport story—a media well paid to lie for Washington's hegemony and crimes?

One final question for skeptics. Where are the photographs of the terrorists during their terrorizing? Surrounding the scenes of violence there were not only abundant security cameras, but also hundreds, even thousands, of people with cell phones that have cameras. With all of these photos, how is it possible that the authorities do not know if some terrorists escaped, and if so, who they are and what they look like? Why are the authorities relying on fake passports for photos of the terrorists?

Terrorism has been unleashed in the Western World, and it is the terrorism of Western governments against Western peoples.

Will The Matrix Prevail?

Paul Craig Roberts, November 18th, 2016

Note that the authorities almost always claim that they had no warning or indication of an attack, but they can almost instantly identify the "mastermind."

The Paris attack is playing out as I expected. The French government is attacking French civil liberty with legislation similar to the USA PATRIOT Act.[38] Readers in France have informed me that 84% of the French people, according to a poll, are content to be spied upon as long as it keeps them safe. This means that only 16% of the French nation is not brain dead.

Another reader informs me that a TV news station read a letter left behind by one of the alleged ISIL bombers, a letter written in perfect English. Really! I mean, Really! Those with their secret agendas know how stupid the Western peoples are, collectively a hopeless basket case. French and American politicians are demanding that NATO Article 5 be used to put NATO boots on the ground in Syria. This is important not in order to fight ISIL, which the Russians are successfully doing, but to overthrow Assad under the pretext of fighting ISIL, a crazy policy that could bring conflict with Russia.[39]

Alternatively, to avoid conflict with Russia, Washington can take advantage of the Russian government's hope that the Paris attack will show the West that Putin was correct that the West should join Russia in opposing ISIL. Once a NATO-Russian coalition, as advocated by French Prime Minister Manuel Valls, is formed, Putin becomes the West's captive in the overthrow of Assad.[40]

To ensure that no one is informed of the true facts by the English language Russian media, such as RT and Sputnik, the US Senate arranged hearings on foreign propaganda. Kenneth Weinstein, a member of the US Broadcasting Board of Governors, that is, the censors, told the senators that RT, Sputnik, and a variety of other truthful news sources are "well-funded state propaganda outlets."[41]

In other words, only believe what you read in Washington-controlled propaganda outlets such as the *New York Times*, *Washington Post*, Fox News, CNN, BBC, NPR, and so forth.

The aftermath of the Paris attack is like the aftermath of the so-called Boston Marathon Bombing. Fifty heavily armed police converged on two people and murdered them. The murdered female is described even by RT as a "female suicide bomber." If the murdered woman is a suicide bomber, how is she still alive to be murdered by police? Not even the "Russian propaganda outlet" RT asks why 50 heavily armed police were unable to capture two people alive and had to kill them![42]

A number of readers have sent to me information that indicates that the Paris attack was reported on both Wikipedia and Twitter before it occurred.[43] I do not know what to make of this. I do remember that the BBC reported the collapse of WTC building 7 prior to its collapse. The BBC reporter is actually standing in front of the still standing WTC 7 as she makes the report of its collapse. In other words, orchestration mistakes occur. But hardly any of the brainwashed pubic notices.

The question that arises is to what extent is this false flag attack in Paris a hoax. Why don't we see the large number of dead and wounded. What we seem to have are uninjured crisis actors.[44] Witnesses in behalf of the official story seem to have performed the same function on other occasions.[45]

Having been at the top of government, journalism, and academia for a lifetime, it is clear to me that there is a great deal wrong with the explanations that people are being given. However, the majority of Western peoples have been thoroughly brainwashed to believe that anyone who doubts official explanations is a "conspiracy theorist." In other words, only governments and their media presstitutes tell the truth.

This makes it simple for governments with their secret agendas to protect their agendas from the facts. Who would believe me when the alternative is to believe Fox News, CNN, the BBC, NPR, Dubya, Obama, Wolfowitz, Hollande, Merkel, Cameron, the Weakly Standard?
If Putin's government and the Chinese people are so desperately determined to be part of the "glorious West" that they will accept a false reality, the world is doomed.

If it is up to Western politicians, the world is doomed for sure. To the man and the woman they are warmongers. Moreover, the response to the false flag/hoax attack is mindless. The morons declare that the West is attacked because it allows women to be educated. The West is attacked because of "French values and French way of life, because we dance" (Foreign Minister Laurent Fabius). In other words, the nonsense that worked for the idiot US president, George W. Bush, works for the French. "We are attacked because we are good." All of us good people here in the West would never be attacked because we have looted and robbed the Middle East for a century and followed up the looting with 14 years of military devastation of seven countries, producing millions of deaths and displaced persons.

Really, it is a wonder that there are not round the clock REAL TER-RORIST ATTACKS on Western countries, who certainly deserve them.

DECODING THE PARIS ATTACKS: ISIS BLOWBACK OR FRENCH-ISRAELI FALSE FLAG?

By Brandon Martinez

Much evidence has come to light that has punctured a litany of holes in the official narrative of the Friday the 13th terror attacks in Paris, which allegedly claimed the lives of 130 civilians.

Mainstream reportage surrounding the event has stimulated a number of intriguing questions about the nature of this operation and how it could have been planned, organized and executed without the knowledge of French and other Western intelligence agencies who, as we know, have constructed a vast and extreme surveillance apparatus over the past 15 years.

Shortly following the Charlie Hebdo attacks in January, the French regime implemented a despotic anti-terror bill that gave authorities virtually unlimited surveillance powers.[46] Yet, despite this amplified power to spy on just about anybody, the French authorities "dropped the ball" once again, failing to stop a highly sophisticated, multi-faceted attack that would have required so much logistical expertise and know-how that it is palpably unfeasible such a plot could succeed without the help of insiders within the French state (and possibly other states).

Alleged Terrorists "Known to Authorities"

As has been the case with all of the staged ISIS attacks over the past year and a half[47]—attacks that only started happening after the West launched its counterfeit "anti-ISIS" bombing campaign in August 2014 —many of the individuals accused of the newest wave of terror in Paris had been well-known to and were being monitored by authorities for years.

Samy Amimour, an alleged gunman at the Bataclan theatre, had been placed on a terror watch list in 2012 after attempting to travel to Yemen, as reported by the *Guardian*[48], the *Telegraph*[49], *Yahoo News*[50] and other mainstream sources. The *International Business Times*, in its article "Paris attacks: Bataclan suicide bomber Samy Amimour previously charged with terror offences," noted Amimour "had been placed under investigation in 2012 for terrorism conspiracy and under judicial supervision," after which authorities sought his capture by issuing an international arrest warrant.[51] He is said to have disappeared in 2013, joining the ISIS insurgency in Syria.

Amimour's back-story mirrors that of the Charlie Hebdo terrorist patsies Cherif and Said Kouachi, both of whom had been tracked by French intelligence for nearly a decade after one of the brothers allegedly tried to join al-Qaeda militants in Iraq in 2005 and was convicted by a French court.[52] Despite being on terror watch lists and the intelligence services trailing them for years, the Kouachi brothers managed to sneak in and out of France, travel to the Middle East to link up with militants, and then make their way back into France without being intercepted by authorities. Most conspicuously, surveillance was pulled off the brothers six months before the Hebdo attack, giving them a perfect window of opportunity to plan and organize the January assault on the satirical magazine's offices.[53] So either the stars just happened to line up for the Kouachis, or they were protected assets of French intelligence. I'll leave it up to the reader to decide which is more likely.

Even the *Telegraph* feigned bewilderment about how French intelligence managed to overlook Amimour's re-entry into France, writing: "The revelations [about Amimour being known to authorities for years] raise questions as to whether French police were aware Amimour had re-entered the country, and if so whether they had placed him under close supervision in the run up to Friday's deadly attacks."[54]

There are also plenty of anomalies surrounding the alleged ringleader of the Paris attackers, Belgium-born Abdelhamid Abaaoud. A *Telegraph* update asked the prudent question, "How did Europe's 'most wanted terrorist' slip into France from Syria unnoticed?" "French and Belgian security services are facing difficult questions as to how one of Europe's most wanted terrorists was able to slip back into the country from Syria and mastermind the Paris attacks from a flat in the city," the report added, further questioning the "ease with which Abaaoud appears to have been able to travel unnoticed back through Europe."[55]

And that is the million-dollar question. How did a high-profile member of ISIS penetrate Europe without security services nabbing him upon entry? This seems especially unlikely in an Orwellian surveillance state like France where the government can track communications without a warrant.

Other questions about Abaaoud linger. Growing up in Brussels, Abaaoud had a history of petty crime and run-ins with the law, including several convictions.[56] So he was known to police. We are told he traveled to Syria and joined ISIS some time in 2013. In February of 2014, he is said to have recruited his younger brother, only 13-years-old at the time, into ISIS. That incident made headlines in Belgium, and

Abaaoud is said to have become "a household name in his native country" by this time.[57] The *Wall Street Journal* reported that Western countries even tracked him while in Syria and sought to assassinate him in an airstrike.[58]

Then, we are told, the now-infamous jihadi "slips back into" Belgium and plots an attack on a police station in the city of Verviers with two accomplices. In January 2015, the CBC tells us, "the ring is broken up in a raid that leads to the deaths of two of Abaaoud's suspected accomplices." But Abaaoud miraculously manages to escape and "then somehow made his way back to Syria."[59] That "somehow" is never explained. There is no possible way Abaaoud could have taken a regular flight in or out of the country, so how did he do it? In July 2015 Abaaoud is sentenced in absentia by a Belgian court to 20 years imprisonment for all of this chicanery.

In an article on the Vocativ website entitled, "Paris Attacks Mastermind Brags About Escaping 'Crusader Intelligence'," we learn that the now-deceased Abaaoud was heavily featured in ISIS propaganda, giving an extensive interview published in the February 2015 issue of "ISIS's magazine" *Dabiq*, in which he boasts of coordinating previous unsuccessful attacks in Europe and of evading authorities.[60] Vocativ reports that Abaaoud "detailed his attempted attack in the Belgian town of Verviers that resulted in the deaths of two militants in January" and bragged of escaping back to Syria after the failed operation "despite being chased by intelligence agencies." Abaaoud specifically said: "My name and picture were all over the news yet I was able to stay in their homeland, plan operations against them, and leave safely when doing so became necessary."

The farcicality of this storyline should already be apparent to the reader, but it gets even more ridiculous.[61] "I was even stopped by an officer who contemplated me so as to compare me to the picture, but he let me go, as he did not see the resemblance!" Abaaoud proclaimed in the *Dabiq* interview, describing his "luck" as "a gift from Allah." So Abaaoud, a "household name" in Belgium, was right within the clutches of the police, but a moronic Belgian cop somehow failed to recognize him with his picture in hand.

Anyone with two brain cells to rub together can deduce that Abaaoud is not simply "lucky"; he is not merely "blessed"; he is most likely a protected asset of NATO, which explains why he was able to slip in and out of Europe undetected like a poltergeist without being nabbed by authorities. And even when he was stopped by police, he was mysteriously let go—not due to incompetence, as the spooks would have us believe, but deliberate connivance.

Another one of the presumed Paris attackers, Ismael Omar Mostefai (a French citizen), was known to authorities as a potential danger. The Huffington Post, in its report titled "Turkey Says It Warned France Twice About Paris Attacker," details how Turkey twice warned France about Mostefai, once in December 2014 and again in June 2015, saying that they came across him during a terror-related investigation on their own soil. "Turkey shared information on Mostefaï with France, but didn't hear anything back—until after Friday's events," the report states.[62]

French police identified Mostefai, allegedly, "by a fingerprint, pulled from a severed finger, found in the carnage of body parts in the concert hall."[63] This story harkens back to 9/11, where authorities claim to have found the DNA of the "hijackers" at the Pentagon and Shanksville crash sites, despite the nearly complete absence of plane debris at either scene. Authorities, needing to explain how they so quickly identify their patsies, sometimes resort to these farfetched claims about fingerprints and DNA recovery, obviously not concerned with how silly such claims sound to intelligent people. Why is nobody asking the question, how does a fingerprint prove that Mostefai was a shooter and not a victim at Bataclan? The fingerprint alone (if that claim is even true, it may be a lie for all we know) may prove he was there but not that he was a perpetrator. Other evidence is required to establish guilt in this respect, but it doesn't seem to be forthcoming, as witnesses have yet to positively identify Mostefai as a shooter.

A CNN profile on Mostefai revealed that he "had been known to authorities as a possible threat" for some time, according to a French prosecutor. The prosecutor, François Molins, also disclosed that Mostefai "had an 'S' file on him for years, which means investigators believe he had been 'radicalized' in some way, though it was not clear whether he would act on his radicalization."[64]

It is not yet proven that he was even a legitimate member of ISIS or traveled to Syria to engage in combat with the group. The Daily Mail tells us that investigators "are now looking into claims that Mostefai spent several months in Syria in late 2013 and early 2014."[65] But, so far, no confirmation. The Mail article also says that "it is thought" he had been radicalized by a hate preacher at a mosque in the French city of Luce. Such speculation is not proof either. The Mail quotes officials at the mosque he was supposedly "radicalized" at who deny he even went there, telling reporters they "had no knowledge of Mostefai, and that neither he nor his family were members or attended." They also told media that, "We expel people who do not respect our rules or behave strangely, and we report them to the authorities."[66]

All of Mostefai's friends, family and neighbours were "stunned" that he would have participated in the attack and say he showed no signs of being radical.[67] So there is so far no evidence that Mostefai physically joined ISIS in Syria, and the only proof he was a radical is an unsubstantiated claim by Jean-Pierre Gorges, the mayor of the French city of Chartres, who could easily be lying to implicate Mostefai.[68]

It's entirely plausible that Mostefai was a total patsy, framed and set-up by authorities, and had nothing to do with this attack. It's also possible that he was involved in some way, likely as a dupe but possibly on his own volition. In any case, the "fingerprint from a severed finger" claim, as well as bare innuendo from a French politician that Mostefai was "radicalized" at a mosque whose leaders say he never attended, does not make for a very convincing case.

More anomalies deserve exploration. A story from the Associated Press titled "'I have no explanation': Key suspect in Paris theatre attack was questioned—then released by police" points out a severe oddity that has yet to be explained.[69] The article states that "[h]ours after the synchronized attacks that terrorized Paris, French police questioned and released the suspect who is now the focus of an international manhunt." The suspect in question, Salah Abdeslam, was said to be "one of three men in a getaway car, headed for France's border with Belgium, when police pulled them over after daybreak Saturday." The article continues:

> The French president had already announced new border controls to prevent the perpetrators from escaping. Hours had passed since investigators identified Abdelslam as the renter of a Volkswagen Polo that carried hostage-takers to the Paris theatre where almost three-quarters of the 129 victims were killed. It's not clear why the local French police, known as gendarmes, didn't take Abdeslam into custody. They checked his identification, but it's not known whether they had been informed of his apparent connection to the attacks.[70]

When asked why police didn't arrest Abdeslam, who, as noted above, had been named as a suspect hours before he was pulled over, a French police official said: "I have no explanation."

Now the storyline emerging contends that Abdeslam "chickened out" of martyrdom and tossed his suicide vest in a dumpster on the outskirts of Paris.[71] Sky News, in its article titled "Suspected Suicide Belt Found In Paris Dustbin," writes:

> Abdeslam is suspected of playing at least a logistical role in the coordinated shooting and suicide bombings on 13 November and police say phone location data places him in Montrouge

that evening. It comes as the 26-year-old fugitive's brother Mohamed suggested Abdeslam may have decided not to go ahead with the attack at the last moment. Another theory suggested by police is that Abdeslam, if he was involved in the attacks, may have had a technical problem with his belt.[72]

Another plausible theory is that Abdeslam is an intelligence asset, which would explain why police failed to arrest him after being stopped, since he's a protected agent whose job was to facilitate the Bataclan attack and then escape. It's also likely that he has been double-crossed by his intelligence handlers who are now pretending he was actually an ISIS operative and not working for them. The story that Abdeslam discarded his suicide vest in a dumpster sounds ludicrous, one of those too-good-to-be-true Hollywood moments. It may well be made up by authorities. Why throw it in a public dumpster instead of someplace hidden? And how did police locate it so quickly? Did they go around rummaging through waste bins in the suburbs of Paris? What did they expect to find in random waste bins? Sounds contrived.

The chances are slim that they'll bring Abdeslam in alive. After all, dead men tell no tales.

Prior Warnings
French authorities cannot claim the attacks took them by surprise because the Iraqi government sent them a warning one day before the deadly incidents. The Associated Press report cited earlier explains:

> The day before the attacks, senior Iraqi intelligence officials warned France and other members of the U.S.-led coalition fighting the Islamic State that assaults by the militant group could be imminent, according to a dispatch obtained by the AP. Abu Bakr al-Baghdadi, the group's leader, had ordered supporters to use guns and bombs and take hostages in the days ahead in coalition countries as well as Iran and Russia, Thursday's dispatch said.[73]

The French downplayed the Iraqi warning by claiming it "wasn't specific" and that they receive similar cautions "all the time." But Iraqi officials later clarified that "they also shared specific details with French authorities before the attack—including the size of a sleeper cell of militants they said was directing attackers sent back to France from Islamic State's de-facto capital in Raqqa, Syria."[74]

There are other examples of forewarning. Back in September of 2015, France24 reported that French authorities had arrested a French jihadist in August who told them that he was sent on a mission by ISIS to attack concerts in France. France24's report on the incident, titled "Arrested French jihadist 'instructed' to attack concert," tells us:

> A French national suspected of planning a terrorist attack in France after returning from the Islamic State group's Syrian stronghold of Raqqa was arrested last month, officials said Friday. The man admitted to police that he had been instructed to carry out an attack on French soil—"preferably" during a concert—but has denied that he had any intention of following through with the plan, according to a judicial source.[75]

So French authorities had known since September that ISIS was sending operatives into France to attack specifically concerts. The French also had a fairly unambiguous and direct warning of an imminent attack provided by the Iraqis; they had received multiple cautions about at least one of the individuals purportedly involved, and had been monitoring several others. In fact, as the Independent is now reporting, "Belgian authorities allegedly had a list of suspected jihadists including the 'mastermind' of the Paris attacks and the two brothers who carried them out—a month before the massacre took place."[76] The list contained "names and addresses of more than 80 people believed to be Islamist militants," including the Abdeslam brothers (Salah and Ibrahim) and Abdelhamid Abaaoud (the "mastermind"). Yet, nothing was done to preemptively thwart these individuals.

Following the Charlie Hebdo attack in January, France essentially declared martial law, dispatching tens of thousands of troops in the streets.[77] Then the government passed an Orwellian surveillance bill that not only gave authorities unlimited powers to wiretap phone communications and snoop on Internet traffic of ordinary citizens, but even the ability to "bug suspects' homes with microphones and cameras and add keyloggers to their computers to track every keystroke."[78]

In spite of all of these forewarnings, in conjunction with their unprecedented surveillance prowess, the French government had "no idea" about what was to come on Friday the 13th?

Do they take us all for fools?

Pot-Smoking "Jihadis"

Reminiscent of the 9/11 hijacker patsies, several of the alleged attackers in Paris don't seem to have been bona fide Islamic fundamentalists or extremists. For example, Ibrahim Abdeslam, who authorities say blew himself up outside a Paris café, reportedly "smoked cannabis every day while he stayed at home listening to Arabic hip hop and claiming unemployment benefits," according to his former wife Naima.[79] The ex-wife told the *Daily Mail* that Abdeslam smoked obscene amounts of pot ("three or four joints a day") and "never went to mosque or prayed."[80] Naima also claimed her ex-husband was not the least bit interested in politics or current affairs and "never watched the news because they did not have a TV." She further suggested that he "had no gripe with the West." Ibrahim and his younger brother Salah, also accused of involvement in the attacks, ran a dodgy bar in Molenbeek, Belgium, where they lived, but it was recently "closed down after [their] drug-dealing ways came to the attention of police," reports the *Mail*.

So the two brothers were petty criminals and drug addicts, but somehow transformed into diehard "jihadis" seeking martyrdom in an unrealistically short time frame.

The *Mail* article claims that Belgian authorities placed Ibrahim on a "terror watch list" at some point, which was confirmed by a report (cited earlier) in the *Independent* stating that Françoise Schepmans, the mayor of the Molenbeek district of Brussels, had a list of "radical Islamists" containing the names of the Abdeslam brothers and Abdelhamid Abaaoud on her desk a month before the Paris attacks. But that is suspicious in itself considering there were no real indications that the Abdeslam brothers were radicals, and plenty of signals to the contrary, most notably the revelations of Ibrahim's ex-wife. Were they put on that list simply for authorities to point at later to "prove" the brothers were "radical Islamists"? It's a possibility worth considering.

A third Abdeslam brother, Mohamed, who is not suspected of any involvement in the Paris attacks, hinted that his brothers may have been set-up, telling a Belgian TV channel: "I deeply believe that my brothers weren't radicalised. That's the reason why we didn't see anything. I rather feel like my brothers were manipulated."[81]

Even more bizarre is the revelation that the alleged "mastermind" of the Paris attacks, Abdelhamid Abaaoud, was spotted "drinking and smoking cannabis" in a Saint-Denis bar after the events of the 13th! "The apparent architect of the Paris attacks was reportedly seen on the streets of Paris shortly after the atrocities, smoking cannabis and drinking with a group of men, witnesses have claimed," reported the *Independent*.[82]

A witness, Amel Alla, claims she is "99.9 per cent sure" she saw Abaaoud with eight to ten other men "smoking joints and drinking beers" on the street after the attacks. Another witness, Jean-Jacques, claims Abaaoud "was sitting in the street with a bottle of whisky and he offered some to me."

So if these witnesses are correct, this battle-hardened ISIS jihadist was publicly lounging around smoking pot and drinking whiskey shortly after the Paris attacks without a worry in the world. Not only does the smoking and drinking betray Abaaoud's "jihadi" credentials, but this inexplicably reckless behaviour does not support the depiction of him as a "terror mastermind." What is being described here is more like a bumbling patsy. We are supposed to believe that this man had just organized the deadliest attack in France since the Second World War, yet instead of keeping a low profile or fleeing the country, which any serious terrorist would do, Abaaoud deliberately goes out of his way to draw attention to himself publicly whilst engaged in activities considered *haram* (forbidden) in Islam. None of this makes any sense.

As detailed earlier, Abaaoud's sensational escapades—traipsing in and out of Europe with remarkable ease, "planning operations" under the noses of authorities and miraculously escaping, then returning to "mastermind" the Paris attacks—are not the least bit believable; unless of course he was a protected asset of NATO.

Indestructible Passports and False Reporting

Another parallel with 9/11 is the claim that two "suicide bombers" who allegedly detonated outside of the Stade de France were identified by their passports conveniently "found" by police at the scene, having survived the explosions in legible condition. A headline in the Independent reads: "Syrian and Egyptian passports found near bodies of suicide bombers at Stade de France."[83]

This mimics the 9/11 fairy tale of an al-Qaeda terrorist's passport that magically managed to survive the explosive plane crash into the tower and a massive fall to the ground, finding its way into the hands of police virtually without a blemish.[84] In total the 9/11 official story contends that four passports belonging to various "hijackers" were recovered at the assorted crash sites and such items were opportunely used as prime evidence of Muslim guilt.[85]

French authorities have now admitted that the Syrian passport they "found" in Paris was fake and bore the name of a Syrian Army soldier,

Ahmad al-Mohammad, who died months ago.[86] Serbian authorities later detained a man carrying a passport with the exact same details as the one "found" in Paris, apparently faked by the same forger in Turkey. So who was the real bomber if there even was one?[87]

Another damning clue that reveals the fabricated nature of the Paris attacks storyline is the false reporting emanating from Fox News that immediately established the "ISIS" connection in the public mind. Within an hour of the attacks becoming news, Fox News ran a false story alleging that a "suspect" had been arrested at the Bataclan theatre and told police "I am from ISIS."[88] Fox hyped the story multiple times on their live news coverage[89]; it was picked up by other mainstream media outlets and spread like wildfire across the Internet. Fox News anchor Shepard Smith said on air:

> There is one man who has been arrested in Paris tonight. Arrested by French authorities who told French authorities "I am from ISIS." I now have further information: that suspect has just told French police within the last hour or so, "I am Syrian, I was here with two others, we were recruited by ISIS and this is … an ISIS mission." [The man] was quoted from inside the [Bataclan] theatre saying, "This is for Syria. Allahu Akbar."[90]

The story cannot be true because none of the alleged shooters/bombers at Bataclan or the other sites were taken into custody—all are now said to have either detonated explosive suicide vests or were shot dead by police.[91] An eighth suspect, Salah Abdeslam, is supposedly still on the run. Yet this incident alleging a phantom "suspect" had been arrested and confessed to being sent by ISIS was trumpeted across the web as the initial "smoking gun proof" of the terrorist group's involvement, alongside widespread news reports that the gunmen were shouting "Allahu Akbar" and "this is for Syria" during the massacre. The latter claim is questionable as well. An early eyewitness in the Bataclan theatre during the attack, radio reporter Julien Pearce, told CNN that the gunmen "didn't shout anything. Not Allah Akbar or something like this. They said nothing. They just shot people."[92] An audio clip of the Bataclan shooting was released and no shouts of "Allah Akbar" can be heard on the tape.[93]

Considering Fox News' well-known status as a factory of lies for the Neocon-Zionist propaganda machine, the fake "I am from ISIS" story appears to have been deliberately planted disinformation intended to build up the "ISIS did it" narrative early on during the tragedy when the public is most gullible.

Mass Shooting Drill

The phenomenon of "drills" or "exercises" that mimic the events that later take place is a staple of the false flag terror formula.

Such "terror drills" took place on 9/11, where authorities mimicked hijackings and jets crashing into buildings[94]; on 7/7 in London, a private security company linked to British intelligence was running a drill simulating tube train explosions[95]; in the weeks leading up to the much-hyped Ottawa shooting of October 22nd, 2014, Canadian authorities had been running drills simulating "ISIS-style attacks"[96]; a year or so before the "Sydney Siege" hostage taking in Australia, a "counter-terrorism" drill was run by Australian authorities that took place in the exact same location as the future event[97]; and on and on.

The Paris attacks were no exception. A telling headline in Bloomberg Business News reads: "Hours Before the Terror Attacks, Paris Practiced for a Mass Shooting."[98] On the morning of the event, a multi-site "attack exercise" coordinated by French EMT authorities and police simulated a mass shooting. "An exercise with the exact same scenario as the one that happened that night," pointed out a guest on a French television show, commenting on the coincidence.[99] French physician and EMT worker Patrick Pelloux revealed the existence of the drill on French radio, stating:

> As luck would have it, in the morning at the Paris SAMU (EMT), a multi-site attack exercise had been planned. So we were prepared. What needs to be known is there was a mobilisation of police forces, firemen, EMTs, associations who came [to participate] and we tried to save as many people as possible.[100]

Pelloux is no stranger to the media. His Wikipedia page says he "became well known in France during the 2003 European heat wave, as he was the first to denounce that thousands of people were dying, the French authorities denying it."[101] Pelloux just happened to be near the headquarters of Charlie Hebdo during that attack, and was one of the first responders on the scene.[102] He purportedly called President Hollande directly to inform him of the incident. Oddly, Pelloux has written articles for the Charlie Hebdo publication since 2004 and has also done some acting work.[103] Some suspect he is an example of the "crisis actor" phenomenon.[104] The Frenchman's eyebrow-raising track record justifies the suspicions.

The Zionist Connection

Zionist Jews seem to have an uncanny knack for possessing foreknowledge of major events, especially terrorist attacks that just so happen to benefit Israel.

On 9/11, Israelis were forewarned over an Israeli instant messaging service called Odigo of a looming terrorist attack in New York.[105] Conspicuously, the World Trade Center was bought by a Jewish-Zionist billionaire, Larry Silverstein, six weeks before the attacks. Silverstein, who is personal friends with Benjamin Netanyahu and a lavish contributor to pro-Israel causes, attributed his absence from a routine business meeting at the top of the North Tower on 9/11 to a "miracle." He then collected billions in terrorism insurance money and his destroyed buildings gave birth to the Israeli-devised "War on Terror."

A similar scenario is unfolding around the Paris attacks. Shortly after the carnage, the *Times of Israel*, a hardline Zionist media outlet, reported that France's Jewish community leaders were tipped off on the morning of the 13th about an "impending large terrorist attack" in the country. The article states:

> Just Friday morning, security officials in France's Jewish community were informed of the very real possibility of an impending large terrorist attack in the country, according to Jonathan-Simon Sellem, a freelance journalist and a representative of French citizens in Israel. The Jewish community, already on high alert ahead of several planned high-profile events Sunday, had been told that after several minor attacks in France this month, a large terrorist event was thought to be on the horizon. Security experts in France, Sellem told *The Times of Israel* from Paris on Saturday morning, are now comparing the country's situation with that of Israel.[106]

The Zionist editors quickly swooped in and revised the story, changing the original wording from "Friday morning" to "for months."[107] The new phrasing implies that the warning was a vague caution that had been ongoing for "months" and was not specific to what happened on the 13th. The attempt at obfuscation notwithstanding, the French Jewish community was clearly provided with some kind of insider information, most likely by the Israeli Mossad, about an imminent major terror attack—information that no other French citizens were privy to.

To add to these suspicions, we know that the Bataclan theatre, where the main massacre allegedly took place during a concert, was until recently under Jewish ownership. French Jew Joel Laloux owned the venue for 40 years but oddly decided to part with it two months before the attack![108] *The Times of Israel*, in its article titled "Jewish owners recently sold Paris's Bataclan theatre, where IS killed dozens," informs us that, "The Bataclan theatre, targeted in Friday night's Paris terror attacks, was Jewish-owned for decades, but was sold two months ago, its former owners said."[109] It adds that the venue "has for years been the target of anti-Zionist groups as the Jewish owners often put on pro-Israel events." The Jewish Telegraphic Agency confirmed the details of the Bataclan owner's pro-Israel credentials in an article headlined "Before terror, Paris' Bataclan theatre threatened for pro-Israel events," which states:

> Before Friday's bloodbath at the Le Bataclan concert venue in Paris, this centrally located hall from the 19th century had received numerous threats over pro-Israel events hosted there. From at least 2006-2009, Le Bataclan was the venue for the annual fundraising gala of Migdal, the French Jewish nonprofit group that supports the Israeli Border Police. Last month, the theater served as the meeting place for a gathering of some 500 Zionist Christians who came there in support of Israel.[110]

Mirroring 9/11, the Zionist ownership of the targeted venue in Paris has kindled much suspicion about the Bataclan's proprietor, Joel Laloux, and what he may have known about the attack in advance. The report that French Jewish community leaders were on "high alert" about an impending large-scale terror attack "for months," and the fact that French intelligence learned in September from an apprehended "French jihadist" that ISIS had ordered attacks on concerts, raises the question whether Laloux was himself made aware of what was to come, prompting him to suddenly sell his business and move to Israel.[111]

These Zionist connections are intriguing and coalesce nicely with the reality that any anti-Western terrorism blamed on Muslims, no matter their orientation, is good for Israel. To no one's surprise, Israel's bellicose Prime Minster Benjamin Netanyahu wasted no time exploiting the tragedy in Paris for political gain. Much like he did after the Charlie Hebdo attack and every other major terror spectacle from 9/11 forward, Netanyahu quickly tried to link the bloodshed in Paris to "what Israel goes through," declaring that "an attack on one of us is an attack on us all."[112] CRIF, the main Jewish lobby umbrella group in France, echoed Netanyahu's propagandistic chorus, publicly calling for a "world war against jihadism" in response to the attacks.[113]

French Leaders are Zionist Puppets

The French political leadership has for some time now been acting almost exclusively in the interests of Jews and Israel. Alongside those of America and Canada, French leaders over the past decade have been consistently and fanatically pro-Zionist.

The French regime has made pro-Palestinian activism exceedingly difficult in France and has desperately moved to scuttle anti-Israel boycotters. France was the first country in the world to ban pro-Palestinian street protests in 2014.[114] At the behest of the Zionist lobby, French courts have even penalized pro-Palestinian activists under the country's "anti-hate" laws. An October 2015 *International Business Times* article on the issue noted:

> Anti-Israel activists have taken to Twitter to protest a French high court decision upholding a ruling that sentenced a group of pro-Palestinian activists in Colmar, France, to pay high fines, for urging grocery store patrons to forgo products made in Israel. The activists were prosecuted under a French law that prohibits speech that "incites racial hatred," and it has often been used to prevent hate speech.[115]

France also plays host to a particularly virulent branch of the Jewish Defense League (JDL), a radical Zionist ISIS of sorts, which enjoys relative impunity to conduct its violent and coercive methods aimed at intimidating and silencing anti-Zionists throughout the country.[116]

Successive French Presidents have all made groveling public displays of affinity for Israel and the domestic Jewish community. Former President Nicolas Sarkozy, a man of partial Jewish heritage who was outed by the French daily *Le Figaro* as a long-time asset of the Israeli Mossad[117], has made no secret of his love affair with Israel, telling a Jewish journalist that Israel's struggles are "the fight of my life."[118]

A *Jerusalem Post* article titled "Unpopular at home, Hollande appreciated in Israel," quotes the French president stating that he "will always remain a friend of Israel."[119] Hollande, like Sarkozy before him, has parroted the Israeli line on Iran, Hezbollah and the conflict with the Palestinians.[120]

Hollande's foreign minister, Laurent Fabius, is Jewish. The Prime Minister Manuel Valls is blessed with a Jewish wife. Valls is a favourite of the French Jewish lobby for his incessant public pledges to stamp out "anti-Semitism" in France. Following the Charlie Hebdo events, Valls decried the prospect of French Jews emigrating to Israel en masse, stating that "if 100,000 Jews leave, France will no longer be France," adding that the Republic "will be judged a failure" if relieved of its Jews. In 2011, Valls told an audience that he is, by virtue of his Jewish wife, "eternally tied to the Jewish community and to Israel."[121] That and other comments sparked former French foreign minister Roland Dumas to state that Valls is "under Jewish influence."[122]

In April 2015, Valls himself spearheaded a government-backed initiative to stifle criticism of Jews, allocating $107 million of taxpayers' money to the censorship project.[123] Reflecting the attitude and wishes of his Zionist backers, Valls has relentlessly pursued a witch-hunt against the wildly popular French comedian Dieudonne, who works anti-Zionist themes into his comedy skits.[124] Under the leadership of Hollande and Valls, the French regime has engaged in endless judicial harassment of Dieudonne, culminating in the comedian's arrest days after the Charlie Hebdo affair on Orwellian trumped up charges of "condoning terrorism."[125]

The West Created ISIS to Help Israel

The ISIS phenomenon itself was deliberately cultivated by Western powers as part of their lunatic bid—primarily in the interests of Israel—to depose Syria's resilient President Bashar al-Assad and bleed the Arab country to death.

The evidence for this has been mounting for years, culminating in a now legendary admission from the former head of the US Defense Intelligence Agency (DIA), Michael Flynn, that Washington made a "willful decision" to support and facilitate the rise of Wahhabist, Salafist and al-Qaeda-linked extremist groups—entities that have metastasized into what is now known as the "Islamic State"—in Syria as a counter-weight against Assad, and by extension Iran and Hezbollah.[126]

A 2012 DIA report, issued under Flynn's leadership, firstly acknowledged that the Syrian rebels were (during this early stage of the conflict) dominated by "Salafist, Muslim Brotherhood and al-Qaeda" extremist elements.[127] Despite the involvement of said extremists and religious fanatics, the intelligence document wrote, "the West, the Gulf States and Turkey" continued to be the primary backers of this violent, extremist-led opposition in Syria in order to topple the Assad regime. Specifically, the document states that "there is the possibility of establishing a … Salafist principality in Eastern Syria," and that such a development was seen by the "supporting powers" (the West, Gulf States and Turkey) of the anti-Assad militants as a strategic opportunity to "isolate the Syrian regime, which is considered the strategic depth of Shia expansion (Iraq and Iran)."

Security scholar Nafeez Ahmed summarized the essence of the DIA document, writing:

> The secret Pentagon document thus provides extraordinary confirmation that the US-led coalition currently fighting ISIS, had three years ago welcomed the emergence of an extremist 'Salafist Principality' in the region as a way to undermine Assad, and block off the strategic expansion of Iran. Crucially, Iraq is labeled as an integral part of this 'Shia expansion.'[128]

Following Washington's lead, France itself has played an indispensible role in that agenda, funneling cash and arms to anti-Assad rebels, including the head-choppers of ISIS and al-Nusra Front, from the outset of the unrest in Syria. A December 2012 *Guardian* report entitled, "France funding Syrian rebels in new push to oust Assad," laid bare France's dirty hands behind Syria's internal woes. "France has emerged as the most prominent backer of Syria's armed opposition and is now directly funding rebel groups around Aleppo as part of a new push to oust the embattled Assad regime," the report, authored by journalist Martin Chulov, explained.[129] Chulov goes on:

> Large sums of cash have been delivered by French government proxies across the Turkish border to rebel commanders in the past month, diplomatic sources have confirmed. The money has been used to buy weapons inside Syria and to fund armed operations against loyalist forces. ... [A]ccording to Western and Turkish officials as well as rebel leaders, the influx of money has made a difference in recent weeks as momentum on the battlefields of the north steadily shifts towards the opposition.[130]

Some of the French cash, Chulov noted, "reached Islamist groups who were desperately short of ammunition and who had increasingly turned for help towards al-Qaida aligned jihadist groups in and around Aleppo." Chulov further revealed that French military advisors "met with rebel groups inside Syria, in an area between Lebanon and Damascus, in further evidence of efforts by Paris to step up pressure on President Assad."

An August 2014 France24 report titled "France delivered arms to Syrian rebels, Hollande confirms" tells us that, "President François Hollande said on Thursday that France had delivered weapons to rebels battling the Syrian regime of Bashar al-Assad 'a few months ago.'"[131]

"French imperialism has been arming Syrian Islamist opposition forces since at least the spring of 2013," writes Pierre Mabut in a World Socialist Web Site report on French support for anti-Assad armed militants.[132] Citing French newspaper *Le Monde*, Mabut writes that France under Hollande's leadership has "provided weapons including 12.7-mm machine guns, rocket launchers, body armour and communications equipment" to Islamist insurgents in Syria.

The West's actions in Syria are, in large part, motivated by its subservience to Israel, which earmarked the Assad regime for extinction years ago. The former Israeli ambassador to the US, Michael Oren, outlined in candid terms Tel Aviv's desire to oust Assad and install a friendly regime in its place. He told the *Jerusalem Post* in a September 2013 interview that Tel Aviv's goal of regime change in Syria was "a position we had well before the outbreak of hostilities in Syria. With the outbreak of hostilities we continued to want Assad to go."[133] Oren further pontificated about Assad's status as a "keystone" in a "strategic arc that extends from Tehran, to Damascus to Beirut" – an alliance that Israel views as a major impediment to its hegemony in the region, and sought to disrupt through proxy warfare.

Hollande Brings Back Pathetic Bushisms

Resurrecting Bush-era neocon propaganda, French President François Hollande said that Islamic extremists, specifically the ones who allegedly attacked Paris, "fight us because France is a country of freedom."[134] If the statement was not an attempt at ironic humour, then Hollande must be delusional.

France is by no means a "free country." It boasts some of the most restrictive laws against free speech in the world (such as draconian "Holocaust denial" and "hate speech" laws), on top of newly minted police state powers sanctioning mass surveillance of the civilian population. In the name of "freedom," Hollande declared a "state of emergency," effectively putting the nation under martial law—that is to say military rule with enforced curfews, totalitarian opinion-monitoring and widespread mass surveillance of the citizenry. The autocrat successfully pushed to revise French law to allow a state of emergency (martial law) to last three months instead of twelve days.[135] Soon enough he'll scrap all existing laws and declare a full-on dictatorship.

Even if we are to accept that "ISIS" did this attack in Paris, it was not because they hate France's illusory "freedom," but because France has taken part in the "anti-ISIS" bombing coalition that was launched by the West more than a year ago. France has ostensibly (although not actually) been hitting ISIS targets for 15 months, which is what ISIS cites as their primary motive for attacks against Western targets. More-over, French politicians themselves funded, armed and trained many of these militants and terrorists in the first place in their failed criminal ef-fort to overthrow Assad. And they are now expressing shock that their own insane and immoral foreign policies have (allegedly) come back to haunt them? No, France's leaders are playing a sick and twisted double game, using their own people as pawns in it.

So even if we are to ignore the fact that Western powers conspired to create and sponsor ISIS to execute a Zionist-inspired regime change policy in Syria; even if we are to ignore all of the anomalies surround-ing this latest terror spectacle in Paris that point to a false flag, or at the very least a "let it happen" scenario; the truth is that President Hollande is a cynical charlatan who is conning his own population with auda-cious lies, and is, like his criminal counterparts in Brussels, London, Ottawa, Canberra and Washington, using staged terror to expedite the Zionist-Globalist agenda, of which he is a loyal servant.

PARIS AGAIN HIT BY (FICTIONAL) TERROR

Nick Kollerstrom

The second Paris outrage of 2015 happened on Friday November 13th, just days after Halloween (October 31st), when a Russian civilian plane had been blown out of the sky. The date—11/13/15, in US terms—was a remarkable sequence of odd numbers.

A year earlier in November 2014, *The Economist* published their "The World in 2015" issue with a front cover widely surmised to contain Illuminati symbolism. Let us inspect its bottom right-hand corner.

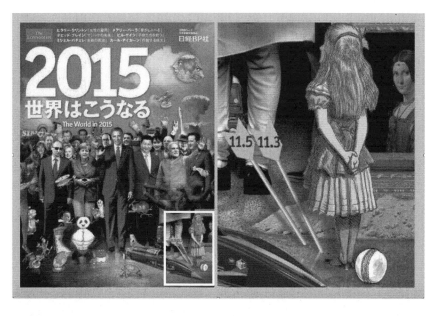

Here is a close-up of the relevant image. We see:
- Two arrows (indicating two attacks)?
- A painting in The Louvre indicating PARIS (which would indeed suffer two attacks in 2015).
- The magazine was pre-viewing the year 2015 so "11" would tend to indicate THE MONTH OF NOVEMBER.
- Alice (portrayed as in "Through the Looking Glass") alludes, I suggest, to a *mirror-delusion* whereby a true enemy creates a virtual enemy that is an image of itself; the reference to "Alice" is a coded confession that THE STATE ITSELF IS THE TERRRORIST creating a false reality for the masses, a "looking-glass world" or "wonderland."

The two arrows have numbers on them (11.3 and 11.5) which are on the same level, suggesting they should be put together. Rearranged we are shown THE VERY DATE OF THE ATTACK 11/13/15 (or 13/11/15 using the French system). In other words, the digits 1, 1, 3, 1, 1, and 5 are a number puzzle with a unique solution. There is only one way to arrange them to form a date in 2015, and that date is the date of the second and larger of the two Paris attacks.

THIS FOREKNOWLEDGE OF THE PARIS EVENT IS UN-EQUIVOCAL.

Thus the manufacturers of the "War on Terror" laugh in the face of humanity as they lead us through lie after lie and war after war towards their desired end. We wonder whether there is a mysterious law, whereby the perpetrators of the fabricated-terror events have to tell us in advance, they have to give the warning! Let us now run through the evidence, indicating who did it.

Anomalous Failure of Intelligence despite heightened surveillance powers

Following the Charlie Hebdo attacks in January, the French regime implemented a despotic anti-terror bill that gave authorities virtually unlimited surveillance powers. France essentially declared martial law, dispatching tens of thousands of troops in the streets. The authorities could wiretap phone communications and snoop on internet traffic of ordinary citizens[136]. Despite this power to spy on just about anybody, they once again failed to stop "a highly sophisticated, multi-faceted attack that would have required so much logistical expertise and know-how that it is palpably unfeasible such a plot could succeed without the help of insiders within the French state (and possibly other states)."[137]

Pre-cognition of the Event

The Event as *predicted* by *Paris Match* on October 2nd was to be a French Style 9/11, "un 11 septembre à la française." Not only was it coming, but it was *impossible to avoid:* "impossible a dejouer"! Judge Trévédic explained in that issue of *Paris Match*: "The attacks in France will be on a scale comparable to 9/11." *Will* be?

How can a senior figure be so confident that a unique event in French history is about to occur?

Intelligence? If they had the Intelligence, they should have been able to prevent the attacks rather than allow the shooters to shoot up the city at their leisure, unmolested, for hours on end.

Drills

As is usual for state-fabricated terror events, drills were planned simulating the event on that very same day: as with 9/11, the London bombing, the Oslo/Breivic event, the Boston Marathon bombing, and others.[138]

Patrick Pelloux appears to be France's version of Peter Power: a character involved in the earlier Charlie Hebdo events, just as Power was for British terror events, who then became a chronicler at Charlie Hebdo. Pelloux explained on *France Info Radio* that Paris police were prepared because, "as luck would have it", they'd **planned an exercise to train for multi-site attacks on that very morning**, Friday November 13th, 2015: *"Exactement la meme scenario"* (exactly the same scenario.)

Although estimates of the actual number of dead keep changing and hover between 125 and 130, are we not astonished that Thomas Loeb, who was responsible for leading the drill's medical services, explained how it had been planned for *"Quelques heures avant la tragédie" (a few hours before the tragedy).* A few hours before—and **it planned for 129 dead?**[139]

> The eight SAMU Ile-de-France met on Friday [13 November] for an exercise pertaining to the simulation of a terrorist attack in Paris. We gathered in the Coordinating meeting room of the defense area Ile-de-France, that morning, to work on the hypothesis [scenario] of an armed group involved in attacks in several locations Paris. This is what we call a tabletop exercise to consider the coordination of our actions... a very clear working hypothesis for months, the idea of multiple simultaneous attacks.

One of the drills was at the actual hotel where the German football team were staying.[140]

Wiki Up Too Soon

The *Wikipedia* account was posted up *while the event was in full swing*! The police did not storm the Bataclan until after midnight, and yet within two hours from the onset of the attacks, at 23:06 a full and detailed account appeared. It was complete with footnotes, and specified "Syria" as being mentioned by a witness at the Bataclan. It had "5 or 6 terrorists" and "three suicide bombers." That initial version specified that in a televised statement at approximately 23:58 (local time), French President François Hollande declared a state of emergency and closing of borders for the whole of France. That was too early—rather like the BBC reporting the collapse of Tower 7 before it had happened on 9/11. A confusion over timezones? Or "precognition"? The too-soon Wikipedia account with its unduly-detailed narrative then hardly changed as events unfolded. We may infer that its purpose was (again, as is the usual practice in False-Flag attacks) to **define and stabilise the narrative.**

Timeline, Evening of 13th November, Paris time

9.17   **Explosions heard in the vicinity of the Stade de France.**
9.20   **Shooting outside Casa Nostra pizzeria.**
9.45   **Bataclan shooting, as "anthem to the devil" being played**
9.50   **Suicide bomber blows up near Stadium**
10.10 **A "hostage situation" in Bataclan.**
11.06 **Wiki site goes up**
00:44 **Police storm the Bataclan**

Jewish foreknowledge and the Israeli Owners of the Bataclan Nightclub

The *Jewish Telegraphic Agency* confirmed the details of the Bataclan owner's pro-Israel credentials in an article headlined "Before terror, Paris":

> Before Friday's bloodbath at the Le Bataclan concert venue in Paris, this centrally located hall from the 19th century had received numerous threats over pro-Israel events hosted there. From at least 2006-2009, Le Bataclan was the venue for the annual fundraising gala of Migdal, the French Jewish nonprofit group that supports the Israeli Border Police. Last month, the theater served as the meeting place for a gathering of some 500 Zionist Christians who came there in support of Israel.

Zionist ownership of the targeted venue in Paris has kindled much suspicion. Questions have arisen about the Bataclan's proprietor, Joel Laloux, and what he may have known about the attack in advance. According to *The Times of Israel*, the Jewish proprietors, who had owned the Bataclan for forty years, for some reason decided to sell shortly before this event—and did so *on September 11th of all days*.[141] They emigrated to Israel after the sale.

Co-owner Joel "told Channel ... he took a call from the theater at the time of the attack and I could hear the gunfire." He added that a member of the Eagles of Death Metal was "hit by a bullet and killed." "There is blood everywhere," he said. "It will take three days just to clean that up." That claim of the band member being hit was incorrect, but it shows a desire to appear knowledgeable on the part of the old owners. After selling the property, did they just happen to be on the phone to the new owners and hear the gunfire? Would the new owners really have wished to phone Israel at such a moment?

Apparently the Bataclan's owners were not the only Jewish (ex-)Parisians with foreknowledge. According to an Israeli newspaper, the "Jewish community" in Paris knew of the impending event on Friday morning. "Just Friday, security officials in France's Jewish community were informed..." wrote *The Times of Israel* the very next day, November 14th, clearly describing foreknowledge of the terror attack. After researchers called attention to the anomaly, the text was soon altered to "for months, security officials... " Those who design these events remain hidden, but is seems they cannot resist adding their signature, as it were.

Bataclan

The world has been shown only one major image of apparent dead bodies that night, and these were in the Bataclan theatre. (David Dees' collage on the front cover of this book includes part of the photo.) Journalists were not allowed to enter this theatre after whatever had happened. The extant photo is a very low-resolution screen-capture image, deliberately so. No emergency medics attend the bodies, nor were any police there, as they should have been. Five unidentified people stand in the background on the upper balcony. If four or five killers had been shooting for ten to fifteen minutes, should there not be a larger number of dead? Eighty or 85 were reported at the Bataclan. Some claim that freshly-killed dead bodies were dragged in to lie there, which accounts for the blood being "swept" on the floor; but this seems unlikely. The bodies resemble dummies with "blood" splashed about and swept strangely into a huge heart-shape upon the bare concrete. None of the normal carpets and chairs for concerts are present—as if the owners did not want them spoiled by this macabre theatre.

Those are more or less the only "dead bodies" seen in available photos of the Friday the 13th Paris event. There are one or two images of blankets covering "corpses," which could have been dummies left over from the drill earlier that day. Suspects are either allegedly dead or escaped, and therefore unavailable for questioning, as with the Charlie Hebdo event. Not one cellphone picture of the alleged dramas is up on Youtube.

"The random slaughter was to go on intermittently for two hours and 40 minutes." Did it take that long for the police to arrive, in central Paris? Attacks began as the band were playing a favourite number Kiss the Devil. "Helen described how the killers chillingly dispatched disabled fans..." (*The Mail*, 16th November). I hope readers are not believing a word of this.

Within an hour of the attacks becoming news, Fox News ran a story alleging that a suspect arrested at the Bataclan told the police "I am from ISIS." (Just as the Charlie Hebdo suspects instructed witnesses to "tell the media it's al-Qaeda in Yemen.") Fox hyped the story multiple times on their live news coverage and it was picked up by other mainstream media outlets and soon spread across the Internet. Fox News anchor Shepard Smith said on air:

> There is one man who has been arrested in Paris tonight. Arrested by French authorities who told French authorities "I am from ISIS." I now have further information: That suspect has just told French police within the last hour or so, "I am Syrian, I was here with two others, we were recruited by ISIS and this is … an ISIS mission." [The man] was quoted from inside the [Bataclan] theatre saying, "This is for Syria. Allahu Akbar."

The story cannot be true (as Brandon Martinez has pointed out) because none of the alleged shooters/bombers at Bataclan or any of the other sites were taken into custody. In the aftermath of state-fabricated terror, the patsies used cannot *ever* be allowed to speak to the media, or to any public figure—they are killed or jailed, or if deemed to be valuable may change their identity after apparently dying.

This Fox News report which at once established the "ISIS" connection in the public mind has to remind us of the US news proclaiming Osama Bin Laden as the culprit almost immediately after the Towers crumbled on 9/11. Such reports inadvertently expose the true perpetrators.

At the Bataclan, a radio presenter witness, Pierre Janaszak described how the gunmen took 20 hostages and he heard one of them tell their captives that "it was Hollande's fault for intervening in Syria." Do we assume those 20 hostages are dead now, hostages that he had time to count?

According to *Daily Mail* (15 November) one of the suicide bombers that blew himself up in the Bataclan was identified after his finger was found. Is this not a mere insult to their readers' intelligence? Can the story get any sillier?

Crisis Actors

Immediate responses, before the official story has stabilised, are valuable. We quote three: "I also knew last night watching Kelly's File on FOX that the 'parade' of 'survivors' on camera with Space Blankets looked very fishy—at least four of these people coming out of the Concert Hall were smiling? laughing? Would you be smiling after witnessing a blood bath massacre as we've been told? People fall back into the same trap and believe the media. Some of it is real. Some of it involved crisis actors... all of it involved the Elite who have been planning this for a long time." (Barbara Joshua).

One must here agree, that the groups of "survivors" seen wearing their gold "space blankets" did look very casual and unharmed. Here is another thoughtful comment made the next morning:

> In the very early hours there were no bloody scenes reported, no eye witnesses telling us what happened, lack of activity from emergency responses (I expect to see a mass rush of emergency calls but nothing) ISIS constantly being blamed, captions in the headlines saying immigrants were shouting for Syria when attacks happened and how emergency measure and tighter control will be needed to deal with this threat. All this to me is the call signs of a false flag event and is very similar to the London bombings. Within minutes it's all being given to us what happened, CCTV footage seems to be hard to come by, it will most likely be confiscated and kept under national security.

Concerning the survivors seen emerging from the concert theatre: "No one is in shock to any degree. People are moving slowly. Others are milling around. No one is in obvious pain. There are no raw gunshot wounds from an AK-47 to be found...No one is suffering from burnt, shredded flesh and/or amputations...These people could be crisis actors...The corpses are also fake."

Of all the people in that concert hall, did not one of them take a photo or record the screams? No video shows the killing spree.

From the Bataclan comes the testimony of the British soft-porn actress Ginnie Watson, which changed on different narrations: She was with one friend, then she was with her two friends. In her Fox News interview the Sunday after she looked as if she could hardly keep a straight face. Such dubious testimonies suggest a set-up job.

White Male Killers

On the Rue de la Fointaine au Roi in the 11th arrondissement a gunman was reported as opening fire on patrons inside the Casa Nostra café. From a *Guardian* report:

> "He was standing in a shooting position," Colclough said. "He had his right leg forward and he was standing with his left leg back. He was holding up to his left shoulder a long automatic machine gun. It was fully intentional, professional bursts of three or four shots. Everything he was wearing was tight, no zippers or collars.Everything was toned black. A man in military uniform, black jumper, black trousers, black shoes or boots and a machine gun."

Despite the heightened security around Paris in the wake of Charlie Hebdo, despite the prediction a month before that something like this could happen, a man dressed all in black could walk along a street carrying a machine gun, set it up, and start spraying restaurant-customers …and then get away. He allegedly killed five or six diners. But do we see any trace of dead bodies?

Here's a different witness in the *Mirror*:

> At about 9:30 p.m. a new-looking black Mercedes pulled up outside with dark tinted windows at the back and the passenger and driver windows down. I could clearly see the passenger's face as he was not wearing a hat or mask. As soon as the car stopped he quietly opened the door and got out in front of the restaurant. That is when I saw he was holding a machine gun that was resting on his hip. I could not take in what I was witnessing.
>
> People outside spotted the shooter approaching with his gun and tried to run inside but he shot them down in the doorway. Then people inside moved forward to see what was happening and he sprayed more bullets into them. I was trying to catch them on my camera phone but the gunman saw the light on my mobile and I ducked down behind the wall as they fired at my hotel. The gunman calmly reloaded his weapon several times. He then shot up at the windows in the street to make sure nobody was filming anything or taking photographs. It lasted over six minutes
>
> He fired lots of bullets. He was **white, clean shaven and had dark hair neatly trimmed.** He was dressed all in black accept for a red scarf. The shooter was aged about 35 and had an extremely muscular build, which you could tell from the size of his arms. He looked like a weightlifter. He was not wearing gloves and his face was expressionless as he walked towards the bar.

The driver had opened his door shortly before the shooting began and stood up with his arm and a machine gun rested on the roof of the car. He stood there with his foot up in the door acting as a lookout. I would describe him as tall, with dark hair and also quite muscular. **They looked like soldiers or mercenaries and carried the whole thing out like a military operation.** It was clear that they were both very heavily armed and the gunman was carrying several magazines on him. They both then coolly sat back in the car and sped off in the direction of the Bataclan Theatre.[142]

These sound like special forces killers, hired mercenaries, trained commandoes. Of course they were not caught, but simply vanished into the night…and then into the memory hole. No mainstream media outlet raised any questions about these white paramilitaries, even after the French authorities blamed the shootings on non-white amateurs.

Oddly, no corpses appear around this café after the event, nor does a single photo record this amazing sight. No one records their license plate number.

One survivor told *Sky News* that he had been in the Bataclan concert hall and saw the attackers who murdered hostages. He added that one of the gunmen had white skin and blonde hair. Another white male killer was reported the next day in the *Metro* newspaper.[143]

Football Stadium: Passports

The attack included a football stadium at which the President was attending: foreknowledge of his location would have required significant planning and preparation. The three suicide bombers (or two on other reports) at the stadium were the unluckiest in history, as they blew themselves up with only one victim.

The *Guardian* laughably reported, "A suicide bomber approached the gate with a match ticket when he was frisked by a security guard who turned him away." This was at 9:15 p.m. French time, meaning he was attempting entry some two hours after the game had begun. The guard said the attacker was discovered wearing an explosives vest when he was searched at the entrance to the stadium![144] We are indeed in some fairy tale from hell, when a "suicide bomber" allows himself to be frisked—and then what happens? We naturally hear nothing from the two hundred CCTV cameras in use around the stadium.

Two "suicide bombers" who allegedly detonated outside of the Stade de France were identified by their passports fortuitously discovered by police at the scene, having survived the explosions in pristine condition. A headline in the *Independent* read: "Syrian and Egyptian

passports found near bodies of suicide bombers at Stade de France."
Just about every state-fabricated terror event features a passport in pristine condition, so this new report stimulated widespread scorn and
derision. French authorities conceded that the Syrian passport they had
allegedly found in Paris was fake and bore the name of a Syrian Army
soldier, Ahmad al-Mohammad, who died months ago. It remains wholly
unclear who was the real bomber if there even was one.

Is that the best that French Intel can manage? The image would
hardly get anyone through passport control.

Inside the stadium, Hollande and his German counterpart were sitting together. Bangs were heard, presumably coming over the PA
system, but *nothing was seen* and the game continued to its end. Hollande was moved to the most conspicuous part of the stadium, inside a
big glass case—just what one would do with a President in case of a
deadly terror attack. At the end of the match the exits were closed and
the spectators are seen milling around on the pitch. No witness outside
sees the "bombers" or any remains of them: it's the usual story.

Alleged Mastermind

"Europe's most wanted man" Abdelhamid Abaaoud was allegedly
among those killed in a police raid on Wednesday November 19th. A
mangled corpse was identified as that of the Belgian national. They also
shot dead "a female suicide bomber" who died crying "I'm not his
boyfriend." The general policy appears to be, "Let's kill all these terrorists. It's not as if we want information from them."

A witness, Amel Alla, claimed she is "99.9 per cent sure" she saw
one of the patsies, Abdelhamid Abaaoud, with eight to ten other men
"smoking joints and drinking beers" on the street *after* the attacks. Another witness, Jean-Jacques, claims Abaaoud "was sitting in the street
with a bottle of whisky and he offered some to me." That doesn't sound
quite like a Muslim extremist who had just organized the deadliest attack in France since the Second World War.

Ibrahim Abdesalam, who allegedly blew himself up outside a Paris
café—without killing anyone[145]—reportedly "smoked cannabis every
day while he stayed at home listening to Arabic hip hop and claiming
unemployment benefits," according to his former wife Naima. The ex-
wife told the *Daily Mail* that Abdeslam smoked pot ("three or four
joints a day") and "never went to mosque or prayed." She also claimed
her ex-husband was not the least bit interested in politics or current affairs and "never watched the news because they did not have a TV."
She further suggested that he "had no gripe with the West." This is

rather remiscent of the Hebrew-speaking "Mohammed Atta" character and the other cocaine-snorting, hard-drinking, stripper-dating, casino-fancying alleged 9/11 hijackers;[146] also the "no interest in politics" reminds us of the four patsies framed for the 7/7 event in London.[147]

Instant National Response: War declared

Right away, the authorities knew and were proclaiming who had done it. Let's listen to professor Michel Chossudovsky of *Global Research:*

> Within minutes following the attacks, which were launched simultaneously, and prior to the release of a preliminary report by the police, France's media went into overdrive. News commentators and intelligence analysts on France's network TV stated with authority that the attacks emanated from Syria and Iraq...The attacks were described without evidence as an act of revenge and retribution against France for having bombed ISIS strongholds in Syria and Iraq as part of Obama's counter-terrorism air campaign.[148]

Are we really meant to believe, that starving, travel weary, ill, weak people with no money, perpetually high on marijuana, somehow managed to pull off a military-precise attack in five different locations without anyone in the French forces knowing anything—despite all the indications of foreknowledge?

Shortly before midnight on that same day November 13th, France's president announced drastic police state measures against an alleged terrorist network operating nationwide. He surely did not take that decision spontaneously that evening, just prior to the cabinet meeting. He averred that jihadists were behind the attacks, but gave no evidence from from police sources to support his claim. We note his words:

> This is a terrible ordeal which once again assails us. We know where it comes from, who these criminals are, who these terrorists are.[149]

That is almost identical to the phrase Tony Blair used, on the afternoon of 7/7! **We accept the absolute truth of his words—he did indeed know who these criminals are, and where "it" comes from!**

Hollande declared a "state of emergency," effectively putting the nation under martial law—that is to say military rule with enforced curfews, totalitarian opinion-monitoring and widespread mass surveillance of the citizenry. French media immediately started comparing the November 13th attacks in Paris to 9/11, intimating that France was at war and that the alleged Islamic State attack was from abroad, i.e. the Middle East. Without debate in France's National Assembly, a State of Emergency was declared throughout France—a lockdown under military law

Wider Geopolitical perspective

France's largest warship, the nuclear-powered aircraft carrier, the Charles de Gaulle, was parked off the coast of Syria, in need of a script and a role. A new round of Western military intervention was needed "in order to save a proxy war that has been all but lost by the West."[150]

It was clearly state-sponsored terror, but by which state?

> The scale of the attack is that of a military operation. It would have required a large group of well-trained militants, well-armed and funded, with experience in planning and executing coordinated military operations, moving large amounts of weapons clandestinely, experts in the use of weapons and explosives, as well as possessing intelligence capabilities used to somehow circumvent France's increasingly colossal surveillance capabilities.
>
> Like the terrorists and their supply lines pouring out of NATO territory into Syria itself, clearly with immense state sponsorship behind them, those involved in the most recent attacks in Paris are also clearly the recipients of state-sponsored funding and training." …
>
> Just as the Islamic terrorist mercenaries always "accidentally on purpose" leave their calling cards behind, so are the dirty CIA-Mossad fingerprints left indelibly written all over virtually every state sponsored terrorism on this planet.[151]

That is by now hardly disputable.

On the 15th, French planes struck the Syrian town of Raqqa. It was announced that thirty air strikes had destroyed an ISIL training camp and munitions dump. However, a media activist in Raqqa told *Al Jazeera* that these air strikes had just targeted abandoned ISIL bases in the suburbs of the city where there were no ISIL fighters. "It has been two insane nights. Abandoned ISIL posts were targeted at the entrance of the city, along with ISIL checkpoints and several other points. Electricity and water have been cut off as supply lines were hit too."

As usual, the French and American strikes claim to be attacking ISIL/ISIS while actually hitting Syrian towns and villages, knocking out their water and electrical supplies. Creating desolate and abandoned Syrian cities appears to be the strategic goal of the bombing campaign, achieving depopulation and forcing refugees to teem across to Europe.

A new theatre of the absurd is needed to do justice to the demented stories we are being given: the suicide bombers who were not allowed into the football stadium because they had not got a ticket, so they instead blew themselves up outside; the terrible attacks outside lovely cafes, leaving no corpses behind; the people teeming out of the back exit of the Bataclan, to the sound of bang-bang-bang, stepping over a body lying on the pavement by the exit—who later gets up to consult his mobile phone; while a pregnant woman hangs out of a window, by one arm. We are being invited to *suspend our disbelief* if you'll excuse the expression. The crisis actors get to wear smart gold thermal-shock foil; they all look unstressed, unwounded: in vain we search for anyone with a real gunshot wound or with real blood coming out.[152]

View of Ken O'Keefe

"The thing that is most important with regard to the latest manipulation in Paris is not whether it is a hoax or not. It is however a very interesting issue, that I will not deny. But the most important matter is that this is a manipulation, staged or not, and those responsible are as always, very easy to identify because essentially they all work for the same masters, whether they know it or not. Getting caught up in technical issues that are truly inferior to the bigger issue of what is at play is a mistake in my view. I am in no way saying we should not look at every angle, hoax, not a hoax, Mossad/CIA responsibility, Russia in on it or not, etc., indeed we should; but let us not be distracted by issues that are more of a footnote than a primary issue of the event. It is an active attempt to manipulate us into yet more war and always it is based on lies, this is the most important matter and we need to guide people to the primary relevance of this fact and not let details marginalise this critical-for-humanity understanding.

Aside from that it is in my opinion a classic false flag, hoax or not. It is yet another "evil Muslims did it" manipulation. Even if those who carried it out are "ISIS" dipshits who were just successfully shepherded to carry out their silly little delusional "jihad," while probably having no idea at all who they actually work for, it is still a classic state orchestrated false flag. This is not blowback, which means unfortunate and unwanted; this is most definitely wanted and encouraged if not overtly carried out by our so-called "intelligence" services. The big white gunman being a pretty good sign of this. The bottom line is no matter what the details it is just another sad and transparent act that is consistent with the agenda of setting the Middle East alight and fostering a third world war by fanning the flames of a clash of civilisations. That theme/agenda is primary. How it ties into

Greater Israel is also, in my opinion, hugely relevant and critical for people to learn. (Nov 18th).

If Hercule Poirot were investigating this case, he'd probably start off by enquiring:

•   How the police managed to take two hours before storming the concert theatre.

•   How can a killing spree go on that long in central Paris?

•   Who and where are the two burly white men dressed in black that turned up in a new-looking black Mercedes with tinted windows, with a machine gun on the roof of the car—and calmly started shooting at the diners.

•   How did a new-looking passport survive after a suicide bomber blew himself up with a huge bang in a football stadium.

•   How did a terror-drill come to be ongoing that same day in Paris.

•   He might interview the two Jewish-Zionist owners of the Bataclan theater, who had owned it for forty years, then sold it on September 11th, two months before the event.

•   He might then visit the Paris mortuary to enquire about their records of corpses from that night: where he would surely receive an "access denied" notification.

Of course we are just being nostalgic here: police no longer need to search for clues in that old-fashioned manner. Why, they can read in the newspaper who did it…like the rest of us.

ANATOMY OF A FALSE FLAG

by Stephen Lendman

Evidence known so far strongly indicates false flag responsibility for Friday's Paris attacks. They're usually identifiable the way fingerprints ID people.

They're strategically timed, most often for what's planned to follow. Post-9/11 horrors are well documented. America declared still ongoing war on humanity.

The 9/11 incident provided a treasure trove of giveaways showing what happened was other than the official narrative. The most obvious was how could a handful of terrorists outwit America's 16 intelligence agencies, including sophisticated NSA eavesdropping on anyone or anything suspicious?

No evidence implicated Al Qaeda. Nothing to this day—yet claims persist. Without verifiable hard facts, they're specious.

The official 9/11 story was beginning-to-end contradictions and Big Lies—still supported by media scoundrels as gospel despite volumes of evidence proving otherwise.

Bin Laden was dying of natural causes in a Pakistan hospital, reported by CBS on 9/10/01. The *New York Times* and other sources reported his death in December 2001. Obama did not kill Osama. Yet the Big Lie persists.

The mother of all all Big Lies still links so-called Arab terrorists to what happened. Most named on the fated flights were discovered alive and well in their home countries, mainly Saudi Arabia.

Claims about Mohamed Atta's luggage found at Boston's Logan Airport containing "decisive evidence" about Al Qaeda's responsibility were false—including a Saudi passport, an alleged letter saying he planned martyrdom to go to heaven, video instructions on flying Boeing airliners, and other belongings. They were planted to blame Al Qaeda for what happened.

A key unanswered question was why Atta's alleged luggage wasn't on the flight he was accused of hijacking and piloting. Travelers don't leave their belongings behind when boarding flights or disembarking to reach destinations.

No one ever explained why Atta went to Portland, ME from Boston on September 10, necessitating an early return the next day to be on Flight 11.

Another passport allegedly belonging to one of the hijackers was mysteriously found near the Twin Towers site, miraculously not burned by ignited jet fuel.

While the events of 9/11 were unfolding, Secret Service agents let George Bush remain at a Sarasota, Florida school for 30 minutes after learning about the second Twin Tower strike. Standard procedure calls for securing his safety immediately in case of potential danger.

Architects, structural engineers and other knowledgeable professionals know it's scientifically impossible for jet fuel to heat high enough to melt or cause rigid steel columns to crumble.

Controlled demolitions destroyed both towers. Building 7 fell the same way. A likely cruise missile, not an aircraft, struck the Pentagon. No bodies or aircraft parts were found at the site.

Numerous other Big Lies and contradictions completely destroyed the official 9/11 narrative. Will Friday's Paris attack unravel the same way? Odds strongly suggest it.

Here's what happened Friday night. At least seven apparently well-coordinated attacks occurred, gunmen with automatic weapons and suicide belts killing over 100 victims. Many others were injured. Stade de France stadium was struck during a football (soccer) match between France and Germany.

So was the Bataclan theater during a concert, restaurants full of patrons, a cinema, and pedestrians on Bichat Street, the Avenue de la Republique and Boulevard Beaumarchais.

Reports indicated other Paris locations were attacked, including the Forum des Halles shopping area attracting an estimated 150,000 daily visitors.

The predictable aftermath so far includes French President François Hollande declaring a state of emergency—effectively suspending constitutional rights under martial law.

"Two decisions will be taken," Hollande announced. "The state of emergency will be decreed, which means several places will be closed off, and traffic will be limited in certain areas."

"The state of emergency will apply across the country. The second decision I have taken is to close the borders, so that the people who have committed these crimes can be apprehended."

"We know where this attack came from. We must show compassion and solidarity, but we must also show we are united. There is much to fear, but we must face these fears as a nation that knows how to muster its forces and will confront the terrorists."

Heavily armed French soldiers were deployed around key Parisian locations. Five metro lines were shut. Orly airport flights were suspended. All city schools and universities were closed.

De facto martial law legitimizes repressive police state powers. Constitutional protections are suspended. Swat teams conducted pre-dawn raids throughout the greater area. Residents were terrorized. Helicopters patrolled overhead. Police and FBI operatives were everywhere. Managed news misinformation substituted for accurate reporting.

Post-9/11, Bush claimed unconstitutional "unitary executive" authority to govern extrajudicially in the name of national security. He declared (phony) war on terror and hot war on Afghanistan. Iraq, Libya, Syria, Donbass and Yemen followed. Police state laws were enacted—still in force. Repressive National Security and Homeland Security Presidential Directives were announced.

Hollande cancelled his G-20 summit participation, scheduled for November 15th and 16th in Turkey. Obama, the world's leading perpetrator of state terrorism, offered France "full support," duplicitously saying America shares the bonds of "liberté, egalité and fraternité."

The US post-9/11 knee-jerk reaction blamed bin Laden and Al Qaeda for the attack—the mother of all Big Lies, we now know.

Likewise, ISIS was automatically blamed for the Paris attacks—despite no evidence so far establishing responsibility. Official statements, actions and media hype created an atmosphere of fear, a likely public willingness to sacrifice freedom for so-called security, a rationale for harsh measures to try stemming the human refugee flood caused by US-led imperial wars, and a desire for revenge.

Perhaps the stage is set for escalated Western wars OF terror instead of unity to battle the scourge of ISIS and likeminded groups. Were Friday attacks state-sponsored terrorism—a carefully staged false flag for whatever may follow?

Herman Goering once explained how easy it is to get people to go along with "the bidding of the leaders...All you have to do is tell them they are being attacked, and denounce the pacifists for lack of patriotism and exposing the country to danger. It works the same in any country," he said.

Friday's Paris attacks were either blowback for Western wars on Islam or a state-sponsored false flag. Odds strongly favor the latter. The sordid Western history of false flags for subsequent planned events suggests it.

On September 20, 2001, George Bush lied to Congress and the public, claiming America was attacked because we are "a beacon of freedom." The attackers were "evil. This is civilization's fight." He suppressed Washington's direct responsibility for what happened, perhaps complicit with Israel's Mossad.

The aftermath of 9/11 is clear—endless US-led imperial wars, a phony Global War on Terrorism (GWOT), an assault on fundamental human and civil rights, police state harshness replacing them, an America unfit to live in.

France and other European countries have planned or already instituted greater repressive measures. Will increased war on humanity follow, complicit with Washington, Israel and other rogue partners?

It's easy blaming ISIS for Friday's Paris attacks. It's the new Enemy Number One. Its creation by Washington for use as proxy foot soldiers is suppressed.

Important clues suggest Friday's incident was a classic false flag. Most important: How could a few terrorists outwit French intelligence? The attacks were a carefully orchestrated, well planned military operation requiring some degree of sophistication. Weeks of planning likely preceded it.

The operatives were armed with automatic weapons and explosive belts. How could they have entered attack sites unnoticed? How was this possible—dressed in black heavily armed?

They were well known to French security agencies, likely kept under surveillance. Why was nothing done to prevent the attacks or intervene straightaway once they began?

Syrian and Egyptian passports were found at the Stade de France stadium, one of the attack sites, begging the obvious question: Why would operatives carry IDs? Clearly they were planted, just as "hijackers' passports" were planted at alleged crash sites after 9/11.

French authorities claim three terrorist teams carried out the well-coordinated attacks. Do they know more than they're telling?

Le Monde reported one team fled Paris by car with a Belgian license plate. Paris police chief Micheal Cadot said all attackers were killed. Then the story changed.

French President François Hollande straightaway blamed ISIS despite no evidence indicating its involvement. His behavior was an automatic red flag.

A so-called ISIS statement claiming responsibility remains unverified, yet it made headlines, likely getting most people to believe it. Anyone can call themselves ISIS and claim responsibility. The statement remains meaningless.

The incident preceded multi-nation November 14 talks in Vienna on Syria and the November 15-16 G-20 meeting. Washington and key

NATO allies likely want so-called war on terror escalated, not re-solved.Why? Resolution defeats America's imperial agenda.

Israel is also suspect. Netanyahu wants justification to keep reigning terror on a defenseless Palestinian population.

France and other European countries need justification to close their borders to the human refugee flood caused by US-led imperial wars. They now have it.

Hollande's low 12% approval rating needed something to boost it. Following the January Charlie Hebdo/kosher market attacks, his popularity increased by 21%.

On 9/10/01, George Bush's approval rating hovered around 50%. A day later, it shot up to 90%. Expect Hollande to get a similar boost, especially after vowing "pitiless war" on ISIS.

The world community now rallies around France the way it did for America post-9/11. Landmark structures were lit in the French blue, white and red tricolors.

The 408-foot One World Trade Center spire, built on the 9/11 attack site, was illuminated Friday night. New York Mayor Bill de Blasio called it "a very painful night."

"(O)ur hearts and our prayers are with the people of Paris. (Y)ou know, we know all about this feeling because of what we experienced on 9/11." De Blasio stopped short of explaining the state-sponsored terrorism behind the fateful attacks.

Brazil's Rio de Janeiro's Christ the Redeemer statue was lit in France's tricolors. So was London's Wembley Stadium, New Zealand's Memorial Museum and Sky Tower, Sydney, Australia's Opera House, Malaysia's Kuala Lumpur Tower, San Francisco's City Hall, Washington, DC's Verizon Center, and numerous other sites.

Paris, called "The City of Light," went dark. Its signature Eiffel Tower turned off its lights. So did New York's Empire State Building, as well as Chicago's Sears Tower and John Hancock Center.

The world community clearly supports whatever response France intends—complicit with Washington, Britain, likely Israel and other rogue allies.

Expect the worst ahead, including greater police state erosion of fundamental freedoms, endless wars of aggression, likely escalating, perhaps new ones initiated, more mass slaughter and destruction, greater numbers of refugees desperate to find safe havens—now likely shunned by Europe.

There was nothing ordinary about Friday's Paris attacks. False flags are planned for a reason. Expect nothing good to follow.

Part 2:
False Flags and Deep States:
Theory and Practice

DEEP STATES:
A THREAT TO DEMOCRACY?

PHILIP GIRALDI

[Editor's note: Portions of this essay first appeared in the *New York Times* and the *American Conservative*.]

Almost immediately after the Paris attacks of 11/13/2015, alternative media began raising the issue of Operation Gladio—a "deep state" program implicated in Cold War era terrorism. To prevent such suspicions from undermining confidence in government, we need to confront the worldwide problem of "deep states."

Citizens in many countries wonder how certain government policies can persist in spite of widespread popular opposition or clear perceptions that they are harmful. This persistence is frequently attributed to a "deep state."

The phrase is often applied to Turkey, where the nation's security services and governing elite pursue the same chauvinistic and inward-looking agenda no matter who is prime minister. Supporting such forces that enforce stability at the cost of democracy buys friendship with no one for the U.S. and empowers radicals.

But every country has a deep state of some kind. "The Establishment" as it's been called in the United States where it evolved from the Washington-New York axis of national security officials and financial services executives. They are said to know what is "best" for the country and to act accordingly no matter who sits in the White House.

This comfortable consensus in America favors the forces that provide a measure of stability in troubled regions, including Turkey and Egypt. Such stability comes at a cost though.

In Turkey deep-state forces support not only oligarchical interests but—it's been plausibly contended—criminals including drug traffickers, money launderers, and weapons merchants when it suits their interests. Some analysts believe Egypt too has developed a dominant deep state that is actually running the government. As in Turkey the Egyptian version has grown out of the national security establishment.

In both countries real democracy has been the first victim. Both Turkey and Egypt are now ruled by autocrats who have among their first steps eliminated an independent press and freedom of speech.

The unwillingness of the United States to seriously confront the effects of supporting forces that enforce stability at the cost of democracy ultimately buys friendship with no one because supporting promoters of strength to repress radicalism largely serves only to empower those same radicals.

Deep states may also pose a threat to American democracy, as University of California-Berkeley professor Peter Dale Scott argues.[153] Some researchers including Sibel Edmonds have argued that elements of the Turkish deep state, perhaps working with Israeli, American and Saudi deep state forces, may have been complicit in the attacks of September 11th, 2001.[154]

Senator Rand Paul, supported by a number of other congressmen, has demanded that the 28 pages of the 9/11 Commission Report that explored the Saudi Arabian role in the terrorist attack be made public. The redacted section of the report, which apparently concluded that the Saudi government itself played no direct role in 9/11, nevertheless contained considerable evidence suggesting that wealthy Saudis and even members of the Royal Family had been supporting and funding al-Qaeda. Some who have actually read the 28 pages were reported to be shocked by what was revealed.

Recent comments by presidential aspirant Donald Trump indicating that he was aware of people celebrating the terrorist attack in New Jersey, whom he described as "Muslims" numbering in their thousands, might well be regarded as misremembering events that took place over fourteen years ago. Or it could just possibly be part of a deliberate scheme to establish a false narrative that would fit nicely with Trump's stated desire to surveil mosques, waterboard suspects and subject all Muslims to extraordinary scrutiny by the police.

The Trump over-the-top comments were greeting with disbelief and debunked by many media pundits. They were even denounced by some Republicans competing with him for the GOP nomination. But what is really astonishing about the reaction was the failure to connect the dots with what actually happened on 9/11. There were indeed people celebrating as the Twin Towers were burning and collapsing, but they were not Muslims. They were Israelis.

If the Saudi role in 9/11 is still classified secret it is regrettable, but the Israeli role, insofar as can be determined, was never seriously investigated at all and any conclusions, if there were any, were never included in the final report. This time around with the story being resurfaced by Trump one would think that a journalist or two just might be able to make the connection and realize that Donald may have actually been referring to a reported incident involving Israelis rather than Arabs and that he is possibly confusing one with the other.

But of course no one in the mainstream media did pick up on the connection, inhibited no doubt by the understanding that there are some things that one just does not write about Israel if one hopes to remain employed. That is true in spite of the fact that the Israeli angle to 9/11 is without a doubt a good story, one that has never been satisfactorily explored, but it is a tale that will have to remain mired in the alternative media where it can be marginalized by critics as a conspiracy theory or the product of anti-Semitism.

So for the benefit of Mr. Trump and for anyone else who might be interested, I will take it upon myself to relate what happened. Quite possibly Senator Paul will read this and decide that giving billions of dollars in aid annually to a country that just might have been linked to what occurred on 9/11 might no longer be a good idea. He might even demand an inquiry or a commission to look into it and determine what exactly the U.S. government does and does not know. That would be very interesting.

In the year 2001 Israel was running a massive spying operation directed against Muslims either resident or traveling in the United States. The operation included the creation of a number of cover companies in New Jersey, Florida and also on the West Coast that served as spying mechanisms for Mossad officers. The effort was supported by the Mossad Station in Washington D.C. and included a large number of volunteers, the so-called "art students" who traveled around the U.S. selling various products at malls and outdoor markets. The FBI was aware of the numerous Israeli students who were routinely overstaying their visas and some in the Bureau certainly believed that they were assisting their country's intelligence service in some way, but it proved difficult to actually link the students to actual undercover operations, so they were regarded as a minor nuisance and were normally left to the tender mercies of the inspectors at the Bureau of Customs and Immigration.

American law enforcement was also painfully aware that the Israelis were running more sophisticated intelligence operations inside the United States, many of which were focused on Washington's military capabilities and intentions. Some specialized intelligence units concentrated on obtaining military and dual use technology. It was also known that Israeli spies had penetrated the phone systems of the U.S. government, including those at the White House.

In its annual classified counterespionage review, the FBI invariably places Israel at the top for "friendly" countries that spy on the U.S. In fact, the pre-9/11 Bureau did its best to stay on top of the problem, but it rarely received any political support from the Justice Department and White House if an espionage case involved Israelis. By one estimate, more than 100 such cases were not prosecuted for political reasons. Any Israeli caught in flagrante would most often be quietly deported and most Americans who were helping Israel were let off with a slap on the wrist.

But the hands-off attitude towards Israel shifted dramatically when, on September 11th, 2001, a New Jersey housewife saw something from the window of her apartment building, which overlooked the World Trade Center. She watched as the buildings burned and crumbled but also noted something strange. Three young men were kneeling on the roof of a white transit van parked by the water's edge, making a movie in which they featured themselves high fiving and laughing in front of the catastrophic scene unfolding behind them. The woman wrote down the license plate number of the van and called the police, who responded quickly. Soon both the local force and the FBI began looking for the vehicle, which was subsequently seen by other witnesses in various locations along the New Jersey waterfront, its occupants "celebrating and filming."

The license plate number revealed that the van belonged to a New Jersey registered company called Urban Moving Systems. At 4 p.m. the vehicle was spotted and pulled over. Five men between the ages of 22 and 27 years old emerged. They were detained at gunpoint and handcuffed. They were all Israelis. One of them had $4,700 in cash hidden in his sock and another had two foreign passports. Bomb sniffing dogs reacted to the smell of explosives in the van.

According to the initial police report, the driver identified as Sivan Kurzberg, stated "We are Israeli. We are not your problem. Your problems are our problems. The Palestinians are the problem." The four other passengers were Sivan's brother Paul, Yaron Shmuel, Oded Ellner and Omer Marmari. The men were detained at the Bergen County jail in New Jersey before being transferred to the FBI's Foreign Counterintelligence Section, which handles allegations of spying.

After the arrest, the FBI obtained a warrant to search Urban Moving System's Weehawken, N.J., offices. Papers and computers were seized. The company owner Dominick Suter, also an Israeli, answered FBI questions but when a follow-up interview was set up a few days later it was learned that he had fled the country for Israel, putting both his business and home up for sale. The office space and warehouse were abandoned. It was later learned that Suter has been associated with at least fourteen businesses in the United States, mostly in New Jersey and

New York but also in Florida. Suter and his wife Omit Levinson Suter were the owners of 1 Stop Cleaner located in Wellington Florida and Dominick was also associated with Basia McDonnell, described as a Polish "holocaust survivor," and as a business partner in yet another business called Value Ad. Florida was a main focus for the Israeli intelligence operation in the U.S. that was directed against Arabs.

The five Israelis were held in Brooklyn, initially on charges relating to visa fraud. FBI interrogators questioned them for more than two months. Several were held in solitary confinement so they could not communicate with each other and two of them were given repeated polygraph exams, which they failed when claiming that they were nothing more than students working summer jobs. The two men that the FBI focused on most intensively were believed to be Mossad staff officers and the other three were volunteers helping with surveillance.

The Israelis were not exactly cooperative, but the FBI concluded from documents obtained at their office in Weehawken that they were targeting Arabs in New York and New Jersey, most particularly in the Paterson N.J. area, which has the second largest Muslim population in the U.S. They were particularly interested in local groups possibly linked to Hamas and Hezbollah as well as in charities that might be used for fund raising. The FBI also concluded that there was a distinct possibility that the Israelis had actually monitored the activities of at least two of the 9/11 hijackers.

To be sure, working on an intelligence operation does not necessarily imply participation in either the planning or execution of something like 9/11, but there are Israeli fingerprints all over the place, with cover companies and intelligence personnel often intersecting with locations frequented by the hijackers. And even possessing bits and pieces relating to the plot does not necessarily imply significant prior knowledge of it.

Apart from the interrogations of the five men from Weehawken, the U.S. government has apparently never sought to find out what else the Israelis might have known or were up to in September 2011. There are a lot of dots that might well have been connected once upon a time, but the trail has grown cold. Police records in New Jersey and New York where the men were held have disappeared and FBI interrogation reports are inaccessible. Media coverage of the case also died, though the five were referred to in the press as the "dancing Israelis" and by some, more disparagingly, as the "dancing Shlomos."

Inevitably, the George W. Bush White House intervened. After 71 days in detention, the five Israelis were released from prison, put on a plane, and deported. Two of the men later spoke about their unpleasant experience in America on an Israeli talk show, one explaining that their filming the fall of the Twin Towers was to "document the event." In 2004 the five men sued the United States government for damages, alleging "that their detention was illegal and that their civil rights were violated, suffering racial slurs, physical violence, religious discrimination, rough interrogations, deprivation of sleep, and many other offenses." They were represented by Nitsana Darshan-Leitner, who in the previous year had founded the Shurat HaDin Israel Law Center which seeks to bankrupt groups that Israel considers to be "terrorists." Shurat HaDin is closely tied to the Israeli government.

Now it is just possible that the Urban Moving Israelis were indeed uninvolved in 9/11 but nevertheless working for Mossad, which one has to suspect is the case. More than fourteen years later it is perhaps past time to reveal what exactly the FBI knew and currently knows about both the scale and modus operandi of Israeli espionage in the United States. Did Israel have critical intelligence either in broad outline or possibly in specific detail about 9/11 and let it happen to bind Washington more closely to it in a "global war on terror?" If Senator Rand Paul wants to learn more about the Saudis, it is fair to ask "What about Israel?" If Donald Trump wants to pillory fictional celebrating Muslims it is perhaps appropriate that he begin to take note of the actual celebrating Israelis who were caught in the act on 9/11.

WAS PARIS 11/13 A FALSE FLAG EVENT? A MATRIX FOR EVALUATING POSSIBILITIES

Robert David Steele #bigideas

It is with sadness that I observe that most people—including extremely intelligent and accomplished people—appear to have lost their critical thinking faculties over the past quarter century. When I have the temerity to suggest that Paris may have been a false flag event intended to:

•   legalize the illegal US war against Syria by invoking the North Atlantic Treaty Organization (NATO) Article 5 protection clause;
•   or that it is a means for the party in power in France to lock down the country (neutralizing the extreme right challenging its loose authority);
•   or that Saudi Arabia and Turkey gain from international publicity consistent with their export of state-sponsored terrorism;
•   or that Israel is always happy to both punish France for supporting the Palestinians and considering a boycott of Israeli products while also frightening more French Jews into moving to Israel to fill up the illegal settlements being built there at U.S. taxpayer expense

I get three reactions:

•   one third tell me that it is high time someone put all this in writing at a time when the mainstream media and even alternative media have been bribed or intimidated into avoiding any challenge to the official narrative;
•   one third tell me I am most certainly a lunatic and perhaps a traitor (remember this is how America treated Daniel Elsberg on VietNam and the Dixie Chicks on Iraq); and
•   one third don't notice—they don't read much and are largely oblivious to world events.

Me? I think for a living. I am a professional intelligence officer who has spent a quarter century trying to reform a terribly dysfunctional secret intelligence community, and for varied reasons, I feel compelled to live up to my personal motto, "the truth at any cost lowers all other costs."

I believe the American public—and other publics—need to know the answer, now, to the question: "Was Paris 11/13 a false flag?"

I have no direct knowledge. I do know how to directly investigate such an event, to include deep examination of the forensics of each scene and each weapon, each body, accounting for every object and person at every moment across the event spectrum. I am pretty sure that has not been done and will not be done in the case of the recent events in Paris. Hence this is a speculative essay intended to provoke thought among those who believe that the truth at any cost lowers all other costs.

What Is a False Flag?

A false flag event is one in which the alleged perpetrators, their motives, and the outcome are fabricated. It generally includes very real dead people and often includes very real terrorists using very real bombs and bullets, but the entire script, the enabling logistics, and the prepared narrative that quickly follow are designed to meet the needs of the "deep state" and its financial masters—both of which are very international in nature, with no national loyalties to speak of... for the "deep state" a few French casualties are no different than, say, a few Palestinian casualties.

The origin of the false flag concept is traced to naval warfare, where ships could achieve a form of tactical surprise in the open ocean by flying the flag of the enemy they planned to attack once close enough to do some unexpected damage.

False flag attacks by authorities against themselves are classic means of justifying internal repressive measures needed to deepen control of the population, or elective wars against others. False flags have been widely used by the US in the aftermath of World War II, generally as a means of deepening the power of controlled puppet regimes, or as a means of inspiring the election of "owned" candidates, or as a means of justifying sanctions or other measures intended to lead to regime change.

False flag operations are used by individuals and organizations—including political parties—not only by governments. From fake death threats to forged poison pen letters to abusive surveys ostensibly from the party to be discredited to orchestrated smear campaigns, the false flag concept is one that is now very common to socio-economic systems in which cheating is considered acceptable behavior, and corruption is inherent in the political and economic environment.

False flags in cyberspace are very common now, and some attacks that have been blamed on international terrorists appear to have originated with the Reservists working for the U.S. Cyber Command associated with the National Security Agency (NSA).

Have False Flag Operations Been Documented?

I find that the one third wishing to think me a lunatic or traitor is quick to dismiss all suggestions that false flag operations may have been documented. Despite hundreds of ably researched and proven studies, this mental group goes deaf, dumb, and blind when presented with facts.

Key Indicators of a Modern False Flag

1. Early Warning and Public Alarm. First give them something to fear, then show them what to fear, and keep them in fear. This includes a constant churning out of alleged local terrorists such as have been produced by the Federal Bureau of Investigation (FBI) in what one author calls "The Terror Factory."[155]

2. Scheduled Official Exercises Coincident with the Event. From 9/11, when Dick Cheney scheduled a national counterterrorism exercise so he could control the government, armed forces, and the day in detail, to the most recent attacks in Paris, scheduled official exercises are the single greatest indicator that a catastrophic event is in fact planned and being orchestrated.

3. Prepared Media Narrative. From the earliest understanding offered up with respect to "Manufactured Consent" and the more recent "Weapons of Mass Deception" that in the case of Paris have also been joined by "Weapons of Mass Migration," we consistently see a media that has been pre-positioned—in some cases leading anchor personalities "coincidentally" being on site—and pre-briefed, with a narrative and story line ready to roll.

4. Blocked Public, Media, and First Responder Access. The sponsors of very public false flags are slowly learning they need to block priests and rabbis from attending to the alleged wounded, they need to block both media and first responders from access to interiors of the locations where the alleged bombs exploded and bullets flew (those pesky upholstered chairs without a sign of shrapnel or fire stand out in the most recent event), and they need to shut down or block hand-held video that may reveal false flag activities—for example, alleged shots to the head of a terrorist with no sign of impact or blood thereafter.[156]

5. "Attackers" Die, Actors Live. Evidence continues to mount that many attackers across multiple incidents have been trained by the US military (some sheep-dipped out as alleged dishonorable or administrative discharges), or are active informants for the FBI or local intelligence or police service (as in France), or think they are contractors participating in an exercise where they are a "Red Team" and everyone is supposed to be shooting blanks. Surviving attackers—and actors hired to play surviving victims or relatives—are generally there to support the narrative.

6. Hospital Triage, Real Estate, and Statistics. The absence of real victims showing up in hospitals (or vastly smaller numbers than alleged to have been killed and wounded), the odd sale of real estate before and immediately after an event, the disappearance of the individuals alleged to have lost relatives, and inconsistent statistics are all indicators of a false flag but must be addressed with care.

7. Prompt Official Refutation or Dismissal of Expert Voices. As modern false flag operations have matured, perpetrators have been learning how difficult it is to counter formal highly qualified critics of the official narrative. While controlling the media is helpful, when families, firefighters, architects, engineers, and military as well as intelligence professionals all converge on facts that are compelling, the authorities are challenged.[157] So far they are able to drown out the experts, but the timeline toward public disclosure is shortening—it took 25 years for the truth about US government involvement in the assassination of John F. Kennedy and Martin Luther King to be fully documented, 9/11 is on a fifteen year disclosure track, these new false flags and regime change operations (Georgia, Ukraine, Syria, Azerbaijan is next) are on a five to ten year track.

8. Crack-Down on Alternative Voices. As the Internet makes it possible for intelligent people with integrity to challenge the official narrative, we are seeing more and more punitive expeditions, from threatened investigations to incarceration to murder disguised as suicide. Those who question authority join the ranks of the unemployed, are libeled and slandered, are black-listed without their knowing, added to spam and "hate crime" lists, "inadvertently" put on the "no fly" list or are blocked from entering specific countries, and when all else fails—for those very rare individuals whose voices gain traction– murder most foul (never mind that Gary Webb needed two bullets in the head to commit suicide). It merits observation that there is no due process by which a blocked individual can challenge their back office assassination.

9. Fast Track Legislation (Already Written) and Bogus Investments. The Patriot Act is a classic example of legislation written before an event and passed immediately after the event without being read or debated. The "deep state" and its financial masters have an agenda that includes an insatiable demand for taxpayer investments (mostly funded by debt levied on future generations). We now know that the Iraq war was based on 935 lies that led to a cost to the taxpayer of over $4 trillion, with the Islamic State of Iraq and Syria (ISIS) as a direct spin-off. In the absence of intelligence and integrity—evidence based strategy and policy—post-event legislation and budget initiatives should be regarded with great suspicion.

10. *Who Benefits?* Following the money is a major part of this, but benefits can be calculated in domestic political advances, military-police-industrial investments, and "coincident" decisions favoring specific financial interests, and more.

So Where Are We on Paris 11/13 as a False Flag?

Paris a False Flag? Matrix for Evaluating Possibilities

Country	United States	France	NATO Gladio	Saudi Arabia	Turkey	Israel
Prior History of Proven False Flags?						
Clear Benefits from a Paris False Flag?						
Suspicious Activities Before Event?						
Suspicious Activities During Event?						
Suspicious Activities After Event?						

Above is a simple matrix for considering the possibilities of each of six major actors—not necessarily the legitimate governments within each of those state, but perhaps rogue actors with undue influence and discretionary authority—being engaged in a false flag campaign to legitimize the US war on Syria, bring France into the war, destabilize Europe, Balkanize the Middle East, and spread the Wahhabist brand of Islamic terrorism.My over-all conclusion is straight-forward. Absent compelling evidence to the contrary, the public must assume that Paris 11/13 was a false flag, and resist all attempts to declare war, increase the militarization of the police, and spend more on domestic surveillance while reducing civil liberties. This was, in my view as an observer and intelligence professional, a false flag operation.

As a citizen and voter and patriot, I will not vote for anyone stupid enough to claim that ISIS has a life of its own apart from Saudi Arabia and Turkey with inputs from Israel, the US, France, and the disenfranchised officers of Iraq. We need adults with intelligence and integrity leading us, not ideologues and traitors who will tell any lie and pay any price in our blood, treasure, and spirit for their personal gain.

Below I will list just a few of references I consider to be helpful.

Ahmed, Nafeez Mosaddeg, "NATO Is Harbouring the Islamic State," InsurgeIntelligence, November 19, 2015.

Ahmed, Nafeez Mosaddeq, "Why Was a Sunday Times report on US government ties to al-Qaeda chief spiked?," *Ceasefire Magazine*, May 17, 2013.

Akleh, Elias, "Another France's False Flag Attack," *Intifada: Voice of Palestine*, November 17, 2015.

Barrett, Kevin. "Another French false flag?, Veterans Today, November 13, 2015.

Burks, Fred. "Origins of ISIS aka Islamic State," WanttoKnow.info, November 26, 2015.

Burks, Fred. *Prescription for a World Crisis. Global Outlook, Issue 13 Annual 2009, False Flag Operations, How Wars Are Started By False Flag Operations, Global Outlook*, 2009.

Chuckman, John. "Friday the 13th in Paris and the Ugly Truth of State Terror," *Foreign Policy Journal*, November 20, 2015.

Crubaugh, Joe. "10 false flags operations that shaped our world," March 7, 2007.

Donahue, Patrick and Rainer Buergin, "Syrian Passport in Paris May Be Planted, German Minister Says, " BloombergBusiness, November 17, 2015.

Editor. "42 ADMITTED False Flag Attacks, " *WashingtonsBlog.com*, February 9, 2015.

Editor. "False Flag," *Wikipedia*, accessed November 21, 2015.

Editor. "Paris Attack – Inside Job – PSY-OP – Like Mumbai and Gladio Attacks," *Shoah: The Palestinian Holocaust*, November 16, 2015.

Hagopian, Joachim. "Paris Attacks: Another False Flag? Sifting through the Evidence," *GlobalResearch*, November 19, 2015.

Judge, Anthony, "Dying to Live, Living to Die, Lying to Live, and Living a Lie, *Laetus in Praesens*, November 13, 2015.

Lendman, Stephen. "Washington Bears Full Responsibility for Paris Attacks," *ThePeoplesVoice.org*, November 19, 2015.

Mathew, Binu, "10 Reasons Why The Paris Terrorist Attack Could Be A False Flag Operation," *CounterCurrents.org*, November 16, 2015.

Mongoose, Erdogan's Dirty Dangerous ISIS Games — Turkey Goes to War on Arabia, Russia, and the West, Phi Beta Iota Public Intelligence Blog, November 26, 2015.

Mongoose, Understanding Paris – NATO, Gladio, Beligium & False Flag Terrorism — the Original Full-Length BBC Movie, Phi Beta Iota Public Intelligence Blog, November 21, 2015.

NEOnline/GK, "All Paris attackers were EU nationals," NewEurope, November 20, 2015.

Onfray, Michel, "French Joined the Americans in War on Afghanistan, Iraq, Libya, Mali...Reap As Ye Sow...," Phi Beta Iota Public Intelligence Blog, November 15, 2015.

Parry, Robert, "Hitting Saudi Arabia Where It Hurts," *Consortiumnews.com*, November 23, 2015.

Parry, Robert. "Tangled Threads of US False Narratives," *Consortiumnews.com*, November 19, 2015.

Quinn, Joe. "Paris Attacks Reveal Bizarre ISIS Strategy and NATO's Strategy of Tension in Europe, Sott.net, November 15, 2015.

Roberts, Paul Craig. "Another Paris False Flag Attack?," *Dissident Voice*, November 14, 2015.

Roberts, Paul Craig. "The Paris Terror Attacks: Washington Refines Its False Flag Operations," GlobalResearch, November 16, 2015.

Rusticus, "Questions for Operation Gladio, German Intelligence Amidst Paris Carnage," *Activist Post*, November 14, 2015.

Swift, Sebastian. "5 Confirmed False Flag Operations and How to Spot Them in the Future," *Anti-Media*, July 14, 2015

NOTE: There are a number of YouTube videos and audio podcats addressing Paris false flag and Gladio themes. I have chosen not to list them, they are easy to find.

ACADEMIC COMPLICITY IN THE GLOBAL WAR OF FALSE FLAG TERRORISM

Anthony Hall

Coming to Terms with the Global War of False Flag Terrorism

I met Dr. Kevin Barrett as planned at a small bookstore near the Notre Dame Cathedral landmark in Paris, France. On that day, December 11th, 2015, the Paris bookstore was the site of a significant academic conference entitled "Islamophobia and the Erosion of Civil Society."

Hours earlier I had exited the last class of the fall term in my third-year Globalization Studies course at the University of Lethbridge in Alberta Canada. I had driven to Calgary, hopped a flight to Dallas, and then transferred onto a big American Airlines 777 for the trans-Atlantic flight to the City of Lights now under martial law.

For the second time in 2015 Paris had been rocked by violent episodes attributed to the independent actions of Islamic terrorists. After the first event last January, Dr. Barrett had coordinated the emergency responses of a team of analytic observers, myself included. Together we uncovered the outlines of an outlandish fraud of an externally-engineered false flag terror event. Dr. Barrett assembled the revelations in his edited book *We Are Not Charlie Hebdo*. Now a sequel volume was in the making as Kevin and I met up in the Paris bookstore where the inner workings of the "Islamophobia Industry" were the subject of scholarly investigation.

The majority of contributors to Dr. Barrett's book on the first Paris shooter event of 2015 concluded that the attacks on the Charlie Hebdo cartoon office and on the customers of a Jewish deli were not as they were made to seem in the mainstream media. The evidence pointed to a continuation of the same type of state-manufactured violence directed at civilian populations in Western Europe during the Cold War by NATO's overseers of Operation Gladio.

The aim of Operation Gladio was to discredit the politics of progressive reform by misrepresenting the nature of NATO-concocted episodes of seemingly arbitrary violence directed at civilian populations. Violent events were engineered by right-wing agents of NATO's occupation of Western Europe to make it appear that left-wing progressives were subject to the control of psychopathic extremists intent on foisting their will on society through coercive methods.

Today, a new wave of false flag terrorism is underway with the objective of turning public opinion against groups slated for state-sanctioned assaults, including aggressive warfare. As demonstrated by the deep state politics of Operation Gladio, false flag terrorism has long been a standard psy-op deployed by the Western intelligence and counter-intelligence agencies to affect public perception, attitude, and behaviour. The deployment of false flag terrorism to bring history's course into conformity with the objectives sought by strategic planners has become the particular specialty of the Israeli deep state.

The most ambitious false flag terror episode ever occurred on September 11th, 2001 in the orchestrated strikes on three World Trade Center Towers, on the Pentagon and on the remnants of integrity in our governing structures. The overwhelming weight of evidence derived from these events points squarely at those in charge of the powerful networks of global influence aligned with the expansionary aspirations of Likudnik Israel. The lies and crimes of 9/11 provided the pretext for the transition from Cold War's demonization of socialism, as manifest in the engineered terrorism of Operation Gladio, to the demonization of Muslims through what might most accurately be described as the Global War of False Flag Terrorism (GWOFFT).

The 9/11 strikes were central episodes that created the core narrative and imagery for a multi-faceted psychological operation that continues yet. This 9/11 psychological operation has been frequently characterized as a global coup d'état. The 9/11 global coup d'état was engineered to entrench neoconservative agendas aimed at concentrating more power in the world's dominant banking, military, media and academic cartels together with the plutocrats that control them. In the Global War of False Flag Terrorism, ruling elites everywhere have attempted to entrench their regimes of fraud and corruption by characterizing their critics and opponents as terrorists, as potential terrorists or as terrorist sympathizers.

Without a doubt it is the Jewish state of Israel that gained most from replacing anti-communism with anti-terrorism as the primary purpose and preoccupation of the world's dominant military-industrial complex. The key to manufacturing consent for this shift has been the incitement and political exploitation of hatred towards Muslims. This engineered hatred of Muslims is often described as Islamophobia.

Convening in Paris to Shed Light on Islamophobia

The study of Islamophobia brought together scholars from Europe and North America at the conference in the Paris bookstore. This convention of scholars was organized under the auspices of the Race and Gender Studies Center at the University of California in Berkeley. The Chair was Prof. Hatem Bazian, Professor of Islamic Law and Theology at Zaytuna College in Berkeley. Part of the U of C, Zaytuna College is the first Muslim liberal arts institution of higher learning in the United States.

Prof. Bazian had assembled about a dozen scholars at various stages in their movement through the academic procedures of tenure and promotion. Generally speaking the assembled scholars have taken on some of the most difficult and fraught subjects covered in our university curricula. To study the institutional workings of the cynical business of purposely turning public attitudes against Muslims is an especially difficult academic mission in the poisoned atmosphere of these times.

In spite of our criticism of their work, the dozen or so colleagues who gathered at the Paris bookstore on December 11th deserve much respect and recognition. These colleagues have persisted in following a very contentious line of investigation in spite of the serious professional recriminations often thrown their way by critics who think nothing of destroying academic careers to advance political agendas.

Kevin Barrett and I took part in the proceedings with the anticipation that we would co-host our own alternative conference the following day at a hotel near the Charles De Gaulle Airport. This plan was a response to the rejection of Dr. Barrett's paper that was originally accepted as part of their conference. Dr. Barrett's proposed contribution highlighted the frequent exclusion of Muslim perspectives from officialdom's accounts of the originating events triggering the 9/11 wars.

Dr. Barrett's academic credentials in the subject matter of the conference are of course very strong as evidenced by the initial warm welcome extended to his offer to contribute to the conference's scholarly proceedings. Then came the events of Friday November 13th 2015, when the world was told Islamic terrorists had murdered over a hundred victims at a concert at the Bataclan music venue, at the Stade de France and at other Paris locations. In the wake of this development Dr. Barrett was informed by Professor Bazian, "Due to state of emergency in France and the on-going active operations, the organizing committee is not able to accommodate your paper at this point in time. Our supporters on the ground are under extreme emergency conditions and the whole program is under stress due to it."

In spite of the declared state of emergency in Paris the organizers had pressed ahead with the conference minus the contribution of Dr. Barrett. No explanation was given of why it was deemed alright to go forward with the other presentations but not the one containing Dr. Barrett's interpretation of Islamophobia. The exclusion of Dr. Barrett, a Muslim himself with advanced degrees and many publications in Islamic Studies, could be seen as an expression of the very same forces that the Paris event had been convened to identify and analyze.

Rather than step aside without a protest, Dr. Barrett took part in the proceedings. I had joined him with the expectation that the next day we would try to put right the lapse that unfortunately seemed indicative of a more general failure of the academy. How is it that, generally speaking, professors in our institutions of higher learning have failed so conspicuously to sort out truth from falsehood, accurate reporting from fraud, when it comes to explaining the origins and ongoing impetuses of the 9/11 wars?

Why have we in the academy mostly failed to rise to the responsibility of our higher calling when it comes to the vital job of identifying the thick web of lies and misrepresentations used to justify the post-9/11 surge of aggressive warfare abroad, the betrayal of human rights and civil liberties at home? How has this treason of the intellectuals been transacted at the very moment society is most in need of evidence-based research to sort out fact from fiction when assessing the claims and assertions of the permanent war economy's primary protagonists?

Through efforts like those of Dr. Barrett's in his personal and public "truth jihad," there have been significant breakthroughs in illuminating fraudulent reporting by presstitutes that often disseminate the disinformation essential to realizing the subversive agendas of false flag terrorism. Less has been done, however, to highlight the failures of the academy to identify the lies and crimes entailed in the wholesale smearing of Muslims essential to the dark objectives of the Global War of False Flag Terrorism.

Islamophobia is the essential mental ingredient in the atmosphere of fear produced by the psychological geo-engineers pushing forward the Global War of False Flag Terrorism. In the words of Prof. Bazian, Islamophobia has to do with "the construction of an imagined and staged world rooted in the mind." The dissemination of the imagery of self-directed, self-financing Islamic terrorists acting autonomously out of no other motivation than their own religious zealotry constitutes the core lie of this malevolent psychological operation. The demonization of Muslim people, Muslim religion, Muslim cultures and Muslim countries forms the basis of the scaffolding on which a global and unbridled police state is being constructed.

This background helps explain how it is that Dr. Barrett and I had converged at the Paris bookstore on the eve of our effort to host our own conference of world-class thinkers expert in deciphering the inner workings of the Global War of False Flag Terrorism. In taking on this responsibility we were moving into the vacuum of truth telling that the academic community has created, for the time being at least, by failing to come up with a viable evidence-based explanation of the origins and ongoing genesis of the 9/11 wars. On December 11th, 2015, the effort to go beyond the issues explored by the academics assembled in the Paris bookstore would take form the next day in a four-hour event entitled "False Flag Islamophobia" broadcast live on No Lies Radio. This event, in turn, helped encourage and hearten some of the contributors to Dr. Barrett's new book.

Introducing the Islamophobia Industry

Sociology Professor David Miller of the University of Bath in Great Britain was one of the senior contributors to the conference at the Paris bookstore. Miller is a prolific scholar whose work on Islamophobia emerges from his important investigations into the relationship between corporate power and public relations as pioneered by the so-called father of media spin, Edward Bernays.

This approach permeates Miller's Spinwatch website and his co-authored volume published in 2008, *A Century of Spin: How Public Relations Became the Cutting Edge of Corporate Power*. In 2011 I had seen Professor Miller offer up a very interesting presentation in the Westminster Parliament in London England. His address in the Mother of All Parliaments helped give rise to his co-authored publication, *The Cold War on British Muslims*.

Professor Miller's presentation in Paris on December 11th 2015 continued the development of themes that have brought on significant wrath from elements of the Jewish-Israeli lobby in Great Britain. For instance the website of the pro-Zionist Gatestone Institute criticized Professor Miller for his work showing the "covert propaganda operations" of several Jewish organizations with preferential access to high-profile media venues.[158]

Along with Professor Bazian, Miller has been prominent in identifying the financing and workings of an interlinked complex of agencies that Nathan Lean and others have dubbed the "The Islamophobia Industry." According to the Legislating Fear report of the Council on

American-Islamic Relations, the dozens of agencies that make up this hate-inciting industry are funded to the tune of several hundreds of millions of dollars. In the words of Bazian, the aim of the well-funded endeavour is "to use fear and hate-mongering to lull our intellect to sleep" and "to implant negative and racist ideas about Muslims and Islam in our collective consciousness."

Prominent among the core institutions of the trans-Atlantic Islamophobia Industry are the Foundation for the Defense of Democracies, the Henry Jackson Society, the Quilliam Foundation, the Gladstone Institute, Daniel Pipe's Middle East Forum, Campus Watch, Islamist Watch, Pam Geller's Atlas Shrugs, Tammi Rossman-Benjamin's AMCHA Initiative, the Clarion Project, the David Horowitz Freedom Center and CAMERA, the Committee for Accuracy in Middle East Reporting.

These and many other agencies whose mission is to incite Islamophobia, derive their funding from a variety of sources including the family foundations of the Koch Brothers, Sheldon Adelson, Sarah Scaife, Harry Bradley, Irving Moskowitz and Canada's Bronfman dynasty. As noted above, the Gladstone Institute has made the work of Professor David Miller, including the content of his website Spinwatch, a particular target of its pro-Zionist defense of the Islamophobia Industry.[159]

Much of the work of David Miller and his colleagues in exposing the pro-Zionist activities of the anti-Muslim hate purveyors involves tracing the money fueling the Islamophobia Industry. This follow-the-money approach could very easily extend to tracking down the sources of financing for the staging of expensive false flag terror events. Throughout the academic presentations I witnessed at the Paris bookstore, there was a persistent resistance by all the presenters to engage in some sort of reckoning with the anti-Muslim thrust of the false flag terrorism currently imposed upon us. In every presentation there was the same conspicuous absence of interest in investigating the primary engine of contemporary Islamophobia, namely the engineering of false flag terror events to be blamed on Muslim fundamentalists said to be acting alone for no other reason than their religious extremism.

According to Kevin Barrett's record of the event, when it came time for questions and answers I posed my query as follows:

> "This is all very interesting, but I'm not hearing any of you get to the root of why there is all this Islamophobia. There is now a huge literature on the fact that these big terror attacks are contrived. It was 9/11 and all of the subsequent events that have created the wave of Islamophobia. I know it's not a good career move, but: Why can't we talk about this? Why can't we –"

I emphasized in my question the observation that the dominant forces animating Islamophobia lie in the extravagant media misrepresentations of false flag terror events. Again and again these episodes of false flag terror are presented as the independent, self-directed work of Islamic extremists acting exclusively out of religious zealotry rather than the actions of mercenaries paid to create the political currency of fear necessary for the maintenance of the permanent war economy. These misrepresentations form the very core of the activities of the Islamophobia Industry as composed by agencies such as the Foundation for the Defense of Democracies. An outgrowth of the Project for the New American Century (PNAC), which in 2000 called for a new Pearl Harbor, the FDD was created a mere two days after the events of 9/11.

It fell to Professor Miller to respond to my question. He began by taking exception to my suggestion that some "psychopaths" might be involved as "assets" in the execution of false flag terrorism. Miller indicated that, in his estimation, Islamic terror events were by and large the product of considered actions on the part of alienated Muslims who had experienced devastating consequences from various forms of hostile invasion into the lives of their own families, communities, and nations. Their violent responses, he indicated, were often the product of long reflection and preparation by mostly intelligent individuals prone to be especially sensitive to the gross abuses of human rights directed at Islamic populations both within the West and on its resource frontiers.

Miller's response was a classic illustration of the "blowback theory" of 9/11. *Blowback: The Costs and Consequences of American Empire* is the name of an iconographic text by a former CIA analyst, Chalmers Johnson. Although Johnson's *Blowback* was first published in 1999, the volume became a bestseller after the events of September 11th, 2001. Johnson believed the United States was imperiled by the flood of recriminations that would inevitably arise from those most negatively affected by the secret incursions of American empire.

Many seized on the central argument of *Blowback* to explain what had transpired on 9/11. I include myself in that category. Until my friend and colleague, the late Mohawk activist Spitting The Sky, insisted in 2008 that I look into the evidence of what did and did not happen on 9/11, I adhered to the blowback theory. I mistakenly believed that the 9/11 attacks were the work of Indigenous peoples resisting repeated rounds of imperial assault on their lands, their persons and their ways of life. I recall it was difficult for me to put this interpretation aside once I began looking at the overwhelming evidence that the various agencies charged to protect us were in fact deeply involved in perpetrating the lies and crimes of 9/11.

The response of Professor Miller to my question seemed to demonstrate the continuing allure of the Blowback theory of 9/11 in spite of the conclusions that have emerged from the elaborate citizens' inquiry into the events of September 11th, 2001. That inquiry demonstrated long ago that the evidence does not support the thesis that all the destruction on 9/11 can be traced back to the independent actions of 19 Saudi jihadists acting to realize a plan hatched by Osama bin Laden.

I found it very instructive to witness how a group of otherwise courageous and conscientious scholars skated around any direct engagement with the origins and genesis of the Global War of False Flag Terrorism. Our collective failure to force on our governments and institutions some basic reckoning with the lies and crimes of 9/11 have made our societies vulnerable to a seemingly endless repetition of the same scenario of manipulation through the incitement of fear towards Muslims. The key to creating these fears lie in the parade of recent false flag terror events in, for instance, London, Madrid, Bali, Ottawa, Paris and San Bernardino to mention only a few.

The event at the Paris bookstore might be characterized as a frontier zone marking the boundary between permitted and prohibited academic discourse. Their proceedings therefore provided an instructive window illuminating the more general failure of the academy to deal in deep and systematic ways with the full extent of the travesty. The potential of humanity is grossly undermined by the absurdity of a never-ending war being waged "on Terror." The War on Truth is the most essential feature of the Global War of False Flag Terrorism.

The Islamophobia Industry and the Deep State Operations of the False Flag Terror Industry

I have learned a lot at the Paris conference and in my subsequent research into the leads provided by the scholars who participated. Professor Miller and others called my attention to, for instance, the dual preoccupations of the same funders and lobby groups that simultaneously instigate hatred of Muslims even as they invest in and promote Jewish settlements on the expansionary frontiers of the Israeli warrior state.

I found particular value in the content of a report by the International Jewish Anti-Zionist Network entitled, "The Business of Backlash: The Attack on the Palestinian Movement and Other Movements of Justice." The document explains in detail the financial, ideological and political community of interests wedding the arms and media industries in the United States to the military and security establishment of Israel.

The channeling of vast treasuries of public funds from the USA to Israel has the effect of creating huge slush funds that end in the coffers of American politicians and in the corporate proprietorships of war profiteers.

The authors go on to explain that this coalition of shared interests is pointed against all manner of progressive movements including environmental groups as well as the decolonization struggles of Blacks, Latinos and Indigenous peoples. It seems the same techniques deployed to cast an aura of criminality over the freedom movement of oppressed Palestinians is being applied more broadly. Accordingly, the demonization of whole populations by practitioners of the Islamophobia Industry casts a very broad shadow. The hate inciting smear campaigns support oppressive structures of top-down power running contrary to the exercise of even the most fundamental principles of universal human rights.

The Islamophobia Industry's assault on human rights extended to an attack on the academic freedom of Professor Rabab Ibrahim Abdulhadi, one of the more prominent participants in the proceedings at the Paris bookstore. Abdulhadi is Director of the Arab and Muslim Ethnicities and Diaspora Initiative at San Francisco State University in California. Recently she has was targeted by a formidable array of Islamophobes led by Tammi Rossman-Benjamin's AMCHA Initiative.

The attack on Professor Abdulhadi was discussed in *The Business of Backlash*. Her Zionist detractors accused the Palestinian-American academic of being "a terrorist supporter as well as a supporter of the anti-Semitic Boycott, Divestment and Sanctions movement." She was said to embody "all that is wrong with radical elements of academia who have all but hijacked the social science and humanities fields. Her obsessive focus on Israel and monomaniacal demonization of the Mideast's only democracy betray a troubling pattern of Judeophobia and overt anti-Semitism."[160]

A formidable coalition of academic colleagues and civil rights organizations rallied to the defense of Professor Abdulhadi who was represented by the lawyers of the Palestinian Solidarity Legal Support network. Abdulhadi's participation in the Paris conference as a working professor attests to their success in persuading the administration of San Francisco State U. to fend off the malicious attempt to end this important scholar's academic career.

It seems very strange that those who participated in the academic conference in Paris, like those who authored *The Business of Backlash*, could make themselves so expert on the relationships between the Islamophobia Industry, Jewish Settlements on the West Bank and the deep state machinations of the Israeli-American power elite but not extend their investigations further. The evidence has become overwhelming that what is portrayed in the media as self-motivated, self-financing, self-directed Islamic terrorism is rather the outcome of a complex network of connections linking intelligence agencies, paid assets, mercenaries and other private sector contractors connected to the operations and objectives of the pro-Zionist Islamophobia Industry.

As my reading on the Islamophobia Industry progressed I came to see the most visible agencies of public hate mongering towards Muslims as but the tip of the iceberg of far larger structures of deceit and corruption. Beneath the overt activities of the Muslim-bashing agencies lie the covert deep state entities devoted to generating the false flag terror events on which the parasitic Islamophobia Industry feeds. This connection can be well illustrated in the reincarnation after 9/11 of the Project for the New American Century as the pro-Zionist, anti-Muslim Foundation for the Defense of Democracies.

The basic aim of this whole sordid complex of deep state and public agencies is to transform Israel's Arab and predominantly Muslim regional enemies, the Palestinians, into one element of a larger global entity presented as the antithesis of the West's self-proclaimed "freedoms." Composed of the worldwide community of Muslims, the Ummah was instrumentalized in public mythology as the aberrant "other" to be guarded against, pacified and sometimes vanquished. The wholesale demonization of Muslims served the purpose of providing the war machine with a new enemy to replace the defunct enemy of the Soviet Union.

The Memes, Symbols and Demonology Deployed in Generating Hatred Towards Muslims

The same banking-military-media establishment that benefited most from the permanent war economy on the capitalist side of the Cold War was reborn, re-energized and refinanced with the launching of the Global War of False Flag Terrorism. In this fashion a degree of continuity was maintained as the same national security establishment created to fight communism was re-deployed in a very strange operation involving both the creation of, and opposition to, Islamic terrorism.

In the decade and a half since 9/11 a powerful Islamophobia Industry has set the tone for the entire mainstream media. In the process, the imagery of Islamic jihad has been rendered an essential part of the visual vocabulary of popular culture. The project of generating fear of Muslims in mainstream media draws on many tried and true techniques of the Public Relations Industry.

The integration of Islamophobia into popular culture often invokes archetypes and symbols from religious mythology like, for instance, the stereotypical demonology of witchcraft and devil worship. Resort is made to mental imagery rooted in children's fables such as Peter and the Wolf. To convey these messages, instant-made-for-TV "terrorist" experts regularly conjure up terms such as "Lone Wolf Terrorist" even as they warn us against the "Homegrown Terrorists" said to be lurking amongst us. In such theatres of normalized hate speech, whole populations are wedged, divided and turned against each other to grease the gears of fear and distrust as primary lubricants for political and commercial exploitation.

The lies and crimes of 9/11 lie at the origins of a Great Transformation for the worse. To fail to deal with what did or did not happen in the Mother of All False Flag Terror Events is to give credence to the interpretation that the saga of misrepresentation essential to the Global War on Terror's genesis did not begin until 2003. According to that gatekeepers' version of reality, the administration of George W. Bush was an innocent victim of Islamic attacks until the executive branch began floating the lie that the government of Saddam Hussein possessed weapons of mass destruction in order to justify the US-led invasion of Iraq.

Much of the responsibility for publicizing the false assertions that Saddam Hussein's government possessed weapons of mass destruction has been laid at the doorstep of the *New York Times* and the work of its star reporter Judith Miller. Miller's primary sources on this story included Richard Perle, Paul Wolfowitz, and Douglas Feith, all prominent Israeli-American members of the Project for a New American Century. In a major report in 2000, PNAC anticipated the events of 9/11 by proclaiming that the realization of their neoconservative agenda could not be achieved "absent some catastrophic and catalyzing event—like a new Pearl Harbour."

Is it credible that a handful of Saudi Muslims led by Osama bin Laden, armed with nothing but box cutters, a smattering of flight training and intense jihadist zeal, acted independently to bring about the elaborate high-tech crime that took place on 9/11? Is it credible that the neocon cabal controlling both the Israeli government and the Bush White House was fortuitously presented by self-directed jihadists with precisely the catalytic event it needed to institute its ambitious agenda of police repression at home and military expansion abroad?

Is it credible that the neocon establishment was only a respondent to, rather than an author of, the cataclysmic events of 9/11? If the events of 9/11 were indeed a surprise attack on power symbols of American prowess in warfare and commerce, why was no one responsible for such a stupendous breach of national security fired for such a spectacular failure? How is it that so many of those who accuse the Bush-Cheney regime of lying about so many subjects refuse to explore the extent of the lies whose effect is to protect the actual perpetrators of the 9/11 crimes?

Part of the problem in the official cover story of 9/11 is that the custodians of the fable keep on changing it to suit the changing currents of political expediency. In the early days following 9/11, the culprits were said to be Osama bin Laden and his coterie of Islamic extremists in al-Qaeda. Then the demonology of 9/11 shifted so that somehow Saddam Hussein and his Iraqi government were made to epitomize the jihadist extremes of Islamic terror. Once Saddam was captured and executed in 2006 the world was briefly introduced to a person or persons identified by the name Khalid Sheik Mohammed. For a time it seemed that the US executive branch would conduct a show trial in New York of Khalid, the supposed "mastermind of 9/11" to commemorate the 10th anniversary of the infamous day.

The plan to try Khalid Sheik Mohammed for war crimes was abandoned. This prisoner remains jailed in the US concentration camp at Guantanamo Bay on the island of Cuba. There he has been tortured through water boarding many dozens of times in order to elicit all manner of confessions including some that found their way into the 9/11 Commission report in the United States. The creation of an official government report, whose conclusions are drawn from supposed evidence obtained from illegal torture, is itself a war crime. Accordingly, those academics, jurists, politicians, journalists, and other public intellectuals who accept the 9/11 Commission report as accurate and satisfactory are rendered complicit in war crimes and crimes against humanity.

Instead of conducting a show trial, the government of US President Barack Obama opted to mark the 10th anniversary of 9/11 by announcing that US Navy Seals had hunted down and killed Osama bin Laden at a compound near Abbottabad Pakistan. In this fashion bin Laden was posthumously returned to the role assigned him by the White House and media agencies within hours of the 9/11 strikes without any formal investigation whatsoever.

According to Seymour Hersh, the White House's story on bin Laden's elimination "might have been written by Lewis Carroll." Bin Laden was supposedly buried at sea. What sense would it make simply to execute the man that would be far and away the world's foremost authority on international jihadism if the mythological demonology attending the 9/11 psychological operation was actually true. The elimination by the Democratic Party President of the Republic Party President's initial 9/11 patsy cleared the way for a new phase in the Global War of False Flag Terrorism overseen by Barack Obama.[161]

This Democratic Party version of the neocon plan for global domination restored al-Qaeda to a role something like it had played in the 1980s as a part of the mujahadeen proxy army army serving US geopolitical strategies. Where al-Qaeda helped overthrow the USSR-backed puppet regime in Afghanistan in the 1980s, in the second decade of the twenty-first century al-Qaeda was reborn as a mercenary instrument of NATO's assault on the Libyan government of Muammar Gaddafi.

The instrumentalization of mercenary armies paid to fight under the banner of Islamic religion has grown in scope so that this historical trajectory lies at the very heart of the international showdown for control of the lands and resources of Syria. Under heavy Israeli pressure, the US government with backing from the governments of Saudi Arabia, Turkey and Qatar has built up al-Qaeda's successor, Jabhat al-Nusra. The aim of this sponsorship of Islamic theocrats hostile to Bashir al-Assad's more secular and pluralistic Russian-backed Syrian government is to balkanize the region and possibly to prepare the ground for the eastward and northward expansion of Israel.

This US backing of al-Qaeda-related fighters was spun as support for a "moderate opposition" to the Assad government. This scenario unfolded concurrently with the rise, in Iraq and Syria, of the entity known variously as the Islamic State in the Levant, ISIL, ISIS, and more recently Daesh. The evidence has become overwhelming that this fighting force is financed, armed and organized in part to embody the memes of hatred and extremism essential to the operations of the Islamophobia Industry and the main protagonists of the Global War of False Flag Terrorism.

The close connection in the international oil business linking governments of Turkey, Israel and the non-state entity dubbed the Islamic State, highlight the many layers of complicity in a very strange operation. The US government presents itself publicly as the world's leading opponent of Islamic terror while it cultivates, assists and facilitates the very forces it says it is fighting.

In a recent post on his website, Voltairenet, Thierry Meyssen has described the prevalent blindness to what has been really taking place in the region of Syria and Iraq. He lays bare the dynamics of a dangerous game that involves "pretending, like NATO, that these [Islamic fighting] groups are independent formations which have suddenly materialised from the void, with all their salaries, armement and spare parts. More seriously, the jihadists are in fact mercenaries in the service of Turkey, Saudi Arabia and Qatar.... to which we must add certain multinationals like Academi, KKR and Exxon-Mobil."[162]

A Reversion to Old Styles of Imperialism in the Name of Anti-Terrorism?

Since bin Laden was supposedly buried at sea by the US Armed Forces in 2010 the role once assigned to al-Qaeda as the all-purpose boogyman of Islamic terrorism has now been re-assigned to the non-state entity dubbed the Islamic State. When acts of false flag terrorism take place as in Ottawa in October 2014, or in Paris in November of 2015, or in San Bernardino a month later, the authorities in charge of pseudo-investigations are prone to announce almost immediately a connection to ISIS/ISIL Daesh.

Criminal law is thereby put aside and the violent events are immediately elevated to "acts of war" justifying quick retaliation by armed forces. Within hours of the Friday the 13th Paris event, for instance, French President François Hollande was ordering the French Air Force to intervene in Syria. While the supposed target was ISIS/ISIL/Daesh encampments and strongholds, there is reason to see the real objective of the supposed anti-terror attacks as the overthrow of the Assad government. This French military intervention could thus be interpreted as a resort to France's old imperial role in the part of the Middle East assigned it by the Eurocentric Sykes-Picot Agreement of 1916.

The point of this foray into the recent history of the Global War of False Flag Terrorism is to encourage colleagues in the academy to address, document and explain the unfolding patterns of deception so integral to the process of enlarging the unaccountable powers of the covert deep state, diminishing the overt role of the public state. I extend this encouragement especially to the colleagues that Dr. Barrett and I met in the Paris bookstore at the event entitled "Islamophobia and the Erosion of Civil Society."

These colleagues and their networks of academic collaborators have made a good start in identifying the institutionalization of hate mongering in the Islamophobia Industry. The time has come, however, to connect the visible workings of this Zionist enterprise of anti-Muslim provocation to the deep state operations in the ongoing Global War of False Flag Terrorism.

THE WAR OF TERRORISM: DRUGS, DEATH SQUADS, CLASS RULE AND RESISTANCE

Gearóid O Colmáin

The day of the November 13ᵗʰ attacks in Paris, two teachers and trade union leaders in Colombia were shot dead in their homes by paramilitaries. The murders did not make international headlines. They never do. But the assassination of labour activists in Colombia is a regular occurrence. The murders of labour activists in the country are carried out by paramilitaries in the service of the oligarchic state.

A Colombian connection to the Paris attacks has been reported. According to the Colombian press a Syrian female terrorist allegedly involved in the Paris attacks had traveled on a false Israeli passport from Bogota, Colombia to the French capital, after having bribed officials there. The significance and veracity of this story has yet to be examined. But another Latin American connection to the Paris attacks has been definitively established. One of the weapons found at the scene of the November 13ᵗʰ Paris attacks was sold by Florida based company, Century Arms, that supplied contra terrorists in the CIA's secret war against Nicaragua during the 1980s. Such reports raise the question of the deep state as a function of the wider class war that subtends imperial geopolitics, a class war deceptively referred to as the "War on Terrorism." So to trace the outlines of the deep state implicated in the apparent false flag attacks in Paris, a detour to Columbia may be illuminating.

The late Hugo Chavez once referred to Colombia as the "Israel of Latin America." In March 2011, the Syrian authorities arrested an Egyptian/American citizen who had been living in Syria. Mohammad Radwan had been paid by a Colombian agent residing in Israel to produce war propaganda videos for the international press, falsely portraying Syria as a country erupting in chaos under the tyranny of a "brutal dictator" who was "killing his own people." During the 1980s, Israeli mercenary and IDF commandant Yair Klein trained paramilitary death squads in Colombia. The death squads were responsible for thousands of atrocities. Klein financed the training through the laundering of drug money in the United States.

The Israeli used his contacts among Jewish rabbis in the United States to have the drug money laundered through Israeli banks. When the rabbis were caught by US law enforcement, powerful interests intervened to get them released. When Klein was arrested in Russia in 2007, Colombian officials half-heartedly attempted to secure his extradition to Colombia but the European Union refused, citing concerns about human rights abuses in Colombian prisons. No such concerns were shown in 2002 when three IRA men were arrested in Colombia in connection with the FARC guerillas, a Marxist-Leninist army who have been protecting poor peasants from state terror for over half a century. The European Union refers to the FARC as "terrorists."

The method used to destablise Syria since 2011 was inspired by the US/Israeli trained death squads of Latin America. US ambassador to Iraq and Syria Robert Ford had worked under John Negroponte, who was US ambassador to Honduras from 1981 to 1985. Negroponte organized the funding and training of the contra terrorists created by Washington to overthrow the democratic government of Nicaragua. He also oversaw the deployment of death squads in Honduras who murdered political opponents of the US-backed military dictatorship. This policy was also carried out in El Salvador. These operations were financed by CIA drug running and illegal arms shipments to Iran. Thanks to the investigative journalism of Gary Webb, who was subsequently murdered, the story became known as the Iran/Contra scandal—and Century Arms, who supplied the Paris terrorists also supplied the Contra death squads, who murdered over 30 thousand people in Nicaragua.

In 2005, the Pentagon revealed that the El Salvador Option was being used in Iraq to crush resistance to the US occupation of the country. Ford became ambassador to Syria shortly before the invasion of that country by death squads. The purpose of the US/Israeli destruction of Syria is to destroy a nation state resisting Zionist hegemony in the Middle East, in preparation for a wider war against Iran, Russia and China.

Although Colombia is a state where speaking up for the rights of the poor will endanger your life, it is considered an ideal country for investment by European and American corporations. French investment in the country has increased by 67 percent in recent years, making the narco-state France's second largest trading partner in Latin America after Brazil.

French propaganda czar Thierry Gaubert, a former advisor to Nicolas Sarkozy, owned a palace in Colombia where he would regularly invite French corporate bosses. Gaubert, who has since been prosecuted for fraud and embezzlement of public money, has also been accused of involvement in organised narco-crime in Colombia. A country where labour leaders and socially engaged teachers are murdered by paramilitaries linked to the state presents ideal investment opportunities for multi-national corporations, which is why the corporate media cover up the crimes of the Colombian narco-state while blaming many of them on those resisting that state terror, namely the Revolutionary Armed Forces of Colombia.

The utilization of drug trafficking gangs by the bourgeoisie against the organisations of the working class has a long history. During the 1947 strike in France's port city of Marseilles, the CIA used its connections with the Socialist Party deputy and Mayor of Marseilles Gaston Deferre to break the labour unions and the power of the French Communist Party (PCF) by tolerating the drug trafficking activities of the Guerini mafia who murdered and terrorized labour activists on behalf of the state. The war led by the Socialist Party against France's working class proves what Marxist-Leninists have always held: That social democrats are the agents of the bourgeoisie in the labour movement. The Socialist Party's CIA funded destruction of France's working class militancy led to one of the world's worst heroin epidemics among the demoralized workers of Marseilles. The petit-bourgeois class collaborationism of Maurice Thorez's PCF, coupled with obsequiousness in the face of Soviet revisionism, completely betrayed working class militancy in France. Today, many white workers vote for the extreme-right-wing National Front. Ruling class internationalism has beaten the working class into racially and ethnically divided factions, fighting each other instead of their class enemies.

Class struggle is at the heart of both the war on terror and the war on drugs—and both wars are deeply inter-related.

In the corporate media the Revolutionary Armed Forces of Colombia are regularly slandered and demonised. They are called "drug-traffickers" and "terrorists." Nothing could be further from the truth. The Revolutionary Armed Forces of Colombia arose out of a civil war after the country's oligarchy refused to allow the Communist Party of Colombia to run in elections in the 1960s. Any attempts made by the FARC to engage in a peace process have been met with state-terrorism. In Colombia, almost 70 percent of the country is owned by less than 0.4 percent of the population, while up to 90 percent of peasants in the countryside live in dire poverty. This is in spite of the fact that Colombia is one of the most resource-rich countries in the world.

Peasants and workers who organise to fight for their rights are subject to the most obscene state terror at the hands of paramilitary death squads trained by the likes of Yair Klein. The crimes of the Colombian death squads eerily resemble those of Daesh in the Middle East—perhaps because the same forces are behind the two seemingly unrelated phenomena. Pregnant women's wombs are ripped open and their infants dismembered, community leaders are raped in front of their wives and children, activists are beheaded and their bodies mutilated. The savagery of the paramilitary crimes comes from a desire to warn other peasants never to support the FARC. Just like the rebels who attacked Libya and Syria, the European Union and the United States implicitly support these crimes against humanity by ignoring or blaming them on the FARC. The FARC have a high percentage of women among their ranks and are creating family-oriented ecological subsistence farming in areas they control. They practice restorative justice and are building schools and hospitals for their people. Were they to succeed in seizing power in Colombia, the movement would inevitably spread to all of Latin America, liberating millions of people from poverty and class oppression.

Such a development would bring an end to corporate profiteering; an end to agri-business; an end to resource-pillage; latifundias; narco-crime, an end to the secret palaces of the world's Thierry Gauberts. So the FARC are terrorists, say the corporate media. That is all you need to know. Colombia might seem like an extreme example in the context of the class war in Europe, but this is what the world will soon look like if the current global dictatorship is not replaced with popular democracy.

An indication of just how strong, consistent and international ruling class networks are is evinced by the recent deployment of Colombian mercenaries to Yemen by the United Arab Emirates, a client-state of NATO. NATO, Israel and their Gulf State clients have been waging a brutal war against the people of Yemen for over a year in an attempt to crush the popular Ansarallah movement, a threat to Zionist domination of the Arabian Peninsula.

Just months after the terrorist attacks on the *Charlie Hebdo* magazine, President François Hollande visited Saudi Arabia to sign lucrative arms deals. Hollande met with the new Saudi monarch King Salman. Salman was accused by democratic opposition leaders in Britain of providing direct financial and logistical support to Al Qaeda terrorists in Afghanistan before and after 9/11. This did not bother the French government. Hollande also met with intelligence Prince Mohammad Bin Najef. In 1999 Najef's close relative had been arrested in Paris smuggling cocaine from Colombia and Venezuela. The operation was being used to finance Al Qaeda terrorists in Afghanistan. The Saudi regime immediately threatened to cancel a military contract for radar technology with the French firm Thales to the tune of seven billion dollars if charges were brought against the Saudi prince.

Just weeks after an Al Qaeda terrorist attack traumatized the French people, the country's president was in Riyah selling arms to the very people financing and arming Al Qaeda, who the French government claims "want to take away our freedoms." Meanwhile, the Afro-French lumpen-proletariat of France's ghettoized banlieux face quotidian police harassment, while thousands languish in overcrowded prisons for selling the drugs brought onto our streets by the agents of the deep state or for practising too fervently the death-cult ideology promoted by the French government's Saudi clients. Openly attempting to insult the intelligence of the French reader, *Liberation*, the "left-wing" news rag of the French imperial establishment, ran the following headline: *François Hollande En Pleine Lune de Miel Saudienne* (François Hollande's Saudi Honeymoon).

The Imperialist Left

Petit bourgeois leftists in Europe love to wax lyrical about the "left-turn" in Latin America, declaring their support and admiration for revolutionaries of the past such as Hugo Chavez and Che Guevara, yet the same people openly declare their support for the death squads massacring the workers of Libya and Syria, in spite of the fact that the leaders of those countries Gaddafi and Assad were close friends and admirers of Venezuela's Bolivarian revolution.

These petit-bourgeois leftists evince a common fault, one for which Lenin repeatedly reproached Trotsky, the inability to engage in concrete political analysis and the masking of a right-wing, reactionary agenda with ultra-leftist phrases and slogans. One only has to recall the references by Noam Chomsky in his BBC interview on the eve of the bombing of Libya, where he agreed that the West had a "duty" to "stop the massacres" being perpetrated by Gaddafi. Of course, there were no massacres carried out by Gaddafi and any honest political analyst who understands how corporate media war propaganda works would have denounced the lies used to demonise Gaddafi and bomb his people.

In his smug BBC interview Chomsky mentioned the "labour struggles" in Egypt that preceded the 2011 uprising. The MIT academic was obviously unaware of the the fact that the CIA front organisation, the American International Federation of Labour had been active in Egypt organising the April 6th Youth movement since at least 2005. The post-revolution outcome of the CIA's "labour struggle" was that henceforth

Egyptian workers would not be paid if they went on strike nor would they receive any wages when corporations decided to cease production due to lack of market demand.

Chomsky's support for the NATO bombing of Libya and subsequent war against Syria is indicative of the treacherous ideology of what Lenin referred to as the "vacillating class," namely the petite-bourgeosie. An indication of just how triumphant petit-bourgeois ideology has become among communists is the fact that both the Libyan and Syrian rebels have had tents at France's annual communist festival "l'Humanité."

In France the imperialist left tends to evince a rabid anti-Americanism. This tendency to blame America for all the world's problems allows the imperialist left to ignore the crimes of French imperialism. For the French imperialist left, the Arab Spring represented the coming of age of the North African youth, who through education had discovered the great thinkers of French civilisation, and were now demanding freedom and democracy French style.

The notion that all Americans are stupid and that therefore the United States government would be incapable of planning and organising such an impressive wave of revolutions in Francophone countries such as Tunisia is unthinkable to the petit-bourgeois anti-American leftist. *Le Monde Diplomatique*, a prominent imperial leftist journal published an anti-conspiracy theory supplement in 2015. A common technique used by the imperial left is the argument from authority. This consists in claiming to be able to distinguish real, proven conspiracies from farfetched nonsense promoted by simpletons.

So on one page an article was published where the author confirms that the US government's National Endowment for Democracy are indeed funding and training opposition activists in Venezuela for the purposes of subverting democracy. Yet on the same page, another article appears claiming that simple-minded people in the Arab world believe the Arab Spring was orchestrated by the United States and Israel to spread chaos among the Arab speaking world. In spite of the fact that the National Endowment for Democracy did not disguise their support for the Arab Spring, but proudly published the information on their website; in spite of the fact that US Secretary of State Condolezza Rice confirmed herself that the US government supported the "revolutionaries"; in spite of the fact that the activists of the Center for Non Violent Actions and Strategies admitted training Arab Spring activists; in spite of the fact that academic studies by conservative researchers from Sciences Po such as Dr. Naoufel Bahimi El Mili have documented this; in spite of the fact that France Inter reported on the role of Gene Sharpe's work and US NGOs as the Arab Spring farce unfolded, even interviewing activists who spoke of receiving money from the US embassy; in spite of the hundreds of articles and numerous books published meticulously documenting all of this, *Le Monde Diplomatique* blocks its ears and compares all of these people to simpletons spreading rumours on the internet.

Of course, *Le Monde Diplomatique* must do this. How else could it, with such callous insouciance, justify the neocolonial invasion of Libya by islamo-fascists, the brutal eight month long carpet bombing of its people and NATO's ongoing genocide in Syria and Yemen? How else could it support neo-colonial wars and genocides while still pretending to be "left-wing" and "progressive"? Attempting to calumniate genuine anti-war activists as red/brown shirts will no longer suffice. The Libyan and Syrian wars, myriad neocolonial wars against Africa and the utterly spurious "War on Terrorism" have shown who the real brown shirts are and they know it.

It is important to critique and expose the lies and disinformation that would claim to be "anti-establishment" or "anti-capitalist," as such publications and the dishonest intellectuals who publish in them are the life-blood of the imperialist military-industrial-media-intelligence complex, the life-blood of a planetary imperialist apparatus murdering millions of innocents in the name of "human rights" and "freedom." One could say that if they did not exist imperialism would have had to invent them, in so far as they create the illusion that genuine dissent is possible within the imperialist system, when in fact the only space left open to genuine critique of the current global order is the Internet and as the reign of terror intensifies, that space is in grave danger of disappearing.

Terrorism: an instrument of the capitalist state

In the 1980s, the Central Intelligence Agency armed, funded and trained "islamist" mujahedeen in Afghanistan to serve as a proxy force for US imperialism against the democratic revolution in that country, a revolution that had brought major land reforms in favour of poor peasants, working class emancipation through mass education and industrialization, women's rights, and most importantly, the Saur Revolution in Afghanistan had brought social hope to a desperately poor and backward country. The CIA soon put an end to that. Within a decade the entire infrastructure of the country had been destroyed, millions killed, women enslaved and the country's social and political institutions were in ruins. Drug lords and warlords roamed the lawless country. The

CIA's mission had been accomplished. The US had prevented the expansion of the Soviet Union's sphere of influence. That was all that mattered. Drug trafficking played a key role in financing the CIA's proxy war against the Soviet Union in Afghanistan. Drugs also financed the wars in Vietnam, Cambodia and Laos. Since NATO's occupation of Afghanistan in 2001, the country's drug trafficking has increased 500 percent, and much of that drug money provided important liquidity to the global banking system after the financial crisis in 2008.

During the 1950s, the Communist Party of Iraq had a newspaper called Al Qaedah (Arabic for the database). This is ironic, given the function Al Qaeda was subsquently to assume as a tool of imperialism against the workers of anti-imperialist nation states. The CIA put Saddam Hussein in power in 1963 in order to crush the power of organized labour represented by the Iraqi communist party, who had made gains under Abdul Karib Qasim's administration. Saddam took power with a list of communists the CIA wanted murdered and dutifully carried out the Empire's orders. Although Saddam had run Iraq on behalf of US geostrategic interests, Israel wanted the country to be annihilated and pushed the US Congress to declare the 2003 war. After the occupation, Al Qaeda terrorism flourished in the devastated country, stoking up ethnic and religious conflict in accordance with US/Zionist divide and conquer occupation tactics.

The word Al Qaedah, a name well known to the CIA, had been given to Osama Bin Laden's network of military intelligence assets during the 1990s, when Bin Laden operated freely out of London using the CIA's Bank of Credit and Commerce International. During the Yugoslav wars of the 1990s, the CIA redeployed terrorists trained in Afghanistan to Bosnia and Serbia to destabilise and break up the Yugoslav Federation. The terrorists committed thousands of atrocities which they blamed on the Yugoslav government. The Kosovo Liberation Army, used by the CIA to pull the province of Kosovo away from Serbia, funded their terrorism with heroin trafficking. Today Kosovo, run by a mafia boss wanted by Interpol for crimes against humanity, is home to Europe's largest US military base, and has the distinction of being referred to as Europe's rubbish bin, whose main exports are illegal arms, prostitution, drugs and terrorism.

Imperialism's "revolutions"

The same networks of terrorists and drug traffickers would be used by NATO to invade and destroy Libya in 2011. The so-called "Arab Spring" had been planned by the United States and Israel more than a decade before the uprisings in 2011. US secretary of State Condolezza Rice announced the US strategy of "creative destruction" to reshape the Middle East during her speech to the American Israeli Public Affairs Committee (AIPAC) in 2006, where she revealed that US foreign policy had "changed" and henceforth Washington would be supporting "democracy" in former US-backed secular dictatorships such as Tunisia and Egypt. Egypt's President Hosni Mubarak, a former air-force pilot, was skeptical about the US government's official explanation for the 9/11 terrorist attacks. He opposed the Iraq war and refused to back the Zionist division of Sudan. As Condolezza Rice would later admit during a press conference "there was a reason why President Mubarak did not go back to the United States after 2003."

US NGOs under the patronage of the National Endowment for Democracy were active across North Africa from 2004, training youth activists in how to use social media and technology for political subversion. By 2011, the mass media was buzzing with phrases such as "popular uprising" and "spontaneous uprising," slogans echoed enthusiastically by an astonishingly large proportion of self-styled leftist and Marxist intellectuals. The "left-wing" consensus surrounding the Arab Spring provided the cover for one of the most brutal neo-colonial wars in modern history. The Great Socialist Libyan People's Arab Jamahirya, Africa's wealthiest, most developed, most democratic and egalitarian state was torn asunder by NATO death squads cheered on by "radical" leftists as the racist, fascist militia massacred all before them. The destruction of Libya caused a humanitarian catastrophe, with over half the population reduced to refugees.

The destabilization soon spread to neighbouring Mali where the French used the pretext of "fighting terrorism" to bomb and invade their former colony, thus bringing the country's resources under the control of French corporations. In 2013, the Central African Republic would fall prey to the same destabilization techniques. For months, a heavily armed Seleka Rebellion massacred village after village, as unnamed French officials told the press that they were "monitoring" the situation, while spokesmen for the rebels had easy access to the French press. The leader of the Central African Republic, François Bozizé had run the country on behalf of Paris since 2002 but had fallen out of favour after he signed a large contract with the Chinese National Petroleum Company giving it extensive oil exploration rights in the Central African Republic, a nation and a people the French ruling elite have always considered to be their private property.

The Seleka rebels were led by Saudi asset Michel Djotodia. After thousands of innocents were massacred, the French military performed a Eurypidean *deux ex machina*. The country was pacified and brought firmly back under neo-colonial control. It is an imperial strategy regularly employed in Africa. The current focus of French, Belgian and American neocolonial terrorism is Burundi, where a terrorist campaign has been launched since April 2015 under the guise of "civil society" and "peaceful protestors" against one of Sub-Saharan Africa's most popular presidents. The NATO-fomented terror has resulted in thousands of deaths and hundreds of thousands of refugees and could possibly lead to a repeat of the genocide by the French and Belgian backed regime that preceded Nkurunziza's rise to power, where up to four million people were exterminated in death camps and killing fields scattered throughout the country. In a country where questioning the genocide of the Jews could land one in prison, outright negation of French neocolonial genocide in Africa is not only legal but is the politically correct norm.

Since the destruction of Libya, millions of Africans have been attempting to flee the continent for Europe. Just as the United States and Israel used the social discontent of the Magrebin youth to bring down recalcitrant secular leaders and replace them with compliant Muslim Brotherhood traitors, the policy of using the problems of imperialism to further imperialism would also come into play during the refugee crisis of 2015.

Coercive Engineered Migration and the Division of the World Island

The US military's grand strategist General Thomas PM Barnett has predicted that Europe will collapse this century under the weight of mass, uncontrolled immigration from Africa and the Middle East. In Halfold Mackinder's geopolitical theory, Eurasia and Africa form a "World Island," the key to the British Empire's domination of the World Island was to gain control over the Eurasian landmass, that is to say predominantly Russia and Central Asia. In his book *Democratic Ideals and Reality* Mackinder wrote "Who rules East Europe commands the Heartland; who rules the Heartland commands the World-Island; who rules the World-Island commands the world."

US leaders have always understood that a marriage of Russian natural resources with German industry would lead to a Eurasian integration which would challenge America's global primacy. In order to prevent this, an intermarium, or Russophobic bloc in Eastern Europe is proposed which will stretch from the Baltic Sea to the Black Sea. Meanwhile, in order to subordinate Africa to US imperial interests, mass migration of Africans to Europe is advocated. US/Israeli global hegemony requires pulling the European peninsula away from the Eurasian landmass.

The CIA has predicted that Europe will descend into Civil War by 2020. In order to precipitate this process, NGOs linked to US intelligence agencies are financing mass migrations of Middle Eastern and African youths to Europe as the Middle East is depopulated in preparation for Greater Israel, while Africa comes under the control of US African Command.

The policy of Coercive Engineered Migration, whereby migrants are used as weapons by one state to destabilize another, is being carried out with ruthless efficiency by US funded NGOs which are also linked to oligarchs such as George Soros and Carlos Slim. NGOs such as We2Eu, Med..., Peng, are all linked to powerful US and Israeli financial institutions, while ORS systems, one of the main project management companies dealing with refugees in Europe, is managed by a company affiliated to Barclays bank. The "refugee crisis" is big business and is part of a global class war which seeks to uproot humans from localities, languages, cultures and traditions, transforming man into an economic nomad eternally worshiping at the alter of commodity fetishism.

As millions of Africans flee countries torn asunder by NATO's mercenaries and death squads, "agri-business" will replace traditional farming, GMOs will replace the fruits of nature and the acculturated automaton from Mali or the Congo who ekes out a living in Europe taking away the bins of the corporate bosses raping his country and people, will earn just enough money to buy a tin of GMO unfood, his daily dose of "soylent green" before he dies and is thrown out with the refuse.

The Project for a New American Century (PNAC), the brainchild of Zionists and neo-conservatives, threatens to enslave humanity. The state of Israel is at the heart of this project. For the state of Israel is perhaps the world's most globalized state, with powerful branches operating in Europe and the United States, registered as lobbies but functioning as de facto shadow governments. Israel is a state but not a country. It has no official borders. It is a global imperial work-in-progress. The war on terror is a creation of Zionism. It is the tool with which Zion seeks to divide and conquer "the nations" (*goyim*) through takfiri proxy armies who mimic the Assassins of the Middle Ages, clearing the ground for the expansion of Zionist hegemony in the Middle East. Daesh and Al Qaeda are and always have been the foreign legions of the Zionist entity. The Gulf monarchies are the ugly sisters of Zion. They promote the Wahhabi death cult, which oppresses and enslaves Muslims and discredits Islam on behalf of Zionism. If the French government was interested in fighting terrorism, President Bashar Al Assad and the Grand Mufti of Damascus, two highly cultured, tolerant leaders of civilization would be the chief interlocutors of French diplomacy in the Middle East. But sadly, this is not the case. The current regime in Paris is among the most belligerent and barbaric in modern French history. Unlike De Gaulle and Mitterand, the French regime has vassalized the French nation to the United States and Israel. This was even admitted by economist Bernard Maris in an article in Le Monde shortly before he was murdered during the Charlie Hebdo terrorist attacks in January 2015.

The Gaza concentration camp is a microcosm of the world to come, for the entire global policy of Zionism is attempting to reduce man to the status of a refugee, an outlaw, a terrorist. The troops on our streets and surveillance in our skies, far from temporary measures designed to protect civilians from terrorism, represent the encroaching Gaza-fication of the world. All of the gains of centuries of class struggle are being taken away by an increasingly organised and globalized oligarchy, acutely conscious of its class interests.

In France, we now have the return of Vichy with Prime Minister Manuel Valls pushing for the introduction of legislation for the creation of concentration camps for whose who may be considering committing acts of terrorism. When one recalls that the same government is recruiting, training and deploying terrorists all over the Middle East and Africa to fight its imperial wars and that the term terrorist is now used to describe "insurrectionist movements" who "threaten French national interests," the sinister agenda of the current French regime becomes all too clear and the question of people's resistance becomes paramount.

What is to be done

Posting articles on social media, attending conferences, financing independent media, convening meetings, organising demonstrations, co-operating with all social and political movements from the left to the right on the basis of a common platform, such actions can and will acquire critical mass. French Foreign Minister Laurent Fabius has declared that Daesh are attempting to create a civil war in France. Translated, this means that the oligarchy have declared class war. Tyranny is no more clement submitted to than resisted. What is required now is what Lenin referred to as a "League of Struggle for the Emancipation of the Working Class." Such a league can have no place for petty bourgeois vacillators, but must constitute a broad, international movement of the working class and the progressive bourgeoisie against the

New World Order, a people's movement united provisionally on the basis of a minimal platform defending national sovereignty, the rule of law and the rights of workers.

French essayist Maurice Barrès once said that the first condition for social peace is that the poor are convinced of their own impotence. We must work to change this through the creation of what Gramsci termed proletarian Cultural Hegemony. This is beginning to occur in the internet through quality independent media, which is why we must resist policing of the world-wide web. Historian Robert Darnton in his book *The Forbidden Bestsellers of Pre-revolutionary France* shows that contrary to official history which sees the philosophical works of the great French philosophers Diderot, Rousseau, Voltaire, Condorcet, inter alia, as being the motor for the French revolution, it was the vast network of forbidden underground pamphlets and radical political treatises, the controversial *livres philosophiques* such as the works in French translation of Irish republican philosopher John Toland, which undermined public confidence in the *ancien regime*. Today, those underground networks are flourishing on the blogospheres, websites, youtube channels and social media of the world wide web, and prestigious Parisien book shops such as Librairie Tropiques are regularly organising conferences and talks, defending the great French tradition of critical inquiry against the barbaric cognitive policing of today's court sycophants. This new enlightenment will continue to grow as the current regime plunges French society into misery and chaos.

Education is the key to emancipation. The ruling class understand this. One is hardly surprised therefore to read in *Le Monde* a few weeks after the November 13th attacks that the "Islamic State" are now complaining about the "judeo-masonic" elite's control over our education system.[163] How hostile to Zionist freemasonry the Islamic State becomes in Europe while fervently massacring all of Israel's enemies in the Middle East. The attempt to criminalise those who criticise freemasonry and Zionism by associating them with the Islamic State is intended to render impossible any criticism of those in power. Given the fact that those suspected of terrorism can simply be and regularly are assassinated, a precedent is being set for the murder of political opponents of the current regime. The equation of terrorism and conspiracy theory is becoming increasingly alarming, given the fact that the real terrorists for the government of the North Atlantic Treaty Organisation are those researchers who understand and are exposing the truth about the war on terror.

We live in a world where the masses are drugged into submission to the status quo.The drug has become a symbol of our cultural decadence.

Pharmaceutical corporations run our health services for profit, forcing millions of citizens to consume toxic drugs that all too often worsen rather than improve their health. Meanwhile our streets are teeming with proletarian youths from immigrant families, whose only livelihood consists in selling recreational drugs, or being recruiting by local imams working for NATO and Israeli intelligence to fight in foreign wars financed by drug-trafficking. Terrorists in the Middle East are now being given drugs to turn them into more effective killing machines. The Pentagon's Director of Net Assessment Andrew Marchall told Wire magazine in 2003 that in the following decade victory in war would depend on what drugs combatants and targeted populations were taking. Irish revolutionary James Connolly once wrote:

> The moment the worker no longer believes in the all-conquering strength of the employer is the moment when the way opens out to the emancipation of our class. The master class realise this, and hence all their agencies bend their energies towards drugging, stupefying and poisoning the minds of the workers—sowing distrust and fear amongst them.[164]

History shows that all tyrannies collapse upon their own contradictions. But endless analysis and critique of globalisation will not end corporate tyranny. Humanity must formulate and implement a viable political alternative. Our education system is replete with anti-communist, anti-working class historiography. Police agents such as George Orwell and Leon Trotsky who spied on progressive working class resistance movements on behalf of the imperialist state are held up as examples and heroes while millions of communists who sacrificed their lives for a better world are demonised and denounced. The oligarchy's masonic symbols and logos pervade our entertainment and advertising industry while the hammer and sickle, symbols of proletarian democracy, are increasingly forbidden in many European states.

Our children are sent into schools that discourage critical analysis and inculcate subordination, conformism and cynicism. The French press abounds with articles about the difficulties faced by teachers in the aftermath of the terror attacks. Pupils are reading "conspiracy theories" on the Internet, are unable to think in an "abstract way" etc. It never occurs to many of these so-called teachers that they themselves may be the ones who lack the ability to critically engage with complex contemporary and historical sources of information, that they themselves may be guilty of misology, logical fallacy, oversimplification and a plentiful lack of "esprit critique" in their pathetic attempts to explain state dogma on the complex geopolitical phenomenon of terrorism. The difference between a pedant and a teacher is that the latter is always open to learning from his pupils. The staffing of our education system with intellectually challenged pedants is one of the primary reasons driving the stultification of so-called Western civilization.

An article in *Le Monde* describing the repression of a philosophy teacher after he suggested there might be a link between French foreign policy and terrorism began with the following sentence "where are the limits of thought." Self-censorship is the key to survival in what sociologist Jean Claude Paye describes as the super-egoistic dictatorship. Kantian epistemology which asks the question "what can I know" is replaced with a pious narratology of what I am allowed to know. Kant's fundamental ethical question "what should I do" is answered with the simple injunction "conform and shut up!"

The war of terror against the working people of this world will never end until the mode of production which extracts surplus value from labour, enriching the few while impoverishing the many is overthrown. The war on terror is a class war waged by the few against the many. The few are internationalist and conscious of their class interests, something the working class have lost.The war will only come to an end when the mode of production driving it is replaced by a non-exploitative, collaborative, mode of production conducive to popular democracy and peace. Understanding the implications of that fact is the first step on the road to victory in this long, global war between oligarchic state terror and the toiling masses.

WARS: US MILITARIST FACTIONS IN COMMAND

James Petras

"Over the past 15 years the US has been engaged in a series of wars, which has led many writers to refer to the "rise of militarism"—the growth of an empire, built primarily by and for the projection of military power—and only secondarily to advance economic imperialism.

The rise of a military-based empire, however, does not preclude the emergence of competing, conflicting and convergent power configurations within the imperial state. These factions of the Washington elite define the objectives and targets of imperial warfare, often on their own terms.

Having stated the obvious general fact of the power of militarism within the imperial state, it is necessary to recognize that the key policymakers, who direct the wars and military policy, will vary according to the country targeted, type of warfare engaged in and their conception of the war. In other words, while US policy is imperialist and highly militaristic, the key policymakers, their approach and the outcomes of their policies will differ. There is no fixed strategy devised by a cohesive Washington policy elite guided by a unified strategic vision of the US Empire.

In order to understand the current, seemingly endless wars, we have to examine the shifting coalitions of elites, who make decisions in Washington but not always primarily for Washington. Some factions of the policy elite have clear conceptions of the American empire, but others improvise and rely on superior "political" or "lobbying" power to successfully push their agenda in the face of repeated failures and suffer no consequences or costs.

We will start by listing US imperial wars during the last decade and a half. We will then identify the main policy-making faction which has been the driving force in each war. We will discuss their successes and failures as imperial policy makers and conclude with an evaluation of "the state of the empire" and its future.

Imperial Wars: From 2001—2015

The current war cycle started in late 2001 with the US invasion and occupation of Afghanistan. This was followed by the invasion and occupation of Iraq in March 2003, the US arms support for Israel's invasion of Lebanon in 2006, the proxy invasion of Somalia in 2006/7; the massive re-escalation of war in Iraq and Afghanistan in 2007–2009; the bombing, invasion "regime change" in Libya in 2011; the ongoing proxy-mercenary war against Syria (since 2012), and the ongoing 2015 Saudi-US invasion and destruction of Yemen. In Europe, the US was behind the 2014 proxy putsch and violent "regime change" in Ukraine which has led to an ongoing war against ethnic Russian speakers in south-east Ukraine, especially the populous industrial heartland of the Donbas region.

Over the past 15 years, there have been overt and covert military interventions, accompanied by an intense, provocative military build-up along Russia's borders in the Baltic States, Eastern Europe (especially Poland), the Balkans (Bulgaria and Romania) and the mammoth US base in Kosovo; in Central Europe with nuclear missiles in Germany and, of course, the annexation of Ukraine and Georgia as US-NATO clients.

Parallel to the military provocations encircling Russia, Washington has launched a major military, political, economic and diplomatic offensive aimed at isolating China and affirming US supremacy in the Pacific.

In South American, US military intervention found expression via Washington-orchestrated business-military coup attempts in Venezuela in 2002 and Bolivia in 2008, and a successful "regime change" in Honduras in 2009, overthrowing its elected president and installing a US puppet.

In summary, the US has been engaged in two, three or more wars since 2001, defining an almost exclusively militarist empire, run by an imperial state directed by civilian and military officials seeking unchallenged global dominance through violence.

Washington: Military Workshop of the World

War and violent regime change are the exclusive means through which the US now advances its foreign policy. However, the various Washington war-makers among the power elite do not form a unified bloc with common priorities. Washington provides the weapons, soldiers and financing for whichever power configuration or faction among the elite is in a position, by design or default, to seize the initiative and push their own war agenda.

The invasion of Afghanistan was significant in so far as it was seen by all sectors of the militarist elite, as the first in a series of wars.

Afghanistan was to set the stage for the launching of higher priority wars elsewhere.

Afghanistan was followed by the infamous "Axis of Evil" speech, dictated by Tel Aviv, penned by presidential speech-writer David Frum and mouthed by the brainless President Bush, II. The "Global War on Terror" was the thinly veiled slogan for serial wars around the world. Washington measured the loyalty of its vassals among the nations of Europe, Asia, Africa and Latin America by their support for the invasion and occupation of Afghanistan. The Afghan invasion provided the template for future wars. It led to an unprecedented increase in the military budget and ushered in "Caesar"-like dictatorial presidential powers to order and execute wars, silencing domestic critics and sending scored of thousands of US and NATO troops to the "Hindu Kush."

In itself, Afghanistan was never any threat and certainly no economic prize for plunder and profit. The Taliban had not attacked the US. Osama Bin Laden could have been turned over to a judicial tribunal —as the governing Taliban had insisted.

The US military (with its "Coalition of the Willing" or COW) successfully invaded and occupied Afghanistan and set up a vassal regime in Kabul. It built scores of military bases and attempted to form an obedient colonial army. In the meantime, the Washington militarist elite had moved on to bigger and, for the Israel-centric Zionist elite, higher priority wars, namely Iraq.

The decision to invade Afghanistan was not opposed by any of Washington's militarist elite factions. They all shared the idea of using a successful military blitz or "cake-walk" against the abysmally impoverished Afghanistan as a way to rabble rouse the American masses into accepting a long period of intense and costly global warfare throughout the world.

Washington"s militarist elites fabricated the link between the attacks on 9/11/2001 and Afghanistan's governing Taliban and the presence of the Saudi warlord Osama Bin Laden. Despite the "fact" that most of the "hijackers" were from the kingdom of Saudi Arabia and none were Afghans, invading and destroying Afghanistan was to be the initial test to gauge the highly manipulated and frightened American public's willingness to shoulder the burden of a huge new cycle of imperial wars. This has been the only aspect of the invasion of Afghanistan that could be viewed as a policy success—it made the costs of endless wars "acceptable" to a relentlessly propagandized public.

Flush with their military victories in the Hindu Kush, the Washington militarists turned to Iraq and fabricated a series of increasingly preposterous pretexts for war: Linking the 9/11 "jihadi hijackers" with the secular regime of Saddam Hussein, whose intolerance for violent Islamists (especially the Saudi variety) was well documented, and concocting a whole fabric of lies about Iraqi "weapons of mass destruction" which provided the propaganda basis for invading an already disarmed, blockaded and starved Iraq in March 2003.

Leading the Washington militarists in designing the war to destroy Iraq were the Zionists, including Paul Wolfowitz, Elliot Abrams, Richard Perle, and a few Israel-centric Gentile militarists, such as Vice President Cheney, Secretary of State Colin Powell and Defense Secretary Rumsfeld. The Zionists had a powerful entourage in key positions in the State Department, Treasury and the Pentagon.

There were "outsiders"—non-Zionists and militarists within these institutions, especially the Pentagon, who voiced reservations—but they were brushed aside, not consulted and "encouraged" to retire.

None of the "old hands" in the State Department or Pentagon bought into the hysteria about Saddam Hussein's weapons of mass destruction, but to voice reservations was to risk one's career. The manufacture and dissemination of the pretext for invading Iraq was orchestrated by a small team of operatives linking Tel Aviv and Deputy Secretary of Defense Paul Wolfowitz's "Office of Special Plans," a tight group of Zionists and some Israelis headed by Abram Shulsky (Sept. 2002—June 2003).

The US war on Iraq was an important part of Israel's agenda to "remake the Middle East" to establish its unchallenged regional hegemony and execute a "final solution" for its own vexing "Arab (native Palestinian) problem": It was made operational by the powerful Zionist faction within the Executive (White House), which had assumed almost dictatorial powers after the attack on 9/11/2001. Zionists planned the war, designed the "occupation policy" and "succeeded wildly" with the eventual dismemberment of a once modern secular nationalist Arab state.

In order to smash the Iraqi state, the US occupation policy was to eliminate (through mass firings, jailing and assassination) all high level, experienced Iraqi civil, military and scientific personnel—down to high school principals. They dismantled any vital infrastructure (which had not been already destroyed by the decades of US sanctions and bombing under President Clinton) and reduced an agriculturally advanced Iraq to a barren wasteland which would take centuries to recover and could never challenge Israel's colonization of Palestine, let alone its military supremacy in the Middle East. Naturally, the large Palestinian Diaspora refugee population in Iraq was targeted for "special treatment."

But Zionist policymakers had a much larger agenda than erasing Iraq as a viable country: They had a longer list of targets: Syria, Iran, Lebanon and Libya, whose destructions were to be carried out with US and NATO blood and treasure (and not a single Israeli soldier).

Despite the fact that Iraq did not even possess a functioning air force or navy in March 2003 and Afghanistan in late 2001 was rather primitive, the invasions of both countries turned out to be very costly to the US. The US completely failed to benefit from its "victory and occupation," despite Paul Wolfowitz's boasts that the pillage of Iraq's oil fields would pay for the entire project in a "few months." This was because the real Zionist plan was to destroy these nations—beyond any possibility for a quick or cheap imperialist economic gain. Scorching the earth and salting the fields is not a very profitable policy for empire builders.

Israel has been the biggest winner with no cost for the "Jewish State." The American Zionist policy elite literally handed them the services of the largest and richest armed forces in history: the US. "Israel-Firsters" played a decisive role among Washington policy-makers and Tel Aviv celebrated in the streets! They came, they dominated policy and they accomplished their mission: Iraq (and millions of its people) was destroyed.

The US gained an unreliable, broken colony, with a devastated economy and systematically destroyed infrastructure and without the functioning civil service needed for a modern state. To pay for the mess, the American people faced a spiraling budget deficit, tens of thousands of American war casualties and massive cuts in their own social programs. Crowning the Washington war-makers' victory was the disarticulation of American civil and constitutional rights and liberties and the construction of a enormous domestic police state.

After the Iraq disaster, the same influential Zionist faction in Washington lost no time in demanding a new war against Israel's bigger enemy—namely Iran. In the ensuing years, they failed to push the US to attack Tehran but they succeeded in imposing crippling sanctions. The Zionist faction secured massive US military support for Israel's abortive invasion of Lebanon and its devastating series of blitzkriegs against the impoverished and trapped people of Gaza.

The Zionist faction successfully shaped US military interventions to meet Israel's regional ambitions against three Arab countries: Yemen, Syria and Libya. The Zionists were not able to manipulate the US into attacking Iran because the traditional militarist faction in Washington balked: With instability in Afghanistan and Iraq, the US was not well positioned to face a major conflagration throughout the Middle East,

South Asia and beyond—which a ground and air war with Iran would involve. However, the Zionist factions did secure brutal economic sanctions and the appointment of key Israel-centric officials within the US Treasury. Secretary Stuart Levey, at the start of the Obama regime, and David Cohen afterwards, were positioned to enforce the sanctions.

Even before the ascendency of Israeli Prime Minister Binyamin Netanyahu, Tel Aviv's military objectives after Iraq, including Iran, Syria, Lebanon, Libya and Yemen had to be spaced over time, because the non-Zionist factions among Washington's elite had been unable to integrate occupied Afghanistan and Iraq into the empire.

Resistance, armed conflict and military advances in both Afghanistan and Iraq never ceased and are continuing into their second decade. As soon as the US would withdraw from a region, declaring it "pacified," the armed resistance would move back in and the local sepoys would defect to the rebels or take off for London or Washington with millions in pillaged loot.

"Unfinished wars," mounting casualties and spiraling costs, with no end in sight, undermined the agreement between the militarist and the Zionist factions in the Executive branch. However, the massively powerful Zionist presence in the US Congress provided a platform to bray for new and even bigger wars.

Israel's vicious invasion of Lebanon in 2006 was defeated despite receiving massive US arms supplies, a US funded "Iron Dome" missile defense system and intelligence assistance. Tel Aviv could not defeat the highly disciplined and motivated Hezbollah fighters in South Lebanon despite resorting to carpet bombing of civilian neighborhoods with millions of banned cluster munitions and picking off ambulances and churches sheltering refugees. Israelis have been much more triumphal murdering lightly armed Palestinian resistance fighters and stone-throwing children.

Libya: A Multi-faction War for the Militarists (without Big Oil)

The war against Libya was a result of multiple factions among the Washington militarist elite, including the Zionists, coming together with French, English and German militarists to smash the most modern, secular, independent state in Africa under President Muammar Gaddafi.

The aerial campaign against the Gaddafi regime had virtually no organized support within Libya with which to reconstruct a viable neocolonial state ripe for pillage. This was another "planned dismemberment" of a complex, modern republic which had been independent of the US Empire.

The war succeeded wildly in shredding Libya's economy, state and society. It unleashed scores of armed terrorist groups (who appropriated the modern weapons of Gaddafi's army and police) and uprooted two million black contract workers and Libyan citizens of South Saharan origin forcing them to flee the rampaging racist militias to the refugee camps of Europe. Untold thousands died in rickety boats in the Mediterranean Sea.

The entire war was carried out to the publicly giddy delight of Secretary of State Hillary Clinton and her "humanitarian interventionist" lieutenants (Susan Rice and Samantha Power), who were utterly ignorant as to who and what the Libyan "opposition" represented. Eventually, even Hillary's own Ambassador to Libya would be slaughtered by ... the same victorious US-backed "rebels" (sic) in the newly liberated Benghazi!

The Zionist faction destroyed Gaddafi (whose capture, grotesque torture and murder was filmed and widely disseminated), eliminating another real adversary of Israel and supporter of Palestinian rights. The US militarist faction, which led the war, got nothing positive—not even a secure naval, air or training base—only a dead Ambassador, millions of desperate refugees flooding Europe and thousands of trained and armed jihadists for the next target: Syria.

For a while Libya became the main supply-line for Islamist mercenaries and arms to invade Syria and fight the secular nationalist government in Damascus.

Once again the least influential faction in Washington turned out to be the oil and gas industry, which lost lucrative contracts it had already signed with the Gaddafi regime. Thousands of highly trained foreign oil workers were withdrawn. After Iraq, it should have been obvious that these wars were not "for oil"!

Ukraine: Coups, Wars & Russia's "Underbelly"

With the US-orchestrated coup and intervention in Ukraine, the militarist factions once again seized the initiative, establishing a puppet regime in Kiev and targeting Russia's strategic "soft underbelly." The plan had been to take over Russia's strategic military bases in Crimea and cut Russia from the vital military-industrial complexes in the Donbas region with its vast iron and coal reserves.

The mechanics of the power grab were relatively well planned, the political clients were put in power, but the US militarists had made no contingencies for propping up the Ukrainian economy, cut loose from its main trading partner and oil and gas supplier, Russia.

The coup led to a "proxy war" in the ethnic-Russian majority regions in the southeast (the Donbas) with four "unanticipated consequences." 1) a country divided east and west along ethno-linguistic lines, (2) a bankrupt economy made even worse by the imposition of an IMF austerity program, (3) a corrupt crony capitalist elite, which was "pro-West by bank account," (4) and, after two years, mass disaffection among voters toward the US puppet regime.

The militarists in Washington and Brussels succeeded in engineering the coup in Ukraine but lacked the domestic allies, plans and preparations to run the country and successfully annex it to the EU and NATO as a viable country.

Apparently the militarist factions in the State Department and Pentagon are much more proficient in stage managing coups and invasions than in establishing a stable regime as part of a New World Order. They succeed in the former and fail repeatedly in the latter.

The Pivot to Asia and the Pirouette to Syria

During most of the previous decade, traditional global strategists in Washington increasingly objected to the Zionist faction's domination and direction of US war policies focused on the Middle East for the benefit of Israel, instead of meeting the growing challenge of the new world economic superpower in Asia, China.

US economic supremacy in Asia had been deeply eroded as China's economy grew at double digits. Beijing was displacing the US as the major trade partner in the Latin American and African markets. Meanwhile, the top 500 US MNC's were heavily invested in China. Three years into President Obama's first term the "China militarist faction" announced a shift from the Middle East and the Israel-centric agenda to a "pivot to Asia," the source of 40% of the world's industrial output.

But it was not profits and markets that motivated Washington's Asia faction among the militarist elites—it was military power. Even trade agreements, like the TransPacific Partnership (TPP), were viewed as tools to encircle and weaken China militarily and undermine its regional influence.

Led by the hysterical Pentagon boss Ashton Carter, Washington prepared a series of major military confrontations with Beijing off the coast of China. The US signed expanded military base agreements with the Philippines, Japan and Australia; it participated in military exercises with Vietnam, South Korea and Malaysia; it dispatched battleships and aircraft carriers into Chinese territorial waters.

The US confrontational trade policy was formulated by the Zionist trio: Secretary of Commerce, Penny Pritzer, Trade Negotiator Michael Froman (who works for both the Asia militarist and Zionist factions) and Treasury Secretary Jake Lew. The result was the Trans-Pacific Partnership (TPP), involving 12 Pacific countries while deliberately excluding China. Washington's Asian militarist faction planned to militarize the entire Pacific Basin, in order to dominate the maritime trade routes and, at a moment's notice, choke off all of China"s overseas markets and suppliers—shades of the series of US provocations against Japan leading up to the US entering WW2. Additionally the "Asia-militarist faction" successfully demanded a bigger military budget to accommodate its vastly more aggressive posture toward China.

Predictably, China has insisted on defending its maritime routes and has increased its naval and air base building and sea and air patrols. Also, predictably, China has countered the US-dominated TPP by setting-up a one hundred billion dollar Asia Infrastructure Investment Bank (AIIB), while contributing to the multi-billion dollar BRICS Bank. Meanwhile, China even signed a separate $30 billion dollar trade agreement with Washington's strategic "partner," Britain. In fact, Britain followed the rest of the EU and joined the Asia Infrastructure Investment Bank—despite objections from Washington's "Asia faction." But while the US depends heavily on its military pacts with South Korea and Japan, the latter nations have been meeting with China— their most significant trading partner—to work on expanding and deepening economic ties.

Up until 2014, the "business-with-China faction" of the Washington elite played a key role in the making of US-Asia policy. However, they have been eclipsed by the Asia militarist-faction, which is taking US policy in a totally different direction: Pushing China out as Asia's economic superpower and escalating military confrontation with Beijing now heads Washington's agenda.

Ashton Carter, the US Defense Secretary, has China, the second most important economy in the world in the Pentagon's "cross-hairs." When the TPP failed to curtail China's expansion, the militarist faction shifted Washington toward a high risk military course, which could destabilize the region and risk a nuclear confrontation.

The Pirouette: China and Syria

Meanwhile in the Levant, Washington's Zionist faction has been busy running a proxy war in Syria. The pivot to Asia has had to compete with the pirouette to Syria and Yemen.

The US joined Saudi Arabia, Turkey, the Gulf Emirates and the EU in staging a replay of the Libyan "regime change"—sponsoring proxy terrorists from around the globe into invading and devastating Syria. Damascus has been attacked from all sides for the "crime" of being secular and multi-ethnic; for being pro-Palestinian; for being allied with Iran and Lebanon; for having an independent foreign policy; and for maintaining a limited representative (but not necessarily democratic) government. For these crimes, the West, Israel and the Saudis would have Syria fractured into ethnically cleansed "tribal state"—something they had accomplished in Iraq and Libya.

The US militarist faction (personified by Secretary of Defense Carter and Senators McCain and Graham) have funded, trained and equipped the terrorists, whom they call "moderates" and had clearly expected their progeny to follow Washington's directions. The emergence of ISIS showed just how close these "moderates" stuck to Washington's script.

Initially, the traditional militarist wing of Washington's elite resisted the Zionist faction's demand for direct US military intervention (American "boots on the ground"). That is changing with recent (very convenient) events in Paris.

Warfare: From Piecemeal Interventions to Nuclear Confrontation

The Washington militarists have again committed more US soldiers to Iraq and Afghanistan; American fighter planes and Special Forces are in Syria and Yemen. Meanwhile, US naval armadas aggressively patrol the coasts of China and Iran. The militarist-Zionist "compromise" over Syria was comprised of an initial contingent of 50 US Special Forces to join in "limited" combat roles with ("loyal" sic) Islamist mercenaries—the so-called "moderates." There are commitments for greater and heavier weaponry to come, including ground to air missiles capable of shooting down Russian and Syrian military jets.

Elite Factional Politics: An Overview

How does the record of these competing factions, formulating US imperial war policies in the Middle East over the past 15 years stack up? Clearly there has been no coherent imperial economic strategy.

The policy toward Afghanistan is remarkable for its failure to end the longest war in US history—over 14 years of occupation! The recent attempts by US-led client NATO forces to withdraw have been immediately followed by military advances by the nationalist-Islamist resistance militia—the Taliban, which controls much of the countryside. The possibility of a collapse of the current puppet in Kabul has forced the militarists in Washington to retain US bases—surrounded by completely hostile rural populations.

The Afghan war's initial appearance of success triggered new wars —inter alia Iraq. But taking the long view, the Afghan war has been a miserable failure in terms of the stated strategic goal of establishing a stable client government. The Afghan economy collapsed; opium production (which had been significantly suppressed by the Taliban's poppy eradication campaign in 2000-2001) is the now predominant crop—with cheap heroin flooding Europe and beyond. Under the weight of massive and all pervasive corruption by "loyal" client officials, the Afghan treasury is empty. The puppet rulers are totally disconnected from the most important regional, ethnic, religious and family clans and associations.

Washington could not "find" any viable economic classes in Afghanistan with which to anchor a development strategy. They did not come to terms with the deep ethno-religious consciousness rooted in rural communities and fought the most popular political force among the majority Pashtu, the Taliban, which had no role in the attack on "9/11."

They artificially slapped together a massive army of surly illiterates under Western imperial command and watched it fall apart at the seams, defect to the Taliban or turn their own guns on the foreign occupation troops. These "mistakes," which accounted for the failure of the militarist faction in the Afghanistan war were due, in no small part, to the pressure and influence of the Zionist faction who wanted to quickly move on to their highest priority, a US war against Israel's first priority enemy—Iraq—without consolidating the US control in Afghanistan. For the Zionists, Afghanistan (envisioned as a "cake-walk" or quick victory) was just a tool to set the stage for a much larger sequence of US wars against Israel's regional Arab and Persian adversaries.

Before the militarists could establish any viable order and an enduring governmental structure in Afghanistan, attention shifted to a Zionist-centered war against Iraq.

The build-up for the US war against Iraq has to be understood as a project wholly engineered by and for the state of Israel, mostly through its agents within the US government and Washington policy elite. The goal was to establish Israel as the unchallenged political-military power in the region using American troops and money and preparing the ground for Tel Aviv's "final solution" for the Palestinian "problem"; total expulsion...

The US military and occupation campaign included the wholesale and systematic destruction of Iraq: Its law and order, culture, economy and society—so there would be no possibility of recovery. Such a vicious campaign did not resonate with any productive sector of the US economy (or for that matter with any Israeli economic interest).

Washington's Zionist faction set about in a parody of Pol Pot's Khmer Rouge to identify and destroy any competent, experienced Iraqi professional, civil servant, scientist, intellectual, or military official capable of re-organizing and re-building the county and war-battered society. They were assassinated, arrested, tortured or driven into exile. The occupation deliberately encouraged religious parties and traditional tribes to engage in inter-communal massacres and ethnic cleansing. In other words, the Zionist faction did not pursue the traditionally understood policy of empire building which would incorporate the second tier functionaries of a conquered state to form a competent client regime and use Iraq's great oil and gas wealth to build its economy. Instead they chose to impose a scorched earth policy; setting loose organized sectarian armies, imposing the rule of grotesquely corrupt ex-pats and placing the most venal, sectarian clients in positions of power. The effect has been to transform the most advanced, secular Arab country into an "Afghanistan" and in less than 15 years destroying centuries of culture and community.

The goal of the "Zionist strategy" was to destroy Iraq as Israel's regional rival. The cost of over a million Iraqi dead and many million refugees did not prick any conscience in Washington or Tel Aviv. After all, Washington's traditional "militarist faction" picked up the bill (costing hundreds of billions) which they passed on to the American taxpayers (well over one trillion dollars) and used the deaths and suffering of tens of thousands of American troops to provide a pretext for spreading more chaos. The result of their mayhem includes the specter of "ISIS," which they may consider to be a success—since hysteria over "ISIS" pushes the West "closer to Israel."

The sheer scale of death and destruction inflicted on the Iraqi population by the Zionist faction led to thousands of highly competent Ba'athist officers, who had survived "Shock and Awe" and the sectarian massacres, to join armed Islamist Sunnis and eventually form the Islamic State in Iraq and Syria (ISIS). This group of experienced Iraqi military officers formed the strategic technical core of ISIS which launched a devastating offensive in Iraq in 2014—taking major cities in the north and completely routing the US-trained puppet armies of the "government" in Baghdad. From there they moved into Syria and beyond. It is fundamental to understanding the roots of ISIS: The Zionist faction among US militarist policymakers imposed a deliberate "scorched earth" occupation policy, which united highly trained nationalist Ba'athist military officers with young Sunni fighters, both locals and increasingly foreign jihadist mercenaries. These deracinated members of the traditional Iraqi nationalist military elite had lost their families to the sectarian massacres; they were persecuted, tortured, driven underground and highly motivated. They literally had nothing left to lose!

This core of the ISIS leadership stands in stark contrast to the colonial, corrupt and demoralized army slapped together by the US military with more cash than morale. ISIS quickly swept through half of Iraq and came within 40 miles of Baghdad.

The US militarist faction faced military defeat after eight years of war. They mobilized, financed and armed their client Kurdish mercenaries in northern Iraq and recruited the Shia Ayatollah Ali al-Sistani to appeal to the Shia militia.

ISIS exploited the Western-backed Islamist uprising in Syria—and extended their sweep well across the border. Syria had accepted a million Iraqi refugees from the US invasion, including many of Iraq's surviving experienced nationalist administrative elite. The US militarists are in a dilemma—another full-scale war would not be politically feasible, and its military outcome uncertain…Moreover the US was aligned with dubious allies—especially the Saudis—who had their own regional ambitions. Turkey and Saudi Arabia, Israel and the Kurds were each eager to expand their power territorially and politically.

In the midst of this, the traditional Washington militarists are left with no overall viable imperialist strategy. Instead they improvise with faux "rebels," who claim to be moderates and democrats, while taking US guns and dollars and ultimately joining the most powerful Islamist groups—like ISIS.

Throwing a wrench into the machinery of Israeli-Saudi hegemonic ambitions, Russia, Iran and Hezbollah have sided with the secular Syrian government. Russia finally moved to bomb ISIS strongholds—after identifying a significant ISIS contingent of militant Chechens whose ultimate aims are to bring war and terror back to Russia.

The US-EU war against Libya unleashed all the retrograde mercenary forces from three continents (Africa, Asia and Europe) and Washington finds itself with no means to control them. Washington could not even protect its own consulate in their "liberated" regional capital of Benghazi—the US ambassador and two intelligence aides were killed by Washington's own "rebels." The competing and cooperating factions of the Washington militarist elite placed Libya on a steaming platter: Serving up invasion, regicide and hundreds of thousands of refugees, which they did not bother to even "season" with any plan or strategy—just unadulterated scorched earth against another opponent of Zionism. And a potentially lucrative strategic neo-colony in North Africa has been lost with no accountability for the Washington architects of such barbarism.

Latin America: Last Outpost of the Multi-Nationals

As we have seen, the major theaters of imperial policy (the Middle East and Asia) have been dominated by militarists, not professional diplomats-linked to the MNCs. Latin America stands as something of an exception. In Latin America, US policymakers have been guided by big business interests. Their main focus has been on pushing the neo-liberal agenda. Eventually this has meant promoting the US-centered "free trade" agreements, joint military exercises, shared military bases, and political backing for the US global military agenda.

The "militarist faction" in Washington worked with the traditional business faction in support of the unsuccessful military coups in Venezuela (2002 and 2014), the attempted coup in Bolivia 2008, and a successful regime change in Honduras (2010).

To harass the independent Argentine government which was developing closer diplomatic and trade ties with Iran, a sector of the US Zionist financial elite (the "vulture fund" magnate Paul Singer) joined forces with the Zionist militarist faction to raise hysterical accusations against President Cristina Kirchner over the "mysterious" suicide of a Israel-linked Argentine prosecutor. The prosecutor, Alberto Nisman, had devoted his career to "cooking up a case" against Iran with the aid of the Mossad and CIA for the unsolved bombing the Buenos Aires Jewish community center in 1994. Various investigations had exonerated Iran and the "Nisman Affaire" was an intense effort to keep Argentina from trading with Iran.

The Washington business faction operated in a mildly hostile Latin America for most of the past decade. However, it was able to recover influence, via a series of bilateral free trade agreements and took advantage of the end of the commodity cycle. The latter weakened the center-left regimes and moved them closer to Washington.

The "excesses" committed by the US backed military dictatorships during the nineteen sixties through eighties, and the crisis of the neoliberal nineties, set the stage for the rise of a relatively moderate business-diplomatic faction to come to the fore in Washington. It is also the case that the various militarist and Zionist factions in Washington were focused elsewhere (Europe, Middle East and Asia). In any case the US political elite operates in Latin America mostly via political and business proxies for the time being.

Conclusion

From our brief survey, it is clear that wars play a key role in US foreign policy in most regions of the world. However, war policies in different regions respond to different factions in the governing elite.

The traditional militarist faction predominates creating confrontations in Ukraine, Asia and along the Russian border. Within that framework the US Army, Air Force and Special Forces play a leading, and fairly conventional, role. In the Far East, the Navy and Air Force predominate.

In the Middle East and South Asia, the military (Army and Air Force) factions share power with the Zionist faction. Fundamentally the Zionists dictate policy on Iraq, Lebanon and Palestine and the militarists follow.

Both factions overlapped in creating the debacle in Libya.

The factions form shifting coalitions, supporting wars of interest to their respective power centers. The militarists and Zionists worked together in launching the Afghan war; but once launched, the Zionists abandoned Kabul and concentrated on preparing for the invasion and occupation of Iraq, which was of far greater interest to Israel.

It should be noted that at no point did the oil and business elite play any significant role in war policy. The Zionist faction pushed hard to secure direct US ground intervention in Libya and Syria, but was not able to force the US to send large contingents of ground troops due to opposition from the Russians as well as a growing sector of the US electorate. Likewise, the Zionists played a leading role in successfully imposing sanctions against Iran and a major role in prosecuting banks around the world accused of violating the sanctions. However, they were not able to block the military faction from securing a diplomatic agreement with Iran over its uranium enrichment program—without going to war.

Clearly, the business faction plays a major role in promoting US trade agreements and tries to lift or avoid sanctions against important real and potential trade partners like China, Iran and Cuba.

The Zionist faction among the Washington elite policymakers takes positions which consistently push for wars and aggressive policies against any regime targeted by Israel. The differences between the traditional militarist and Zionist factions are blurred by most writers who scrupulously avoid identifying Zionist decision-makers, but there is no question of who benefits and who loses.

The kind of war which the Zionists promote and implement—the utter destruction of enemy countries—undermines any plans by the traditional militarist faction and the military to consolidate power in an occupied country and incorporate it into a stable empire.

It is a serious error to lump these factions together: the business, Zionist and various militarist factions of the Washington policy making elite are not one homogeneous group. They may overlap at times, but they also differ as to interests, liabilities, ideology and loyalties. They also differ in their institutional allegiances.

The overarching militarist ideology, which permeates US imperial foreign policy obscures a deep and recurrent weakness—US policymakers master the mechanics of war but have no strategy for ruling after intervening. This has been glaringly evident in all recent wars: Iraq, Syria, Libya, Ukraine etc. Improvisation has repeatedly led to monumental failures: from financing phantom armies to bleeding billions to prop-up incompetent, kleptocratic puppet regimes. Despite the hundreds of billions of public money wasted in these serial disasters, no policy-maker has been held to account.

Long wars and short memories are the norm for Washington's militarist rulers who do not lose sleep over their blunders. The Zionists, for their part, do not even need a strategy for rule. They push the US into wars for Israel, and once having destroyed "the enemy country" they leave a vacuum to be filled by chaos. The American public provides the gold and blood for these misadventures and reaps nothing but domestic deterioration and greater international strife.

THE URGENCY OF NOW

Barry Kissin

We are at a terrifying moment in human history. The world is bristling with weapons, including WMDs. Hostilities are accelerating almost everywhere.

For some, war is always the answer. And the "greatest purveyor of violence"[165] continues to be the U.S.A., which lately has been squaring off with Russia for want of a worthy adversary. The U.S. has put nuclear terror back into play; this Damocles sword is again weighing over the heads of most living beings on the planet.

Strangely, there is practically a total absence of recognition of this effect of our recent escapades in Ukraine and current ones in Syria. The rapid and ongoing demonization of Putin is very frightening. The uniformity in Western media in portraying Russia as the aggressor in Ukraine is appalling—unadulterated propaganda.

The U.S. is now sharing nuclear weapons with (formerly non-nuclear) NATO members Belgium, Germany, Italy, the Netherlands and Turkey. Poland is probably next in line. It is all couched in terms of the brand new (reworked) threat of the Russian hordes swarming over Europe.[166]

No one seems to notice that in our supposed zeal to bolster national security, we are conjuring a confrontation that threatens worldwide annihilation. Americans are thoroughly distracted and numbed and jaded by the constant reminder of the terrorist threat. The next U.S. President will almost certainly be more aggressive and dangerous than the current one. This cannot go on.

In both Ukraine and Syria, there are now numerous potential scenarios in which a direct confrontation between Russia and the U.S. (NATO) could arise. The chances of an accident have multiplied. Mutually-reinforcing escalations could result. And there are so many armed players with their own interests in directing conflict.

I write this shortly after Turkey has shot down a Russian military jet; and not long after ISIS was said to be responsible for destroying a Russian commercial plane carrying 224 passengers in retaliation for Russia's attacks on ISIS in Syria.

Russia is in Syria at the request of the Syrian government. The U.S. (NATO) is in Syria explicitly committed to "regime change"—this time, essentially without a pretext. Attention to pretext has dissipated as of NATO's decimation of Libya ("Hillary's war"[167]).

In fact, the U.S. has been supporting al Qaeda and ISIS in Syria (and Iraq).[168] Our close allies, Saudi Arabia, Israel and Turkey, are doing the same.[169] When teaming up with so-called terrorists promotes the desired "regime change," then so be it. The Global War on Terror (GWOT) has always been nothing more than a disguise to conceal the hegemonic policy of "regime change."

This is the context of the attacks in France. It is secondary as to whether or the Charlie Hebdo and November 13 attacks were staged (false-flag) or amount to our ISIS/al Qaeda Frankenstein acting out-of-control. Ultimately, it is a fine line that separates the two possibilities.

We already know that false-flag attacks have repeatedly served as pretexts for the commencement and intensification of the so-called war on terror. This is established by evidence that is cumulative, corroborative and conclusive.

I was invited by Dr. Barrett to contribute to this book largely because of my expertise regarding the anthrax attacks that swiftly followed the attacks of 9/11. Ultimately, the U.S. government was compelled to officially acknowledge that the anthrax attacks were an inside job; that is, that they came out of our own so-called bio-defense program.[170]

The five recovered "anthrax letters" that accompanied these attacks (all dated 09-11-01) all contained the following language: "Death to America, Death to Israel, Allah is Great."[171] The anthrax attacks thus amount to an officially acknowledged false-flag attack.

How did this amazing situation arise? The perpetrators were so blasé, they used anthrax whose strain (Ames strain) was almost exclusively American. What was most telling was the extremely advanced weaponization technology involved in the processing of the attack anthrax featuring an additive (silicon) long associated with the American bio-weapons program. And there was a momentous leak into the mainstream just before these attacks began—a leak mainstream media ever since has pretended never happened.

On September 4th, 2001, on the front page of the *New York Times*, it was revealed that up-until-then secret anthrax weaponization projects were being conducted by the Army, the CIA and the DIA in Ohio and at Dugway Proving Ground in Utah.[172]

The attempt by the FBI and Department of Justice to pin the attacks on a "lone nut" Army scientist (just after he died in 2008) completely failed, partly because of this scientist's total absence of exposure to, much less experience in the weaponization technology involved.[173] That the FBI/DOJ manufactured evidence in its failed attempt to frame Fort Detrick, Maryland scientist Bruce Ivins has made its way into the mainstream,[174] as has the fact that our (arms control treaty-violating) bioweaponization technology required an "institutional effort."[175]

In his recently published *The 2001 Anthrax Deception: The Case for a Domestic Conspiracy* (2014: Clarity Press), Professor Graeme MacQueen documents instance after instance of the leaders of the Bush Administration (Bush, Cheney, Rumsfeld, Powell, Rice, Ashcroft as well as their media mouthpieces) reading off the same script both before (with apparent foreknowledge) and (for months) after the anthrax attacks.[176] This script contained multiple ways Americans were manipulated to believe that the 9/11 attacks and the anthrax attacks were a one-two punch delivered by al Qaeda (Muslim terrorists) with Iraqi support. Later when the fact could no longer be denied that the source of the anthrax attacks was an American military-intelligence biolab, all the elaborate claims and stories about the apparent connections between 9/11 and anthrax vanished.[177]

Indeed 9/11 and anthrax were connected; and the false-flag, inside job characteristic that inexorably became part of the official version of the anthrax attacks must also apply to 9/11.

As I am writing this, the breaking news is 20 shot, at least 12 killed, at a Social Services office in San Bernardino, California, by heavily armed shooters possibly wearing body armor, "multiple SWAT agencies on the scene."

Two days later (December 4th), Reuters headlines "California Massacre Shooter May Be linked to Islamic State." "[O]ne U.S. official said that [the female shooter] had made a pledge to [ISIS chief] al Baghdadi in a posting on Facebook the day of the attack, under an account that used a different name ... [T]wo U.S. officials ... said the finding, if confirmed, could be a 'game changer' in the investigation."[178]

Six days later (December 8th), the Associated Press reported: "Newly released emergency radio transmissions from the fast-moving tragedy show that police identified Farook as a suspect almost immediately ... It was unclear how he was identified so quickly, given that witnesses said the attackers wore black ski masks. [David] Bowdich [chief of the FBI's Los Angeles office] would not address that question."[179]

Is this unfolding incident another "false-flag," another staged terror incident? Probably.

But again, whether or not San Bernardino was staged is secondary. In either case, this incident like the 2015 attacks in France, will fraudulently be applied to buttress the fraudulent Global War on Terror.

This is the world we live in. And, yes, the U.S. government continues to be the "greatest purveyor" of the violence that is escalating almost everywhere.

Martin Luther King also said: "We still have a choice today: nonviolent coexistence or violent co-annihilation. This may well be mankind's last chance to choose between chaos and community."[180] And: "If modern man continues to flirt unhesitatingly with war, he will transform his earthly habitat into an inferno such as even the mind of Dante could not imagine."[181] And: "We are confronted with the fierce urgency of now."[182]

Postscript I: Terror Drills Go Live

I will contribute to the analysis of whether or not the attacks in Paris of November were staged with a brief discussion of one phenomenon that many of the terror events beginning with 9/11 have in common.

It has already come to light that there were "active-shooter drills every month or so" at the Social Services office that was the site of the San Bernardino attack. On the day of the attack (December 2nd) the *Los Angeles Times* reported that the first reaction of a nurse working at this Social Services office was to text her husband, "Drill started," as law enforcement sprinted toward the building. Later, standing outside a police barricade, the husband is quoted: "They train for this. They know it's going to happen."[183]

The same "coincidental" scenario—terror drills going live—also applies to the Paris attacks of November. According to Bloomberg News, on the day of those attacks, there was an exercise that "simulated … a mass shooting." "Because Paris emergency physicians work 24-hour shifts, virtually every ER doctor on duty in the city Friday night had already taken part in the exercise earlier that day."[184]

This is reminiscent of what many of us have learned about 9/11: At 8:38 AM when an air traffic controller at the FAA's Boston Center initiated contact with the Air Force's Aerospace Defense Command about the hijacking of Flight #11 headed to New York, the response of Technical Sergeant Jeremy Powell was to ask, "Is this real-world or exercise?"[185]

Historian Webster Tarpley has compiled a chart that details the existence of 22 different exercises and drills happening on 9/11, one of which simulated a "plane crash into high-rise government building," and another that occupied air defenses with a simulated "live-fly hijacking."[186] There were also more than twenty drills prior to that day that apparently paved the way for the attacks.[187]

The same drills-gone-live scenario also applies to the 2005 London bombings. On July 7th of that year, four bombs detonated in the heart of London (the UK's 9/11). Three of these bombs exploded almost simultaneously at separate locations on the London subway system. 52 died, and more than 700 were injured. In a BBC radio interview, the managing director of a firm "on contract to the London Metropolitan Police" described the "anti-terror drill" he had organized and conducted as one that simulated bombs exploding at the same time and same places as in the actual event.[188]

On July 22nd, 2011, a car bomb exploded in Oslo, Norway. Two hours later, on a Norwegian island, a mass shooting took place. In all, 77 died. "Only hours before [the mass shooting], the [Norwegian] police emergency squad concluded an exercise where they practiced an almost identical situation."[189]

Also see "The Terror Drills That Became Real" by Christopher Bollyn[190] and "Training exercises dovetail with mass shootings" by Jon Rappoport[191] that cite the July 20th, 2012 Aurora, Colorado mass shooting, the December 14th, 2012 Sandy Hook school shooting, the April 15th, 2013 Boston Marathon attack, and the June 17th, 2015 Charleston, South Carolina church shooting as additional examples of this phenomenon.

Postscript II: The Devil's Chessboard

I am currently reading David Talbot's recently published *The Devil's Chessboard: Allen Dulles, the CIA, and the Rise of America's Secret Government* (HarperCollins 2015). Sixty years after the emergence of what Talbot calls our "secret government," much of the record has been declassified. The record now affords us a comprehensive view of the makings of what is destroying today's world.

I had to stop in revulsion as Talbot outlined the CIA's part (under Dulles) in the 1953 overthrow of Iran's democratically elected, hugely popular Prime Minister, Mohammad Mossadegh. This was a maiden voyage for our fledgling CIA.

Here are some of the facts Talbot substantiates:

1.) The Dulles brothers started out as partners in the most prestigious law firm on Wall Street. (A separate part of the book details the large extent of collaboration among the Dulles brothers, their Wall Street clients and the German Nazis throughout the 1930s, but also during World War II as well as afterwards.)[192] In 1949, Allen Dulles, as attorney for a consortium of eleven large U.S. engineering firms, negotiated an agreement with the Shah of Iran for a "stunningly lucrative deal." Mossadegh led the opposition to the deal which he "denounced as a massive give away that would 'break the back of future generations '"—Mossadegh went on to become Prime Minister.[193]

2.) Eisenhower was initially understanding of Mossadegh's nationalization of the Anglo-Iranian Oil Company (today's British Petroleum). Clearly, as Mossadegh put it, for years this company had "exploited Iran's oil resources," "interfered in the internal life of [Iran]," and then rejected "fair compensation for its losses."[194]

3.) "Realizing that Eisenhower was not inclined to defend British imperial interests, the Dulles brothers reframed their argument in Cold War terms," arguing that Iran could go Communist. This is what procured Eisenhower's approval of their coup.[195]

4.) The CIA hired bands of mercenaries and paid Iranian military leaders to betray their country. Leaders who remained loyal to Mossadegh were tortured and/or murdered to set an example.[196]

5.) On August 19, 1953, "street gangs whose pockets were literally stuffed with CIA cash" as well as armament that included two U.S.-built Sherman tanks descended upon Mossadegh's home. Prime Minister Mossadegh was arrested, "thereby ending Iran's brief interlude of democracy."[197]

6.) Allen Dulles was intimately involved in persuading the Shah to take back his throne, thus beginning a 26-year reign that relied upon a savage secret police, trained and equipped by the U.S.[198]

7.) The Shah proceeded to denationalize Iran's oil "with 40 per cent of the spoils now going to American oil companies."[199]

8.) "Dulles not only persuaded his high-placed friends in the press to throw a cloak over the CIA's operation, he convinced them to share his exuberance over its success." *Washington Post*: The overthrow was a "cause to rejoice." *New York Times*: Mossadegh was "a rabid, self-seeking nationalist." Elsewhere in the media: This was a "popular uprising" and a "nation's revolt."[200] (Like today's "uprisings" in Libya, Ukraine and Syria?)

Dulles was directly involved in the assassination of Patrice Lumumba, the first legally elected prime minister of Congo, a terrible turning point in African history.[201]

Time has also rendered explicit the nature of the JFK assassination, another coup d'état involving Allen Dulles in both perpetration and cover-up.[202]

What Talbot refers to as our "secret government" has been growing in power ever since. And it is malignant. False-flag attacks are one facet of its vast repertoire.

Postscript III: A Sign of Life in Congress

On the day of the Charlie Hebdo attack in Paris, January 7th, 2015, there was a (previously planned) press conference conducted at the Capitol convened in order to publicize the reintroduction of a House Resolution to declassify 28 pages of the 2003 report by the Joint Senate-House Intelligence Committees regarding its investigation of 9/11.[203]

In introductory remarks, Representative Walter Jones (R-N.C.) stated: "Just like the tragedy in France today, no nation can defend itself unless the nation knows the truth, and especially when there's been an attack like 9/11."[204] Former U.S. Senator Bob Graham (D-Fla.) was the chairman of the Senate Intelligence Committee when it co-authored the 9/11 report. He stated: "[The] events in Paris this morning … bring this matter into its proper focus …"[205] Graham elsewhere has said: "The 28 pages primarily relate to who financed 9/11, and they point a very strong finger at Saudi Arabia as being the principal financier."[206] Graham has also referred to Saudi Arabia as "essentially a co-conspirator in 9/11 …"[207] And: "ISIS is a product of Saudi ideals, Saudi money, and Saudi organizational support."[208] At the press conference, Graham added: "Al-Qaeda was a creature of Saudi Arabia; … and now, ISIS is the latest creature!" And: "[What] we saw this morning in Paris … [is a] consequence of our passivity to Saudi Arabia."[209] (Graham's use of the word "passivity" amounts to transparent understatement.)[210]

The House Resolution to declassify, H.R. 14, now has a counterpart in the Senate, thanks to the introduction of S. 1471 by Senator Rand Paul in June, 2015.[211]

I submit that the pending legislation to declassify is not only about Saudi Arabia. There is a growing emphasis on the cover-up of these 28 pages, first perpetrated by the Bush administration, but now upheld by the Obama administration (despite President Obama's personal promise on two occasions to two different family members of 9/11 victims that he would release the 28 pages).[212]

Graham has charged the FBI with "aggressive deception."[213] During a PBS interview about the still secret 28 pages in August, 2015, Graham stated that support for 9/11 "could have come" from "foreign governments" and also "domestic groups."[214] Graham and other reputable sources have made it clear that much of the financing of the alleged 9/11 hijackers was funneled through the Saudi Embassy whose Ambassador at the time was none other than Prince Bandar bin Sultan, nicknamed by George W. Bush himself "Bandar Bush" for his close and longstanding affiliation with the Bush family.[215] The source of particular funds that went to two of the alleged 9/11 hijackers has been traced to Bandar's wife.[216] (This helps account for Michael Moore's focus on Bandar and George W. smoking cigars on the Truman Balcony of the White House on the evening of Sept. 13th, 2001 in Moore's largely forgotten documentary *Fahrenheit 911* released in 2004.[217] Cheney and Condoleezza Rice were also present.[218])

For decades, Bandar has been involved in "numerous covert activities of U.S. and Saudi intelligence" going back to organizing and facilitating the mujahideen in Afghanistan.[219] Bandar has admitted his role in moving arms to Iran and money to the Contras during George H.W. Bush's "Iran-Contra" operation[220] (which is what gave rise to Senator Daniel Inouye's coining of the term "shadow government."[221]) Most recently, Bandar has been implicated in setting up the false-flag chemical attack in Syria in August, 2013 that came very close to providing the Obama Administration with the pretext for bombing Damascus.[222]

The 28 pages campaign has unique potential for unraveling the cover-up of Inouye's "shadow government," Talbot's "secret government," Peter Dale Scott's "Deep State."[223] I do not believe the American people can possibly mount the urgently necessary challenge of the Deep State without Congressional participation. To help, visit the website 28-pages.org.

WHY PARIS 11/13?

Mujahid Kamran

Two forms of terrorism can provoke such a situation [breakdown of state]: blind terrorism (committing massacres indiscriminately which cause a large number of victims), and selective terrorism (eliminate chosen persons) ... This destruction of the state must be carried out under the cover of "communist activities." Popular opinion must be polarized ... that we are the only instrument capable of salvation.
                    – Captain Yves Guerin-Serac, French Gladio terrorist

You had to attack the civilians, the people, women, children, unknown people far from any political game. The reason was quite simple—to force the people to turn to the state to ask for greater security.
                    – Vincenzo Vinguerra, convicted Italian terrorist

If you infiltrate a group and then carry out terror operations with that group, without that group knowing that it has been infiltrated and is being "steered," that is one of the strategically most sophisticated operations imaginable. To any strategist that is beautiful, just as it is ugly from a moral perspective.
                    – Daniele Ganser, author, *NATO's Secret Armies*

In order to comprehend the current global scenario with reference to the so called Global War On Terrorism (GWOT) a review of the first phase of Operation Gladio is indispensable. Despite the enormous cover-up and disinformation apparatus employed by NATO agencies, and despite the highly questionable role of the so-called "mainstream" media, dedicated researchers in the West have been able to expose the holes in every official and "mainstream" media narrative about all major acts of terrorism that have afflicted the West, and increasingly, the rest of the world.[224] The discovery of the existence of secret stay-behind armies in West European countries in the aftermath of World War II remains the key to all acts of blind terrorism, murder of leaders, and general subversion in the West, in South America, and in Turkey in its first phase. The purpose of these stay-behind armies, commonly known in the literature as Gladio units, was to offer resistance to the USSR in case it invaded a West European country. These armies were set up as a result of an understanding between a few members of the US military and espionage hierarchy who were deeply loyal to the international bankers, without the knowledge and approval of the US government. The initial funding of $200 million came from the banksters—through the Rockefeller and Mellon Foundations [ref 3, p 29]. Subsequently the Gladio units were funded through drug trafficking. But increasingly these stay-behind armies have been used to subvert European democracies, in particular, in the first phase, to prevent the left wing from being elected to office and to prevent these countries from pursuing a foreign policy independent of the Anglo-US-Israel group. During the heyday of the USSR, all such acts of terrorism, which were always carried out by secret stay-behind armies (called Gladio units), were, as a matter of strategy, routinely blamed on left wing elements. After the USSR was dismantled and 9/11 staged, the communist bogey was replaced by Islam (the current phase of Gladio). As Richard Cottrell wrote in the Author's Preface of his book:

> Every NATO state, and some that were not, had such a secretive force. As the prospect of an attack from the East receded, so did the fear of the Soviets. To preserve the myth of the Red Peril, these secret or sleeping soldiers were released in a wave of synthetic violence against innocent European citizens. It lasted two decades, the years remembered by the Italians as the anni di piombi—years of the lead.[225]

The modern day manufactured war on terror comes from the same staple of synthetic violence. With the communist bogey exhausted, we are told of an insidious new peril in our midst: the fearful prospect of minarets and Sharia law marching across the European landscape, destroying Christian civilization. But for fear to work in tangible form, as was discovered in the years of lead, we must have the visible impact of terror all around us. That is where we are now.

Acts of terrorism committed by the deep state are now routinely blamed on Muslim extremists. The whole situation requires a dispassionate analysis and the question "Who benefits" must be the first to be raised and addressed. It is highly significant that the mainstream media never raises this question. Yet the question of who benefits is asked as a matter of routine in all homicide cases. Major acts of terrorism committed in the West and elsewhere are the only exceptions. As soon as the act has been committed the mainstream media places the blame on Muslim extremists, even before any analysis whatsoever is done. The people, who are in a state of shock, and are therefore in a highly suggestible state, are deeply influenced by the media. At the same time draconian legislation is passed, security measures are taken, and civil liberties are targeted, leading to warrantless surveillance, warrantless arrests, etc. The overall effect is two-fold: public anger is directed towards Muslims, and the powers of the state are irreversibly enhanced overnight. The twin consequences then enable NATO to increasingly attack and dismantle resource-rich Muslim countries and plunder their resources, particularly oil and gas. The goal is to bring China and Russia to their knees after capturing all major oil and gas resources in the world. Once this is achieved nation states will be merged into a global organization which will be under the absolute control of the international banking families, all of whom are freemasonic Zionists[226]. There will be no freedom of expression and even our very thought processes will be controlled using advances in science and technology. Further, under the New World Order, there will be no freedom of movement—movements of all individuals will be tracked through microchips linked to computers.

The reasons for the rapid and predesigned erosion of democratic rights in the West were spelled out by the Elite mouthpiece and "thinker" Zbigniew Brzezinski in his 1997 book:

> America is too democratic at home to be autocratic abroad. This limits the use of America's power, especially its capacity for military intimidation. Never before has a popular democracy attained international supremacy. But the pursuit of power is not a goal that commands popular passion, except in conditions of a sudden threat or challenge to the public's sense of domestic well-being. The economic self-denial (that is defense spending) and the human sacrifice (casualties among professional soldiers) required in the effort are uncongenial to democratic instincts. Democracy is inimical to imperial mobilization.[227]

Please note, these views represent the views of the Elite as thrashed out in various think tanks, and as expressed, first in journals like *Foreign Affairs*, and then in book form, to give these brutal and anti-mankind ideas ideological respectability. Those who control America are busy bringing America, as well as European governments, in line— democratic instincts are being replaced by fear of an Islamic threat, in the manner pointed out by Cottrell. All over the Western countries civil liberties are being rapidly eroded and the powers of the state enhanced. False flag operations are the key to this "systemic destabilization" as pointed out by Professor Peter Dale Scott[228]. The purpose of this destabilization, this strategy of tension, was summed up by "God's Terrorist," author of the Gladio manual, Yves Geurin-Serac in the following words (emphasis added):

> Our belief is that the first phase of political activity ought to be to create conditions favoring the institution of chaos in all the regime's

structures. In our view the first move we should make is to destroy the structure of democratic states under the cover of Communist and pro-Chinese activities . . . (at) the same time we must raise up a defender of the citizenry against the disintegration brought about by terrorism and subversion.

Obviously we will have to tailor our actions to the ethos of the milieu —propaganda and action of a sort which will seem to have emanated from our Communist adversaries. [These operations] will create a feeling of hostility towards those who threaten the peace of each and every nation [i.e. the Left].[229]

All one has to do is to replace the word Communist by Muslim to arrive at the present phase of Gladio subversion.

In its present phase, Gladio has become something more than merely holding the people of the West captive and spellbound in a state of terror so they may surrender their liberties and the Communists or leftists do not get elected to power, or the Western democracies dare not pursue a foreign policy independent of the Anglo-US-Israel group. Gladio now provides the additional motive for wars abroad in the name of GWOT. The present worldwide phase of Gladio subversion is to create a pretext for interventions abroad as happened in Libya and is happening currently in Syria. The hostility generated in the public mind as a result of propaganda that these acts of terrorism have been carried out by Muslim extremists makes foreign interventions easier for those who control the Anglo-US-Israel alliance.

Cottrell has also pointed out another important fact about Gladio subversion that is currently applicable to the "Muslim extremists":

A common stripe ran through all the urban revolutionary forces that arose in Europe. They were riddled with double agents planted by the secret intelligence services to provoke takeaway terror to order.

There is agreement among alternate history researchers that almost the entire gamut of "Islamic" fighter groups, from Al Qaeda to ISIS / ISIL, Daesh, al-Nusra, etc. have been erected by the Anglo-US-Israel agencies and "retired" intelligence operatives. A declassified DIA document obtained by Judicial Watch reveals that the West intentionally supported violent Islamist groups to destabilize Assad [e.g. 10-13].[230] The DIA report shows that the DIA foresaw that this kind of backing of violent extremist groups with the intention of toppling or weakening Bashar al-Assad's regime in Syria would lead to the emergence of an Islamic State in Syria in the form of a "Salafist Principality." This document may still be regarded as a smokescreen that hides the true nature and extent of the involvement of US agencies in creating, training, building and controlling these militant groups, all of which are serving the purpose of the Anglo-US-Israel empire building coalition. No wonder Professor Chossudovsky, who from his office, has waged an incessant war against the lies, brutalities, inhumanity, illegality and deceptions of these powers, wrote recently (emphasis in original):

> **Al Qaeda and its affiliated organizations are creations of the CIA. They are not the product of Muslim society.** Terrorist attacks are undertaken by jihadist entities which are CIA intelligence assets.
> The Islamic State (ISIS) is an intelligence construct which is used essentially for two related purposes.
> **1. They are the foot soldiers of the Western military alliance, the instruments of destabilization,** recruited, trained, financed by the Western military alliance. The various al Qaeda entities are the instruments of destabilization in US-NATO sponsored proxy wars (AQIM in Mali, Boko Haram in Nigeria, ISIS in Syria and Iraq). At the same time, they constitute a pretext and a justification to intervene under the banner of a "counter-terrorism" bombing campaign.
> 2. On the home front, the various Al Qaeda/ ISIS terrorist cells –supported covertly by Western intelligence—are **the instruments of a diabolical and criminal propaganda operation which consists in killing innocent civilians** with a view to providing legitimacy to the instatement of police state measures allegedly in support of democracy. These false flag attacks allegedly perpetrated by terrorist organizations are then used to harness Western public opinion against Muslims. The underlying objective is to wage an illegal war of conquest in the Middle East and beyond under the banner of the "global war on terrorism." According to Western politicians, "we are defending ourselves against the terrorists." According to our governments, the bombing raids allegedly directed against the terrorists in Syria are "not an act of war," they are presented to Western public opinion as an "act of self-defense." "The West is under attack by the ISIS terrorists," the ISIS is based in Raqqa, Northern Syria, "we must defend ourselves" by bombing ISIS.[231]

Earlier, on 19 September 2014, Garikai Chengu had written:

> Much like Al Qaeda, the Islamic State is made-in-USA, an instrument of terror designed to divide and conquer the oil-rich Middle East and to counter Iran's growing influence in the region.

There is undeniable evidence that Western agencies, in particular the Anglo-US-Israel group, have been luring, manipulating and trapping Muslims residing in the West or elsewhere into carrying out activities that can establish that Muslims harbor terrorists. The FBI, for example, has itself created the vast majority of alleged "radical Islamist" terror plots in the USA.[232] Similarly a recent terror trial against a Swedish national Bashir Behrin Gildo in Old Bailey, London, collapsed after his lawyers argued that British security and intelligence agencies were supporting the same Syrian opposition groups as he was.[233] *Veterans Today* has also reported that the ISIL leader al-Baghdadi is a Mossad agent, a son of Jewish parents whose original name is Simon Elliot.[234] In fact, as noted astutely by Anthony Hall: "Netanyahu is cunning in his condemnation of ISIL, the hugely hyped Islamic group that tellingly wants only to fight other Muslim groups and strangely never wants to fight Israel."[235] As Barbara Honegger, who epitomizes the true American spirit of integrity, wrote (emphasis in original):

> The whole purpose of the CIA-NATO-Mossad Operation Gladio was, and is, to frighten European civilians—in the "American Gladio" attacks of September 11th, U.S. civilians as well. In particular, according to NSA documents revealed by whistleblower Edward Snowden, American, British and Israeli intelligence worked together to **create** the brutal Sunni jihadist organization Islamic State of Iraq and Syria (ISIS; also known as IS or ISIL), whose leader is supposed to be Mossad trained agent Simon Elliot and which President Obama is seeking a new Authorization for the Use of Military Force from the Congress and billions of U.S. taxpayer dollars to fight. Stinger and TOW missiles used by ISIS are reported to be from Israeli stockpiles, and in 2014, Netanyahu confirmed that the Israeli Defense Force is supporting Al Qaeda terrorists in Syria through a logistics base in the Golan Heights. And Netenyahu had the unmitigated gall to address a joint session of Congress in early March 2015, only weeks after the Paris shootings, in an attempt to rally the American public in the fight **against** "radical Islam."[236]

We now have the traditional Gladio units and we have the so-called Islamic groups whose members can be used to create terror in the West as well as abroad. All major terrorism in the world has to be analyzed in this context. That is precisely why the official and mainstream media narrative in each and every such incident turns out to be false on closer inspection. The Charlie Hebdo incident has been analyzed in detail by scholars and the book edited by Kevin J. Barrett has blown apart the myth that Islamic extremists as such were behind the Charlie Hebdo incident. Who benefitted from Charlie Hebdo?

To begin with the Charlie Hebdo incident was staged after French President Hollande had announced, on January 5th, 2015, that a) France would not send its troops to Libya; b) restrictions on Ukraine must go; and c) it was up to the Greeks to decide whether or not they wanted to stay in the EU. All three points were in direct conflict with the Anglo-US-Israel policy dictated as usual by a secret cabal, the international bankers. Further, France had committed the crime of being sympathetic to the human rights of Palestinians. And above all one must not forget the veiled threat given by Israeli leader Benjamin Netanyahu that France would face terrorism if it recognized Palestinian rights. Alain Soral writes [24]:

> He [Netenyahu] declared to the French people on August 7th 2014, in an interview with iTele: "This is not Israel's battle. It is your battle. If they succeed here, if Israel is criticized instead of the terrorists, if we do not stand in solidarity, this plague of terrorism will come to your country."
>
> If we do not understand Netanyahu's statement as a disguised threat, it is absurd, since there is obviously no reason why recognizing Palestine and standing is solidarity with Gaza would provoke Islamist attacks on France.[237]

Referring to the Charlie Hebdo march, Alain Soral further points out [25]:

> It's the triumvirate of the police state, media propaganda, and Zionism. With this threesome one approaches a dictatorship of great modernity and subtlety. Valerie Percresse, former minister and government spokeswoman, issued a Tweet demanding a "French Patriot Act," that is to say, a state of emergency in the name of a "terrorist threat." This much-vaunted "terrorism" is an abstraction that is never defined, in order to impose an anti-historical, anti-political and anti-rational approach that uses emotion to prevent thinking. This is extremely disturbing, since the forces resisting such manipulation are miniscule.[238]

The Charlie Hebdo murders changed all that overnight. The greatest beneficiary of these murders was the Anglo-US-Israel war-mongering alliance, in particular Israel.

The Paris massacres of November 13th, 2015 took place against the backdrop of the gloomy situation for the Anglo-US-Israeli war against Syria. The situation had suddenly changed when the Russian planes began bombing ISIS/ISIL forces inside Syria. The tide of the war turned and this led to the ugly massacre in Paris, just as it had previously led to the explosion aboard the Russian airliner in Egypt. The Anglo-US-Israel cabal smelled isolation and defeat; it needed more allies and it needed to protect its assets in its war against Syria. The Russians had inflicted heavy damage on a most important ISIS/ISIL funding source: illegal oil. Russian airstrikes halved the income of ISIS/ISIL, from $3 million per day to $1.5 million per day.[239] Does ISIS have the expertise to man and to pump oil from oil fields in a war torn region? Who trained them? Are there Western operatives at these oil fields? Or have they held workers at the oil fields captive? I remember a British taxi driver in Lancaster, who had fought in Iraq, telling me that "all we seemed to be doing in Iraq was pumping out huge amounts of oil and looking for Saddam's gold."

It was quite clear that Western airstrikes were not doing any harm to ISIS/ISIL. Were these airstrikes an eye wash? Almost certainly they were. The long convoys of vehicles with arms-bearing terrorists, the long convoys of trucks carrying oil to Turkey, the long convoys of trucks carrying arms into terrorist-controlled territory from Turkey, all these remained practically unscathed until Russian air power came into play. The whole lid was blown off the Anglo-US-Israel deception in this war, by the Russian success in dealing heavy blows to ISIS et al.

The extent of oil theft has been exposed very recently by the Russian leadership:

> The image taken on November 16 shows up to 360 oil tanker trucks and heavy vehicles close to the Syrian border...
>
> The space images of this ports dated November 25, 2015, show a concentration of petrol tank vehicles, which are waiting for shipment...
>
> 395 petrol tank vehicles were detected in Dörtyol, and 60 in Scanderoon...
>
> In the area of Deir-ez-Zor, space intelligence means detected 1722 oil transporting vehicles on October 18, 2015. Most vehicles were on the unequipped parking areas...
>
> On 28 November, 50 oil trucks were registered near Karachok on the territory of oil transferring point...
>
> The photo demonstrates waiting areas of oil trucks located at the Syrian-Iraqi borderline near Cham Khanik. There were registered 380 vehicles in August. Everything has remained the same...
>
> Reconnaissance is still registering movement of a large number of tanker vehicles crossing the Turkish and Iraqi borders. Even more tanker vehicles are registered on the Iraqi-Turkish border. Their amount has not decreased for the last three months...
>
> Therefore, footage, dating from November 14, allowed detecting 1,104 oil trucks and heavy vehicles near Zakho and Tatvan.[240]

After the Paris massacres, the situation has changed in favor of wider war in Syria the way the Anglo-US-Israel war-mongering alliance wanted it. And it was a momentous change in such a short span of time. Now other countries including France have decided to go into Syria in a heavy way, without regard to public opinion. On December 2nd, 2015, twenty days after the Paris massacre, the US announced an expeditionary force for combat in Syria. On December 5th, 2015 the German parliament voted for military intervention in Syria. As Urlich Rippert noted:

> Not since World War II has a decision on participation in war been taken so quickly. The government could count on a compliant parliament, whose members regard themselves as its agents. These tactics served to suppress all public discussion of the significance of the Syrian mission, its risks, its consequences and its lack of an international legal and constitutional basis.[241]

On December 8th, 2015 Johannes Stern wrote:

> Developments have proceeded rapidly following the decision by the German parliament on Friday in favour of military participation in Syria. Just a few hours after the vote, the German frigate Augsburg was under way for Syria. According to a spokesman for the Mission Command in Potsdam, it has been alongside the French aircraft carrier Charles de Gaulle since Sunday. At a Luftwaffe (air force) base near Kiel, German Tornado combat aircraft are being prepared for their deployment to Turkey.

Following a vote by the British parliament in favor of bombing Syria, the British Defense Secretary Michael Fallon authorized an immediate strike by RAF bombers on Syria. The parliament voted at 10:30 pm on Wednesday December 2nd, 1915 and by 11:30 pm two RAF bombers took off from a Cyprus airbase "each loaded with three Paveway missiles, worth more than 100,000 pounds each. An hour later two more Tornados took off armed with Paveways."[242]

The Israelis also decided to escalate their already hidden involvement in the Syrian conflict after the Paris massacres. Near the end of November 2015, the Director of the Israeli Political-Security Division Amos Gilad reportedly said that "Syria is a dead state and Israel must understand this and prepare accordingly." As for Israel's role in creating and promoting conflict in Syria, Jean Shaoul wrote on December 3rd 2015:

In July, Defense Minister Ya'alon admitted that Israel had been aiding Islamist groups, something that Israeli officials had previously denied. Speaking about Israeli medical aid to the Islamists fighting with the al-Qaeda affiliated al-Nusra Front, he said, "We've assisted them under two conditions. That they don't get too close to the border, and that they don't touch the Druze."

Last February, a report by the UN Disengagement Observer Force (UNDOF) in the Golan Heights, submitted to the UN Security Council and buried by the Western media, showed that the IDF had been in regular contact with Syrian rebels, including Islamic State militants, since May 2013.

UNDOF has been subject to attacks by the al-Nusra Front, including kidnappings, killings, theft of UN weapons and ammunition, vehicles and other property, and the looting and destruction of its facilities, in a clear bid to drive it from the Golan border area. Only a small contingent is still stationed on the Syrian side of the border.[243]

When questioned by i24News, as to whether Israel had given medical treatment to ISIS and al-Nusra members, an Israeli military spokesman stated: "In the past two years the Israeli Defence Forces have been engaged in humanitarian, life-saving aid to wounded Syrians, irrespective of their identity." Humanitarian? Life-saving? Ask the Palestinians whose children and unarmed men and women are murdered in cold blood day after day, week after week, month after month, by the Israeli forces. The brutality of the Israelis surpasses that of Hitler—it has been going on for almost seven decades whereas Hitlerian repression lasted less than a decade and a half.

There are numerous questions that may be raised about what happened on Paris on November 13th, 2015. There were apparently seven coordinated attacks on a Friday night beginning at 21:20 hrs, when merry-making and happiness would be at its peak (which reminds one of the Oktoberfest attack in Germany, a case which has been reopened after three decades). These seven attacks took place within a span of 33 minutes, the first one at 9:20 pm and the last one at 9:53 pm.[244] According to the mainstream media narrative, at 9:20 a suicide bomber detonated an explosives belt close to the Stadium (Gate D), Stade de France, where a soccer match between France and Germany was in progress. Two bodies, including that of the suicide bomber were found. Only five minutes later, at 9:25, gunmen in a black vehicle indiscriminately shot 15 people sitting in restaurant and wounded ten others. At 9:30 another suicide bomber exploded 437 yards from the stadium (near Gate H) killing only himself/herself. The fourth restaurant shooting took place two minutes later, at 9:32, killing five people. Four minutes later, at 9.36 gunmen in a black car killed 19 people in a restaurant shooting—the victims were sitting on the terrace of La Belle Equipe—and nine others were critically wounded. At 9.40 two simultaneous attacks took place. A suicide bomber managed to kill only himself in one attack. In the other attack a concert hall was the target. Around 9.40 three men with assault rifles emerged from a black Volkswagon Polo, entered the two storey ball room of a concert hall, threw grenades at the spectators, and also fired with rifles. In the shootings and suicide attacks at the concert hall 89 people were killed. The gunmen took those spectators who could not flee as hostages. After a standoff of two hours the security forces stormed the club. Two men died by activating their suicide vests and the suicide vest of the third exploded due to police gunfire. At 9:53 an explosion occurred at some distance from the stadium. A body was subsequently found at the site of the explosion presumed to be the body of a suicide bomber. The total number of injured in the carnage was more than 300. The number of dead stood at 129.

Seven coordinated attacks in a city like Paris could not take place without military planning and without involvement of the deep state—most likely Anglo-US-Israel (with possibly French joining in out of fear) based on the past record. One very important fact was covered up and completely ignored by the media as it went into a (presumably pre-planned) overdrive. This was noted by Professor Chossudovsky.[245] He pointed out on November 14th, 2015 that on October 2nd *Paris Match* had predicted that a French 9/11 was expected, citing a judge who dealt with terrorism cases and also citing intelligence agencies. It is noteworthy that the same story also pointed out that the attacks could not be avoided (*"impossible à dejouer"*). This story was never brought up in the French media when the attacks took place. Why was this suggestion made? Was the story suggesting that French intelligence had given up hope of averting such an attack? Was it to suggest that the agencies were inept? Or was it a part of the agenda of the agencies, or sections of the agencies, to let it happen, as in Pearl Harbor? Has anyone subsequently asked the reporter of *Paris Match*, and the judge who was cited, as to exactly what were their sources?

In Pakistan, which has suffered numerous terrorist attacks, and which is not only a target of the Anglo-US-Israel coalition, but additionally of India as well, such an attack in several different places concurrently, has not taken place, and probably cannot take place. Why not? Because such an attack can only take pace with help from intelligence agencies and the military. Are the French law enforcement authorities inferior to those of Pakistan? It is hard to believe.

What makes the entire massacre suspicious is the response of the French authorities and the French media. Professor Chossudovsky states:

> Within minutes following the attacks, which were launched simultaneously, and prior to the release of a preliminary report by the police, France's media went into overdrive. News commentators and intelligence analysts on France's network TV stated with authority that attacks emanated from Syria and Iraq. The media coverage of these tragic events was casually linked up with the war in the Middle East, highlighting France's commitment—alongside its allies—in waging a "humanitarian war" against the terrorists.[246]

If within minutes, without any investigation, the media and intelligence analysts had concluded that the attacks emanated from Syria and Iraq, then one must conclude that the very aim of these attacks was to drive France into deeper involvement in the Mideast war. The hate campaign against Muslims is a strategic ploy that will allow the Anglo-US-Israel coalition and their "allies" (who became allies through arm twisting and false flag operations) to massacre Muslim populations in huge numbers, with the general acquiescence of Western people. Also, one must ask how the pundits immediately knew that the attacks had emanated from Syria and Iraq? As observed by Laurent Guyenot:

> The key to the success of a false flag attack is the speed with which the official version, that is to say, the guilt of the patsy, is imposed. The most important task is to cut short any alternative theory, which can then be denied as baseless rumor. Official pronouncements must drown out the public's efforts to discover its own meaning in the event, express doubts, or debate. If, during and after the initial shock, the government speaks with confidence, authority and unanimity, it will convince the naïve and intimidate skeptics. Studies show that information received in a time of emotional stress, during which rationality is suspended, are integrated into the memory of the trauma, so the distinction between facts and their explanation is abolished.[247]

The media overdrive and the instant consonance between the government and the media smells of a false flag. A Reuters report mentions that the French President clearly stated that "this was an act of war committed by Daesh that was prepared, organized and planned from outside [France]" with help from within the country.[248]

Another aspect of false flag operations has been noted by Guyenot:

The second rule of a good false flag attack is to quickly eliminate the patsy. Once he understands that he has nothing to lose by proclaiming what he knows ... Therefore, a good patsy is a dead patsy.[249]

So the chances of any perpetrator of the Paris massacre being caught alive are practically zero. Three perpetrators died in individual suicides, three others inside the concert hall also were killed or committed suicide. Those who fired at people in restaurants have disappeared and have not been apprehended! They were probably Gladio operatives or Mossad agents.

The story that has been put up is that the mastermind was a Belgian citizen named Abdelhamid Abaaoud, who returned to Belgium and travelled to Syria freely despite being on the radar of the authorities! This is a pattern one also sees with some 9/11 hijackers as shown by Kevin Fenton in his book *Disconnecting the Dots*. He establishes that each time the FBI wished to arrest two terrorists it was tracking the unseen hand of the CIA would intervene to stop them from doing so. Is Abdelhamid Abaaoud a similar case? Similarly other names that have been floated seem to fit the same pattern. Salah Abdeslam lived a few blocks from Abdelhamid Abaaoud, and the police are convinced that they knew each other. However the Belgian police said that "the investigation showed no sign of him actively going to terrorism." He was caught by the Turkish authorities while trying to cross into Syria. Ismail Omar Mostefai was another terrorist. Turkey had informed France about him in December 2014 and in June 2015 but there was no response from the French authorities until after the Paris massacres.[250]

Apparently ISIS/ISIL claimed responsibility for the attacks of November 13th, 2015. Who heads ISIL/ISIS? Mossad agent Simon Elliot, masquerading as a Muslim jihadi with the name al-Baghdadi. The true identity of al-Baghdadi has been revealed through Snowden leaks and other sources. Why is the question of the true identity of al-Baghdadi not raised in the Western media? The reporters and the media personalities are well aware who employs them—the media is owned by Zionists and it is all a question of saving one's bacon. The greatest beneficiary of the 11/13 attacks and the Charlie Hebdo murders, and of every major terrorist incident in the West that is attributed to Muslims, is Israel. Since the media owners are mostly Zionists, the question "Who benefits?" dare not be raised in Western media.

The reaction of the French President indicates that 11/13 had, at least for the time being, the same consequences for France that 9/11 had for the U.S. The French President speedily declared a state of emergency without even consulting his cabinet. He also sealed the borders. As Hollande stated:

> Two decisions will be taken. The state of emergency will be decreed, which means several places will be closed off, and traffic will be limited in certain areas. The state of emergency will be applied across the country. The second decision I have taken is to close the borders, so that people who have committed these crimes can be apprehended.[251]

As Professor Peter Dale Scott writes in his 2015 book: "Finally, still in the ninety-day 'shadow government' period after 9/11, President Bush proclaimed two important emergencies that are still in force today."[252] Will the French emergency follow the same pattern? Most likely, yes. Any attempt to lift it may be met with further false flag acts of terrorism sponsored by the Anglo-US-Israel alliance—an alliance for world domination under the Zionist flag, the flag of the international bankers. So it is now highly probable that the emergency in France will become almost permanent. The President could not impose an official emergency after the Charlie Hebdo murders because the Parliament turned down the proposal. This time he bypassed not just the Parliament, but the cabinet also. They had to sacrifice at least 129 human beings to get to where they are now. Such opportunities are not available frequently, although given the increasing tempo of false flag events one cannot rule out a repeat of such killings unless France succumbs completely and absolutely to the will of the Anglo-US-Israel Zionist cabal.

Part 3: Who IS ISIS?

WE ARE ISIS

Ken O'Keefe[253]

Here is an edited transcript of my appearance on Press TV shortly after the 11/13/15 Paris attacks.[254] I think it necessary at this point to spread the understanding that WE, the West and all of our puppet governments, are in very real terms, so-called "ISIS." We created this monster, we use it to foster more insane policies in the Middle East, to demonize Muslims, to take away more rights from the people ... and it serves one agenda above all others, the Greater Israel Project. I say WE are responsible because WE have not done all that we are capable of to stop it, when we do it will stop, and the truth is the most powerful weapon WE have. We need to spread this truth further and further and use the mainstream media's incessant lies against them to wake up more people. These false flags are exposing the powers that be and their agents more and more; in a tactical sense these are great opportunities for humanity, so let us keep exposing the truth on every level and also start pushing for war crimes and crimes against humanity charges for mass media as well as military and government "officials." It may seem impossible to think this could happen right now, but it will if we make it so and the transformation to a better world can occur much, much faster then people currently realize.

Hello, welcome back to Press TV's live coverage of the terrorist attacks in Paris. Joining us for the analytical part of this live coverage is Ken O'Keefe, a former US Marine, who joins us in the studios here in Tehran...
Ken O'Keefe, this should, I would think, be a warning signal to some of the countries supporting the terrorists in the war on Syria —in particular the US, Turkey, and Saudi Arabia.

Yes. And I hope it's even more of a wake-up call for us to realize that WE ARE ISIS—that the Western governments that are in bed with Saudi Arabia, who is the primary funder of ISIS, along with Qatar and other Gulf states. We not only provide political cover and military assistance to Saudi Arabia while it slaughters innocent people in Yemen, but we also provide the cover for them to go ahead and do their dirty dealing with these ISIS psychopaths who are running around Syria, Iraq, and other parts of the world. Let us remember that before the United States invaded Iraq there was no al-Qaeda in Iraq. Look at it today. Let us also remember that when Qaddafi was in power in Libya there was very little al-Qaeda. And now look at it. It's an absolute basket case, full of these operatives. And we can look to Syria as well as yet another example of where these problems, in terms of al-Qaeda, were actually under control. In fact, Bashar al-Assad was assisting the United States —this is all on record. Many of the tortures were being carried out (on behalf of the US) by Bashar al-Assad or at least his regime, to extract information from people that we were supposedly fighting.

Not only is the United States providing the financial, political, and military cover for these terrorists, through our proxies, but we've also provided them training in Jordan. And Turkey, another of our best friends, has been shuttling these psychopaths into Syria for a long time now. So the idea that the West is actually fighting a war against ISIS is beyond ridiculous. So what we really need to do is start realizing that we *are* ISIS. And the reason our corrupt, treasonous governments are carrying out these policies is that they do not represent us. They represent the bankers. And the bankers make a hell of a lot of money from war. And more importantly, as long as we're all fighting each other, as long as we're all not trusting each other, as long as we're all being played as pawns, over and over, then they can maintain this tyrannical system of never-ending war.

So this is really a wake-up call. What has happened in Paris is us. We are responsible through our corrupt governments. And even if these individuals who carried this out are not directly working for Mossad, CIA, ISIS, al-Qaeda—all the same thing—even if they did this organically and of their own volition, believe me, that is exactly what our own so-called governments want. That is the policy that we have been fostering over and over. And quite frankly, if we are to look closer at ISIS, it stands for Israeli Secret Intelligence Service. They never attack Israel. And that tells you a lot about who these individuals are.

Some of the events we've been talking about, in terms of Islamophobia, more policies against Muslims ... maybe this is what the intent is behind these attacks, if there are hidden hands behind the scenes in some of the countries involved in this so-called war on terror.

Indeed, that is the case. And it's just more of the same now, isn't it? I'm a non-Muslim, and I'm angry at the way Muslims have been portrayed around the world. I have lived in Muslim lands, and I have experienced some of the greatest hospitality and generosity that you will ever experience. And yet Muslims in general are being associated with this monstrosity known as ISIS—which again I say is Israeli Secret Intelligence Service. And also, before that, al-Qaeda, the al-Nusra Front. All of these are intended to smear Islam as a whole, all 1.8 billion on this planet, to associate them with this sort of madness, when in fact it is us in the West who are creating this stuff, funding it, protecting it. In fact, America has been providing air cover to these psychopaths in Syria and Iraq. And we see that when Russia comes in and actually does something constructive, look at how many of these ISIS men are shaving their beards and running off with their tails between their legs. It is really disgusting that people have been conned into thinking that Muslims have anything to do with this.

And let us harken back to the original incident which has caused this madness known as the war on terror. "The So-Called Hijackers and Osama Bin Laden" is one of the greatest fairy stories ever created. The idea that this man in a cave in Afghanistan on dialysis masterminded this incredible operation against the United States with 19 so-called hijackers wielding box cutters, Mohamed Atta among them, snorting cocaine and hanging out with strippers in Florida, that these people are responsible for this event, in defiance of the greatest military machine in the history of mankind, never mind all of the evidence that has come forward that makes the official version of 9/11 beyond ridiculous ... Muslims did not carry out 9/11. In fact, those who blame the Muslims, primarily the Jewish-supremacist-Zionist-controlled media of America, and the government that is controlled by these Jewish-supremacist Zionists—all of them parrot the same ridiculous tired old line that Muslims were responsible. This is an agenda that is intended to create a clash of civilizations. Those who are collaborating in this agenda need to be held to account for war crimes and crimes against humanity. And I'm including not just the politicians and the military, but those in the media who have perpetuated these lies. Because there is no way that they could possibly believe this nonsense. These people have sold their souls in service to the devil.

There has been a piece of breaking news, a message from Assad to Hollande: "France suffered the brutality of terrorism that has plagued Syria for more than five years." That's quite telling in terms of what Syria has experienced. Your reaction?

It is truly incredible that we listen to anyone, whether it is François Hollande or Obama or any of these other puppets, as if anything they say has any merit whatsoever. There is no moral authority at all in the West. These people are an embarrassment to all of us who have a functioning brain and a heart. These people are traitors. Whether they come from France or whether they come from Britain or America. And everything they say is to be taken as complete and total rubbish. The idea that France and the West are not directly responsible for the mayhem that has been occurring in Syria is, again, beyond ridiculous. We know for a fact how we've been funding and supporting the supposedly "moderate rebels." There is no such thing. Recently a US general admitted that there might be four or five of these people in Syria.

The entire policy is intended to create havoc in the Middle East. And it is extremely important that people around the world begin to comprehend that these policies that are being carried out in the Middle East are actually not failures. I'm getting sick of hearing so-called experts talking about geopolitics and how America is failing to learn from its mistakes and all of this nonsense. These are not mistakes! These are intentional polices to wreak havoc, to sow the seeds of sectarian hatred. Again, let me cite the fact that before we took Saddam Hussein out in Iraq there was no al-Qaeda in Iraq. Before we played this game in Libya there was no such thing as ISIS and all of this madness that's going on in Libya today. Syria, while it had its problems—and it certainly had its human rights abuses—most definitely did not have the problem that it has today. Every country that we, the West, touch in the Middle East is full of these monsters.

Let's look to Iran, the country the US claims is the biggest threat to everyone. The Israeli Jewish-supremacists constantly tell us that Iran is the biggest threat to the world, and that it wants to "wipe Israel off the map." Let's look at Iran, at how many attacks by al-Qaeda and ISIS are occurring here. Let's look at how Iran has been fighting MEK, a true terrorist force that has killed over 20,000 people in the last 20 years or so. This nation, Iran, is fighting terrorism, legitimately. It has provided sanctuary to Jews and Christians historically over the millennia. It has not indulged in any war for hundreds of years other than the imposed war which we, the US, with our attack dog Saddam Hussein, forced on it. And yet we are being told that Iran is the threat. Here I sit in Tehran and I can tell you that the threat from ISIS is next-to-none. The reason is that Iran is not a player in this nasty game in which Saudia Arabia, Qatar, other Gulf states, Turkey, Jordan, the US, Britain, France, all fund, train, support and ultimately are responsible for these monsters whose latest brand name is ISIS, which I repeat a third time stands for Israeli Secret Intelligence Service.

HOW WE KNOW ISIS WAS "MADE IN THE USA"

Jim Fetzer

For those who may have missed the memo, 9/11 was brought to us by the CIA, the Neo-Cons in the Department of Defense (most of whom were dual US-Israel citizens) and the Mossad. Its objective was to trans-form US foreign policy from one in which we (at least, officially) never attacked any nation that had not attacked us first to one in which we would become the greatest aggressor nation in the world.[255]

Wesley Clark, upon his return from serving as Supreme Comman-der, Allied Forces Europe (the military chief of NATO), learned the plan was to take out the governments of seven nations in the next five years, beginning with Iraq and Libya and ending with Syria and Iran, which he shared with us during a speech at The Commonwealth Club in San Francisco, which may have been the most honorable act of his life.[256]

That it has not played out that way has not been from lack of trying. The brilliant intervention of Russia on behalf of Syria and its people and in defense of its maligned president, Bashar al-Assad, a staunch ally, has thrown a monkey wrench into the master plan, which would enable Israel to become "the Greater Israel" and fulfill "its destiny" by dominating the Middle East from the Tigris-Euphrates to the Nile.[257]

The massive control of the mainstream media in the United States, however, has obfuscated the grim reality of the situation, where the Obama administration was thwarted in its plan to lob cruise missiles into Syria on the fabricated context that Assad had gassed his own peo-ple, which Russia refuted with a 50-page dossier to the United Nations. This required the Neo-Cons who dominate his administration to regroup and contrive a more subtle rationale for attacking Syria.[258]

A plan to take out 7 governments in the next 5 years

Thus was ISIS born in a directive from the DIA, Defense Intelligence Agency, which Judicial Watch was able to obtain under a Freedom of Information request, which has revealed the hypocrisy that underlies US involvement in the Middle East, where we are performing "the dirty work" on behalf of Israel, which cleverly contrives to use our military, our money and our political resources to benefit Israel, where there have been no benefits to the United States from our intervention.[259]

That ISIS was "made in the USA" can be substantiated by a great many sources. Here are (what might be called) the "top twelve" reasons we know that ISIS was created by our government to promote its political agenda, which has nothing to do with bringing "freedom and democracy to Syria" but only in pursuing the master plan to create "the Greater Israel":

(1) On 23 February 2015, FARS reported that the (much maligned) Iraqi Army had downed 2 UK cargo planes carrying weapons for ISIL, which was among the first signs that things were not as the world was being told by Western—and especially US—news sources.[260]

(2) On 1 March 2015, FARS reported that Iraqi popular forces known as "Al-Hashad Al-Shabi" shot down a US helicopter carrying weapons for ISIL in Al-Anbar province of which they had photographs.[261]

(3) On 10 April 2015, PressTV reported that, in response to a request by Syria that ISIL be named a terrorist organization, the US, Britain, France and Jordan refused, which was rather baffling on its face.[262]

(4) Photographs were appearing contemporaneously showing ISIS members sporting "US Army" tattoos, which the American media has yet to acknowledge.[263]

(5) On 19 May 2015, Brad Hoof of levantreport.com, "2012 Defense intelligence Agency document: West will facilitate rise of Islamic State in order to isolate the Syrian regime," based upon the release of a selection of formerly classified documents obtained by Judicial Watch from the US Department of Defense and Department of State.[264] [265]

(6) On 22 June 2015, ex-CIA contractor Steven Kelley explained the US "created ISIL for sake of Israel" and to have a "never-ending war" in the Middle East, which would make the countries there "unable to stand up to Israel" and to provide "the constant flow of orders for weapons from the military-industrial complex at home, which is feeding a lot of money to the senators pushing for these wars."[266]

(7) On 11 July 2015, Gordon Duff, Senior Editor at veteranstoday.com, broke the story that a video of staged ISIS beheading videos had been hacked from the computer files of an assistant to Sen. John McCain.[267]

(8) On 12 July 2015, *Time Magazine*, a mainstream publication, admitted that ISIS was bringing arms and fighters in from NATO nations, which received extensive coverage from alternative media but unsurprisingly would not be reported by US news and TV media.[268]

(9) On 4 October 2015, Alexi Pushkov, head of the International Affairs Committee of the Russian Parliament, asserted the US is "not bombing ISIS at all . . . Obama is lying to the American people."[269]

(10) On 18 November 2015, Vladimir Putin exposed that 40 countries —including some of the G20—are financially supporting ISIS, which begins to reveal the extent of the duplicity of the Western nations, including especially the United States, which has been using feigned attacks on ISIS to damage or destroy the infrastructure of Syria.[270]

(11) On 22 November 2015, multiple sources reported that the fuel trucks transporting oil from Syria to Turkey are "off limits" and that the truck drivers have to be warned before US planes attack them.[271]

(12) On 26 November 2015, Russia's Foreign Minister, Sergey Lavrov, was reported to have told his Turkish counterpart, Mevlut Cavusoglu, that the shooting down of a Russian plane appeared to have been "a planned provocation", where zerohedge.com identified Bilal Erdogan, the son of the President of Turkey, as having been responsible for the shoot down and for the management of oil from Syria into Turkey.[272]

There are many other sources that confirm that ISIS was created by the US and is being supported by Western powers to promote their own political agenda. Since the nullification of the Smith-Mundt Act of 1948 (which precluded the techniques of propaganda and disinformation within the United States) by the NDAA 2013, there are no trustworthy news sources in the US, not even *The New York Times*.[273]

From a sound stage in Tel Aviv or even Hollywood

The *Times* deserves emphasis because it is the nation's "newspaper of record," which records what it officially taken to be the history of the United States. The *Times* has served as a conduit for propaganda in the past, including a series of articles demonizing Saddam Hussein and publishing unfounded claims about weapons of mass destruction, which were used to justify the invasion of Iraq, even though none were ever found.

No doubt because ISIS is commonly called "John McCain's Army" in Washington, D.C., The *Times* has published articles attempting to exonerate him from any connection to ISIS, even though he has been photographed with some of its leaders. The *Times* claims that McCain was among "the earliest advocates of military action" against ISIS, but the reality appears to be that he was fostering the policy of using the cover of those attacks to take out the infrastructure of Syria.[274]

Recent articles suggest that Turkey has an agenda and appears to be engaging in a proxy war with Russia. Peter Koenig observes that Turkey had to know that the Russian SU-24 fighter jet was within the borders of Syria, yet the G-20 members all agreed to stand together as "voices in unison." This raises serious doubt about the extent of the Turkish commitment, given that Russia was taking the lead in the attack on ISIS.[275]

Finian Cunningham has driven deeper by suggesting that the shootdown may have been a deliberate provocation to scuttle cooperation between the members of the G-20 in fighting the extremist network in Syria. "Such a coalition might seem reasonable, even desirable, to most people. But it is profoundly unacceptable to Washington because it would further expose the criminal nature of the Western-sponsored regime-change operation in Syria." That may be the heart of the matter.[276]

And what could be more absurd than to blame Syria for the Paris attacks, when ISIS has claimed responsibility? Syria is at war with ISIS. And ISIS is a creation of the United States. For the United States to go to war with ISIS is for the United States to go to war with itself. The attempt to spin responsibility onto Syria is beyond ridiculous and into the theater of the absurd. Yet that appears to be the US position.[277]

For all its espousal of the principles of freedom and democracy, the Obama administration has been extremely aggressive in conducting military operations in other nations. The US does not have the right to determine the leadership of Syria, which is a sovereign nation, even to benefit Israel, whose leaders appear to be exercising a remarkable degree of control over the course of events. Like the psy-ops Charlie Hebdo and now Paris, the benefits appear to be accruing to Israel, not to any other nation (including the United States) and certainly not to the people of the world.[278]

ALL THIS HAS NOTHING TO DO WITH ISLAM

Alain Soral (translated by Kevin Barrett)

First Reaction

The natural first reaction to these events is compassion for the victims. Unfortunately, the emotional escalation imposed by the media on a Hollywood model—which is to say, a Judeo-American model—is so artificial that it is difficult to relate to even when it is authentic; one does not like having one's tears yanked out.

This kind of media-manipulated compassion has little to do with what I call our Hellenic-Christian tradition of modesty. We never would have handled events like this during the time of General de Gaulle, or the 1920s or 1930s.

Instead of virtual compassion on the Internet—which is cheap— what I have done, and what I am inciting others to do, is to go on the Internet and look at the face and name of each of the dead. We then see that they killed mainly young French whites from the middle bourgeoisie. This touches me personally, since the Bastille neighborhood is where I hung out when I was their age. It was us, the trendy ones of that time, who launched these neighborhoods. I can therefore say that had I been born at a different time, I could have been one of the victims.

This leads us to a digression on the lie of universal compassion without borders: We are terribly shocked because the victims are young French men and women. I note that a few days before the massacre, two hundred Russians were killed in an airliner explosion; yet no torrents of compassion were unleashed. And since the first Gulf War, in which we participated, we have massacred Arab and Middle Eastern populations on a daily basis, as well as the populations of the Maghreb and Libya; and we are surviving quite well emotionally.

This difference in reaction is anthropologically normal: We are primarily sensitive to the suffering of our own people. To pretend otherwise is a typical lie of the universalist defender-of-human-rights: a lie that fits well in the mouths of such professional liars as Bernard-Henry Lévy. The fact that the victims of November 13th were close to us made us suddenly aware of the reality of these dead people. So let us also be aware of what we have, since 1991, inflicted on the people of Iraq: Each week in Iraq a bomb explodes in a market, causing a similar number of deaths, mainly of women and children. This has been a constant reality in Iraq for more than twenty years. It is now also a reality in Libya through the fault of M. Bernard Henry-Levy and Sarkozy. And it is equally a reality in Syria, where we have been inflicting terror and death on the Syrian people for more than five years, for reasons that are very difficult to justify. Nobody any longer believes the lie about needing to replace the "dictator" Assad—actually the legitimate leader of a republican, democratic and multiconfessional state—with the famous Al-Nusra Front (a.k.a. al-Qaeda), about which our Minister of Foreign Affairs recently said, "They do a good job."

It is also interesting to note that France, which has not managed to sell one of its Rafale aircraft for twenty years, found a new market a few weeks before the massacre. Who are these new customers? Qatar, Saudi Arabia and the United Arab Emirates: that is to say the countries that finance ISIS. Could these aircraft purchases be a reward to French elites for their complicity in the mass murder? For in reality, as more and more people say, "ISIS is us"—meaning our political elites.

Geopolitical analysis

To understand the events in Paris, you must place them in the global context that I explain in my book *Understanding the Empire: Tomorrow Global Governance—or the Revolt of Nations.* In Western societies, facing a social crisis they lack the will to resolve, our oligarchic elites have chosen to divert the class struggle into a religious struggle. For this, they have in France all the necessary means: a large, poorly-integrated Muslim population, and a global geopolitical context dominated by the American desire to colonize the Middle East.

It should be noted that the bobo population (a contraction of "bourgeois bohemian") of the 11th arrondissement of Paris is predominantly from the French middle-class, which is traditionally the most anti-racist and sensitive to the Palestinian cause. For the alleged jihadists of ISIS, targeting these people is hardly in the interest of Muslims. The practical result of the attacks is to influence young people who, heretofore, were not amenable to the "clash of civilizations" and were not anti-Islamic (as are other social categories in France)—and to incite them to anti-Arab racism. These events, which resemble a French 9/11, are well-timed; they are clearly part of a program that is reaching a crescendo, designed to bring the French to submit to the neoconservative ideology of the "clash of civilizations."

Who benefits? Let us repeat: this crime does not benefit the Muslims of France, who now find themselves more worried than ever about their future in the country and fear the rise of Islamophobia. The crime also certainly does not benefit the French people, who are now living in fear of terrorism and suffer the restriction of their freedom due to the state of emergency.

So who are the beneficiaries? Messieurs Cukierman (President of the Representative Council of Jewish Institutions in France) and Netanyahu explained it recently to the French: "Now you see what we are living through in Israel." This suggests that the real beneficiaries are the American-Zionist empire—and the Jewish community in France, which now has the means to bring the bobos into the Zionist camp.

These attacks represent a clear progression from those of Charlie Hebdo last January. There is an increase in the number of deaths. At Charlie Hebdo, people were killed ostensibly because they had insultingly caricatured the Prophet. Now the dead are random innocents.

This crescendo universalizes the jihadist threat. This may correspond either to a program of ISIS, or of those who manipulate ISIS and have an interest in creating a collective psychosis in France with respect to Muslims. We also note that the media are going all-out on behalf of that agenda.

Micro-social analysis

Alongside this geopolitical analysis, I can make a micro-social analysis, which does not contradict the previous one. Seeing these young suburban "re-Salafized" thugs from our former colonies attacking the native French, reminds me of my own experiences when I was a teenager hanging out near the Bastille. They flocked to the Bastille neighborhood (from immigrant ghettos) to attack young whites. It was the "scum" against the "bolos" (a contraction meaning "bourgeois fag"). This involved a process that has a lot to do with the Boulevard Périphérique, the freeway ringing Paris that forms a border between two worlds: outside, the young descendants of immigrants crammed into places of banishment known as suburban ghettos, excluded from growth and social welfare; they had a jealous relationship, a mixture of hatred and fascination, with the young salaried middle classes who led a good life in the beautiful heart of Paris. They took to the youthful bohemian neighborhoods and enjoyed assaulting and humiliating their victims, a kind of palliative for the pleasure they could not share. Today, the phenomenon has reached a much higher level of violence. We have moved in the 1990s from suburban violence against the petty bourgeoisie, which was limited to minor assaults, to the violence of the Kalashnikov —because it is no longer the Socialist Party and SOS-Racism handling these young outcasts, but the Mossad and the CIA. And this is where sociological analysis meets geopolitical analysis.

The role of Islam

We must understand that in reality, Islam is not central to any of this. What is at stake is a French society in which there is fear, symbolic violence, and mutual hatred between the native French—who are themselves often descended from former immigrants, but from white European Christian populations—and people who have arrived more recently and are poorly integrated. At root it is an ethno-social violence, that is to say both social and racial. This violence can be more or less instrumentalized and mediated by national or international political forces. At one time, the Socialist Party, after abandoning the working class, made use of this violence to substitute the issue of race for that of social justice. That is why they created SOS Racism (which Alain Finkelkraut tells us was actually about saving racism, since there was so little of it). Today, that same violence is used by others to validate the clash of civilizations—that American-Zionist theory set up after the Cold War, when it became necessary to replace the communist enemy with a new villain, the radicalized Muslim.

The proof that radical Islam is a desired artificial creation of the West, not a spontaneous evolution of the Arab world, is that the heyday of European colonial domination never produced any such radical Islam. Rather, it produced the secular nationalist movements like that of Abdel Nasser. Why was this radical Islam, which now undeniably exists, born precisely when US geopolitical theorists needed it? To put it another way: I think that this mutation of Islam into "radical Islam" did not come from Islam.

The evolution of Western policy

We recently observed a shift in Western policy towards ISIS. One might think that this is due to the massacre on Friday the 13th. But that is not the case. In reality, it is due to Putin's entering the game. Russia is currently on the ground in an actual struggle against ISIS, and they now have the ability to show the world that the French government has been merely pretending to fight ISIS for two years. Not only is France pretending to fight ISIS, but it is part of the coalition of powers that support ISIS, with England, Israel, Turkey, Jordan, the United States and the financiers Saudi Arabia and Qatar. Today, the French government pretends to do something, because it has to respond to a legitimate popular anger. Indeed, people are beginning to understand that if young

French people are dead, it's because of the political choices of their elites who are not serving the best interests of France: Syria has never done anything to us; it is not a problem. So why put so much energy into pushing for regime change in Syria? On what basis could we have a mandate to choose the government of such a distant country, especially when the alternative to Assad is ISIS? I think the real impetus is Putin, not the 130 deaths in Paris. Since Putin entered the game, he is in a position to expose the lies of the Atlanticist coalition in which the French State is complicit. For whenever Putin gets mad, he threatens, for example, to become interested in Apollo 11, or to open the archives of the liberation of the Nazi camps, which, it must be remembered, were liberated by the Russians, not the Americans.

What to do ?

What are the possible outcomes? Among the immediate reactions, we find people who are calling for civil war, with the following logic: Muslims have declared war on us, therefore we must expel the Muslims from France. Many angry young people think that this is the solution. I appeal to people of a certain age to explain that civil war is easier to start than to end; and that it's not a video game.

Many people were taken in this direction by the way the media reacted, and by the way the French president responded by declaring that we were at war. If we are at war, he should say against whom: Is it against Muslims, against the suburbs? Either François Hollande is grossly irresponsible, or he is not working for the best interests of his country. As for Prime Minister Manuel Valls, we know that he is not "forever attached" to France, but rather to a state that has a vested interest in anti-Islamism developing in France, so that the French situation will resemble that of Israel. From this point of view, Friday the 13th is a continuation of the strategy of Tel Aviv-sur-Seine. From Tel Aviv-sur-Seine, we get ISIS-sur-Seine.

Civil war is not desirable. So some look a little further and talk about "re-migration." This "re-migration" is a real issue. To understand this, we must go back to 1975 when President Giscard d'Estaing instituted "family reunification," creating an immigration that was not justified by the need for labor, since we had already gone through the first oil shock, come to the end of the Thirty Glorious Years of post-WWII growth, and entered into a period of high unemployment. This open immigration policy was not justified, as in the time of De Gaulle, by a need for workers. The real reasons may be found in the Masonic lodges, the ideology of miscegenation, and what some call the "great replacement"—a term which I once found excessive, but which acquires some credibility when one sees migrants crashing into Europe by way of Turkey.

Given this historical context, some now suggest the need for a re-migration. The country is saturated, cohabitation has taken a wrong turn for ethnic and religious reasons, so we should make these immigrants go back where they came from. This is the thesis of Philippe Val, former director of *Charlie Hebdo*, who went from singing the anti-racist refrain "immigrant, make yourself at home," to calling for the expulsion of that same immigrant. But you have to imagine the implications of the idea of re-migration, politically and in terms of enforcement. We are talking about removing French citizenship from people who were born here, and deporting them to countries where they are not citizens. This would require not only a national revolution in France, but also a European revolution—as well as the agreement of the countries receiving them. It is a political fiction scenario with a very high level of violence. In the world as it is, it is impossible.

However, re-migration at the individual level makes sense. There are people who tell me that they feel increasingly ill at ease in France and want to return to their country of origin. Their social prospects are blocked, they feel under suspicion and cannot practice their religion in peace. One can understand that voluntary re-migration could be an option for these people. But this re-migration could only be a solution at the individual or family level.

The "Third Way"

There is a third way: that of our organization Equality and Reconciliation. France is what it is—that is to say, as De Gaulle put it, "a white European country, of Greco-Roman culture and Christian religion." But there was a colonial adventure, ardently desired by the freemasonic Third Republic. This colonization amounted to forcing people to be French—people who had never asked for any such thing. Then there was decolonization, followed by immigration from our former colonies. This is what created the current French situation. This immigration has become dysfunctional, absurd and disastrous since the family reunification law imposed by our irresponsible elites in 1975—especially since, on top of that, they have been promoting multiculturalism to prevent assimilation. But a multiracial country is a multi-racist country. Given this situation, we will have to work hard to re-assimilate assimilation, that is to say, to make Muslims of immigrant origin into French people—good French people, people who love their country.

It's a real challenge. For if these young people do not like France, they have plenty of good reasons not to. Into what kind of France are we going to assimilate these people? The France of François Hollande, Manuel Valls, Bernard-Henry Levi, Jacques Attali? If it was the France of De Gaulle, Eric Tabarly, Bayard, Du Guesclin, and Saint Louis, it would certainly be easier, even for Muslims. The real problem today is that if we want to save France by assimilating struggling populations, we will first have to dislodge the illegitimate elites who have been speaking on behalf of France. And we will have to rid ourselves through the electoral process—because it is the least violent way—of all the people who claim to speak on our behalf and who purport to be managing a crisis they themselves have entirely created since 1975. The guilt is shared by both left and right.

"Equality and Reconciliation" is possible provided we re-commit ourselves to assimilation. We all have to find ourselves fully French and loving France. This requires that France become lovable again. Yet to-day France is odious to young people from the suburban ghettos, and it is not very pleasant for ethnic French people either. On the one side are people who hate it, and on the other people who have a hard time liking it. Why would I, if I were twenty, love the France of François Hollande and Manuel Valls? That France is neither likable nor respectable; and moreover it is no longer respected— because of its foreign policy, its grotesque elites, and even its lousy writers. We have totally lost our prestige and respectability. And so our youth, whether of native or immigrant origin, does not like this country. The former can no longer love her; while the latter, whose roots harken back to colonial conflict, hate her.

Jihadism and instrumentalization of the young

"Jihadism" is a symptom of the instrumentalization of young people through the ideology of "the young." The jihadists are not people 40 or 50 years old. They are not scholars of Islam, ready to sacrifice themselves to rejoin God. These are adolescents and post-adolescents, raised in rough neighborhoods of mob rule and de-socialization, re-Islamized recently and superficially, participating in a crisis initiated in the year 1968 as part of a strategy of domination: the apotheosis of the adolescent. It is the ideology of "wild at heart" and the "rebel without a cause"— whose other name is "obnoxious little bastard." This ideology essentially aimed at killing the father: that is to say the reasonable adult male, the patriarch, the one who could withstand the onslaught of capital, the vulgarity of money, and the immorality of consumption. The father is the one who conveys authority and, through identification with him, the transition from teenage to adult status. They destroyed the father with feminism and with "young" ideology.

Jihadism today is a cancer emanating from this strategy of the omnipotence of adolescence in our societies. All these jihadists are teenagers who fail to make the transition to adulthood and therefore are unable to plan for a future. The thing all these scum have in common is that they are unable to think ahead beyond a few weeks. That is why they are so easily manipulated. They act quickly and impulsively, unable to see themselves in jail or dead. According to recordings, the night before the attack, one of the Bataclan jihadists was screaming that he wanted to get paid right away, without understanding that he would die the next day. When you are preparing to die for God, you do not think of your dough the day before.[279]

We recognize here typical teenage behavior of someone unable to move forward into adulthood with a life plan: find a wife, start a family, have children, and be able to support them by working. The real cause of the events of November 13th is the manipulation of young people who have failed to become adults, with all their energy exploding into violence because they are unable to project themselves into the role of a responsible adult, for lack of a model with which to identify.

Ultimately, all this has nothing to do with Islam. But it has everything to do with a catastrophic crisis of the adolescent strategy of degenerate capitalism.

This whole story is a story of mindless young idiots: young wankers on the side of the bobos, and hysterically violent young men on the side of the scum. This hyperviolence is a teenage thing. Men at 45 or 50 don't do collective brawls. The people sent to die in wars are twenty-year-olds. Being prepared to die to prove you're a man, full of testosterone and energy, is a characteristic of teenagers.

CALLING TAKFIR ON TAKFIRIS AND TERRORISM

Rasheed al Ḥājj

Murder of innocents, even in the context of war, is strictly forbidden in the Qur'ān (5:32). This is incontrovertible. Suicide is also explicitly forbidden in the Qur'ān (4:29-30). Therefore, whether the terror attack of 11.13.15—Paris part deux—proves to be a political "false flag" or not, it is unalterably a religious imposter. This is to say that, whether the atrocities were carried out by ISIS sympathizers or by Israeli Mossad and French black ops forces, to attribute these actions to Islām is to raise a false flag over acts of terror.

Calling takfīr is a dangerous practice fraught with pitfalls. (Editor's note: To *call takfir* means to accuse a person who considers herself Muslim of being outside of Islam; it is roughly comparable to excommunication in Catholicism. *Takfiris* are extremists who habitually excommunicate, or even execute, their fellow Muslims, while frequently oppressing and killing non-Muslims as well. Daesh/ISIS is an exemplary takfiri group.)

Calling takfīr on takfīris and takfīrism is to court irony, at the very least. To call takfīr on a person or a group is to say that this person or group of people who claim to be Muslim are not truly Muslim. It is uniquely according to takfīri illogic that, in calling takfīr, the takfīri assumes a right to kill the other that the takfīri has deemed to be non-Muslim. This is the exact opposite of Islām.

Claiming to know a person's heart, or their relationship with God, is impossible. Even if the issue of what is in another person's heart were knowable, no one can judge a person's status in the eyes of God but God, and God's judgment is not based on a person's religion. In contrast, the Qur'ān clearly states: "To each of you have We prescribed a law and a way. If Allāh had so willed, He would have made you a single people, but you are to be tested in what He has given you. So race with one another to do good works." (Qur'ān 5:48) It does not say now go out and race to denounce and kill someone because of their faith.

To claim to commit murder and suicide in the name of Islām is an utter abomination. It is not merely a lie. It is a blasphemy. Whoever it is who did commit the 2015 Paris terror attacks, it is unequivocally stated here that these are not acts of people who have submitted to God. They are definitely not the actions of anyone who understands and follows the Qur'ān on even the most simplistic basis, no less on any more refined or subtle levels.

ISIS and Al Qaeda and their ilk are described as self-proclaimed takfīris. This means that, against the uniform and consistent teachings of the Qur'ān, they claim the right to kill other Muslims by declaring that they are not Muslim. This is what makes them unique. Takfīris are as much outlaws to the Qur'ān as they are to the world. Their doctrine is so completely misguided as to constitute a form of insanity, as their own behavior repeatedly attests.

There are multiple flaws in the basic takfīri arguments at all levels. In the Qur'ān, Muslims are never given leave to kill anyone simply for being non-Muslim. Nor is permission ever given for causing any harm to someone who leaves the religion. To the contrary, the Qur'ān repeatedly asserts the validity of the Torah and the Gospels (Q 2:62, Q 5:69). It proclaims the spiritual friendship of faithful Muslims, Christians, and Jews (Q 48:29), and assures the worldly protection and the soteriological validity of the practices of all sincere Christians and Jews (Q 3:3, Q 5:44-48, Q 5:59-70, Q 5:109-119, Q 6:48, Q 7:157-162).

Indeed, it is categorically asserted in the Qur'ān (2:256) without any reservations or qualifications: "There is no compulsion in religion." *La ikrāha fi deen.* In fact, the Qur'ān directly commands Muslims to give shelter and travel assistance to wayfaring polytheists (Q 9:6). And the Constitution of Medina instituted by the Prophet Muḥammad (peace be upon him) even safeguarded the rights of atheists.

Thus, nothing in the fundamental takfīri schema bears any resemblance whatsoever to a single basic tenet or theme enunciated in the Qur'ān, or in the original practice of Islām as implemented by the Prophet himself (pbuh). Takfīrism is nothing but a deceitful form of theological sophistry that is being employed to create a false justification for murdering and making war primarily against Muslims, as well as against members of other faiths.

As far as promoting an Islāmic state, takfīrism is completely flawed existentially. In every historical form and setting in which it has arisen, it has resoundingly failed as a means to nurture and sustain, to serve and protect life. This is God's chief charge to humankind in the Qur'ān—for humankind to serve as vicegerents, as caretakers of life on earth (Q 2:30). Takfīris fail miserably in this most basic duty. Eleven hundred years ago the Qaramatīya formed a so-called "Islāmic" state. The Qaramatīya were such inept caretakers of life, yet lovers of takfīr, that they slaughtered thousands of innocent Muslim religious pilgrims who were on ḥajj.

But doesn't the Qur'ān promote war? No, it counsels peace over war (8:61). The Qur'ān sets limits on who may be killed and on the levels of destruction even in war (2:190), and it declares as transgressions acts that are also listed as war crimes in the Geneva Conventions. A vast multitude of scholars of Islām from every era agree that it is clearly prohibited to kill children, the elderly, and adult non-combatants, or to destroy trees, livestock, agricultural crops or land, i.e. Islām forbids the targeting of societal infrastructure or innocent civilians.

Compare that to the deaths in Gaza of 1,500 Palestinians, of whom 500 were children, in a three week long Israeli operation known as "Cast Lead" in 2009, wherein the skin melting banned weapon White Phosphorous was used by Israeli forces against the Palestinians; or the millions of tons of Depleted Uranium ordnance fired by the U.S. which is causing grotesque birth anomalies and widespread cancer throughout the theatre of the global war of terror; or the continuing murder of thousands of innocent civilians in over a decade of drone strikes by the U.S. across the Muslim world; or the millions killed in the wars begun by the U.S. coalition in Afghanistan in 2001 and with the "Shock and Awe" bombing of Iraq in 2003; or the U.N. sanctions during the first Gulf War that led to the deaths of 500,000 to 1,500,000 Iraqi children in the 1990s; or the destruction of ninety percent of the 20 million acre date forest bordering the Shatt al Arab/Arvand Rūd waterway and its delta on the Persian Gulf that was destroyed in the eight year long Iran Iraq war in the 1980s, in which millions of innocent citizens of both nations were killed. Both sides were trained, armed, and supplied by the U.S. and NATO countries, with banned chemical weapons being sold to Iraq. And let's not forget the defoliation and cancerous toxification of Viet Nam, when the U.S. military drenched it with Agent Orange (2,4,5-T & 2,4-D) in the 1960s and 70s; or the millions of souls in Cambodia and Laos wiped out in the carpet bombing ordered by Henry Kissinger in 1969; not least the 100 million indigenous Native Americans who were slaughtered along with tens of millions of bison, both nearly to extinction, in the genocidal settling/invasion of North America by Europeans after 1492. And that barely scratches the surface of the West's monument of war crimes against people who never attacked them.

Takfīrism operates in similar fashion, by killing and destroying indiscriminately, and by promoting oppression and violence which is directed both externally, and internally within its own society. A brutal form of official control, it promotes a war/military/police ideology of state violence against civilians. Being the projections of Western style police state militarism, Al Qaeda and ISIS are both takfīri groups in their methods and stated beliefs, and their publicized horrors are well known. But from whence did they arise? According to its own documents, the CIA first attempted to stir up and organize takfīri "jihadism" among Uzbeks to destabilize the USSR in 1952. This nascent campaign was reinvigorated in 1979 in Afghanistan under Kissinger's successor as U.S. National Security Advisor, Zbigniew Breszinski. This led to the creation of Al Qaeda, "the Base," which was simply the CIA's database of its jihadist operatives, later blamed for the 9/11 false flag attack. No wonder that in some circles it is known as al-CIA-duh. When asked about the CIA and Al Qaeda by *Le Nouvel Observateur* in January 1998, Breszinski famously stated:

> Breszinski: "That secret operation was an excellent idea. It had the effect of drawing the Russians into the Afghan trap and you want me to regret it? The day that the Soviets officially crossed the border, I wrote to President Carter we now have the opportunity of giving to the USSR its Vietnam war. Indeed, for almost ten years, Moscow had to carry on a war unsupportable by the government, a conflict that brought about the demoralization and finally the breakup of the Soviet empire."

> Q: And neither do you regret having supported the Islamic fundamentalism, having given arms and advice to future terrorists?

> Breszinski: "What is most important to the history of the world? The Taliban or the collapse of the Soviet empire? Some stirred-up Muslims or the liberation of Central Europe and the end of the Cold War?"

What about ISIS? It consists of some 30,000 mercenaries from over eighty-five countries. Paid by the Saudis, armed by the U.S., trained by U.S./NATO forces in Turkey and Jordan, supplied by U.S. air-dropped shipments in Iraq, provided U.S. surface to air missiles transferred from Libya after its fall, their wounded are treated in Israeli run hospitals in the Golan Heights. Of note is the 5 August 1990 CSPAN interview of Dan Raviv, co-author of *Every Spy A Prince*, the first published history of the Mossad. After personally questioning then Israeli Prime Minister Yitzhak Shamir about what English acronym or initials he should use to designate the Mossad, he was told that the proper designation was ISIS, for Israeli Secret Intelligence Services. It came straight from the horse's mouth.

We watch wan troglodyte takfīris, addled with the power ceded to them by their imperialist handlers, commit unspeakable atrocities, videos of which are bandied about to the public on television and the internet, after being discovered by/on U.S. and Israeli-linked intelligence gathering, i.e. agitprop generating, websites. While photographic evidence shows us ISIS videos being created on sound stages, Paris is dramatically hit twice. Media-fueled public fear of false flag horrors now revives the motivation, the will, and a precipitating excuse to spur globalist imperialists to work harder to destroy Muslim culture and kill Muslims by waging highly profitable wars of division and conquest across the entire Muslim world, from East Asia to Eastern Europe, the Middle East and Africa, all planned and directed out of the united power centers of Washington, D.C., New York, London, Paris, and Tel Aviv.

The evil behind the ill begotten misconception of calling fatal takfīr has deep historical roots. The Muslims who first concocted takfīrism were the khawārij, over thirteen centuries ago. It is by no means a modern invention. Nor is it limited to Muslims or Islām. Universally committed, it is a human failing that knows no boundaries of culture, religion, place, or era. Fatal takfīr has been practiced by Tibetan Buddhist monks in the governments of various Panchen and Dalai Lamas, as well as by the Chinese invaders who have more recently sought to politically control or exterminate them. Fatal takfīr was the chief activity of the Catholic Inquisitions, and it was one of the *raisons d'être* of the Catholic crusaders and missionaries in both the Old and New Worlds. It is the force that motivated the Holocaust and the Nakba.

Takfīr, taken to its endpoint, embodies the essence of genocide. The practice of takfīr creates a meme of group otherization. It draws a line around a community of people, as defined by perceived differences in, or false assertions about, their religious and cultural beliefs and practices, and then denounces them as coverers of the truth, the truth being whatever the takfīri decides it to be. Takfīris then use their spuriously derived conclusions as the excuse to target Muslims whom they have marked for elimination, dispossessing them of their human rights to the exercise of free will and to life, and seizing their worldly goods, their lands and resources amidst the carnage. It thus conforms to the definition of genocide.

Similar behavior is seen elsewhere in the animal kingdom only among insects, in a subset of species of ants and bees known as kleptoparasites. They invade and occupy the nests or hives of other species, kill or enslave the inhabitants, eat the young, and replace the queen with their own. Takfīrism finds its only behavioral parallel in the kleptoparasitism of the insect world. It is insectoid behavior which we as humans must evolve beyond.

Takfīrism is but a variant of age old xenophobic iterations. Would-be conquerors first call names before they kill en masse. Pejorative terms like barbarians, cannibals, redskins, darkies, gooks, dirty A-rabs, among others, have all been used to reduce our natural inhibitions against hatred and killing other human beings, to soften and direct the wills of the speakers and the hearers of those epithets. The strategic aim to exterminate finds its implementation via this otherization which eliminates a people's identity as human beings. After targeting the culture of the people, ultimately the people themselves are eliminated.

The Islāmophobia industry practices its own form of takfīr in the media. To use the meme "radical Muslim terrorism," or to call all Muslims terrorists or jihadists, is to call takfīr on them in the context of Western civil society, to otherize and dehumanize all Muslims, and to make them ripe for extermination. Takfīris are thus dupes, "useful idiots" to oppressors whom they claim to fight, but who are manipulating them to bring about their extinction.

Regardless of what degree of sincerity may be present in any modern Muslim takfīri's heart, anyone choosing to follow that doctrine commits a truly horrific error of judgement.

Takfīrism is now a tool of engineered global imperialist policy, both by design and default. Either way, it is projected by means of ghastly acts of mass terrorism against innocents, including proxy wars of aggression against other Muslims. Terrible casualties of every kind—physical, spiritual, social, ecological, and economic—are inflicted with malevolent intentions to discredit, to otherize, to demonize, and finally to completely destroy Islām as a religion and as a culture, and as a positive force for human civilization.

Thus, without fear of irony, takfīr has been called on takfīris, takfīrism, and terrorism.

There is yet hope. "Those who have been driven from their homes unjustly only because they said 'Our lord is God,' were it not for God checking one people by another, surely many monasteries, churches, synagogues, and mosques where the names of God are mentioned frequently would have been destroyed." (Q 22:40) "O you who believe, remain steadfast for Allah in witness to justice and let not hatred of a people cause you to deviate from justice. Be just. It is closer to piety." (Q 5:8)

Calling takfīr on takfīris is risky.
    Ironic or not, it's a duty that's necessary.
YouAintNoMuslimBruv, not when you kill.
    Murder is not surrender to God. It is ill.
You ain't no Muslim, bro, not when you rape.
    That puts you far below on the scale, beneath apes.
You ain't no Muslim, akh, ruling through fear.
    Take your portrait down. Who needs to see it all year?
Talk can be cheap. Yet some speech is so dear
    that it costs human lives. Truth wracks tyrants with fear.
Dicis de mortuis nil nisi bonum.
    Say nothing but good of the dead. Aught. Say quonam?
Whether or not you believe in the akhira,
    It is still best to develop good character.
Character here in the here and the now
    will not fail you, no matter what, who, why, where, how.
Building good character, that was his mission,
    not bullets nor warheads, not fusion nor fission.
Try letting live, being loving and kind.
    The rewards you receive will blow your human mind.
Nevertheless, has the West bombed the Muslim world?
    Yes. It has sought to destroy, commit genocide,
Trump up invasions from falsified terror,
    a plague of wars brought by war jobbers inside.
Inside, they are all corrupt to the core,
    these self dealers in war, pimps and whores on a ride.
Minarets, mosques, culture, ummah are targeted.
    Centuries wiped away. Millions have died.
False flag militias are made to fight wars.
    These scum murder the ummah. They spread suicide.
They blow up everything, make themselves corpses.
    Their doctrines are poison Islām can't abide.
Nor are they equal, the good and the evil deeds. Q41:34
    Drive away evil with that which is better.   Q41:34
Save someone's life, you save all of humanity.   Q5:32
    Murder one soul, murder all of humanity.   Q5:32
These are the words of Allāh ~ love, not hatred ~
    And all people, each human life, God made sacred.
Strive to be merciful. Practice compassion.
    Allāh's names show qualities with which we're fashioned.
Strive for the Truth and be truthful.
    Al Ḥaqq is the goal of sincere seekers, not golden clocks.

Since Al Musawwir shapes form out of function ~
    aesthetics, perception are made in conjunction.
This friend gives thanks to Allāh for sensation.
    But one needed organ now suffers negation.
We've nearly lost our most precious of senses.
    We need and must cultivate digital genesis ~
Not limned by zeroes and ones, but our thumbs.
    We've lost touch with what is truly human, gone numb.
We need to reclaim and regain our thumbs,
    and not focus on screens, but on faces from wombs.
True elevation means that of all humankind.
    Otherwise our race will be to our tombs.
Many appear not to have moral thumbs.
    They can't grasp life's significance. They have no qualms.
We want our thumbs. We're opposed to those lacking
    opposable thumbs, those without moral backing.
Moral negation means not being human.
    Primordial nature provides the solution.
We must attune to our fiṭra ~ the gift of
    God's nature. Primordial deen heals the rift. Q30:30
War hawks will seek to promote revolution.
    Ignore that. What we need is more evolution.
More than mere political nomenclature,
    we need that which brings out our most human nature.
We need advancement in moral behavior.
    Islām improves character ~ fiṭra's its nature. Q30:30
Do not apologize for people over whom
    you have no power. Don't give them that cover.
They are not Muslims who torture and wantonly
    kill and destroy. Don't succumb to the taunting.
Don't try to justify. Do not excuse.
    Don't accept the presumptions from those who accuse.
They do not practice Islām. These takfīri
    warmongers are innovators, mercenaries,
Cutouts, imperial stooges and shills,
    kafirūn, so misguided it gives one the chills.
Do not apologize. Morally educate.
    Guide on the path to becoming more human.
Do not surrender your thumbs. Get a grip.
    Wield your moral free will. Use Allāh's greatest gift.

THE KHAWARIJ PHENOMENON: A FALSE-FLAG WAR ON THE MUSLIM UMMAH

Zaid Hamid

"Turkey is dead and will never rise again, because we have destroyed its moral strength, the Caliphate and Islam."
                                              –Lord Curzon, 1924.[280]

The above-quoted proclamation of then British foreign secretary Curzon gaudily established two fundamental aspects of long term strategic planning of Western powers vis-a-vis the Muslim world and Islam. Firstly, the division of Muslim lands into many nation states, under secret agreement between Britain and France, was part of a greater a political scheme which completely changed the world's geography and politics. Secondly, the destruction of political Islamic ideals like *Caliphate* and *Sharia laws* was the pivot of this Western strategy.

Apart from these obvious realities there is a hidden message embedded in this proclamation as well: the determination to not let the Muslim world gain its political, military and moral strength to challenge Western political and financial models like Western democracy, communism, capitalism, socialism, nationalism and international money lending empires run through the likes of the Bank of England and the Federal Reserve.

The crisis has deep historical roots. Plans to topple the Ottoman Empire were hatched in the late 15ᵗʰ century, shortly after the conquest of Constantinople by Ottoman Turk general Sultan Muhammad Fateh. For the following two hundred years, the Islamic Caliphate continued to expand in Eastern and Central Europe. By the end of the 17ᵗʰ century, the Empire was at its political zenith. But this vast expansion created its own share of political, administrative and social problems for the Caliphate, including the rise of regionalism and tribal nationalism.

In the battle of Zenta, in 1699, the Ottoman side was defeated and lost huge territories comprising modern day Hungary, Bosnia and Herzegovina, Croatia, and Slavonia. This battle was the last clash of the Austro-Ottoman Wars which lasted for 14 years (1683-97).[281] These protracted and costly wars against the expanding Russian influence had put the Muslim Caliphate under huge debt to French banks which were actually owned by Jewish bankers. So the financial stagnation of the Muslim Empire also began around the same time. The nexus between these bankers and Western anti-Islamic political forces was natural because Islam, in its political incarnation, had emerged as the ultimate challenge for the Western political as well as financial models.

Ottoman Empire at its political Zenith

In order to maintain their political and financial clout in Europe, it was imperative for these two forces to conspire against the Ottoman Empire. Social and political disorder along with weak administration was prevalent in some parts of the Ottoman Empire since the late 18th century. But large scale political upheaval in the central provinces of Hijaz, Syria and Iraq by Arab tribes against the Caliphate began in the 19th century when European countries started to penetrate these provinces and launch their covert subversive operations. Western bankers and strategists had found new allies against the Caliphate: the Arab tribes. By the end of the 19th century, the Ottoman Empire was reduced to modern day Turkey and a few parts of the Middle East. The first World War ended with Western colonial powers occupying virtually all of the Ottoman provinces. In order to gain its present day territory back, Turkey had to accept treaty of Lausanne which effectively ended the institution of the Caliphate in 1924. The decision saved Turkey—but destroyed the central governing institution Muslims had maintained since the Rashideen Caliphate almost 1300 years earlier.

The real Zionist plans for the Ottoman Empire (and for the entire Muslim world) came to light after the Balfour declaration, in which the British Crown decided to create the state of Israel on Palestinian lands. A letter was sent from then British foreign secretary Lord Balfour to the Zionist banker Baron Rothschild at a crucial moment during World War One, essentially accepting the Zionist offer to break the military deadlock by using Jewish financial and media influence to drag the US into the war and hand victory to the British—in return for the British promise to hand over Palestine. The "Balfour Declaration" was later incorporated into the Sèvres peace treaty which was signed before the treaty of Lausanne extending the British mandate to Palestine. This was at least 30 years before the creation of the state of Israel. But this letter openly outlined the British Empire's policies for the future as well.

The map of the Muslim world was redrawn, creating different nation states based on Arab nationalism. It was later revealed by the British that their policy was to instigate a conflict amongst the Arabs through the Arabs themselves, so the world would not blame the West for the destruction of the Muslim lands. Now if Damascus fell, it would be to Arabs. If Baghdad were captured, Arab groups would be blamed. This is exactly what began to happen as the Muslim Ottoman Empire remained oblivious to internal challenges. At the beginning of the 20th century, the political turmoil had crossed the critical threshold. Abdul Aziz ibn Saud attacked and occupied the fortress at Riyadh, killing the Ottoman governor.[282]

This history is relevant today as once again, the geography of the entire Muslim world is being redrawn to further divide the Muslim nation states along ethnic, sectarian and linguistic lines with the end goal of expanding the borders of the State of Israel. Once again local tribal and religious groups have resurfaced to help the Zionist forces in pursuance of their ultimate political agenda in the region.

Who are these militant groups? How do they emerge? And from where do they gain so much power enabling them to challenge the entire Islamic World? What is the historical background of the present rise of extremism and terrorism within Muslim world? What is the role of major global players in creating the present chaos? And most importantly, how can Muslim societies be saved from this violent frenzy?

Emergence of Khawarijism
As told in ahadeeth of Prophet Muhammad (sm)
In Islamic history the first emergence of such groups was recorded during the time of Prophet Muhammad (sm) when Muslim forces returned from the battle of Hunain and war booty was being distributed among the poor and the needy. What transpired there has been recorded in many authentic narrations. These ahadeeth not only explain the emergence of Khawarijism in the time of Prophet Muhammad (sm) but also expose the mindset, character, thought process and strategy of these "dogs of hell" (as they have been called in sayings of the Holy Prophet).

By carefully analyzing these ahadeeth, the identifying traits of the Khawarij can be summarized as follows:
- They would recite the Quran but it won't go down their throats. They will exit the Deen like an arrow going through prey and emerging without a trace. In salat and fasting they would pretend to be better than others.
- They would talk as if their words were the best among the creatures. But they would be worst of the creatures under the sky. They are dogs of hell!

- They would have shaved heads. They would be people of young age with no wisdom of deen at all.
- They will appear from the east. They will keep emerging till the Day of Judgment. Their last group would emerge along with Dajjal (Antichrist).
- The Khawarij would raise slogans from Quran like "there is no command but Allah's." This is true—but Khawarij would use it for the wrong cause. Similarly, they would twist other verses of Quran against Muslims, even those verses which are directed at infidels. In this process, they would call takfir on Muslims who would not agree with their beliefs.
- The Khawarij would emerge whenever there is dissension amongst the Muslims.
- Battling the Khawarij would be rewarded on the Day of Judgment and the army that would fight against these people would be the best army.

Khawarijism During the Rashideen Caliphate

Certain tribes never accepted Islam as their new code of life but instead had their own pre-Islamic political and financial agendas to follow. During the times of first Caliph Abu Bakar (R.A.) these tribes fought in Ridda wars against the apostates who had refused to pay Zakat. After these wars, they were remunerated with the highest pay in the Muslim army; and they also got trusteeship of most fertile lands in the area. As their motives were desire for political clout and wealth, they came to regard these lands as their private domain—which contradicted Islamic teachings. These conquered lands belonged to the Islamic state and not to any individual.

In Iraq, these groups gained considerable influence around Kufa and came to be known as Qurra and later as the Khawarij, due to their political and military revolts against the Islamic Caliphate. Many historians have recorded the events of that time illustrating the selfishness and greed of these tribes. In "Modern Intellectual Readings of Kharijites", historian M.A. Saban writes: "The Qurra received stipends varying from 2000 to 3000 Dirhams while the majority (of Muslim forces) received only 250 to 300 Dirhams."[283]

These Qurra launched their rebellion against Caliph Usman (R.A) when the Caliph decided to reduce their undue status and demands, and declined to give them more lands in Persia.[284] The Caliph took these measures following his predecessor Caliph Umar Ibn Al-Khattab (R.A.) when he refused to allot lands to the Muslim soldiers and commanders in the areas conquered by Muslims in Iran, Iraq and Syria. [285] This move by Umar (R.A) infuriated these tribes. Later on, the Caliph had to make the ultimate sacrifice to uphold Islamic principles.

These Qurra (later known as Khawarij) never accepted the basic principle of equality and justice in Islam and kept on demanding more and more privileges, just like in the pre-Islamic days of the Persian-Byzantine Wars. To ensure fairness, Caliph Usman (R.A) later removed the distinction between the Ridda and pre-Ridda tribesmen, which was not to their liking as it lessened their prestige.[286]

After many years of constant troublemaking, the Qurra/Khawarij split up and went to different Muslim power centers and started fomenting rebellion, particularly in Egypt.

At the same time, Caliph Usman (R.A.) was busy planning to launch a major military campaign to Constantinople through the Mediterranean Sea. Muawiyah (R.A.) was ordered to prepare a Muslim naval armada to open up the sea for future expeditions. The first major naval battle between the Islamic naval fleet and the Byzantine navy took place in the Battle of Masts in which, within a matters of days, the Muslim navy demolished the Byzantine navy completely with Emperor Constans retreating back to Constantinople.[287] This battle took place in 655 AD. Victory here was significant as now Islamic forces were poised to launch more naval campaigns towards Constantinople. But the gravest tragedy in Muslim history occurred the following year; Caliph Usman (R.A.) was assassinated by Qurra (Khawarij) tribes in Madina. Suddenly, the Byzantine Empire had found a new strategic ally within the ranks of the Muslims. (Unfortunately, this nefarious nexus exists even today.)

Events which took place after the assassination of Caliph Usman (R.A.) severely damaged the Muslim military campaigns towards the Roman Empire. Though the Qurra (Khawarij) were responsible for assassination of the Caliph, they began to confuse everyone in Madina by adopting a very shrewd stratagem to create division among the Muslims. They deliberately raised the issue of Qisas (blood money) of Caliph Usman's martyrdom through their propaganda and deception. Muslims were without any caliph or any nominee to be the next ruler. It was a complete political breakdown. For the Muslim elite, finding the next Caliph posed a huge problem. A group of people asked Ali (R.A.) to take the matters in hand which he did but very reluctantly.

This fact has been recorded by Ali (R.A.) himself in Nehj ul Balagah: "I did not approach the people to get their oath of allegiance but they came to me with their desire to make me their Amir (ruler). I did not extend my hands towards them so that they might swear the oath of allegiance to me but they themselves extended their hands towards me."[288]

The selection of Ali (R.A.) as next Caliph of Islam was a bad omen for those who had actually assassinated Usman (R.A.). They started to spread rumors and made getting Qisas (retribution) for Usman (R.A.) a more urgent issue than the political stability of the Muslim State. Ali (R.A.) wanted to punish the assassins of Usman (R.A) after settling the political crisis, but the Khawarij understood that a former judge and man of unquestioned integrity like Ali (R.A.) would soon expose them. They upped the ante and started to spread the confusion among the Muslims which led to the first intra-Muslim civil war. The battle of Saffin and the later Battle of Jamal occurred due to their propaganda. Muslims killed each other in thousands during these wars.[289] The only beneficiaries were the Khawarij and the crumbling Byzantine Empire.

During the rule of Ali (R.A.) the fitna of Khawarij became a serious threat to the entire Muslim state, to the point that the Caliph himself had to lead military expeditions against these rebels who were defeated during the battle of Naharwan in 658 AD.[290] Most of the Khawarij were eliminated during the battle but few of them survived and reappeared three years later when, in 661 AD, they plotted a triple assassination plan against Ali (RA), Muawiyah (RA) and Amar Ibn al-As (R.A.). Both Muawiyah and Amar Ibn al-As survived the attempts but the strike against Ali (R.A) in Kufa proved fatal.

After these initial troubles which created undying divisions among the Muslims, the Khawarij kept emerging during the coming centuries and creating troubles within the Muslim Caliphate. The radical anarchist ideology of the Assassins emerged later during the 10th century and wreaked havoc within Muslim society for almost 200 years, during and after the times of Crusades. The great Kurdish Sultan of Syria and Egypt, Salahuddin Ayubi, had to fight and subdue the Assassins within Muslim society before he could attack and counterattack the invading Crusaders from the West. Salahuddin, like the early caliphs, suffered assassination attempts by the same Khawarij.

It is interesting that the English word Assassin has come from the Arabic word Hashashin, meaning those who use Hashish or intoxicating drugs.[291] The murderous thugs of the Order of the Assassins cult were drugged with hashish and then sent on dangerous suicide missions within the Muslim world, committing murders, sabotage and terrorism. Hence the word *assassin* came to be used in Western languages to mean a hidden, terrorist murderer. In mid-nineteenth century, a German historian, Von Hammer, wrote *The History of the Assassins*, in which he vividly explains their murderous practices and cult ideology, which almost succeeded in overrunning the entire Muslim heartland, and even came close to assassinating Sultan Salahuddin during the peak of the Crusades.[292] Even Salahuddin could not finish off the cloak and dagger cult of the Order of the Assassins, who were finally, decisively and ruthlessly eliminated by the rampaging Mongol armies which had also overrun the Capital of the Caliphate in Baghdad in the 13th century AD. But just as they had done after the battle of Naharwan, a few of them escaped to resurface yet again—which is what they have been doing ever since.

And they are still with us. Bernard Lewis, a Zionist Jew and leading advisor to British and Israeli intelligence agencies, is widely viewed as the chief architect of the West's geostrategic plan to to create an army of mercenary terrorists and fanatics, modeled on the Assassins, to undermine the Islamic world and enable Israeli expansionism. In his article "Islamic Terrorism?" Lewis implicitly called for the West to create a wave of phony "Islamic terrorism" to rally the West against Islam on behalf of Israel; this, Lewis suggests, is *How the West Can Win* (the title of Netanyahu's book in which Lewis's essay appears.) Lewis's Western-manufactured pseudo-Muslim terrorists of al-Qaeda and ISIS are today's khawarij.

So once again today, just like during the Crusades, the Muslim world is again facing two prongs of opposing violent, fascist, political ideologies—Crusading Zionists and the Assassin Khawarij— fighting within the Muslim world for control, power, influence and turf.

The Way Forward

We need to understand that there are only three major Muslim countries left which can play any decisive role in the Ummah. They are Turkey, Iran and Pakistan; there is no more Iraq, Syria, Jordan, Saudi Arabia or Egypt left in real terms! It is a sad reality of regional geopolitics. These countries are all on the verge of collapse, too weak to play any substantial role now, and about to become part of "Greater Israel."

Multiple fault lines have been activated in these countries by internal and external enemies. Sectarian, ISIS, TTP, FSA, PKK and other Khawarij gangs are waging civil wars while US/NATO/India are planning to expand their military intervention to create further anarchy in the region.

Building and Presenting Our Own Narrative

The Khawarij's biggest strength is their narrative which provides the basis for their strategy of deception. Destroying this twisted narrative remains the most fundamental imperative for any counter-strategy.

Keeping in view the sensitivity of these matters and ensuing sectarian intolerance this is a delicate undertaking which cannot be left to any single state in Muslim world.

Since all present day Khawarij gangs claim to be "sunnis," it is the primary responsibility of the Sunni Muslims and Sunni-majority countries to respond to the Khawarij ruthlessly using Sunni narratives and scholarly work. The Shia narrative cannot help to destroy the ideological basis of the Khawarij, who have hijacked Sunni Islam.

The Khawarij are a common threat to both Sunni and Shia Muslims. The Khawarij are NOT Sunnis, despite their claims, and in authentic Sunni traditions they are considered as damnable heretics. So ideally, Sunni Muslims states must lead and form a panel of prominent scholars to build a counter-narrative on issues like terrorism, takfir and Khawarijism. In the next phase, Muslim states and policymakers should transform that narrative into state policies regarding the aforementioned issues. A political consensus among Muslim nation states is the most fundamental requirement to cope with strategic challenges posed by the state of Israel and other foreign hostile forces occupying different parts of the Muslim heartland.

Combined Military Alliance

The last 100 years of history of the Muslim world in the colonial and post-colonial era provide irrefutable testimony that Muslim nation states continue to face perils to their sovereignty and territorial integrity if they fail to develop a collective security response.

Redrawing the Middle East to create "Greater Israel" is a nefarious plan hatched by the West/NATO/US which poses a combined military threat to the sovereignty of every Muslim nation state. Iraq, Libya, Tunisia, Syria, Jordan, Yemen, and Somalia, have already been neutralized. Pakistan is already under advanced levels of attack. Iran and Turkey are the next on the target list.

Today none of these countries is capable of defeating the military prong of this existential threat alone. This necessitates a combined Muslim military alliance along the lines of NATO. Due to prevailing geopolitical issues within the Muslim world, inclusion of all the states in this alliance may not be possible initially. But Pakistan, Iran and Turkey must establish a combined forum of defense experts, foreign policymakers and military chiefs to work out the broader contours of a military alliance with its own charter to undertake not only a military response to internal and external threats faced by Muslim nation states but also to conduct humanitarian security operations all across the Muslim world. The concept of a Muslim peacekeeping force must be seriously developed into a working strategy.

Evaluation of Warfare and Khawarijism

In 21st century geopolitics, the lines between political, religious and military conflicts have become blurred. This makes response building extremely difficult, as holistic threat perception itself becomes a cumbersome task. For these reasons new era warfare has been categorized as "4th Generation Warfare" also known as 4GW.

In simplistic terms, 4GW is political and psychological conflict using distributed, non-state and violent elements from within the targeted enemy state itself. Creating mistrust among enemy communities and propagating uncertainty among enemy nations are amongst the many goals of any 4th generation endeavor. 4th generation warfare is very different from high-intensity physical conflict between nations. 4GW is entirely based on asymmetrical warfare tactics, while the major front is psychological, and not physical as in a real conflict. Broadly analyzed, it can be said that national cohesion becomes a primary target of such a warfare model. The importance of destroying national unity and creating mistrust becomes all the more relevant when the enemy is an ideological state like Pakistan.

At the tactical level, various maneuvers and elements are employed to achieve these goals like rear area operations and supporting armed insurgencies and terrorism on one hand, and centrifugal forces in the enemy's political system, media and civil society on the other. The information and political war waged by the fifth columnists and traitors within the country supporting armed insurgences can demoralize the nation and the armed forces into submission, confusion and surrender.

Economic manipulation, whenever possible, can also serve as a tool in this kind of warfare. Fragile economic conditions in enemy states have always proved conducive in 4th generation warfare, as economic crisis makes it much easier to manipulate the masses into agitation and civil disorders.

What is transpiring across the entire swathe of the Muslim heartland —from Pakistan to the Middle East to Northern Africa—is a continuation of the old wars with the old political agenda of keeping Muslim populaces divided on religious, political, sectarian and economic lines in order to debilitate the idea of a United State of Islam or a united Islamic Caliphate. The internal violent forces of Khawarij have become an integral element in destroying Muslim societies from within, fully backed and armed by the invading Western Crusaders and Hindu Zionists.

Since the collapse of communism, capitalism and democracy have been on the brink of failure, and humanity has been in search of an alternate political and financial model. Islam, as a political and financial system, has remained a viable model. This explains the present phase of the Crusades against the Muslim heartland. Revival of Islam as a political force would pose serious challenges to the Western powers; and more importantly it would end the Zionist dream of creating "Greater Israel" in the heart of the Muslim world.

In the post-9/11 scenario, new 4th Generation war strategy and tactics employed to further divide the Muslim lands have been so complex that very few analysts from within the Muslim world have been able to understand the entire spectrum. The American "Global War on Terrorism" (GWOT) has engulfed the entire West Asia, Middle East and Northern Africa. The very foundations of the nation states in this region are being shaken, and a violent phenomenon of religious militancy and terrorism has emerged.

To further understand the present crisis and role of Khawarij along with other militant forces (both homegrown and foreign-funded) let's analyze the two states, as case studies, which have been affected the most during the current phase of this war.

Case Study: Iraq

Today, nearly 100 years after the Balfour declaration, Israel is planning to greatly expand its borders. After WWI, the concept of a state of Israel was declared. After WWII, Israel was created in 1948 and now a new World War has been launched whose objective is the creation of "Greater Israel" on the lands which belong to the Muslim States of Syria, Iraq, Jordan, Egypt, Lebanon and even Saudi Arabia. The destruction of the Muslim countries falling within this region of "Greater Israel" is the critical objective of this war.

The proposed map of "Greater Israel"—the area that Israel considers its "promised land"—can be found on the Web. It will span from the outskirts of Baghdad, through Kurdistan and Syria, and will include all of Israel, Lebanon, Jordan and parts of Egypt all the way to Medina. It looks like a big snake that plans to engulf the Muslim world. To destroy all the Muslim countries, they are using these so-called "Muslim" groups, just like they used Arab tribes after WWI to destroy the Ottoman Empire. It's the same strategy, the same policy. (It's impossible that a real Islamic "caliphate" could arise in the heart of "Greater Israel" and America, Israel and UK would do nothing about it.)

After the first Gulf War in 1991-2, all of Saudi Arabia effectively became an American colony. American military fleets came and stayed permanently. The first Gulf war attacked not only the Iraqi State, but also targeted the Iraqi people with a decade of sanctions which killed nearly five million people through disease and famine. Iraq was finally destroyed after 9/11 and the subsequent occupation and civil war, which effectively turned it into a failed state on the verge of dismemberment. The creation of the autonomous Kurd region within Iraq and rise of the Khawarij gangs of ISIS have now sealed that fate.

Usually it is believed that when Al Baghdadi announced his "caliphate," the US, UK and Israel expressed their concern and considered ISIS a genuine Muslim threat. The reality is exactly the opposite. Just as the public perception was stage-managed on the "Iraqi WMDs," the drama of ISIS is also being choreographed in carefully crafted media campaigns by the Western powers.

There is no legitimate caliphate in the Muslim world today. But there is a strong possibility that some day Muslim societies will adopt this model once again. The phony ISIS "caliphate" is a pre-emptive strike intended to de-legitimize the concept.

The current wave of Khawarijism is the most devastating phenomenon in Islamic history. They are not just taking over Muslim lands, they are not just making it easier for the West to create "Greater Israel," they are not just exploiting Muslim women, they are not just burning libraries, they are not just destroying the tombs and graves of the Prophets. They are hijacking Islam as a whole, destroying the entire Muslim civilization from within and creating a false caliphate, made by Khawarij, to represent Islam as a violent political and religious cult. It is a new strategy to eradicate Islam from European societies and present the Caliphate as violent and demonic!

Interestingly, all the ISIS videos feature British youth from various British cities. They're being recruited under the protection of MI6 by an organization called Al Muhajirun. They are openly recruiting ISIS comrades in the UK, cursing the West and calling for the slaughter of Westerners. They are inviting boys to fight against Shias in Syria and Iraq, triggering the sectarian wars within the Muslim world. British government, police and intelligence agencies are complicit and now distributing ISIS flyers and pamphlets, calling for "jihad" in Syria and Iraq, outside British mosques.

The UK and the rest of Europe will greatly benefit from this strategy. They have been able to identify and weed out the Muslims within their societies whom they suspect of having a militant mentality. They hand them a one-way ticket to Syria. This strategy serves multiple objectives. The UK and Europe will rid themselves of extremists and militants while simultaneously instigating sectarian and ethnic battles in the Muslim heartland. Muslim States would be seen to be destroyed by Muslim themselves, with no blame on the West, and the path to "greater Israel" will be paved when Muslim states implode one after another.

Now the European Union has approved the policy of arming Kurd militant groups to fight against ISIS[293]. The question remains, why on earth is the West not supporting the democratic government of Iraq (which they installed themselves after Saddam) to fight against ISIS? The Western strategy is to weaken the states of Syria and Iraq, while strengthening the autonomous militant gangs, who later on will fight against each other, ultimately helping the cause of "Greater Israel."

The most disturbing aspect of this Western strategy is the way Islam as a civilization, ideology and religion is being slandered. The world will perceive that Muslims as a whole, even those living in Europe, are also terrorists, due to the videos released by ISIS, in which the militants are shown committing horrendous crimes—while the viewer is told that they have come here from cities like Manchester and Birmingham. The West is trying to kill many birds with one stone and ISIS Khawarij are their strategic tool in this reshaping of the greater Middle East plan aimed at destroying Islam as an alternate benevolent ideology.

Washington is actually providing ISIS with $500 million dollars in aid, under the label of supporting Syria's 'moderate resistance'.[294] The term "moderate" is used by the US as a mere smoke screen in order to conceal their covert support to ISIS.

The CIA has also been recruiting militants from Guantanamo Bay for future black operations against Muslim countries. Abdullah Mehsud, founder of the so-called Pakistani Taliban (TTP), was a Guantanamo Bay prisoner for three years. In 2004, he was released and created the TTP under the CIA's patronage to wage asymmetric urban war against Pakistan. Similarly, Abu Bakr Baghdadi, ISIS chief, is another prisoner-turned-agent for the CIA, doing in Iraq and Syria exactly what the TTP is doing in Pakistan.

Yet another proof of Zionist forces and Takfiri Khawarij Nexus

Though there are over 100 authentic ahadeeth on Khawarij in the Sunni traditions of Islam, Holy Prophet Muhammad (sm) has also categorically warned us about ISIS! There is a valid hadeeth from Naeem bin Hamad's book, with several others with strong and accepted references proving its authenticity.

The Prophet (sm) said the following about Iraq: that a group of Khawarij will rise and they will create a "daulat." (The word "daulat" is used in hadeeth). ISIS also calls itself Daulat-e Islami. The Prophet also mentioned that they will call themselves by their 'kuniyat' (teknonym) and associate themselves with cities. AbuBakr is his Kuniyat and Baghdadi is the name of his city.

Then there is Abu Musab Zarqawi: Abu Musab is the kuniyat and Zarqa is his city. The Prophet also said that their hearts will be like hard rocks and steel (having no mercy) and they will keep their hair long like women. He also warned that when such groups come out, ordinary people should stay in their homes and not confront them because they will be vicious and brutal and the common man cannot stand up to them. And then the Prophet informs us that Allah will create conflict within these groups through internal strife, and then decide their fate.

Another hadeeth in Sunni traditions tells us that these Khawarij will ultimately take over Damascus. They haven't conquered it yet, but in the future, ISIS may take control of that city. US president Obama has announced an expansion of the battlefield from Iraq to Syria just as he pushed war from Afghanistan to Pakistan using the Af-Pak military strategy and CIA drone wars. It was Af-Pak in Pakistan. It is going to be Sy-Raq in Middle East. Khawarij remain the key tool in both wars for the CIA/Zionists.

Case Study: Pakistan

Pakistan's strategic geography, nuclear capability and most importantly its Islamic ideology makes it the natural guardian, protector and brother of the entire Muslim Ummah, and a foe to all the hostile anti-Islamic forces of the East and the West. Pakistan, despite all its internal problems, has been able to establish the 5th largest standing army of the world including a nuclear arsenal. Pakistan's armed forces are the only armed forces in the Muslim world to have fought against India, Israel and former Soviet Union and to have shot down fighter aircraft from all three enemy states.

Along with ISIS, the most brutal and ruthless terrorist organization in the world today and the most prized asset of the Zionist forces, is the TTP. Emerging in 2005 under direct support of the CIA and Indian RAW, TTP acted as an umbrella organization for many Deobandi militant groups fighting against the Pakistani state, under the ideology of takfir. TTP is led by Indian-backed deobandi militants but consists of Pakistani, Arab, Uzbek and Afghan nationals.

Following their khariji strategy, TTP declared the whole of the Pakistani nation as infidels and declared a ruthless and brutal war on the state of Pakistan. To gain moral and religious legitimacy, TTP adopted the slogan of Jihad against US occupation of Afghanistan to get more recruits from Pakistani tribal areas in order to intensify and expand its war against Pakistan. In the last nine years of its operations, TTP has never fired a single bullet on US forces in Afghanistan and its entire war has remained against Muslims in Pakistan, both against the state and the civilians, with a particular focus on Pakistan's army and its intelligence organizations. Nearly 100,000 Pakistanis have died in a brutal campaign of terror which is threatening the very foundations of the state itself.

TTP's war against Pakistan armed forces to help India/Israel

TTP established its foothold in South Waziristan agency, on the border of Afghanistan, in FATA (Federally Administrated Tribal Areas) of Pakistan in 2004. Soon it expanded its influence in other agencies of FATA as well. There were several incidents where Pakistani security personnel were beheaded by the cold blooded TTP operatives. Apart from that, the phenomenon of suicide bombings in Pakistan was introduced by the TTP.

The Pakistan government has declared TTP as a terrorist organization. In 2009, Pakistan's army launched massive military operations against TTP in South Waziristan, where TTP had established its illegal state. Now in 2014, the Pakistani Army has launched another major offensive against TTP terrorists in North Waziristan as well. TTP is now on the run, as the Pakistan army has almost overrun their last strongholds.

The Pakistani Army's discoveries during anti-TTP operations have left no doubt that the TTP militants are actually khawarij. Their war planning, strategy, narrative and tactics are based on khawarijism. They claim to be Muslim warriors but actually are working hand in hand with Zionist forces to implode the only Islamic ideological and nuclear state from within.

Fourth generation warfare revolves around the idea of creating complete political and social paralysis in the targeted state. The first targets of the TTP were political and social figures of influence. Their elimination created an environment of fear and hopelessness among the local masses. The same exact strategy has been employed by ISIS in SYRAQ region. Absence of political leadership created an atmosphere of lawlessness and chaos, giving TTP a free hand to recruit, train and arm locals against the state by imposing its own ideology and political views on people through brutal bloodletting. Swat was the first major urban region of Pakistan to be captured and overrun by these Khawarij. Pakistan's army had to fight a bloody battle in this urban center in 2009 to liberate it.

But phenomenon of Khawarij and insurgencies in Pakistan is more complex than it is in the Middle East, as the state is faced with both religious and secular insurgencies. The geopolitics of the subcontinent, in which unresolved issues like Kashmir play a major role, has complicated the issue further. Establishing strategic hegemony in South Asia is a primeval Indian dream. Pakistan is not only a major military rival of India but also a serious obstacle in the realization of "Greater India." The Indian establishment has been working to remove this obstacle since the independence of Pakistan in 1947. Pakistan has never been accepted as an independent Islamic state in the collective psyche of the Hindu Zionists.

Greater India plan—creating a Hindu empire from Malaysia to Afghanistan

India achieved a major breakthrough in 1971 with the secession of East Pakistan. The Indian-backed proxy Mukti Bahini terrorist group played a central role in this secession. Further dismemberment of what remains of Pakistan into smaller states on ethnic lines is something India has been trying to achieve since 1971.

Only now, the emergence of Khawarij has given an added opportunity to the Hindus as well to use religious militant gangs to attack the Pakistani state. The interests of the CIA and Indian RAW have converged against Pakistan. The Khawarij of TTP have emerged as useful mercenary terrorists gangs for both the CIA and the RAW.

Nearly a hundred thousand Pakistani troops are stationed along the Afghan border now fighting an array of enemies from TTP terrorists to Arab militants to local tribal sympathizers to Uzbek infiltrators sent from Kabul and India. The scenario is not just complex, it is downright dirty.

While the Zionists from US and Israel have their own objectives in attacking Pakistan, India wants to accomplish its own multiple strategic goals through this insurgency:

- To bring Pakistan to its knees by imploding it as a failed state.
- Building a case against Pakistan being a failed state with nuclear arms which can fall into the "wrong" hands.
- Once declared a failed state, Pakistan will be denuclearized by the international community under various global agreements.
- A weak, denuclearized Pakistan can then be invaded and dismembered, clearing the way for creating "greater India" or Akand Bharat, as Hindus call their dream.

Just as ISIS is a tool in creating a "Greater Israel" dream, the TTP are a weapon in the hands of Hindu Zionists and the CIA for a "greater India" and "dismember Pakistan" plan.

To get Pakistan denuclearized is the first step of a bigger strategic Indian plan and is in complete harmony with US/West's designs for Pakistan. TTP's attacks on Pakistan's security apparatus and bases help create the propaganda myth that Pakistan's nuclear weapons are unsafe. The UN can be mobilized, just as in the case of fake Iraqi WMDs, to "secure" Pakistan's nuclear weapons.

The next phase is to invade Pakistan physically, which is not currently possible due to nuclear deterrence. So the denuclearization of Pakistan is a common agenda of the Israeli, American and Indian foreign policies for Pakistan.

The TTP insurgency was created and is being kept alive through massive support of weapons, money and infiltrators in the garb of "Muslim militants" and "Arab Mujahideen" or "AlQaeda." Israeli Mossad and CIA are handling the Arab connection, while RAW and RAMA manages the Deobandi TTP, Uzbeks and local Pashtun and Pakistani terrorist elements.

Along with waging a war against the state itself, the Takfiri Khawarij have also been aggressively active in igniting the sectarian wars in both Iraq and Pakistan. Both ISIS and TTP have strong sectarian agendas and ruthlessly kill Shia Muslims to bring more fissures within the Muslim societies. LeJ, the sectarian Takfiri terrorist organization in Pakistan is now a subsidiary of the Khawarij TTP.

The fascist religious ideology of Takfir against the Pakistani State has been aggressively promoted through planted Arab spies like Ayman al-Zawahiri and Abu Yazid. Local terrorists like TTP are further supported by Uzbek militants from ruthless Communist warlord Rasheed Dostum's gangs under the guise of the "Islamic movement of Uzbekistan." Pakistani sectarian terrorists groups like SSP and LeJ have also been absorbed in the ranks of TTP for protection and survival, and have expanded their role from anti-Shia militancy to anti-state and anti-Pakistani warfare. The entire campaign of terrorism against Pakistan is based in Afghanistan under the patronage of a hornet's nest of CIA, Mossad, RAW and RAMA. Almost all of the Khawarij gangs in Pakistan belong to the Deobandi sect, which originated from a pro-Hindu religious seminary of Darul Uloom deoband in India with branches in Pakistan as well.

All these facets of 4GW are being unleashed by the hostile forces who want to create a specific narrative regarding Pakistan. Unfortunately, till this day, successive Pakistani governments have perceived these compounded threats as separate law and order issues and have failed miserably in developing a holistic response to the deployed 4th GW.

Only the military response axis has been largely successful. Pakistan's army has eradicated the Khawarij's strongholds in North Western FATA regions, pushing them back into Afghanistan. But even this success has come at a very high cost; it was only possible after the Pakistani army adopted and introduced a strong anti-Khawarij ideological narrative in its rank and file. Khawarij are NOT just a military threat. They must be defeated ideologically first, based on strong Islamic scholarly arguments, to destroy their twisted narrative of Islam. Once their argument is defeated, they can be crushed on the battlefield too.

But despite this success, Pakistan cannot claim a complete victory against these hidden internal gangs as long as they sustain their bases and staging areas across the border in Afghanistan protected by NATO/US.

Conclusion

In 21st century warfare, the phenomenon of terrorism is being deployed as a strategic weapon of war, and the Muslim world is the region most affected by this menace. Muslim states are being dismembered once again, for the first time since their present maps were drawn about 100 years ago. Greater Israel is in the making now.

The Muslim masses in the occupied lands are at the mercy of the aggressors and their paid proxy terrorist gangs like TTP, ISIS, and Al-Qaeda. Not just the Muslim lands but the entire Islamic civilization and way of life is under existential threat. The most unfortunate aspect of this entire crisis is the complete lack of understanding within Muslim societies of modern dynamics of global political order and its historical background, as well as understanding 4th generation warfare and the use of religion by Western powers and Khawarij as a major destabilizing factor.

To crawl out of this geopolitical abyss, the Muslim world—at every level of society and the state—will have to comprehend the current political pandemonium along with its covert dynamics in complete historical context. The issue of terrorism faced by Muslim societies is not a mere law and order crisis. It is not a sectarian war either. It is not just about oil or grabbing pipeline routes. It is not a war against Iraq or Syria or Iran alone. It is a total war against the Muslim Ummah—an ideological war to create "Greater Israel" and "greater India" and to destroy Islam as an ideological, spiritual, political and financial alternative. A collective response strategy, based on a holistic political and ideological narrative, is the need of the hour. The sooner the Muslim ruling elite understands this, the swifter will be the response.

The crisis is unprecedented. Our response must also be unparalleled.

FRANCE—THE GUINEA PIG FOR WAR ON RUSSIA?

Imran N. Hosein

With Allah's Blessed Name

And with a prayer for peace and blessings on His Noble Messenger

"The Rabbis who support the State of Israel will one day realize to their astonishment and terror, that there must be a hidden Mossad inside the Israeli Mossad committing horrendous acts of terror for which Jews will be blamed. The ensuing universal condemnation will be so great that even trees and stones will also cry out calling for them to be punished! It is because of eschatology that we know that false-flag chickens will one day come home to roost."

A Different False-Flag

Although it is as yet too soon to deliver a mature analysis in response to the recent terrorist attack in France, it is already possible to recognize a significant connection between this event and the previous Charlie 9/11 Hebdo terrorism.

That terrorism was a public relations adventure meant to galvanize French public opinion in a manner favorable for those who want to use France as a guinea pig for initiating Zionist military adventures in advancement of a mysterious messianic agenda for which modern Western civilization was itself created.

This follow-up act of terrorism on the other hand, seems designed to open the way to push France, willingly or unwillingly, on a significant military adventure that will eventually allow NATO to wage war on Russia.

Those who planned this attack know very well that war on Russia will certainly be nuclear war, and that France will be destroyed in such a war. But they do not care for the French, or any other people. All of mankind are their sacrificial lambs, as they relentlessly pursue their arrogant goal of imposing their messianic rule over the whole world.

From Islam for the French: A Warning

It is time for the French people to wake up and realize that they are being taken for a "guinea-pig" ride, and that this will be the last ride they will ever experience. It should not be long before the truth of my analysis stares them in their horrified eyes since I expect that nuclear war to take place within a year from now—or even less than that. It should not be difficult for the French, and others resident in France, to anticipate the horrible consequences of Western nuclear war with Russia.

The immediate consequence of this new French terrorism is a dramatic increase in France's military profile in the Syria/Iraq war theatre. Whoever planned and executed the terrorist attack in Paris, wanted to provide France with an opening that could be exploited to justify a progressive escalation of France's military involvement in that war theatre in which ISIS is entrenched, and which Russia has now entered so dramatically. If the French government were to hesitate in escalating its military profile in in that war theatre, then it is certain that another act of terrorism will take place to pave the way for NATO's war on Russia. Indeed, the very recent Turkish destruction of a Russian fighter-jet may very well qualify as that act of state terrorism which will finally succeed in lifting the curtain for war.

The mysterious shadowy actors who created, programmed, armed and financed ISIS are almost certainly the ones who planned the latest terrorist attack on France. Whoever those actors may be, I am absolutely certain that the CIA, the Israeli Mossad and the Turkish secret service are amongst them.

I am now beginning to have doubts about the nature and extent of Saudi Arabia's involvement in the creation of ISIS since I am leaning towards the view that the Saudis may have been double-crossed, deceived and trapped into giving birth to a baby who will eventually replace their rule over Arabia. However, there are other analysts, more skilled than this writer, who may shed greater light in the matter of the Saudi role in the creation of ISIS and the present awesome Saudi dilemma.

The positive (official) identification of the attackers will certainly not end the search for those responsible for planning this French terrorism since there are many innocent young French and Belgian Muslims who have been the target of devilish Western anti-Islam and anti-Muslim psychological warfare, in addition to being deliberately harassed and persecuted for the longest while. Many are now so scared that they do not want the cameras (which record my public lectures) to even show their faces, while others are too scared to reveal their identity when they write to me.

There must be no scarcity of such angry young Muslims who can be bought with USD and Euros and who would be only too happy to end their wretched lives in a lucrative blaze of fiery revenge.

In allowing themselves to be bought and sold in such a way, such Muslims render themselves a shame and a disgrace to the noble religion of Islam. The ranks of ISIS are filled with such cattle. But such Muslims do not represent the greatest evil in this sordid affair. That distinction belongs to the evil ones who plan and finance such acts of terrorism and who are past masters of the art of framing innocent Muslims (why does it always have to be passports that are conveniently located in the pockets of dead men?) with responsibility for their acts of terrorism.

My view is that this was too big and too strategically important an act of terrorism to be left to angry Muslims amateurs, and that it must have been committed by the most highly-trained professionals. As much as they take care to conceal their evil footprints, Allah Most High can still ensure that some footprints will eventually surface to confirm yet another act of false-flag Israeli Mossad terrorism, or something far worse than that.

France was chosen for the terrorist attack since it was the most favorably placed candidate in the Western alliance—more acceptable than Britain and the USA—to lead the way for NATO's eventual military response to the alarming Russian military intervention in Syria. Now that France's military profile in Syria/Iraq war theatre is being dramatically enhanced with nary a squawk from the French people, it has already paved the way for eventual British and US military profiles to be also enhanced with little or no objections from the British and American peoples.

The actors who created ISIS have done so in order, among so many other things, to target Russia and to lure Russia into a trap in which they can resume their unfinished and unvarnished military agenda that was last pursued in the Crimean war of 1853–56. The enhanced French military profile in the Syria/Iraq war theatre not only paves the way for Britain and USA to follow France, but now makes it very clear that war with Russia is absolutely certain to take place. I expect that war to occur sooner rather than later because the longer NATO waits to wage war on Russia, the stronger will Russia become as a military power.

It is time enough for the world of Islam to remember that Turkey is not only a NATO member-state but is also actively involved in assisting NATO in the pursuit of the Western military agenda.

War with Russia will certainly be nuclear war that will result in unprecedented devastation in Europe and North America. Indeed modern Western secular civilization will probably be erased from the map of the post-nuclear world.

I believe that the Zionist master-plan at work is for the rump of mankind that survives nuclear war to be told that mankind now has a chance to build a new post-secular world in which religion will replace secularism. Zionist Jews would then seek to lead the world to a deceptive new golden age that would promise Jewish justice and moral values to replace the godlessness, decadence, injustice and oppression which now prevails. It would be deceptive since true religion has zero tolerance for oppression, and only those with the intellectual acumen of cattle can fail to recognize the Jewish State of Israel as an oppressor state.

History cannot end until truth triumphs over all rivals, and justice replaces injustice and oppression. That was the message sent when the waters parted in the Red Sea, and that dramatic history is destined to be repeated when Jesus the true Messiah (peace and blessings be upon him) returns.

The Qur'an has declared that Allah Most High created the world with Truth so that each soul may receive an award that is appropriate for what it has earned. The implication is that the hidden perpetrators of false flag terrorism have a great End-time surprise in store for them. Divine justice is certainly coming, and when it does come, they will eventually find themselves being blamed for horrendous acts of terrorism which they did not commit. The Rabbis who support the State of Israel will one day realize to their astonishment and terror, that there must be a hidden Mossad inside the Israeli Mossad committing horrendous acts of terror for which Jews will be blamed. The ensuing universal condemnation will be so great that even trees and stones will also cry out calling for them to be punished! It is because of eschatology that we know that false-flag chickens will one day come home to roost.

Islamic eschatology has, of course, much more than the above to offer as an explanation of a post-nuclear world, and our readers, particularly those in France, would be well-advised to devote an effort to study the subject. My books on Islamic eschatology can hopefully assist those who would like to pursue such studies.

Website: www.imranhosein.org; Bookstore: www.imranhosein.com
Email: inhosein@hotmail.com

THE TERROR WHICH COULD END ALL WESTERN DEMOCRACIES:
BUT WHO KILLED THE FRENCH MARIANNE?

Catherine Shakdam

As France is slowly coming to terms with the tragedy which befell its people, looking to make sense of the murderous irrationality of terrorism, it is not reason which its officials have professed, but violence and social erosion.

And while ultimately France stands to further betray its future by playing directly into the hands of fascism, as it answers one radicalism with another—that of radical secularism—Western powers have remained stubbornly true to their agenda: spitting hatred and intolerance against those communities they seek to ostracize to better manifest their new paradigm of fear.

Islam once more was pinpointed as the axis upon which radicalism has risen to power. But this terror the West is facing today, this evil which rejects the sanctity of life and wishes only to instill fear so that its hordes can rule and enslave, is devoid of any religious consciousness. Ayatollah Ali Khamenei explains this well in his second letter to the Western Youth (included in this book) where he calls for unity against the universal evil of extremism.

ISIL's ideology is rooted not in Islam but in Wahhabism. Charles Allen postulated in 2007 that Wahhabism represents a fascist devolution born from the mind of a pseudo-scholar: Muhammad ibn Abdul Wahhab, a tyrant whose sole purpose was to raise an empire of fear, right at the heart of Islam, to deceptively draw on its religious legitimacy.[295]

Wahhabism is nothing more than a cult, a heresy rooted in bloodletting, slavery, and violence—an abomination of the mind so revolting that it can only be compared in its madness to Nazism.

The Wahhabi tribe, extreme Islamist fundamentalists, set out at the turn of the 18th century to restore purity to their faith by declaring violent jihad on all who opposed them. And while their history has long been forgotten, their vicious political ideology lives on. Wahhabism deeply influenced not only the formation of modern Saudi Arabia, but Osama bin Laden and the Taliban, as Allen explains in his research.

Today this Wahhabist crusade has reached the shores of the Old Continent. But Islam had no part and no hand in this attack. And yet, voices have already risen calling for a witch-hunt against those [Muslims] whose guilt has already been proclaimed on account their faith "does not belong."

Paris, we were told, was targeted because radicals hate the freedom Western capitals enjoy. Paris, we were told, was earmarked for destruction and its people condemned to death because their liberties are offensive to the fascism of ISIL. But that would imply that democracy is alive and well, and of course for such statements to ring true, it would imply that France stands as a real democratic state.

Questions have arisen since the Paris attack about the real state of Western democracy. Western powers have long presented themselves as the guardians of democracy, the custodian even of those republican values, we were told, are best expressed in Western institutions; where such principles as personal freedom and political self-determination are inalienable rights under the Constitution. From Washington to London, Paris and Berlin, heads of states have clamored their moral superiority, positioning themselves as models to be emulated and emblems to be adored.

But on-the-ground realities betray a very different truth indeed. Western democracy offers only a moral facade; while its substance, the freedom and liberties it promises, remain very much out of reach. Our modern-day Western countries are anything but democratic; rather, they are autocratic in nature, profoundly reactionary in practice and utterly violent in their political expressions.

And yet we have been told ad nauseam that it is in the West that liberty's flame shines the brightest. That of course is the grandest lie of all.

Francis Fukuyama,an American author and intellectual, proposed an interesting overview of what he refers to as the "political decay of democracy" in the West. He suggests that for a democracy to be truly functional the state needs to realize popular legitimacy, separation of powers and democratic accountability.[296]

Looking at France today, it appears the state has failed on all accounts: the state serves not its people but a corporate and political elite. All three branches of power (judicial, legislative and executive) have become patsies in the hands of lobbies. There is no democratic accountability, as the media have become the grand censors of the powerful elite.

France today resembles not the republican and democratic ideals the likes of Robespierre, Voltaire and Montesquieu once hoped would become institutional realities. Instead, it has reached a terrible, and yet many will argue, inevitable crossroads as its republican state has been raided and defiled to make way to a new form of radicalization—a new nepotism whose expression is found in the militarization of all state institutions.

France's republican values, one can argue, have withered away so completely that its people can hardly recognize those principles their forefathers so valiantly stood for and bled for. Would Voltaire and Montesquieu today look upon France's institutions and applaud, or would they instead deplore the sad institutional devolution the Fifth Republic has become under the thumb of a capitalist oligarchy?

Once upon a time, freedom of religion and tolerance stood at the center of French philosophers' political ideals. It was Voltaire[297] (18th century) who argued that religious intolerance was against the law of nature and was worse than the "right of the tiger."

Towards the end of his long life Voltaire took the courageous stand of defending a Protestant family against religious intolerance and legal persecution. Voltaire wrote:

> Human law must in every case be based on natural law. All over the earth the great principle of both is: Do not unto others what you would that they do not unto you. Now, in virtue of this principle, one man cannot say to another: Believe what I believe, and what thou canst not believe, or thou shalt perish." Thus do men speak in Portugal, Spain, and Goa. In some other countries they are now content to say: "Believe, or I detest thee; believe, or I will do thee all the harm I can. Monster, thou sharest not my religion, and therefore hast no religion; thou shalt be a thing of horror to thy neighbours, thy city, and thy province." ... The supposed right of intolerance is absurd and barbaric. It is the right of the tiger; nay, it is far worse, for tigers do but tear in order to have food, while we rend each other for paragraphs.[298]

France today no longer stands for such principles.

In early 2015, Pierre Cassen, founder of Riposte Laique and Christine Tasin, President of Resistance Republicaine, both French far-right leaders offered to initiate a national movement against Muslims, calling for their expulsion and a ban on their religious rights. In effect they have lobbied for the criminalization of Islam in France, a trend which has found many supporters across Europe and the Americas. "We propose to initiate what should become a succession of rallies and patriotic demonstrations, a popular movement in the image of PEGIDA in Germany, a movement which rallies all individuals, associations, political parties... marking the refusal of the Islamisation of our country with all its consequences. We will demand that all Islamists be driven out of France," they wrote in a common statement to the press.

With religious liberties standing to be obliterated in the name of secularism, France also stands to become a bona fide police state, devoid of all democratic characteristics as its legitimacy will be based not on popular will, but popular repression.

Militarization within and without

It is often believe that a person's true nature will be revealed at times of great hardship and duress, as one's ability to self-censor and reason are impeded by passions. At this particular juncture in its history France did not exactly put its best foot forward—or we should say, its leaders did not.

While the Paris attacks offered an opportunity for peace and social cohesion, in that France's rejection of terror should have acted a universal rallying cry regardless of internal ethnic, religious, social and political divisions, politicians chose to play ISIL to the tune of their own prejudices.

The rise of the far right to the political stratospheres attests to French society's new descent into the darkness of fascism, a repeat some intellectuals have argued of the Vichy government (1940-1944) when Marechal Philippe Petain paused the IV Republic to better collaborate with Nazi Germany. Even Bernard-Henri Levy is terrified:

> Will the Front National, a despicable party led by a nepotistic clique replete with ex-cons pining for the good old days of wedge politics, gain control of entire regions of the country? In the second round of regional elections, will France concede part of its territory to the heirs of the Vichy regime, to those nostalgic for "French Algeria" and the OAS, to perennial enemies of republican democracy? ...Will we stand by fatalistically while smug, vulgar, ignorance makes France the laughing stock and the pity of Europe? Will we resign ourselves to the posthumous revenge of Charles Maurras, Robert Brasillach and Marshal Pétain, the revenge of a cabal that sought to assassinate Charles de Gaulle, of a party led by people who hate the best of France, who never stop trying to make France smaller, less influential, less glorious than she is?[299]

Where France government could have chosen to defy terror by flying democracy's flag, President François Hollande called instead for a democratic pause. On November 19th, France's parliament extended the state of emergency proclaimed by President Hollande on the day of the attack by another three months, thus allowing for the police and all other security services to wield immense powers against all residents. Then on December 23rd President Hollande and Prime Minister Manuel Valls called for the State of Emergency to be enshrined in the Constitution and made permanent, effectively abolishing the Republic and transforming France into a dictatorship.[300]

Such measures give the police powers including the ability to keep people in their homes without trial, searching homes without a warrant from a judge, and the power to block any website that the government doesn't like. French officials have rationalized the decision by arguing that in order to protect democracy, freedoms had to be taken away ... an interesting paradox indeed.

"This is the fast response of a democracy faced with barbarism. This is the effective legal response in the face of an ideology of chaos," Prime Minister Emmanuel Valls told parliament. Valls also stressed that such measures were "modern and effective tools to fight the terrorist threat."

Undeniably France, and Europe, have become increasingly militarized. On November 20th, the Guardian spoke of a new European border crackdown. The report read: "EU ministers are to hold emergency talks on Friday on tightening border checks after the killing of the alleged ringleader of the Paris attacks in an apartment in the French capital put European leaders under intense pressure to get a grip on Europe's external and internal borders."

Under France's impetus, Europe is losing its democratic character. Following Paris attack French Interior Minister Bernard Cazeneuve called on his fellow ministers to agree on a Europe-wide passenger information register, improved controls along Europe's external borders, and better coordination against arms trafficking. "France has been calling for these measures for more than 18 months, and some progress has been made," he said. "But it is not fast enough, and it does not go far enough ... Everyone must understand Europe has to organize, recover, defend itself against the terrorist threat."[301]

The ministers are set to unveil a battery of mainly electronic measures aimed at combating terror and improving controls, including tightening checks on all travelers at the Schengen zone's external borders. And while such measures have been portrayed as legitimate measures against terror, they nevertheless betray the very values officials claim to want to protect.

And so the real question remains, which of the two terrors, wahhabism or secular radicalism, killed the French Marianne?

The rise of secular radicalism

Today, it is not just Islam which stands in the line of fire. Freedom of religion is under unprecedented attack by an elite—a vicious group of militant secularists in government, academia and the media who are determined to expunge God from every corner of public life. Their goal is to replace faith with religious syncretism and moral relativism as the foundations of a new secular world order.

Such a wicked campaign to annul religion in the West has been carried out in the name of secularism, freedom, tolerance, pluralism, and the all too famous separation between the religious and the state. Extremists have misappropriated these terms and hijacked them, twisting and distorting their true meaning in order to advance their sinister anti-religious agenda.

Radical secularists[302] have so thoroughly distorted the terms "secularism" and "secular" that they have become the equivalent of the term "non-religious." But that is not the original meaning of the words or what nations have understood them to mean. The term "secular" was simply used to distinguish civil society or the state from religious bodies. Something that is distinct from something else is not necessarily the enemy of that other thing. Such were the ideas expressed by the French Enlightenment philosopher Montesquieu.

Yet in the modern age we have been trained to think the opposite. Religion and society, faith and reason, faith and science, love and truth, public and private life, the spiritual and material worlds, are now commonly regarded as polar opposites: inherently contradictory and opposing realms that must be hermetically sealed off from each other. Professor Tariq Ramadan, the prominent Swiss academic, has long rejected such a binary way of thinking.[303]

This great divorce between distinct realms that are in fact mutually compatible, complementary, and interdependent is a bitter fruit of the relativistic and materialistic philosophies that increasingly dominate our postmodern society and that provide a basis for the destructive totalitarian ideology of radical secularism. Relativism[304], of course, is the irrational idea that there is no such thing as absolute religious, moral or spiritual truth, whether accessible to human reason alone or divinely revealed. Rather than being gifts of God and paths to absolute truth that tend to unite mankind, faith, morality, spirituality, and reason are viewed as purely human attempts to impose order on a chaotic and meaningless cosmos. In this great sea of relativistic truth, it's up to each individual to decide for himself or herself, in a hermetically sealed vacuum, what to believe (if anything) and what is morally right and wrong.

The only absolute truth that can be known for certain by all humanity is what can be discovered about the material world through scientific research. And there we have just defined materialism—-the even more irrational idea that nothing exists beyond what we can see and hear and measure and quantify. Relativism pushes God out of the picture, while materialism denies his existence a priori.

These two unreasonable atheistic philosophies, which contradict human experience and common sense, form the backbone of the radically secularist ideology that is now infecting our world. This totalitarian ideology carries within itself the potential to destroy society.

The new nationalism and religion as an ethnicity

Much can be said about society when it cries over a police dog more than its own human members on account of geography and ethnicity. How far has democracy fallen when it no longer sees men, women and children but color, faiths and differences?

In the wake of the Paris attack, as police broke into homes and businesses, armed with the newly established state of emergency, a police dog was shot dead in a brawl. Decried as a national hero by his masters, yet another victim of Islamists' irrational wrath, the world trended the loss on social media, carrying the hashtag #Jesuischien (I am dog) as new emblem for freedom lost.

Through grand displays of grief and international calls for solidarity, much of the world reached out to the French nation, joining in this global stand against terror, radicalization and bigotry—only solidarity and sorrow were reserved for a selected few, a chosen elite which we have been told is more worthy of our tears than the many "others": those thousands and tens of thousands of souls lost to terror across the world, mainly in Asia, the Middle East and Africa.

They are blinded by their own sense of white colonial entitlement[305], this ingrained belief that the West knows better, does better and thinks better. France has unwittingly told the world what it is it has been hiding in its republican belly: that the Republic will only ever be White, that its people have a greater right to life than those third world degenerates it has been at war against for well over a decade, and before that, for almost two centuries.

But how many innocent civilians have been killed by drones over the past decade? How many lives were cut short under NATO intervention, in the name of democracy building? How many times have Western politicians owned up to their crimes and offered an apology?

The Paris attacks laid bare one of the West's ugliest little secrets: its innate fascist streak, the diseased rationale which once upon a time allowed for the rise of the Third Reich. By once more playing into chauvinism and racism France insulted those brave warriors who, during the Resistance, fought to end fascism's reign of terror, and reclaim those values of liberty and equality the French nation was built upon. So while the Paris attack could have become a rallying cry against terror, the cornerstone of a new movement against theo-fascism and all forms of violent oppression, the Western powers exploited France's grief to serve their xenophobic and totalitarian agenda.

It was never solidarity for all against the plague which is ISIL, but rather Western solidarity against the "other," the foreign, the unwanted and the undesirable—this imported element of society which remains like a stain on an otherwise proud Christian society, or rather an increasingly secular white society.

Here is one of France's most interesting paradoxes: on the one hand officials can argue secularism and republicanism to defend their innate aversion of so-called "Islamic values"—essentially the headscarf; and on the other, those same officials have no qualms about attending Church services to honor their martyrs.

Not only has France claimed monopoly on grief for its tragedy—never mind that only a few days before the Paris attacks Beirut burned under the fire of ISIS, never mind Yemeni civilians dying under the advances of Wahhabism and never mind the Kurds, Yezidis, Alawites, Sunni and Shia Muslims drowning under the rubbles of their homes ... those losses are not as trendy as Parisians' candle and flower displays; and France chose to mourn a dog more than human lives.

So what does it say about Western society when the death of a dog trends more than that of thousands of Africans, Asians and Middle Easterners? Are those the values the world is supposed to get on board with and fawn over? Or has Western society self-cannibalized its humanity to the point where it has become THE devolution to be opposed, right alongside ISIL?

Part 4:
Media Lies, Bias, Cover-Ups and Complicity

THE ROLE OF THE MEDIA IN AGENDA-DRIVEN COVERAGE OF TERRORIST EVENTS

A. K. Dewdney

An analysis of the characteristics of all media, from newspapers to the Internet, leads to a useful distinction that helps to explain the power of the print and broadcast media over our minds. With that understanding in place, we examine just some of the techniques used by the media to preserve a terrorism story from being undermined by countervailing facts.

A typology of media

The world is awash in media. Traditional forms, such as print and broadcast media, have been crowded out to some degree by other forms. People who used to read the newspapers or watch television news, now spend more time getting news from the internet (or even Facebook or Twitter). Although we refer to all of these sources as "media," that name tends to ignore a crucial distinction between two classes of media, each with a special name used in this article.

The traditional (print and broadcast) media have one important psychological element in common: simultaneity. When we watch the news on television, we can't help being aware, subliminally perhaps, that a great many other people are watching the same newscast—or ones with essentially the same content—at the same moment. This gives rise to a feeling of group cohesion in the sense that what we now "know" is also known by a great many other people. Newspapers operate in a similar way, albeit with a slightly expanded time frame. As we read our news-paper, we are subliminally aware that others are doing the same thing—or have just done it or are about to do it. Again, a sense of social cohe-sion implies that what we are told in the newspaper is being told to a great many other people. "Did you read that story in The *Free Press* about the guy who imprisoned his wife in the basement?" "Yeah. Isn't that awful?"

Additionally, the "other" people who absorb the news along with us usually live in the same local area. They are our neighbours, in effect, and we regard ourselves as part of the local social group. A sense of community arises from the feeling that we all understand the world in the same way, both locally and globally. And this applies with equal force to those who scorn the public media and hold opposing views. After all, if they share opinions that seem contrary to the shared world view they become outcasts to that extent. If being outcasts saddens then or makes them angry, that's simply a sign of the same social pressure in operation.

On the basis of the attributes of simultaneity and proximity one might define the print and broadcast media as "public media." The internet might accordingly be called a "private medium" itself populated by other, private media. The term "private" applies to an attribute that differs radically from the two "public" ones. First, there is little or no sense of simultaneity, as we may be looking at yesterday's news or even last week's. (Many news sites change their content less frequently.) As far as the moment is concerned, we are, for all we know, the only person accessing the website. The *feeling*, accordingly, is somewhat lonely. We are also physically isolated at such times, alone at our computer screen, knowing that anyone who happens to be staring at the same screen might live in Hong Kong or Hungary. We have no idea who they are or where they are. The experience is essentially private, the very opposite of what we were once told would amount to a "global village."

When it comes to content, public and private media are cross-connected to a degree. Public news stories may occasionally refer to a website (rarely a news website), but usually some pointless distraction that is newsworthy partly because it is "going viral" (even when it actually isn't). Private news stories refer to public stories far more commonly, especially in our line of research. This discrepancy amounts to a de facto firewall, even without censorship.

In cases where the private media are running a story that contradicts a public story, or calls into question its veracity, the public media may avoid any reference to the private content. This is especially true in the case of news content generated by operations of what some call the "New World Order," the "Deep State," "Shadow Government," or some other term. This provides a thought experiment that probes the psychological gulf between private and public media. Let us say that citizen Bill, who believes the official story of a terrorist attack in Paris, stumbles across a website that gives a very different story. Alarm bells go off in the citizen's psyche: "What! That's crazy." And instead of reading the article in question, Bill deletes the website immediately, regarding it as simply irrelevant nonsense, an isolated anomaly. Now suppose that a sea change has taken place in the public media and that Citizen Bill opens the paper one morning to be greeted by the following headline:

FRENCH OFFICIALS DECLARE PARIS ATTACKS FAKED

Instantly Bill is pouring over the text of the article to see who is saying what, exactly. He puts down the paper, shaking his head, and turns on the TV, there to see the same story. Bill is now deeply concerned and far from dismissive; he has absorbed the new message but suffers inner tension between his old beliefs and his newer ones. Much of that tension centers on worrying how other people in his audience-group are dealing with the surprising news. The *credibility* of the public media rests ultimately not on logic or facts, but on the social cohesion of the audience. The *credulity* of the audience rests ultimately on the desire to identify with and belong to that social group. In reviewing the earlier web experience, we see that Bill has no sense of audience or of any social group whatever.

One can take this analysis a little further to explain the phenomenon of "political correctness," a wonderful term that means nothing and everything. It is applied to everything from concerns about bullying to second-hand tobacco smoke (currently in the process of being replaced by marijuana smoke). Indeed, political correctness is itself a disguised form of bullying, one that induces fear in certain sensitive persons who not only follow the new directives to the letter, but get out in front of the crowd to lead and thus forever place themselves above criticism, not to mention giving them a kind of social power hitherto lacking in their lives.

Terrorist-cum-media operations

In this section we will examine how these factors explained above come into play, with special references to the Paris shootings of 11/13. Let us analyze how such operations are designed with the public media in mind.

The main elements of the operation include
1. a) determining the type of operation
2. b) choosing a target venue and selecting patsies to take the blame
3. c) assigning a shooting and/or bombing team to the operation
4. d) dividing the operation into two parts, the attack per se and the take-down

The operation must be slick enough to fool low-level public media reporters (not difficult) but can allow loose ends between the act of terror and the apprehension or termination of the patsies. After all, the transition between the two phases is covered by claims of "confusion" in the aftermath of the act. Somebody saw two shooters, somebody saw just one—or three.

"Move along folks. Nothing to see here!"

The transition is a busy time for those involved in managing the act and shepherding the media. They keep a close eye on reporters, of course. If one of them spots an anomaly, he or she can be talked out if it by an official on the scene or, failing that, threatening the reporter with a violation of national security. In fact the transition is a time when valid information is still alive, when pedestrians or residents who have actually witnessed the act of terror, having clearly seen the perpetrators and what they did, try to tell police or reporters what they have seen.

A startling example of this very phenomenon occurred during the Paris shootings at Le Belle Equipe restaurant. Mr Mahoud Admo was staying at the Salvation Army hostel right across the street from the restaurant, watching the proceedings from a second-story window:

> I was just in my room and had the window open on to the street below. I could see lots [of] people [sitting] outside the bar eating dinner and enjoying a drink. The place was full of people just enjoying themselves. At about 9.30 pm a new-looking black Mercedes pulled up outside with dark tinted windows at the back and the passenger and driver windows down. I could clearly see the passenger's face as he was not wearing a hat or mask.
>
> As soon as the car stopped he quietly opened the door and got out in front of the restaurant. That is when I saw he was holding a machine gun that was resting on his hip. I could not take in what I was witnessing. People outside spotted the shooter approaching with his gun and tried to run inside, but he shot them down in the doorway. The gunman showed no emotion at all as he began spraying bullets into the diners. He just kept reloading his machine gun and firing, without saying a thing. The people outside the bar were dead straight away. There were streams of blood everywhere and broken glass. It was carnage.[306]

Admo went on to describe a second shooter: "The driver had opened his door shortly before the shooting began and stood up with his arm and a machine gun rest[ing] on the roof of the car. He stood there with his foot up on the door, acting as a lookout. I would describe him as tall, with dark hair and quite muscular." Admo went on to provide not only details of appearance (including being white and clean-shaven), but the general military impression. "They both looked like soldiers or mercenaries and carried the whole thing out like a military operation . . . They both then cooly sat back in the car and sped off in the direction of the Bataclan Theatre."

As far as the author knows, this account did not appear in any public medium of the day—or any succeeding day. And of course the real shooters morphed into the two alleged shooters, Brahim Abdeslam and Abdelhamid Abaaoud, who do not answer the description given by the eyewitness quoted above. But at least the media could report two shooters, matching at least to that extent what was seen at the restaurant.

As for as the Bataclan Theatre is concerned, it's not clear to what extent the shooters described by Mr Abdo were active in the resulting massacre. Or indeed to what extent there was a massacre in the first place. The website NoDisinfo[307] contains a detailed analysis of the bodies spread out on the floor of the theatre where a rock concert was being held at the time of the shooting. (See this book's front cover.) The bodies may not be real, but dummies, dragged across the floor, leaving large smears of blood that refuses to dry properly, and not covered by blankets or sheets, as is customary. Presumably this was to make sure that as much gore as possible, or the appearance thereof, would be visible.

A key element of current terror operations is the parallel terror exercises. Almost every terrorist incident since 2001 has been accompanied by a drill that involved the same scenario that occurred in the incident in question. These drills are never part of the main story in the public media, but provide a cover that permits the deployment of police in time to deal with the event, not to mention the provision of patsies to take the blame, who start out as party to the exercise. An interesting incident occurred on a French television news channel when two (talking head) reporters were interviewing the Chief of Emergency Services for the city of Paris. Asked to recount his impressions of November 13th, the chief began as follows:

Chief: "That evening had started that morning because we were doing an exercise with the exact same scenario of the November 13th attacks."

Reporter: "Hang on. That morning you had a real world condition drill for an attack? You couldn't imagine that same evening it would happen for real?"

Chief: "We were repeating the scenario."

The reporters question the Chief further about this, even as he begins to demur, admitting the extreme unlikelihood of such a coincidence, then casting his eyes downward.[308]

In general, public coverage of all terrorist attacks since the 9/11 kickoff have one important feature in common, one that is rarely noticed: A necessary accompaniment to the underlying subtext that all Muslims are potential terrorists is to keep out any mention of saving graces or counter-indications. Imagine, for example, that every report of terrorism was accompanied not by the timid op-ed piece of an all-too-polite Islamic scholar, but a front-page news story:

MUSLIMS CLAIM NO RESPONSIBILITY FOR TERRORISM

or, better still,

MUSLIMS NOT TO BLAME FOR TERROR ATTACKS

Such stories would accurately reflect polling data showing that the majority of Muslims does not believe official accounts of 9/11 and other iconic attacks attributed to "radical Islamists."[309] They would also make a central point out of two of the strongest prohibitions in Islam. First, it is forbidden to take the lives of innocent people, whatever race or nation they may belong to. Second, it is forbidden to die by one's own hand, whether falling on a sword, firing a pistol or triggering a suicide belt. Period. "You have pre-empted me," says God in the Qur'an. Any violation of these prohibitions leads directly to a place not inhabited by virgins, but well-known for its complete lack of air conditioning. Again, full stop.

Strangely, the public media have adopted a peculiar terminology to get around these uncomfortable facts. Instead of talking about "Muslims," they use the following suite of bizarre terms: "extreme Muslims," "Muslim extremists," "Jihadists," "Islamists," "Islamofascists," "radicalists," and so on. The word "extreme" is the most frequently used adjective to describe alleged perpetrators, as though to imply that taking Islam to an extreme, perhaps by praying too much or becoming too engrossed in the Qur'an, leads automatically to terrorism. In reality, one can only describe the members of Al Qaeda, ISIS—or the terror flavour of the day—as "extreme non-Muslims."

The terminology used by the media leads to some interesting implications about the concerns that drive the actual perpetrators of today's worldwide terrorism; they are apparently deeply concerned about Islam, not because it leads to terrorism, but because of its appeal of a peaceful life lived in harmony with God's will. Too many people are entering Islam in spite of the campaign currently being waged against the Faith. This may explain why so many members of ISIS are described as "converts" to Islam. Such a description, it must be said, also helps to cover the presence of mercenaries from European countries who look very little like Middle Easterners. Well, they're converts. Of course!

Finally, the author of this article has been a Muslim for 40 years. He has visited many mosques in North America and the Middle East, has interviewed and held discussions with many hundreds of Muslims from around the world, and not once has there been any mention of resentment against the West, much less any talk of "jihad." ("Shhh. Don't use the J-word," say some Muslims.) Only occasionally has he heard words of despair that Western nations turn a blind eye to Israel's genocidal activities on the West Bank and in Gaza. Frankly, he has heard many more complaints from non-Muslim academics who have been involved in campus demonstrations over such operations. As for being "jealous of our freedoms," one may well ask, "What freedoms?"

The almost complete absence of investigative journalism in today's public media is due to the media owners. Virtually all American public media are now owned, directly or indirectly, by just five persons, all of them active neoconservatives who endorse regime change in the Middle East, along with a redrawing of boundaries. The infamous map by Ralph Peters shows a new, much larger Kurdistan, now being hacked out of Syria and Iraq (by ISIS) and holding the great bulk of oil reserves currently belonging to those countries. Instructions from the owners to the senior media managers do not need to be detailed, as in a possible message sent out shortly after 9/11: "Broadcast or print nothing that would tend to undermine the War on Terror." Sounds patriotic, doesn't it?

COVERING 11/13: THE STAGECRAFT OF "RELIABLE" SOURCES

James F. Tracy

Modern Journalism and the Secular Worldview

An unquestioning faith in the integrity of journalistic institutions is a cornerstone of modern secularism which has to a large degree replaced religious faith in France and throughout the West. Journalism holds power in check, so this catechism goes, ensuring free exchange in the "open society." In this line of thinking, close study of news reports and the information contained therein suggests apostasy to the secular credo, perhaps even "conspiracy theory" if the analysis is developed alongside careful consideration of political power to any significant degree.

This chapter interrogates an important feature of news coverage as it pertains to the Paris 11/13 "attacks." As with reportage of most any significant event in social life, the coverage of a terrorist attack is only as credible as the testimony of eyewitnesses, those otherwise immediately impacted, such as victims' family members and close friends, and relevant government officials. In fact, fundamental journalism ethics codes theoretically adhered to by news gathering organizations emphasize the importance of tapping trustworthy sources, disclosing their identities, and discerning whether they may have certain motives for providing information.

This very principal aids in developing the secular faith in such institutions by developing trust in news media, and was recognized as such almost a century ago when journalism was becoming professionalized throughout the United States and Europe. "Good faith with the readers is the foundation of good journalism," the 1922 American Society of Newspaper Editors Canons of Journalism declares. "Every effort must be made to assure that the news content is accurate, free from bias and in context, and that all sites are presented fairly."[310]

To this day the professional tenet emphasizing accuracy is echoed in virtually all professional journalism codes of ethics. In these various documents there is express concern with securing credibility and the public's trust, and it is suggested that these are maintained largely through the quality of sources and appropriate attribution. "No reader should find cause to suspect that the paper would knowingly alter facts," the *New York Times* declares in its "Guidelines on Our Integrity."[311]

The authenticity of information is thus key, and if a reporter hasn't witnessed the event the editorial expectation is that s/he must access reliable sources. For example, the BBC emphasizes how its reporters "should try to witness events and gather information first hand. When this is not possible, we should talk to first hand sources and, where necessary, corroborate their evidence."[312] There is an understanding, Reuters likewise counsels its reporters, that "every statement in every story" must be sourced "unless it is an established fact or is information clearly in the public domain, such as court documents or in instances when the reporter, photographer or camera operator was on the scene."[313]

Along these lines reporters are expected to hold to greater scrutiny information from sources that seek partial or complete anonymity. For example, the *New York Times* states that "the general rule is to tell readers as much as we can about the placement and known motivations of the source." The Society of Professional Journalists similarly recommends assessing "sources motives before promising anonymity."[314] The *Washington Post* seeks "to disclose the source of all information when at all possible," and that "before any information is accepted without full attribution reporters must make every reasonable effort to get it on the record. If that is not possible, reporters should consider seeking the information elsewhere."[315] Full disclosure of sources, Reuters maintains, is necessary to safeguard against reporting false information and contrived events: "Good sources and well-defined sourcing help to protect the integrity of the file from overt outside pressures and manipulation and such hazards as hoaxes" [sic].[316]

With the above in mind, what journalistic institutions theoretically espouse and how they go about their craft are two entirely different things, and this has not been lost on the public. The secular faith in journalism and democracy is hardly monolithic, and is in decline even in recent years. A 2015 Gallup poll found that forty percent of Americans proclaim "'a great deal'" or "'a fair amount' of trust and confidence in mass media to report the news fully, accurately, and fairly." This figure was fifty-three percent in 1997.[317] What makes the news media an integral but by no means exclusive element of enforcing belief in events such as Paris 11/13 is the fact that political and administrative officials are journalists' foremost sources for information, and in the wake of a terror attack there is a tendency to unquestioningly accept their pronouncements.

The basic journalistic tenets concerning the quality and careful identification of sources witnessing or impacted by the 11/13 Paris "attacks" was seriously lacking, with many of the stories unrealistic and broader context of the events pointing to a false flag. Yet the still powerful secular impulse toward the news media collectively allowed for these anomalies to be overlooked. Much like reportage of other complex events ostensibly involving Islamic-inspired terrorism, such as 9/11, the London 7/7 attacks, the Boston Marathon bombing, or the large number of mass shootings in the US, is that overriding belief in the "free press."

As of this writing most 11/13 coverage has not been appropriately revisited or amended and thus cannot be accepted as a trustworthy or valid record of the event. There should be little wonder, then, that the public is left with a set of subjective impressions on the Paris attacks that is far distanced from what actually took place that night. Is it possible that the event was manufactured by state actors with the aid of media and public relations practitioners strategically positioned to provide quotable information for on-the-scene reporters? Close study of many sources providing key information indicates an unusual number of linkages to media-related entities. One such figure is directly related to a "training exercise" that transpired on the morning of November 13th, while others are in especially advantageous proximity to the specific events as they occur, or claim a relationship to the deceased. The verbal or visual testimony of each source is carried widely by major news outlets in the immediate wake of November 13th, thus decisively shaping how the public came to understand and accept the incident.

The Doctor, the Actor, and the Drill

In the aftermath of the Paris attacks Pierre Carli, Director of the Anesthesia-Intensive Care Department of the Hôpital Necker-Enfants Malades of Paris and the Medical Director of the SAMU (medical emergency service) of Paris, explained his key involvement in overseeing several complex "training exercises," one of which took place on the morning of November 13th, 2015. In two separate interviews on French television Carli laid out the specific mechanics of how the morning drill was conducted. In one interview he discusses how it began "at 10:00 AM" with

> all 8 SAMUs ... We had an exercise with computers, phone calls, lists of victims, all the elements we'd need to dispatch the victims to hospitals and dispatch our forces to sites as they became known. [The drill] helped everyone enormously. We were right there ready. And it's

something we'd done several times—practicing for treating victims with gunshot wounds, which requires special treatment, you understand. And that particular day we had the organizational part. Meaning based on the victim analysis, how many and where they were, get them to hospitals and better coordinate amongst ourselves—doctors, firemen, police—to perform like that ... So at 10 AM—it's an unannounced exercise. Very few people know—we're calling hospitals asking, "Can you handle seriously wounded victims?" "How many? When?" "Do you have sufficient staff? Do you need people?

At this point the interviewer stops Carli. "The hospitals weren't overloaded because that same morning you'd just realized the need to equally distribute the wounded?"

Carli nods in affirmation. "A certain amount of, not really lessons but rather our observations were implemented that very evening because a larger part of the morning's exercise corresponded to the medical organization the SAMU needed that evening."

Further along in the exchange Carli explains that the 11/13 Paris exercise included an array of participants and observers from other countries. "We prepared our teams by working with people who know how to do this," he explains. "We don't invent it all. Using military doctors who are in Afghanistan, using the experience of our colleagues in other countries, Israel, Spain, England, where they've had this type of attack."[318]

Despite these revelation Carli's statements are almost entirely overlooked by Western media. A LexisNexis search for references to the medical administrator yields just a single article. "We were dealing with injuries caused by weapons of war. This isn't our normal job. This is normally the work of people operating in conflict zones." The UK *Guardian* also briefly notes Carli's observation of "a rehearsal on Friday morning. As we know now we were close to reality. We could never have imagined reality would have been worse."[319] Days later Carli and his colleagues lay out the 11/13 evening developments in a leading medical journal.[320]

While Carli is a primary administrator behind the Paris attack drills, it is Patrick Pelloux who is designated as a principal spokesman to explain how such exercises coincidentally transpired on the morning of November 13th. He is also one of many witnesses affiliated with the media tapped as a source in coverage of the 11/13 events. According to his Wikipedia profile Pelloux has acted in two films, *Incognito* (2009) and *Bad Girl* (2012), wrote a medical column at the *Charlie Hebdo* humor magazine, and is president of a French trade union representing emergency physicians, Association des medecins urgentistes de France. Pel-loux' s Facebook profile lists his profession as "writer," while a nondescript Linkedin page only references his position as head of Asso-ciation des medecins urgentistes.[321]

News stories typically refer to Pelloux as a physician. Unlike Carli, however, publicly-available evidence or references to Pelloux's specific medical credentials are difficult to locate. Pelloux was previously de-picted in various news media as the initial first responder to the January 7th, 2015 shooting at the Charlie Hebdo editorial offices in Paris, where he claimed to have personally telephoned French President François Hollande to inform him of the attack. In addition to Pelloux's close ties with Hollande, he now has a personal government security detail con-sisting of "armed soldiers."[322]

Still Pelloux is unstintingly used as a credible source during the Charlie Hebdo attack and again in November. A *Guardian* article de-picts the writer/actor dramatically proclaiming how "'the reaction'" to 11/13 "'should be European. We musn't be afraid, we must all stand to-gether to find a Churchill spirit.' Pelloux," the story continues,

> was one of the first at the scene of the massacre at the satirical [*Char-lie Hebdo*] weekly. He gave his colleagues emergency treatment as many of his friends lay dead, after two French gunmen opened fire with Kalashnikovs, killing 12 people. Ten months later, on Friday night, Pelloux was in a Paris A&E department treating some of those seriously injured in the latest series of coordinated attacks that left at least 129 people dead and hundreds injured.

The reader also learns that Pelloux's new book on the Hebdo attacks was coincidentally released on November 12th. "'As soon as I heard of Friday night's attacks, I rushed straight to A&E,'" Pelloux recounts.

> That morning, the emergency services in Paris had actually done a training exercise for a major terrorist attack. We were well prepared. But the type of the attack is significant. It is a methodical gunning down of everyone, a little like a video game." Some of the attackers appeared to have been very young, he added. "The question that now has to be asked is why did these people who are so young take up arms and fight?" "The fact that there was an attack at a place where the French president was and then that gunmen mowed down people in the street is incredible. We've moved into another phase. We're re-ally in a war where they will stop at nothing."[323]

As a source Pelloux makes comments that are political and well beyond his areas of expertise in labor organizing, writing, or acting. Further, with the exception of Carli he is among the very few emergency response personnel interviewed by journalists in the wake of the attack. Pelloux's posturing alongside the amazing coincidence of his close involvement in both terror attacks appears to escape the scrutiny of *Guardian* staff. Or does it?

"Spontaneous" Video Footage Produced Professionally

Today the iPhone and similar personal electronic devices allow everyday people to capture high-quality video and photos in an instant. Yet few such spontaneous videos of the Paris attacks exist. Two key clips that have emerged from the November 13th events were shot by established professionals—one of whom travelled from Moscow on the morning of November 13th for a three-day stay where he was quartered in unusually close proximity to the rear exit of the Bataclan Theatre. There he or his his apparent neighbor, a professional journalist, captured footage of shooting victims and survivors being dragged from the building and hanging from the facility's second and third story windows.

Russian Victor Boyko is a well-established professional photographer, as his portfolio suggests. His clients feature some of the world's foremost entertainment and pop culture luminaries, including film director David Lynch, fashion designer Ralph Lauren, rock musician Lenny Kravitz, and singer/model/actress Paris Hilton.

A post on Mr. Boyko's Facebook page reveals that he arrived at Charles De Gaulle airport at around 5:00AM on February 13th. That morning Boyko proceeded to a rented flat ideally positioned at the rear of the Bataclan Theatre, as noted in a Facebook post and accompanying photograph taken at mid-day on November 14th. Perhaps coincidentally Daniel Psenny, a journalist working for *Le Monde*, was in a room or apartment next door, where he claimed to film horrified Bataclan concert goers exiting the facility through its rear entrance and upstairs windows.[324]

In the text of Boyko's November 14th Facebook post he explains that he was out on the town on the evening of November 13th and "went through hell" in his attempt to return to his flat behind the Bataclan. "There were lots of police at the restaurant on the corner of the Boulevard Voltaire and they literally pushed people inside the cafe and the waiter shut the door and locked it," he recalls.

After 15 minutes all hell broke loose. Ten or more people appeared on stretchers and others were being carried by hand and loaded into ambulances. President Hollande arrived along with the woman-mayor of Paris ... The police stopped with automatic weapons, roughly searching those present. A group of survivors from the Bataclan sat in the fence, many of them lacked clothing and shook in the cold. I arrived back early this morning, the door of my flat opposite the rear entrance of the Bataclan, where they ran away. I opened the door and there was blood all over the place. The lever to the elevator was covered in blood...

Here Boyko refers to *Le Monde*'s Psenny, but oddly fails to point out that Psenny is also a journalist who has remarkably produced the same photos and videos attributed in some news outlets to Boyko that are taken from almost the same vantage point opposite the Bataclan. Upon Boyko's return he

went up in the elevator to my floor, and there is no neighbor. The door was wide open... [Psenny] saw people running out of the club from the window and went to help [the] injured. He fell under some of those exiting the theatre and they shot him through hand. He's now in hospital and had to have surgery. Even today, the street is covered in blood.

Psenny is also noted in the end credits of a short video produced by the *New York Times* that includes voice-overs of Bataclan Theatre shooting survivors.[325]

In fact, the *New York Times* credits this video footage to Psenny and Boyko, with similar reports suggesting that Psenny captured the video from his apartment. Yet the video was clearly taken very close to if not from the identical vantage point that Boyko maintains are his quarters. (There are only two unedited shots in the *Times* video—one inside the Bataclan as the terrorists appear to begin shooting and one of the rear entrance scene.)

Did Boyko in fact take the video and allow Psenny and *Le Monde* to appropriate it? After all, these are among the services professional photographers provide. This is suggested in the end credits of a *New York Times/Le Monde* video which lists Boyko as one of the sources of the "social video" and Psenny as having created the "video." One may safely conclude that Boyko could not have been Psenny's guest because he refers to Psenny as his neighbor in the above account. Indeed, their joint positioning at the scene is highly unusual, yet clearly acknowledged in the end credits to the *New York Times* short. Even more puzzling is a report from Canadian Television which states that "Boyko lives three doors down from the Bataclan and arrived home 'a few minutes after the initial shooting.'"[326]

Similar to Boyko's breathtaking story of his return to his rented quarters, Psenny relates to the UK *Telegraph* a somewhat sensational account of rescuing an American who cryptically goes by the name of "Matthew" from the Bataclan shooting scene. "Monsieur Psenny," the *Telegraph* notes, "who had been in his apartment filming panic stricken concert goers rushing from the scene—including a pregnant woman hanging form [sic] an upstairs window—managed to drag [Matthew] to safety but was himself shot by one of the gunmen."

Indeed, this was "Matthew's" second "narrow escape from a terrorist strike." According to the *Telegraph* account, "He was at the foot of the World Trade Center on September 11th, 2001 heading to a work meeting when a United Airlines plan struck one of the towers."[327]

Further, the sole video to emerge out of an audience of up to 1,000 that coincidentally captured the initial stages of the terrorist attack was shot by professional graphic designer and illustrator "Seb Snow," according to the end credits of the *Times'* "Video of Attack on Paris Concert Hall."

Reliable Sources?

Several prominent news outlets tapped various sources following the Paris attacks and depicted them as everyday citizens who've been profoundly shaken by the events. But like Pelloux, Boyko, and Psenny many are either employed by or have close affiliations with the media or public relations industries. A handful of these interviewees are identified as journalists. Yet others with such professional credentials either have these referenced obliquely or not at all. Their testimonies taken as a whole, and more complete disclosure, might have called their credibility into question.

For example, a November 14th *New York Times* story describes the ordeal of "Delphine De Peretti, a 35-year-old project manager," who

> learned of the attacks last night after leaving the theater in London, where she lives. She immediately called her sister, Aurelie, 33, who was in Paris and had attended the concert at the Bataclan. There was no answer. On Saturday morning, Ms. De Peretti said she took the Eurostar train from London to Paris and joined her mother, who had come up from her home in the south of France. "We spent all morning looking for her," she said. Then her mother got a call from the Paris

medical examiner's office asking to come by. "They told us my sister was dead but they did not let us see her," she said, adding, "I am like a robot. I don't know what to do next. I have not watched the news or slept since last night." Speaking outside a counseling center, still holding a suitcase, Ms. De Peretti described her sister as fond of music and culture; she had loved to draw since she was a child. "My only concern right now is to be able to bring back her body and bring her with us to the south of France," she said.[328]

A few days later the *New York Times'* international edition carried a similar story citing De Peretti. "At the Town Hall for the 11th Arrondissement in Paris, Delphine De Peretti, 35, said she had learned early Saturday afternoon that her sister Aurelie, who was at the Bataclan music hall, had been killed. The family had been desperately trying to reach Aurelie all night. 'They told us my sister was dead, but they did not let us see her.'"[329]

Yet *Time* magazine published a piece contradicting de Peretti's account in the *Times*. After attempting to telephone her sister

> she called her parents in Saint Tropez, but they had gone to bed early, and had not heard about the Paris attacks. So Delphine spent the night with close friends in Paris, and at 5 a.m. hopped an almost empty train to Paris [sic], arriving to find her grief-stricken mother at the Gare du Nord station in the French capital. A call from the Paris police had confirmed that Aurélie was among the 89 people killed in the Bataclan concert hall.

In addition to the conflicting information on where de Peretti stayed on November 13th, the *Times* claims the family received a call from the medical examiner, while *Time* magazine claims it was received from police. "Smiling and without tears, she apologized for appearing to have little emotion about the family tragedy. 'I must seem cold right now,' she said. 'But I just cannot believe that I just lost a part of myself.'"[330]

Delphine Lacroix de Peretti is Chief Communications Director at the Paris bureau of the Thomas Cook travel firm. She has over a decade of experience in corporate and crisis communications, previously working as communications executive at CleKom Conseil, PAUL Restaurants, and Edmond de Rothschild, whose family's newspaper Libération printed five million copies of Charlie Hebdo after the January 7th terror attack on the paper.[331]

A similar and widely-covered story involves a woman's loss of her cousin at the Bataclan. "Standing before a makeshift memorial to the dead, strewn with candles, flowers and scribbled notes," Reuters reports,

Caroline Pallut hid her tears behind dark glasses. Her cousin, 37-year-old Maud Serrault, died on Friday night when Islamist gunmen attacked a Paris rock concert in a coordinated series of strikes across the city that killed 129 people and injured a further 352. "We are living a nightmare," Pallut said. "It is all so senseless. She had only just got married." Her husband managed to flee the assault, but lost his wife in the confusion. The family's frantic searches eventually led them to the city morgue.[332]

Pallut is the director of communications and marketing at Biocoop, a retail distributor of organic food, cosmetics, and fair trade products with 2,700 employees. Yet there are two Maud Serraults in the Paris area, and both work in public relations. The one who allegedly died at the Bataclan was Chief Director of Communications at Best Western France. The other is employed in communications and digital advertising at Agence Vianova, a Paris-based media and public relations firm involved in aiding clients "to emerge in a rapidly changing world and build lasting relationships with all public whether media, experts, associations, consumers, from the blogosphere and social networks."[333]

The *New York Daily News* ran a story centering on the riveting account of Erin Allweiss, another public relations practitioner with overt political ties who for

six terrifying hours … was stranded in a Parisian restaurant, her mind reeling from the horrific events … "There were so many things happening at once," Allweiss told the *Daily News* on Saturday. "The people in the restaurant were terrified. (People outside) were screaming at us to stay in." "If I'd walked, I'd have run straight into the gunmen," she said on the morning after ISIS-linked terrorists killed 129 people. "A minute later, we heard gunfire … it was so loud." "The people in the restaurant were terrified," she recounted. "Somebody who saw what happened came into the restaurant—a member of the staff and another woman, who was hysterically crying. She had been shot at in her car … She stayed in the restaurant with us for the rest of the night."[334]

The *Daily News* notes that Allweiss is "a Manhattan public relations executive" who was in Paris for a "dinner hosted by the United Nations Educational, Scientific and Cultural Organization." In fact, the dinner was in celebration of the seventieth anniversary of UNESCO's founding, and Allweiss' boutique public relations firm, No. 29 Communications, has several prestigious clients, including TED and Aqua Spark, "a global investment fund that supports sustainable aquaculture." Prior to starting her own firm Allweiss served as press secretary for the Natural Resources Defense Council and communications director for longtime Oregon Democratic Representative Earl Blumenauer, who achieved national prominence after sponsoring an amendment to the Affordable Care Act for Medicare-funded "end of life counseling."[335]

Shortly after the Paris events Australian political leaders were prominently featured proclaiming the plight of Tasmanian teen Emma Parkinson. Australian Prime Minister Malcolm Turnbull described Parkinson as a "'brave girl," after "the 19-year-old was shot, possibly multiple times, while lining up at the Bataclan to see the concert by the band Eagles of Death Metal," the *Herald Sun* reports.[336]

"I spoke to her on the phone and did my best to cheer her up. I told her that we were all thinking of her, all of us, every parent can sympathise with the thought that their child has been injured in something like this," Turnbull states in another report. "She's a brave girl and in all the circumstances, in good spirits ... I think [Ambassador] Stephen Brady's company and my call, discussion with her, cheered her up a bit."[337]

Parkinson's aunt, Sam Gunner, told the *Guardian* that Parkinson's mother was traveling to France to be with her. "'Emma was under anaesthetic by the time we spoke to her but we got the impression that there had been multiple shots to her hip,' Gunner told reporters in Hobart, Australia."[338]

Samantha Gunner describes herself as an "artist, beauty therapist, and blogger" with skills in marketing and public relations, and knowledge of "entertainment," "social media marketing," "public speaking" and "editing." Gunner was employed for six years as the "principal" at the "Break it down school of entertainment."[339]

Another Australian describing the scene at the Bataclan was "Melbourne's Sophie Doran, who had resided and worked in Paris for over five years." Doran "hid behind chairs in the Bataclan as the terrorists rampaged around her." Michael Doran, her father, explained to Australian television that "she wept as she revealed what had unfolded. 'From what she tells me, the carnage as it's described and the bloodbath seems to be an accurate reflection of what they all saw in there,' he said."[340]

Sophie Doran is also employed in the media industries as managing director and former editor-in-chief of Luxury Society, a marketing company that devises strategies to solicit high-end products and services to "the elusive High Net Worth Individual," according to the company's website. Doran's activities at Luxury Society, which include "design and production of private conference events in London, New York,

Paris, Hong Kong and Shanghai," allows her to associate with a super elite clientele.[341]

Australian-born Sam Davies told Reuters he was inside a club just a few blocks from one of the attacks. "'We were locked in the bar initially and then I was able to get out because the soul singer gave me a ride home,'" he explains.

> "I'm camped out on the outskirts of Paris ... but my house, there was snipers [sic] on the roof just earlier. There was bodies [sic] very close to it. I think there was about 10 or so people hit at the local bar. It's frightening. I certainly never thought I'd be caught up in these kind of things. These are places that I go to, that I went to last night, that I could have gone to tonight and my friends go to and look, it's a shocking thing."[342]

Reuters describes Davies as "an Australian journalist living in Paris." In fact, Mr. Davies' professional credentials are much closer to advertising and public relations than journalism. He is Head of English content operations and business development at TakePart media, and was previously social media strategist at the International Chamber of Commerce. Davies is a self-described "communications consultant with more than 10 years' international experience, specializing in B2B digital content, copyrighting and social media strategy. Paris has been my base since 2008, where I supported France's top-40 companies with their communications across many mediums in English."[343]

Another media professional who figures centrally in the eyewitness accounts provides vivid testimony on the Bataclan siege. "'It was a scene of carnage,' Julien Pearce, a radio reporter who was inside the Bataclan, told Europe 1 radio." "Mr. Pearce told CNN that he saw two of the men enter and begin to fire randomly. He said the gunmen wore black and said nothing." When the broadcaster "walked out into the street, he saw 25 bodies on the ground. 'It lasted for 10 minutes, 10 minutes, 10 horrific minutes when everybody was on the floor covering their heads and we heard so many gunshots, and the terrorists were very calm, very determined, and they reloaded three or four times their weapons'" [sic].[344]

Both the *Times* and CNN refer to Pearce merely as "a radio reporter." In fact, according to his LinkedIn and Twitter profiles he is employed as a journalist/reporter by one of France's leading broadcast networks, Europe 1. As Pearce speaks with CNN's Wolf Blitzer he becomes uncertain of the terrorists' appearance and Blitzer must redirect him to what is perhaps a scripted storyline.

Blitzer: Julien Pearce is joining us. He's a radio reporter. Julien, I understand you were inside the Bataclan theater during this concert that American rock band Eagles of Death Metal were performing, but now you have made it outside. Tell us what you have seen and what you have heard.

Pearce: Well, I have seen two terrorists from my point of view with AK-47s, Kalashnikovs, entering the concert room and firing randomly to the crowd [sic] ... They were in masks and they were wearing black clothes. And they were shooting at people on the floor and—shooting them ...

Blitzer: Julien, with these terrorists you say you saw three or four, you say they were dressed in black. Were their faces covered with masks?

Pearce: They were not wearing mask. They were unmasked. I've seen the face of one guy, one terrorist. He was very young. He was like 20 years old, 25 maximum. He wasn't wearing a beard or something. Like a random guy holding a gun, that's all. There were not masks.[345]

Another "witness" at the Bataclan put words in the terrorists' mouths, explaining how they articulated political rationales for their actions. According to the *Los Angeles Times*, "Several witnesses at the Bataclan concert hall mentioned hearing attackers say the words "Syria" and "vengeance," yet the paper proceeds to quote only one source—another media worker. "'I clearly heard them tell the hostages, 'It's the fault of Hollande, it's the fault of your president, he shouldn't have intervened in Syria'" [sic], Pierre Janaszak, a radio and TV presenter, told Agence France-Presse news agency. 'They also spoke about Iraq.'"[346] According to his Twitter account Janaszak is an animator at Enorme TV, a broadcast outlet featuring comedy and reality television-style fare, and head of publishing at another online entertainment outlet.

Another journalist living in very close proximity to the Bataclan was Patrick Smith, "who lives 50 metres from the concert hall." A spectator who lingered to observe the volatile scene, Smith provided a highly detailed account of what took place during the attack to at least one broadcast outlet. "'The Bataclan concert hall ... can take about 1,200 people at maximum and this evening the attackers stormed in the front of it," Smith explains.

"They shot up a lot of people, made their way into the main concert hall and there were at least three attackers it's believed and then they more or less held the entire audience, which could have been as many as 1,000 people, they held them hostage for about an hour." Mr. Smith said he watched as police placed ladders against the building before throwing in stun grenades. "You see the white flashes of the stun grenades and then there were a series of very big explosions and it may be that some of the hostage takers are actually, they had suicide packs on and they blew themselves up. But some of the survivors are now telling us that they got out by hiding in the seats and a lot of the people had just been shot in cold blood by the hostage takers."[347]

Smith is an editor at Africa Confidential, a news outlet publishing fortnightly and covering political and economic affairs. While Smith may indeed have a primary or secondary residence in Paris, all of Africa Confidential's editorial operations are located in Cambridge and London. What is especially curious is the detail afforded in Smith's account, which at the time was imparted just as the event's aftermath was unfolding. For example, Smith is a journalist and one must conclude that he is relatively careful with facts, but he knows the amount of time the concertgoers were held hostage, the specifics of what took place in the theatre, and infers how some of the "hostage takers ... had suicide packs on and they blew themselves up." As with the other eyewitness accounts laid out above, Smith's observations may appear sound. It is only when these are juxtaposed together that they become potentially suspect.

Conclusion

The foregoing aspects of news coverage on the Paris 11/13 attacks, coupled with the fact that a drill closely resembling the actual events took place 12 hours prior, suggest that this was a false flag. Many of the sources furnishing eyewitness accounts either have ties to the media, public relations or marketing industries, while others are referenced only by first names, and thus the information they impart must be even more carefully scrutinized. The remaining sources consulted were government or government-affiliated parties, the foremost being Carli, Pelloux, and President Hollande, who was present at the Stade de France where one of the apparent bombing attempts took place.

Another closely related and curious feature of the coverage is the clear lack of photos and videos relayed via social media from the scene. This is highly unlikely in an era when most individuals routinely carry cell phones with such advanced capacities, especially those in the twenty-to-thirty-something age demographic attending the Bataclan. Yet the only videos to have emerged from there are produced by professionals. The sole video of alleged terrorist gunfire inside the theatre includes an accompanying soundtrack which sounds uncannily similar to a string of firecrackers exploding.

Finally, the fact that officials and their associates readily admit to a complex emergency exercise closely resembling the attacks taking place just twelve hours before those events is a characteristic shared with many other confirmed false flag events, including 9/11,[348] the London 7/7/2005 attacks,[349] and an array of poorly understood mass shooter events in the US.

The 11/13 events are nevertheless now part of the official journalistic and historical record that, upon acceptance by the body politic, rationalizes government policies—in this and so many similar incidents accelerated police state measures and military involvement abroad to contain the supposed threat. France's "second 9/11" further establishes the mythic threat of Islamic-inspired terror, and the uncertainty surrounding whatever irrational force propels Muslims to such acts is the perceived countervailing force to the secular worldview, where an unquestioning faith in the authority of modern journalism remains key.

THE PARIS ATTACKS AND THE WHITE LIVES MATTER MOVEMENT

Ajamu Baraka

I received a message from one of my friends in Lebanon who asked with feigned curiosity why the U.S. media only gave a passing reference to the bombing in Beirut before turning to non-stop coverage of the attacks in Paris. Of course, like many of us she already knew the answer—that in the consciousness of the White West there is a premium on the value of White life.

Acknowledging this fact is neither new nor should it be particularly controversial. Its obviousness is apparent to anyone who is honest. We saw it in the response to the Charlie Hebdo attacks where the world (meaning the White West) engaged in a gratuitous expression of moral outrage against terrorism. But that outrage against terrorism didn't extent to the two thousand Nigerians who were murdered by Boko Haram the same weekend that a massive rally in Paris took place to condemn the Charlie Hebdo attack. At that rally not one word of solidarity or condemnation of terrorism in Nigeria was expressed by the speakers or the thousands gathered that day.

What my friend and all of us who have been the victims of the selected morality and oppressive violence of Western civilization over the last five hundred years have come to understand is that non-European life simply does not have equal value. How else can one explain the complete lack of attention to the humanity of the victims of ISIS attacks in Beirut and in Bagdad the day before, or the lack of concern for the lives of the over 7,000 people in Yemen murdered by the Saudi Arabia dictatorship with U.S. and NATO support?

And is it unfair to suggest that it is the diminished value of the lives of people in the global South that allows supporters of Bernie Sanders to dismiss his support for U.S. war-mongering policies in the global South?

The Liberal Roots of White Supremacist Psychopathology
In the classrooms of Western universities and occasionally in civic courses in high schools, students are introduced to the ideas of liberal humanitarianism that are supposed to characterize the core values of the European enlightenment. The enlightenment is supposed to represent the progressive advancement of all of humanity by the thinkers of Eu-

rope who, of course, represented the leading edge of collective humanity.

But what is not sufficiently interrogated in these classes is the fact that while these grand theories of "mankind's" inherent equality, rationality and even "perfectibility," were being discussed, those theorists had already arrived at a consensus. This consensus was on the criteria for determining which individuals and groups would be recognized as having equal membership in the human family, what Hannah Arendt referred to as those people who had the "right to have rights." According to the criteria, women and the non-European world were excluded or assigned to a lower order of humanity.

Eurocentric academicians, still a hegemonic force in the West, don't historicize the "great" humanitarian theories of Europe and critically juxtapose the rise of those theories with the concrete practices of European powers. Those practices involved the systematic slaughter of millions of Indigenous people throughout the Americas and the African slave trade that made Europe fat and rich and allowed for the creation of a class of intellectuals freed-up from the struggle to earn a living and able to engage in the higher contemplations of life.

However, Eurocentric liberalism was never just confined to the academy. It became the hegemonic ideological force that embedded itself in the culture and collective consciousness of the Western project and with it the de-valuation of non-European life and culture. In other words, the white supremacist ideology and world-view, normalized and thus unrecognized by most, has become a form of psychopathology. It is the cognitive dissonance that Fanon talks about regarding white supremacy as part of the colonial mindset and what James Baldwin refers to as the "lie of white supremacy" that has distorted the personalities, lives and the very ability of many white people to grasp reality.

However, the contradictions in the spheres of ideas and culture are not the real threat. The construction of a Western collective consciousness that is unable to cognitively process information and consider knowledge beyond the assumptions of its own world-views and values is dangerous enough, but the ease with which humanity is stratified with Europeans and their societies representing the apex of human development is the real threat, because that belief has resulted in the rationalization for the crimes of colonialism, slavery and genocide, and the politics of permanent war.

Despite the spirited defense of the positive aspects of liberalism from John Rawls to radicals like Slavoj Zizek, the racist and sexist contradictions of liberalism were once again confirmed by the obscenely disproportionate response to the attacks in Paris that once again demonstrated that liberalism is no more than a racist ideological construct posing as trans-historical philosophy.

However, let me be clear, my critique of the moral hypocrisy of the West should not be read as a rationalization for the horrific crimes committed in Paris a few days ago. The intentional murder of non-combatants is a recognizable war crime that can rise to the level of a crime against humanity and should always be condemned with the perpetrators brought to justice. That legal principle is based on the moral principle of the equal value of all life and everyone's human right to life. The defense and enforcement of those principles requires, however, that all states and groups be subjected to the same legal and ethical standards and that all are held accountable.

But in the context of the existing global power relations, crimes committed by Western states and those states aligned with the West as well as their paramilitary institutions escape accountability for crimes committed in the non-European world. In fact some states—like the United States—proudly claim their "exceptionality," meaning impunity from international norms, as a self-evident natural right.

And in that sense, while the victims of the violence in Paris may have been innocent, France was not. French crimes against Arabs, Muslims and Africans are ever-present in the historical memory and discourse of many members of those populations living in France. Those memories, the systemic discrimination experienced by many Muslims and the collaboration of French authorities with the U.S. and others that gave aid and logistical support to extremist elements in Syria and turned their backs while their citizens traveled to Syria to topple President Assad, became the toxic mix that resulted in the blowback on November 13th.

Although a number of the dead in Paris are young Arabs, Muslims and Africans, in the global popular imagination, France, like the U.S. (even under a Black president), is still white.

So in Iraq the Shia will continue to die in the thousands from ISIS bombs; the Saudis will continue to slaughter Houthis with U.S. and NATO assistance; and Palestinian mothers will continue to bury their children, murdered by Zionist thugs in and out of uniform, without any outcry from the West. CNN and others will give non-stop coverage to the attacks in Paris because in the end we all really know that the lives that really matter are white.

Part 4:
False Flags and the New World Order

SIGNS OF SATANISM: OCCULT FINGER-PRINTS ALL OVER PARIS ATTACKS

Ole Dammegard (interviewed by Kevin Barrett)[350]

Being an expert on false flag terrorism in Europe, I imagine that your immediate   reaction on Friday the 13th was "it looks like another false flag."

I think it's really important, when you come to a crime scene, not to jump to conclusions without really looking into the evidence. But during the last few years, it has been absolutely crazy what has been going on. And I've come to realize, after thirty years of deep investigation, that what we're seeing is like a theater group on a global terror tour being used by the powers behind the New World Order. I believe we are seeing the same people running around in SWAT team uniforms in Paris, Ottawa, Sydney, Copenhagen, and so on. The same crisis actors, the same media people in the background, the same marketing agencies, the same directors. We're looking at a small group, like a rock group on a global tour, repeating the same performance again and again and again, flown from country to country in military planes, then being transported to locations in buses, helped by local back-ups. I spoke to CIA whistleblower Chip Tatum about this, and he said it's not only possible, it's very probable.

So we're talking about a troupe of traveling terror troubadours, coming soon to a theater of operations near you.

That is my deep conviction. And I've done a lot of work trying to identify people in the background, people in the uniforms. There's a reason why police SWAT teams these days are running around with face masks. It's because they don't want us to recognize them. They claim it's for their protection. But I say, what is the difference these days between what a so-called terrorist looks like and a SWAT team member? And I would suggest that this is why, when false flag terror attacks are carried out, the shooters—most recently in Paris and San Bernardino—are dressed in dark military-looking clothes. And the reason is, they go in, do the shooting, disappear somewhere, inside a building. The SWAT teams arrive. Ten police officers in SWAT team uniforms go in. And then twelve leave the building. Nobody notices the shooters being taken out from the area that way. It's a perfect disguise. So all the shooters have to do is pull on a bullet-proof vest and a facemask, and that's it—you won't recognize them. They did it at the JFK assassination where one of the shooters was in a police uniform.

I was able to predict last February's attack in Copenhagen. And once again, the signs were very strong that they were going to hit again in November. I thought the big terror attack would be in Copenhagen on the 11th of November, because there was a major terror drill there at the university. There was also a major naval drill off the west coast of Denmark, where they planned for a nuclear disaster with two vessels that collided.

We don't have mass shootings in Europe, because the people are not armed here. So they have no need to stage mass shootings on behalf of gun confiscation. But this time they had a mass shooting drill at the University in Copenhagen. Swedish police came over and were playing the terrorists. They brought in the SWAT teams, the helicopters. And when they came out with the two "terrorists" they took these gold-colored metal blankets like we saw in Paris, and put them like tinfoil hats on the two cops playing the terrorists. So when they were taken in front of the cameras they had tinfoil hats on.

Tinfoil hat terrorists? It sounds like they're starting to demonize "conspiracy theorists." We saw that after the Paris attacks, when the government told us that ISIS is now talking about the freemasonic-Zionist conspiracy. So anybody who talks about such things must be part of ISIS.

So I had people on location in Copenhagen, filming, but nothing happened. And then—BOOM!—two days later, it happened in Paris.

I wasn't the only one who saw it coming. There was a Twitter account called PZFeed Ebooks. Two days before the attacks it Tweeted: "BREAKING: DEATH TOLL FROM PARIS ATTACKS 120 WITH 270 OTHERS INJURED." That exact same Twitter account went with the exact same Tweet when there was the so-called mass shooting in Peshawar in Pakistan on December 26th, 2014, where one of the claimed victims was Noah Posner, who had officially died two years earlier in Sandy Hook. Prior to the massacre, the Tweet from PZFeed Ebooks said: "BREAKING: DEATH TOLL FROM PESHAWAR ATTACKS RISES TO 120 WITH 270 OTHERS INJURED." And during the Ebola outbreak, the Ebola hoax, it was the same PZFeed Ebooks Tweet: "BREAKING: DEATH TOLL FROM EBOLA VIRUS RISES TO 120 WITH 270 OTHERS INJURED." So the same Twitter account, with the same Tweet, was used in three different operations. And then there is Wikipedia. Less than two hours after the attacks started in Paris,

Wikipedia had a full description of the whole event, with all the numbers of killed and wounded, all the different sites of the attacks. Everything—including the speech of French President François Hollande about "we have to close the border." When we backtracked the updates to this account, when it was, at 23:06 in the evening it was talking about Hollande's speech to the nation. Only one slight problem: That speech was given at 23:58, fifty-two minutes *after* it had been reported in Wikipedia.

Sounds like somebody's getting ahead of themselves feeding the script to the media, like when CNN and BBC reported World Trade Center Building 7 had collapsed before it happened.

This is the sign of a black op. Also there's a computer game called Battlefield 3. On almost the same date as the first Paris attack on Charlie Hebdo, it came out with a new version. And in that version, there is a terror attack on Paris on November 13th. There is the even stronger indication of foreknowledge with the *Economist Magazine* cover (see page 55). And Kerry Cassidy of Project Camelot was contacted by someone in London who saw Wembley being lit up in the French colors one hour before the attack happened.

There's also an occult, satanic element. It seems the people behind these things are interested in numerology, symbols of ritual human sacrifice. Tom Breidenbach has done brilliant work on this with respect to 9/11. In Paris, the only footage that was released of the carnage in the Bataclan nightclub (see front cover collage) shows bodies apparently having been dragged around the floor to create what appears to be a painting of a heart shape in blood. (Some have suggested an eye of Horus.) It's a very strange picture, especially considering it was the only one released. Ole, I understand you've found traces of an occult or satanic connection to the Paris attacks.

There are so many of them! That photo, for one, is absolutely incredible. I want to point out that when you look at this photo, it looks like a massive paintbrush had been painting in blood, going around in a one-meter wide heart-shaped pattern around these bodies. On November 18th, 2014—the day of sacrifice, also an important date in witchcraft—there was an attack on a synagogue in Jerusalem. They said some Palestinian guys went into this synagogue and killed four people. And there was exactly the same kind of weird blood pattern going out in the long corridor. That was one year, minus one week, before the Paris attacks. The same kind of blood pattern in both cases; it's not natural in any way, shape or form.

At the Bataclan, it's said that at least 80 people were killed. But in the photo we only see 25. There is no-one except the bodies spread around. No police, no medical, no emergency workers. And if you look closely, if you zoom in, you see the body of a woman—she's lying straight, the first body closest to the heart, underneath it. Look at her legs. You cannot do what she's doing with her legs. Not with a human body. What she is, and what these bodies are, I would strongly suggest are what are called capper bodies, stunt bodies, used for film stunts, not real bodies. There are quite a few of them when you look closely at the details—which is very difficult, because it's not sharp. But they're lying in ways that you cannot do with a human body. And in the lower left corner, there's a big open area on the floor—there's no glass, there's no nothing that should have been there, since this was a bar and there was a rock concert. But there's nothing, just these bodies spread around. Look down in the left corner. And if you really enlarge it, you will see there's a big golden death mask. It looks like it has a strong connection to Aztec death masks. Also in the audience, up at the top of the image, if you change the contrast and put a lot of light in the dark areas you will see that there are five or six men, or persons, dressed in black. And it looks like they're holding candles. I've put these Bataclan images next to those of satanic rituals. They're almost identical.

A former Canadian intelligence officer told me that some of the bodies in that picture must be dummies, not real bodies, because of the positions they're in.

How much blood is in one body, how many bodies have been dragged around, to make a meter-wide heart-shaped pattern all around the room? You'd need a lot. It almost looks like it was done by one of those clean-ing vehicles they drive around in airports, in supermarkets, only they put some ketchup in rather than cleaning fluid. And also, there are sup-posed to have been one to four suicide bombers who blew themselves up inside this building as well. No signs of them at all. These stunt bod-ies, they're called dapper cadavers. If you do a Google images search, you'll find that often they're lying in similar positions to some of these bodies at the Bataclan. And Scott Bennett, a former military guy, said that an AK-47, which is supposed to have been used here, with four shooters—he says the impact on the human body of an AK-47 makes holes the size of an orange, bigger than a golf ball. But here, on most of these bodies, there are no holes at all, no blood. And the blood (on the floor) is running in different directions away from the body. It should run in the same direction, due to slight floor tilt. There are so many things that are wrong with this photo. We tried to find out the photo data for this photo—what kind of camera, what time it was taken, who took it—and it turns out it's a screen dump from a computer. So there's absolutely no photo ID in the photo itself. I think they're becoming aware of the work of people like us, so they're trying to avoid all of these ways of tracking them.

There is another problematic photo depicting the audience at the Bataclan as seen from the stage, supposedly taken before the shoot-ing.[351] It says if you use this photo, you have to pay 500 pounds or dollars to the Eagles of Death Metal. [Who are satanic Zionists, by the way.][352] You can see the whole crowd. Many are holding their fists in the air making signs of the devil. And it's like the cover of Sgt. Peppers Lonely Hearts Club Band—an obvious photoshop composite, very poorly done.

It does look a little to good to be true. But I ran this by Massimo Mazzucco, a professional photographer, filmmaker and photo expert who is currently producing a documentary on the moon landing photos. Here is what he told me: "I see nothing strange in the picture at all. Yes, *each face has bright studio illumination*— Most likely someone turned a stage spot-light towards the crowd, in order to take the picture. *Each image on a separate image layer and each character with its own focus?* Not true. The shadows of each person fall properly and accurately on the people behind. It would take a master in photoshopping to re-create those shadows on each single individual. *The crowd doesn't interact as a crowd?* Of course they don't interact: everybody is focused on the photographer at that particular moment. Obviously somebody has called their attention just before the picture was taken. *A very artificial focus and loss of depth in the image, with each figure pasted in separately?* Not true. In fact, it is the opposite. Focus sharpness degrades as you get more distant from the photographer, which is exactly what you would get in that kind of situation (artificial light, wide lens aperture). *Claims that the ginger-bearded fellow holding up a glass to the right is duplicated on the far-left further back?* Wrong! He is not duplicated. They look alike, but on close examination they are two different people.

I do not agree with him. Absolutely not. I've spent many years with photoshop. That is a crap job. If I'd done a job like that, I would never get paid. If you really look into details—I've got a high resolution im-age—it is extremely badly done. The question is, why has someone put such an effort into making a photo like that? It's almost like they're rubbing it in our face. According to sources—and I've been contacted from the inside—they say that the people behind the New World Order have their own interpretation of the law of karma: "If you show your victim what's going to happen, and the victim does not react, then the karma is on the shoulders of the victim, and the attacker goes free." So they put it out there, right in our face. And if we do not react, it's on us.

Well, we're reacting here. Putting them on notice.

I've asked Chip Tatum about this. He was involved in taking out a lot of people on the orders of George Bush Sr. He said he has never heard of it, but it makes total sense, because he and his (assassination) team always had to confront the victim verbally first and give them a chance to "conform." And if they did not, it was a green light. They could be taken out. And Chip was very uncomfortable with that. It was so dangerous for him and his teams, because you never knew how anyone would react. But he said "we always had to do that."

So to continue with the Bataclan: There were two really spooky videos released one week before by an artist called Pantero666. We're back to the satanic theme. His work is described as "a combination of ancient Aztec rituals"—in my world these are blood rituals. You can find them on youtube with the search terms "Bataclan Halloween videos." They were released just one week before the massacre. The first one shows a young girl walking in the forest in a beautiful white dress. And she comes across a dance group. Eight or ten young kids in white T shirts, covered with blood. It looks like they have been shot to pieces. And they're dancing around: "Shoot shoot shoot, blood blood blood," miming shooting gestures, looking like zombies, with blood everywhere. In the middle of the song, they sort of lie on top of her. When they let her go, she has blood on her dress. She walks straight into the camera. And she's got the mask of Hannibal Lecter.

The second Bataclan Halloween video is about a young guy running around the alleys next to the Bataclan, exactly where the shootings were filmed. He's running around looking paranoid, then runs into the Bataclan, around the open area, walks up on stage. There is product placement, with Nike logos all over the place. When he goes up on stage there is a white mask. He puts it on. When he takes it off, the whole place is on fire, everybody's dancing.

In this video there are ten subliminal images that flash by at one-twenty-fifth of a second per image. I've frozen these images and taken them out. They show people's faces, and next to each one, the same Hannibal Lecter mask. I enlarged one of the images. The face beside the Hannibal Lecter mask is the girlfriend of Nick Alexander, one of the victims, who was connected to the band Eagles of Death Metal. And it's the same Hannibal Lecter mask as in the first video.

And it gets stranger than that. A couple was interviewed, the same couple who started the story about the shooters saying "Allahu akbar, this is for Syria." That story came from just one couple. It turned out their names are Benjamin and Celia Vial. He's the co-owner of a record company called Death Proof Recordings. And she is the legal advisor to the movie *Hannibal Rising*, the film in which they use the same mask again.

It's very bizarre. Many of the witnesses had records released just before this happened. So they're really hot now. And some of these crisis actors like Jeannie Watson just had a record come out on— September 11th! Also on September 11th, the Bataclan's long-time Zionist owners sold it to a media conglomerate, Lagardière, which was also in charge of the stadium, and indirectly owned the management company of Eagles of Death Metal. Lagardière also owns the radio and TV stations where many of the people involved, as witnesses and so on, were working. (See James Tracy's article in this book.) We're looking at a theater group here with a marketing agency preparing logos, slogos —all of that is on standby when an operation like this is carried out. Just look at how fast this whole Facebook thing, where you could put the French flag as your profile photo, was there within an hour!

Just like the *Je suis Charlie* slogo that instantly appeared and was blasted all over the world immediately after the January 7th shootings. It was as if a PR agency had designed the Charlie Hebdo shooting with this in mind, that they were going to instantly blast *Je suis Charlie* to the world using media money power. Here the same thing has happened with the French flag.

It is standard procedure. This is how it's done. They've got whole themes. In Ottawa it was what I call the Lassie theme. The poor soldier that was killed there, they say, Nathan Cirillo—if you look him up, you'll find there are a great many photos of this very good-looking soldier who is supposed to have been killed, with dogs. Dogs with Canadian flags, while he's in uniform. But it's not the same dog! I don't know how many dogs this guy is supposed to have had. And if you compare the photos, he's got exactly the same haircut, exactly the same way of being unshaven, the length of his, well, not a beard, it's more of the scruffy look. They've taken a day with this guy and had him take I don't know how many selfies with different dogs, to get the emotions going. It's the Lassie theme for Ottawa.

In the Charlie Hebdo event, all of the signs that thousands of people are holding up are the same: black background, white text, same font. Where did that come from?

It came from a PR agency.

Exactly. If you have a printer, would you print black background? You wouldn't do that. It would be too expensive.

Though I guess you wouldn't have to worry about that if you've got the Rothschilds behind it. Anyway, a little over two weeks after Paris comes the apparent sequel in San Bernardino. What was your reaction?

For me, I almost fall asleep. Because it's so badly carried out. I don't know how many of these crap operations they're going to do. And here, once again, right in our faces, the news reports talk about actors. I've heard at least three news agencies talk about deceased actors.

As Chip Tatum, who has a background in black operations, says, these shootings are just business as usual. They have their meetings, discussing what is the desired effect, how is it going to be carried out. They've got a storyboard. And then BOOM, the operation goes live. They're there, controlling the whole thing. And then they have a direct follow-up meeting. And if the desired effect has not been accomplished, they do a follow-up operation with an identical theme but aiming for an amped-up emotional reaction so they can step in with their solution.

For instance, when they did the Woolwich beheading in London, they didn't get the full effect they wanted. So the next day, BOOM! A very similar thing happened in Paris, to get the impact they needed.

So here, everybody's looking at Paris. Some of us are looking too deeply into it. So they distract us, and amplify the impact, with San Bernar dino. By the way, one of the songs by the Eagles of Death Metal, San Berdoo Sunburn, is about making plans with a "girlfriend who's a swinger" and heading out to San Bernardino. "Next town, San Bernardino."

Another connection between the Paris and San Bernardino events is that in both cases, multiple witnesses reported that the shooter teams were white paramilitaries, not the brown-skinned patsies.

It was so badly carried out. It wasn't even the same car being chased as the one in the crime scene photos. But I didn't look deeply into San Bernardino because I felt they're trying to distract us by diverting our attention. So I needed to keep my focus on Paris. When three separate news agencies openly discuss "actors," when they let reporters totally wreck the alleged crime scene, go in there and turn the whole place upside-down, they openly report that it was three paramilitary white guys doing the shooting—and then try to blame a Muslim couple. How did *that* happen? I posted a photo of the patsy Muslim couple with the caption, "here is a photo of the three white paramilitary guys seen doing the shooting in San Bernardino."

And there is the tie-in between Paris and San Bernardino of really *obvious* drills. In Paris, how could they get more obvious than Patrick Pelloux revealing that multiple-location active shooter exercises were ongoing on Friday the 13th—drills that turned into the real, or so-called real, event. And then in San Bernardino, they say this happened at a facility for disabled people where they have an active shooter drill *every month*. It must be the only such facility in the world where they have an active shooter drill every month. And it's also the only one that got targeted by supposed ISIS terrorists. In both Paris and San Bernardino, it seems they're being way too obvious.

I can only agree. It has come to a point where it's right in our face.

It reminds me of hypnotists who sometimes run a test to see if their hypnotic subject is still in a deep trance. They want to see whether the person is still totally hypnotized. So they'll pull out an onion and say, "take a bite of this delicious apple." If the person eats the onion, believing it's an apple, they know that person is deeply hypnotized. Likewise, the perpetrators of these operations seem to be making what they're doing obvious, to see to what extent the population is so hypnotized they'll accept anything they're told.

That is very possible.

COGNITIVE DISSONANCE:
MEDIA MASKS GHASTLY TRUTH BEHIND TERROR

Henry Makow, Ph.D.

Editor's Introduction

Henry Makow is one of the four contributors to this book who were witch-hunted out of academic careers for investigating topics that Big Brother does not want investigated. But only Makow's work—with which I am not always in agreement, but which courageously raises important issues and shatters prevailing taboos—is so controversial that even people I respect urged me not to include it. "I think the article drags the book down and could damage your efforts," wrote a Religious Studies professor. Here is what I wrote back:

"Have you studied the history of the Jewish-heretical satanic-masonic cults that began (or surfaced in their current form) with Shabatai Zvi and Jacob Frank about 350 years ago? (And constitute the basis of modern Zionism-freemasonry, which forms the esoteric religion of the pinnacle of the Western elite?) I have been reading on this topic, and I think there are reasons to suspect that Makow is, if not right, at least supported by a fair amount of evidence. At the very least, I think this is something that needs to be investigated and pursued. And I think your reaction is precisely equivalent to the reactions of people who would say that "including a truther article in a university press book will drag the book down." In both cases, the topic is of tremendous (potential) importance, and for that reason protected by powerful, manufactured taboos.

"While in Paris I met Youssef Hindi and read his book Occident et Islam: Sources et genèse messianiques du sionisme de l'Europe médiévale au choc des civilisations. *Hindi makes a very strong case that Zionism began many centuries ago, with a satanic Jewish heretical tradition holding that they could force the Messiah to return and establish absolute global "Jewish" domination over the goyim (other tribes) from his throne in Jerusalem by (1) staging a Jewish invasion of Jerusalem AGAINST the will of God, i.e. Zionism, and (2) "religiously" committing abominations—satanic rituals, blood sacrifices, outrageous lies, orgies including horrific acts, and other extreme violations of divinely-sanctioned morality. This appears to be the "religious" outlook*

of the highest level(s) of freemasonry and of the biggest Western banking families. If true, it explains a lot, including the 'satanic' strand in 9/11 (beautifully explored by Tom Breidenbach)[353] and Paris (discussed by Ole Dammegard in the book). Note that the cover of the book, a collage including the Satanic heart/Eye of Horus painted in blood on the floor of the Bataclan, references this area of investigation.

"A great many Muslim intellectuals are aware, to various degrees and from various perspectives, of the above-sketched interpretation of Zionism ... I believe a majority worldwide would be sympathetic to it. Suppressing it would be yet another act of censorship against Muslims (and others who have investigated this domain). It needs to be discussed. If you or anyone else would care to write an article outlining the case against this interpretation I would be happy to include it in the ebook version."

–Kevin Barrett

We are doomed unless we face bitter truths that we've been trained to deny. Society has been subverted; terrorism is state sponsored; politicians and media are complicit.

We must overcome our cognitive dissonance. The "Jewish Conspiracy for World Domination" is not only genuine but has been a fait accompli for a 100 years and more. Despite the corporate media and academe saying the opposite, The Protocols of Zion are in fact 100% genuine.

This centuries-old plot jeopardizes Jews as well as Gentiles because most Jews like myself are not privy to it. We are human shields. Non-Jewish Freemasons are in on this plot in greater numbers, so the question of anti-Semitism is irrelevant, a ruse used to disarm resistance.

Western society has been colonized by a satanic cult, Cabalist Judaism (Illuminism.) The true occult meaning of "revolution" is inverting reality and replacing God at the top with Lucifer. Lucifer represents their perversions and pretensions. They invert good and evil, healthy and sick, true and false, beautiful and ugly.

In *The Red Symphony* insider Christian Rakowski explained that "war is revolutionary."[354] This is because war destroys and demoralizes humanity while concentrating power and wealth in the hands of the Illuminati, who naturally initiate all wars. War is satanic human sacrifice expressing the Illuminati's hatred of mankind.

Their power originates in the private central banking cartel which produces the means of exchange (currency) in the form of a debt to itself. Currency is nothing but a coupon that government could easily produce debt-and-interest free. The Masonic Jewish bankers must prevent any country from doing this by establishing a world tyranny ("world government, globalism"). As soon as one country tries to escape the net, the others will invade.

They use false flag terror to concentrate totalitarian power in the State (which they control.) They are not satisfied with a monopoly over credit. They seek a complete monopoly on human life—political, economic, mental, cultural and spiritual. They want your property. More important, they want your soul. They want your spouse and your children (feminism, homosexuality, sex ed). This is the meaning of Communism and the goal of the NWO.

Because of "debt," most governments (and nation states) are nothing but facades for the bankers. I liken them to high school student councils.

According to *The Protocols of Zion* (15), "the people of the world and even their governments" will be "as children under-age."[355]

Cognitive Dissonance

The Illuminati imagine that society will acquiesce, and so far they've been right.

We are like prisoners in Plato's cave. The Illuminati media projects a picture of reality on the wall which allows them to initiate endless war, terror psy ops or climate change hoaxes.

We suffer from cognitive dissonance.

ISIS commits gruesome atrocities and acts of terror. Yet it is armed and financed by the West who pretend to fight it.

(Donald Trump talks about banning Muslims when he knows perfectly well the CIA and Mossad are behind ISIS and terror.)

A jetliner crashed into the Pentagon on Sept. 11th yet there is no wreckage. World Trade Center 7 was wired for demolition on Sept 11th but the Twin Towers weren't?

Robbie Parker, the grieving Sandy Hook father is laughing seconds before going on camera. The so-called child victims of Sandy Hook sing at the Superbowl two months later. The *Economist* announced the date of the Paris attack on their front cover 11 months prior and so on...These mass shootings are all followed by resolutions to disarm law abiding Americans.

All major social institutions have been subverted. But thanks to the media, the public is none the wiser. Their secret societies control government, business, the church, military, education and law. It is considered a breach of good taste to even mention this.

Democracy is a form of social control and a charade. The Illuminati sponsor most "grass roots" activism.

Our political leaders are Freemasons. The only difference is the speed with which they enact the NWO agenda.

We have de facto Communism. The news consists of psy ops and propaganda. Entertainment is social engineering and satanism. Religion is suppressed.

Would so many Fortune 500 companies spontaneously promote diversity and homosexuality if they weren't all controlled by the bankers? "Political correctness" is an old Communist Party term.

Intelligence Agencies Implement Terror

Western intelligence services like the CIA and MI-6 serve the bankers, not the taxpayers who pay for them. They are responsible for most terrorism. Politicians and media make this charade possible.

The Israeli Mossad seems to coordinate things. In a book, entitled *Coups et Blessures* (Assaults and Injuries), former French Foreign Minister Roland Dumas wrote, "The Israelis are doing whatever they want in France, and are controlling the French Intelligence with what serves them."

French Intelligence certainly carried out Charlie Hebdo and the Paris attacks. Mahoud Admo, an eye witness of the Nov. 13th massacre of 20 people at the Cafe Le Belle Equippe said the shooter arrived in a chauffeur driven black Mercedes:

> He fired lots of bullets. He was white, clean shaven and had dark hair neatly trimmed. He was dressed all in black accept for a red scarf. The shooter was aged about 35 and had an extremely muscular build, which you could tell from the size of his arms. He looked like a weightlifter...They looked like soldiers or mercenaries and carried the whole thing out like a military operation. It was clear that they were both very heavily armed and the gunman was carrying several magazines on him. They both then coolly sat back in the car and sped off in the direction of the Bataclan.[356]

We never know how many actually die in these psy ops. In the Paris attack for example, it seems unlikely that the Illuminati, who are Satanists, would mow down a theatre full of young people celebrating Satanic music. More likely such audience would be collaborators in a psy op. There are reports that the picture of bodies show dummies, and the pattern of smeared "blood" makes no sense.

These psy ops all have the same hallmarks. There is a "drill" happening at the same time. There are crisis actors, fake wounds and no convincing pictures of the so-called victims.

False flag terror is the oldest trick in the Zionist tool bag. "We wage war by means of deception," is the actual Mossad motto. I won't rehash the scores of attacks designed to alienate the West from the Muslim world. Some of the highlights would be the Lavon Affair (1954), the destruction of the USS Liberty in 1967 (killing and wounding 200 in an attack which they wanted to blame on Egypt) and of course 9/11.

Often Jews are the targets of these false flags. The Haganah admitted that in 1940, they blew up the ship "Patria" killing 252 Jews and pretended this was a Masada-like gesture by the passengers whom the British wouldn't allow to disembark. And of course the holocaust itself was the biggest false flag of all time.

In 1951, Zionists staged a series of "anti-Semitic" bombing attacks against Baghdad Jews to force them to leave to Israel where they were shamelessly exploited by Zionists. Google my article "Terror is Longterm Zionist Strategy for World Domination" for more examples.

The Game Plan

The Paris attack and subsequent false flags have created a wave of anti-Muslim hysteria and prepared the ground for the Third World War planned in Albert Pike's famous 1871 letter to Giuseppe Mazzini:

> The Third World War must be fomented by taking advantage of the differences caused by the "agentur" of the "Illuminati" between the political Zionists and the leaders of Islamic World. The war must be conducted in such a way that Islam and political Zionism mutually destroy each other. Meanwhile the other nations, once more divided on this issue will be constrained to fight to the point of complete physical, moral, spiritual and economical exhaustion...

Putin is a member of the illuminati who realized the NWO agenda involved the subjugation and rape of Russia. I like to believe his opposition to this agenda is sincere and not a pretext for world war.

Hitler probably was false opposition that allowed the Illuminati to manufacture World War Two and slaughter 60 million people, mainly Gentiles.

We can rely on Jews themselves to understand the Jewish Conspiracy. The Jewish World of Feb 9th, 1883 stated:

> The dispersion of the Jews has rendered them a cosmopolitan people. They are the only cosmopolitan people and in this capacity must act and are acting, as a solvent of national and racial differences. The great Ideal of Judaism is ...that the whole world shall be imbued with Jewish teachings, and that in a universal Brotherhood of Nations—a greater Judaism, in fact—all the separate races and religions shall disappear.
>
> As a cosmopolitan people, Jews have passed the stage that the national form of separatism represents in social life. They have made the whole world their home. By their activities in literature and science,

by their dominant position in all branches of public activity, they are gradually moulding gentile thinking and systems into Jewish moulds.

Organized Jewry is a also a solvent of family and morality. Multiculturalism, miscegenation, homosexuality and feminism are not about "tolerance and human rights." They are about shredding the social fabric, dissolving European Christian culture and civilization.

In my website article, "Destructive Cabala Doctrine Dooms Humanity," I detail why Judaism as defined by Talmud and Cabala is satanic.

"Secularism" and "Humanism" are masks for this Satanism. So when we read that 135 years ago, they were already "moulding Gentile thinking into Jewish moulds," it means humanity has been inducted into a satanic cult to serve the Cabalist Jewish banker.

Certainly this agenda is nearing fruition. At Hanukah, we saw politicians from every background lighting the Menorahs in front of the White House lawn and Eiffel Tower. Clearly the "whole world has been imbued with Jewish teaching."

We see Masonic politicians rushing to welcome millions of refugees into the West after the psy op where a three-year-old refugee Alan Kurdi, or a convincing replica, washed up on shore.

Illuminati Jews make no secret that, "all the races and religions shall disappear." Migrants cross boundaries as if nation states don't exist.

Society has been brainwashed to deny reality. The Illuminati (Masonic) Jewish agenda is to enslave mankind, mentally and spiritually if not physically. And they have largely succeeded. In the future, they will rely increasingly on false flag terror to galvanize their plot. Western society has a cancer that cannot be treated unless it is first recognized.

Part Six:
Questioning the False Flag Paradigm

FALSE FLAG? REFLECTIONS ON SPECULATION, CERTAINTY, AND RESISTANCE[357]

Gilad Atzmon

The common tendency to attribute the catchy "false flag operation" to an act of violence we struggle to explain is a dangerous political habit. When taken to an extreme, it suggests that behind every act of martyrdom, there must be a Mossad puppeteer. In the following pages I attempt to set a clear categorical dichotomy between the notions of false flag and the conspiratorial.

A false flag operation refers to a covert activity intended to deceive the public into believing that an act has been carried out by perpetrators other than those who actually planned or executed it.

In current political discourse, when we suggest a false flag operation, we basically deliver a simple message—we don't believe what we are told. We don't trust our politicians, nor can we trust the media outlets that echo the given official narrative. Our profound distrust of our information sources leads us to insist that there is a deeply concealed plot that may actually explain everything.

Within contemporary emerging dissent, the reference to a false flag operation often indicates that we are convinced that some devious forces are operating behind the scenes in an effort to make people believe that some people (mostly Muslims and Arabs) are uniquely and particularly bad.

Accordingly, those amongst us who occasionally point at false flag operations are in an understandable state of disbelief and have good reason to suspect the official narrative. Such analysts reject the ridiculous notion of a "clash of civilizations," as a duplicitous Zio-centric dichotomy, designed to separate "us" (the "Judeo-Christians") from "them" (the Arabs and the Muslims). Growing numbers of sceptics who search for evidence of possible false flag operations, understand that the "Judeo-Christian legacy" is a delusional political construction promulgated to recruit the West to launch and fight Zionist immoral interventionist wars.

False Flag vs. Conspiracy Theory

One may wonder at this stage whether there is a categorical difference between the notions of false flag operation and a conspiracy theory.

While conspiracy theory is an explanatory hypothesis, one would expect any given false flag narrative to take us beyond mere hypothesis and into the domain of proof. A thesis of a false flag operation ought to aim for certainty—an account supported by probative or substantial evidence. In an ideal world, concrete evidence would evaporate the conspiratorial theoretical cloud and expose the flag of falsehood, clearly delineated in the sky.

In order to achieve this ideal we must set clear categorical and epistemological standards to define and qualify the type of evidence that tends to establish the existence of a genuine false flag operation.

Epistemology

The fact that X is a prime beneficiary of a terror act perpetrated by Y against Z does not mean that X and Y are working in concert or that Y is X (in disguise). It does suggest, however, that X is a prime suspect. Specifically, in spite of the fact that false flag operations are established Israeli modus operandi, and "by way of deception" is Mossad's motto, the attribution of a false flag operation to any particular act must be supported by direct and conclusive evidence. The notion that Israel may benefit politically from a given terror act performed by an Arab or a Muslim doesn't necessarily show that Israel has funded, facilitated or operationally supported that act. It also doesn't necessarily mean that Israel was working in concert with any particular terror suspects. It only suggests that Israel is a prime suspect in such wrongdoings. Similarly, the fact that our rulers use such acts as an excuse to increase oppressive measures and restrict our elementary freedoms does not prove that it is our rulers who instigate terror acts against us; it only suggests that our rulers may be involved in some devious plots. Particularly, the embarrassing fact that French President François Hollande and his PM Manuel Valls have been shamelessly grovelling before the Jewish lobby (CRIF) for more than a while doesn't prove that the recent Paris attack was a French false flag operation. It merely indicates that the Israeli and French administrations are prime suspects in the murder of more than a hundred innocent civilians. However, in order to indict Israel, the Mossad, the Lobby, the league of Israeli sayanim or the French Administration, we must unveil the truth by producing convincing evidence, the prototypical "smoking gun."

I am obviously frustrated by the manner in which, too often, too many of us attribute the catchy and populist "false flag operation" to every event we struggle to cope with, let alone fully understand. Too often we let the crucial demarcation between the hypothetical (the conspiratorial) and the factual to be blurred or loose. We treat speculations and assumptions as if they were conclusive evidence. The result of this lax promulgation of theories has not been positive. We are submerged in an ocean of conspiratorial ideas that diminish the seriousness of the problem we face. Instead of identifying the true culprits and the supremacist culture behind the destruction of the West and whatever is left of Athens, we often misidentify the problem and as a result, let the criminals off. More troubling, this often allows the dissent discourse to be subject to ridicule.

It may be more productive to present the direct evidence that defies a given "official narrative" rather than insisting upon presenting a speculative interpretation that cannot be substantiated in present time. We do not want to fall into the trap of allowing the theory to dictate the evidence.

For example, in considering 9/11, rather than producing a score of conspiracy theories that cannot be verified as yet, we may be better off concentrating on the evidence that contradicts the official narrative such as the collapse of Building Number 7 and the active concealment of evidence from the crime scene.

The temptation to speculate and attempt an explanation is difficult to resist. I have also fallen into this trap. Just a few hours after the Charlie Hebdo massacre I pointed at a possible false flag operation.[358] I wrote, "While every anti-terror expert has agreed that the attack on Charlie Hebdo yesterday was a professional job, it seems pretty amateurish for a 'highly trained terrorist' to leave his ID behind. And since when does a terrorist take his ID on an operation? One possible explanation is that the so-called terrorists needed a few extra hours to leave France or disappear. They had to fool the French police and intelligence into searching the wrong places and the wrong people. Is it possible that they simply planted a stolen or forged ID card in the car they left behind? If this was the scenario, it is possible that the attack yesterday had nothing to do with 'Jihadi terrorism.' It is quite probable that this was another false flag operation."

However, in retrospect I realise that the false ID narrative that keeps reappearing in these spectacular homicidal events, including the recent massacre in Paris Bataclan, proves little. It may even indicate that the people behind these acts of terror are at least as sophisticated as the conspiracy theorists.

Apparently, right after Paris attack, there was speculation that the fake Syrian ID was planted on the scene by the police or another French governmental agency. Counter Current News wrote in that regard:

> This really only leaves us with one logical possibility: that the fake Syrian passports were planted by law enforcement. The motivation is obvious: to bolster the government's position that a military invasion of Syria is both necessary and a direct response to attacks from Syrian nationals. France has moved to attack Syria in spite of the fact that these passports have now been confirmed fakes, with no logical connection to the terrorists they were found by. If law enforcement didn't plant them near the bodies, then who did?[359]

The above explanation sounds plausible, but it is hypothetical and not supported by any factual evidence as yet. In fact, analysis of that hypothetical narrative reveals some problems. Prior to the attack, the French Government was fully in line with its Jewish paymasters at the CRIF—committed to the removal of Assad and his regime. But following the Bataclan massacre, the French began dropping bombs on Assad's enemies. The motivation is, at the least, confusing.

When we examine the information available to us, (and it is an open question whether enough or sufficient facts are available) we must try to examine all possibilities and theories. We can accept the idea that fake IDs are often planted by a governmental agencies, while still understanding that the fake ID may have been placed by an anti-immigration agent or even by the perpetrators of the act themselves. After all, if the terror act was dependent on a local support operation, then the actors needed to buy precious time that would allow them to leave France and disappear.

Identity vs. Identification

Before we move further, an elementary and necessary observation must be made in reference to religiously and ideologically motivated conflicts.

Religions and ideologies do not kill. It is always people who kill in the name of religion and "great ideas." Accordingly, instead of asking what a religion or an idea stands for, we should amend the question and try to understand what those people who attest to a given religion or an ideology may mean by it.

Some pious rabbinical Jews, for instance, insist that Judaism is a peaceful precept, guided by the Torah, and God loving. Such a reading of the Jewish religion is supported by the fact that Torah Jews and the

Satmar community, both ultra orthodox Jewish groups, are unambiguously critical of Zionism and Israel. Yet, at the same time, the most radical pro-Zionist genocidal and supremacist calls against Palestinians and Goyim in general are also voiced by ultra orthodox rabbinical characters, amongst them renowned Israeli Sepharadi chief Rabbi Ovadia Yosef.[360]

Therefore, instead of passing a judgment on Judaism or trying to verify what Judaism is, it is more productive to ascertain what those who claim to follow Judaism read into their religion. Instead of asking what a given "identity" means, we should examine what a given "identification" entails.

This approach may be helpful in our attempt to untangle some problematic questions about Islamic resistance, militancy and liberation. Hopefully, it will provide us with the necessary tools to distinguish between ISIS and Islam. It will also help us to differentiate between home-grown Islamic liberation forces such as Hamas and Hezbollah on one hand and Daesh brutality on the other. Rather than formulating any judgment of Islam, we will examine and deconstruct the militant actions of some people who identify as Muslims.

Terror Is a Message

If terrorism is the use of violence and intimidation in the pursuit of political aims then we need to accept that terrorism can be understood as a means to deliver a political message. If that is the case, we ought at a minimum, to attempt to grasp what that message is.

As painful as it may be, our intellectual task is to seek the rational mode that drives those who may be keen to kill us and often, also themselves. Unfortunately, efforts to designate as a "false flag operation" every act that appears to be an Arab or an Islamic related aggression undermines the intellectual task described above and is a dangerous mistake. Instead of attempting to determine the message, we reduce the messenger into an "Israeli marionette." In so doing, we occasionally succumb to the supremacist Zionist and Western colonial ethos we claim to oppose.

Arab Nationalism vs. Ummah

Unlike European nationalism that evolved organically in accordance with scientific, technological and cultural progress, Arab nationalism wasn't exactly an authentic home grown development. It was imposed by foreign imperial powers and proved to be a colossal disaster. Arab nationalism rose initially after the fall of the Ottoman Empire in the early 20th century and declined sharply following the humiliating defeat of six Arab armies in 1967. It saw its peak in the 1950-60's in the form of a secular call for a celebration of Arab liberation and civilization. The central premise of Arab Nationalism was that the peoples of the Arab world constitute one nation and should be emancipated collectively from Western colonial powers and influence.

In the last two decades, the Zionised West has used all available means to destroy the last few proud Arab secular states: Iraq and Libya were wiped out completely and Syria was shrunken into a corridor, a tenth the size of its original territory. But at the same time, the Western military elite has been forced to realise that while it is relatively easy to militarily dismantle an Arab nation state, there is no military power in the world that can fight Islamic resistance. This is understandable. Arab nationalism didn't mean much to the Arabs. The Arab soldier wasn't willing to die for Nasser or Sadam. For many of them, the true and real Arab Nation is the Ummah.

The Arab Spirit

Ummah is the Arabic word for the collective community of Islamic believers. It is an abstract term that transcends territory, geography, ethnicity, sovereignty or any other material or positivistic measure. Ummah is a synonym for *ummat al-Islamiyah*, the Islamic Nation, and is a different concept than Sha'b, a term that refers to the modern secular state united by a common ancestry or geography. In the context of Pan-Islamism and politics, the word Ummah can be used to describe the concept of a commonwealth of Believers—it is essentially a loosely defined spiritual bond.

Unlike the Arab nation state that struggled to sustain itself, Ummah unites the Muslims or at least many Muslims. Ummah transforms Arabs and Muslims into an effective and sophisticated collective with a strategic vision, a long term (prophetic) political agenda and most important, a glorious past based upon an historical narrative.

The Israeli army was pretty effective militarily against Arab armies, the PLO and other secular Palestinian paramilitary organisations, but has been totally hopeless in its battle against Hamas militancy and the Shia Hezbollah in Lebanon. The IDF has successfully sustained its destructive power, it knows how to flatten cities and kill indiscriminately, yet it has failed to accomplish a single military goal in its war against Islamic resistance.

The American and British military have had similar results. The English speaking empire was able to defeat the Iraqi and Libyan armies, yet was completely unprepared for Islamic insurgency. Both British and American forces faced a problem; while bombs and shells can cause huge destruction, they are often useless or even counter-productive in defeating the human spirit.[361] And since Ummah is a spiritual and meta-physical abstract notion that extends beyond territory or typical military assets, the materialistically oriented Western military paradigm cannot address or even contemplate the means to defeat it.

And there is another layer to this story. The Israeli military expert Ron Ben Yishai acknowledged recently that the Palestinian shift from "suicidal militancy" into "popular sacrifice" has abolished whatever was left of the IDF's "power of deterrence." Universalising Ben Yishai's observation suggests that as martyrdom becomes a popular ad-venture, Western military thought has, for practical purposes, finished its role and better clear the stage. The reason is simple: People who are excited by sacrifice are impervious to the notion of deterrence—they have lost their fear.

I would love to believe that the Israeli, American and British in-competent elite have realized by now that supporting and facilitating counter-Islamic militancy has been a guaranteed recipe for disaster. These religiously/ideologically driven groups are more than happy to receive American dollars and the latest anti tank missiles, but they quickly manifest their own dynamic. They are astoundingly quick to disregard their foreign backers and weapons suppliers.

The problem goes further. While Western military elites openly ad-mit that they lack the means to counter Islamic militancy, Western political leadership repeatedly evinces a complete lack of understanding of the parameters of the conflict. The French President's immediate re-sponse to the recent Paris attack was a banal populist "eye for an eye" reaction—more air strikes on Iraq were his solution. It makes me think of a person who goes to doctor with a broken leg and whose doctor pulls out a tooth as a counter measure. One may reasonably ask, how can bombing Raqqa solve home-grown Islamic militancy in Paris or Europe? Interestingly, no one within the co-operative media asks this crucial and elementary question.

It seems that like Cameron and Obama, Hollande reduces the con-flict into material measures. Instead of understanding that terror is a message and attempting to grasp what that message is, our so-called "democratically elected" leaders revert to body counts. They vow to kill them as they kill us.

The Primacy Of The Ear

Clearly, our political and military establishments are confused by Islam. The complete domination of the Jewish lobby in American, British and French foreign affairs doesn't help the problem. However, the few who struggle to identify the deep political malaise we are mired in should know better. We must make sure that we do not fall into the same ideological trap. We had better attempt to present an alternative agenda.

We must ask what is at the heart of martyrdom? What motivates young Muslims to lose their lives in such a brutal manner? Is it possible that the notorious "Jihadi John" as the *Guardian* of Judea named him, actually attempted to deliver a message when he called out to President Obama: "I'm back, Obama, and I'm back because of your arrogant foreign policy towards the Islamic State—your insistence on continuing your bombings despite our serious warnings...So just as your missiles continue to strike our people, our knife will continue to strike the necks of your people."[362]

Is it possible that the youngsters who turned the Bataclan into a blood bath were actually trying to tell us something? We can listen to Jihadi John or we can dismiss him as an Israeli shill, a Saudi puppet or a false flag operator. In choosing the latter option, we willingly and consciously choose deafness.

The warning here is unequivocal. We must make sure that pointing at a false flag narrative doesn't blind us to the possibility that we have failed to comprehend a crucial message. In assuming that behind every Islamic militant homicidal act there must be a devious Zionist, we reduce Muslims and their struggle into puppets in a calculated Zionist game. By adopting such a line of thought, we actually succumb to the most radical form of Judeo-centric supremacy. We are in practice dismissing Muslims, Arabs and their humanity.

INTERPRETING OUR LONG HISTORY OF 9/11S

Eric Walberg

When we first learn of spectacular acts of violence from the mainstream media, how should we react? Should we believe the reported facts and accept the interpretations being offered by the big corporate news channels? Or should we react with skepticism? And if so, how much skepticism?

In World Public Opinion Polls in 2007 and 2008, 46% of world citizens, including 78% of Americans (40% 100% sure, 38% had some doubts) accepted the official version of 9/11. A 2011 poll in the Muslim world by Pew Global found most Muslims did not believe that "a groups of Arabs carried out the 9/11 attacks on the US." The poll found a low of 9% of Turks believed the official version, 12% in Pakistan, 22 in the Palestinian territories, 27% in Israel, 28% in Lebanon.[363]

Contributors to this book and its predecessor *We Are NOT Charlie Hebdo*, represent some of the leading public intellectuals, East and West, who not only agree with Muslim opinion on 9/11, but who also raise questions about the official version of this year's events in Paris, seeing them as 9/11 type state-sponsored false-flag events.

I will not focus here on the details of the two French 9/11s, as some call them. My focus is broader and of course starts with 9/11 itself. Let me warn you: I am a doubting Thomas on all-encompassing conspiracy theories in general. No one denies that 9/11 was a conspiracy of some kind, but so far, in my view, claims of such a conspiracy being MHOP (made it happen on purpose) by a secret cabal of hundreds of high level officials are even more incredible that the conventional wisdom which accepts the inexplicable without bothering to get hard facts about what happened that day and who dunnit. But I believe that 19 hijackers crashed their planes that day, whether or not they were being used by someone else, because of Ockham's Razor, which states that among competing hypotheses, the one with the fewest assumptions should be selected.[364]

At this point, neither official or alternative scenarios of what happened are believable. Certainly not proven and quite possibly unprovable. That said, my thesis is that indeed we live in a world of conspiracy, a systemic one called capitalism, that shapes our actions and our thinking.

The moment 9/11 happened, as I watched the towers fall in real time from Tashkent, Uzbekistan, I thought "Is this a Zionist plot?" I have great respect for Jewish know-how and determination. It has been honed year after year since 1947 in the Holy Land, where a Jewish settler-state has faced overwhelming opposition from the angry native Arabs, displaced to compensate European and American Jews for the crimes of European Germans—the most glaring "conspiracy" around, one which most people accept—inciting, of course, many lesser plots of all kinds.

Surprise, surprise, cui bono (who benefits) points the finger at Israel in 9/11. There were tantalizing hints of cell phone warnings to Jews from an Israeli server, and a remarkable absence of Israelis among the dead, airline stock options mysteriously sold just days before the event, the famous dancing Israelis watching the collapse from across New York Bay in Jersey City, comments of delight from Israeli leaders (quickly adjusted to condolences), etc, etc.

But no smoking gun. Ditto, shadowy Pentagon figures. Lots of cui bono but no identifiable figures caught with their fingers in the pie in the sky. The one clear example of a false-flag attack at the time of 9/11 was the anthrax attack a few days afterwards, later implicitly acknowledged by the US government as a false-flag attack from an American germ warfare lab, designed to incite hatred of Muslims and solidarity with Israel. As Barrett argues in *We Are Not Charlie Hebdo*, "Scrawled on the anthrax letters was the message: 'Death to America. Death to Israel. Allah is great.' The Islamophobic pro-Israel propagandist(s) who mailed these letters succeeded in killing four Americans, infecting another seventeen, and convincing Americans that Muslims could deliver weapons of mass destruction to anyone with a mailbox." The perp was never convicted, but the evidence was clear. This conspiracy was either by an independent crank or, at worst, undermines the credibility of claims of a far grander conspiracy behind 9/11.

But I will keep looking for what I consider credible smoking guns. I tell Kevin Barrett: "Keep up your important search for evidence that can convince us skeptics. I wish you well."

Right from the first articles I published after 9/11 in yellowtimes.org, beginning my creative journalist career (thank you 9/11!), I have been a sympathetic skeptic of the view that 9/11 was primarily a cynical, uber-Machiavellian conspiracy by the shadowy forces behind Western society (neocon, Zionist, banker, Freemason, Illuminati...). But I encourage you, whether a truther or not, to read further. I swear that you will agree with me, whatever your take on 9/11 and its offspring.

9/11 as uber-conspiracy

Conspiracy theories surrounding September 11th were granted a certain legitimacy in the Holy of Holies. Alan Riding (*New York Times* 26/6/02) predictably ridiculed the bestseller *L'Effroyable Imposture* (The Horrifying Fraud) by the leading conspiracy theorist Thierry Meyssan, which goes so far as to claim that the Pentagon was struck by an air-to-ground missile fired by the US Air Force and the planes which struck the World Trade Center were flown by similar elements in the US government.

Meyssan's book was quickly followed up by a critique *L'Effroyable Mensonge* (The Horrifying Lie) by Jean Guisnel and Guillaume Dasique. Dasique earlier wrote *Osama bin Laden: The Forbidden Truth* with Jean-Charles Brisard, describing a no less conspiratorial connection between September 11th (but starring Bin Laden) and a stalled plan for Unocal to build a pipeline to exploit the vast natural gas fields along the Caspian Sea in Turkmenistan. Their story pointed damning fingers at American petroleum companies and the Bush administration, citing instances where US anti-terrorism efforts were thwarted in order to smooth the way for the pipeline deal.

Dasique exonerates the CIA and FBI, pointing to the fact that FBI deputy director responsible for the search for Bin Laden John O'Neill quit the FBI in disgust at that time, for the Bush administration's refusal to do anything about all the evidence pointing to a major al-Qaeda attack, and then himself was pulverized at the Trade Center on 9/11. To say these facts do not inspire confidence is an understatement. Nor do the facts that soon-to-be Afghan President Hamid Karzai and then US advisor on Afghanistan Zalmay Khalilzad were former Unocal consultants. But these are not smoking guns, and don't tell us who dunnit.

The Unocal theory behind 9/11 has since been discredited, but the outrageous incompetence of Bush and Condaleezza Rice and Bush's love affair with Saudis, even the family of Osama Bin Laden, are well documented. 9/11 most certainly gave to Bush, Cheney and Rumsfeld the blank check necessary to pursue their own conspiratorial activities to put in place a grand New World Order. Cui bono.

Conspiracy theory today

History is littered with real and imagined conspiracies, especially where the Cold War is concerned. We can laugh in retrospect at attempts to poison Fidel Castro's cigars, but the far more serious shenanigans of the radical rightwing at critical junctures, when their agenda is threatened, show that with or without blatant conspiracies, the bad guys will fight tooth and nail to push their agenda, using whatever pretext is at hand. We should be careful not to be sidetracked from this broader picture.

The great turning points in the past century where militarism triumphed have all contained elements of conspiracy—the turning back of detente at crucial points during the 1930s, 60s, 70s, and 80s, and the refusal to honor the "peace dividend" promised following the collapse of the Soviet Union. Despite, in each case, mass peace movements creating pressure on politicians to resist militarism, the right was always able to triumph. When necessary, using subversion and overt conspiracy. Sometimes, by merely orchestrating and latching onto imagined threats.

Turning point 1

The Reichstag fire facilitated Hitler's seizure of power in 1933, and was officially solved, but continues to be debated. It certainly was convenient for the Nazis, but pinning down the responsibility for the Reichstag fire remains a problem. Did the accused, the communist Van der Lubbe, act alone, as he said, to protest the condition of the German working class? The Nazis accused the Comintern of the act. A few historians endorse the conspiracy theory proposed by the Communist Party: that the arson was planned and ordered by the Nazis as a "false flag" operation. Whatever the truth, the Nazis used the fire to solidify their power and eliminate the communists as political rivals.

The term "Reichstag fire" has even entered the political lexicon along with "false flag" to denote a calamitous event staged by a political movement and orchestrated so as to cast blame on one's opponents. This is an ancient political tradition, which can be dated to the destruction of the palace of Diocletian at Nicomedia, which has been described as a "fourth-century Reichstag fire" used to justify an extensive persecution of Christians.

Turning point 2

The most convincing claim of a political conspiracy orchestrated by individuals is Pearl Harbor. There are individuals who can be identified—there were many in the US government, including FDR, that were eager for an excuse to declare war on Japan—but the fact stands: the Japanese attacked the US. They were not paying attention to what was happening in Europe, gambled on an Axis victory, and lost. But if your conspiracy is "good" and you win, it is no longer a conspiracy.

Turning point 3

Consider the first great post-WWII crossroads, which was closed with the assassination of President Kennedy. The Nuclear Test Ban Treaty had just gone into effect and the 1962 Peace Prize awarded (a year late) to Linus Pauling, the major public figure behind the test ban campaign (a controversial award, delayed a year with two members of the selection committee resigning in protest, saying that Pauling was too pro-Soviet).

In his acceptance speech Pauling said: "The world has now begun its metamorphosis from its primitive period of history, when disputes between nations were settled by war, to its period of maturity, in which war will be abolished and world law will take its place." He saw the test ban treaty as "the first of a series of treaties that will lead to the new world from which war has been abolished forever."

This was surely the high point of the postwar detente. The Cuban missile crisis was safely behind us, and Kennedy, chastened by both it and the Bay of Pigs scandal, looked ready to talk seriously with Khrushchev, who had denounced Stalin and launched a policy of detente with the West, about a new world order, one which would include the Soviet Union.

If we are to believe the Oliver Stone school of thought, Kennedy was assassinated, a few months after the test ban treaty, in a conspiracy, precisely because he was about to make a sea change in US foreign policy, embracing detente and making an about-face on Vietnam. Instead, the US war in Vietnam went into full gear, and Khrushchev was deposed.

Was this a conspiracy? I don't know. Again, there are tantalizing hints and lots of cui bono. Whatever really happened, it was nonetheless followed by "Full speed ahead!" for the US war machine. It's not all that important if it was a personally orchestrated conspiracy by a few nasties. It was really just part of the capitalist conspiracy holding us all hostage.

Turning point 4

Then there is the culmination of the anti-Vietnam war movement and the disarmament struggle in the 1970s, when popular pressure and a weakened US forced the government to sign major disarmament treaties and to cooperate with the Soviets in outer space—the Apollo-Soyuz program. The Olympics were about to be held in Moscow, when the world was suddenly shocked by the Soviet invasion of Afghanistan.

Surely, this was not the fault of the American right (though we all know that it went on to arm the anti-Christ Bin Laden himself)?

Now we find out that the story was more complex, that in fact, the US had already begun a program of covert aid to the Afghan guerrillas six months before the Soviets invaded. Former CIA director Robert Gates in his 1996 memoir From the Shadows revealed that peace-loving Jimmy Carter approved this secret $500 million aid program designed to counter the Soviet support to the pro-Soviet regime that had over-thrown the dictator Daud (who had just overthrown his cousin, the king) in Kabul.

Some elements in the Carter administration wanted to lure the Soviets into a Vietnam-like entanglement. There were no strategic US interests at stake there (unless you argue that the US has strategic stakes everywhere at all times), as the Soviets had been close to Kabul since the 1920s. However, a pro-Soviet regime in Kabul was simply not acceptable to the right, and to inject poison into the underbelly of the Soviet empire was just too tempting to resist.

According to Gates, at a meeting on March 30th, 1979, Under Secretary of Defense Walter Slocumbe suggested "there was value in keeping the Afghan insurgency going, 'sucking the Soviets into a Vietnamese quagmire.'" In a 1998 interview in *Le Nouvel Observateur* former National Security Adviser Zbigniew Brzezinski admitted, "We didn't push the Russians to intervene, but we knowingly increased the probability that they would."

Yet Carter, who authorized the covert program on July 3rd, 1979, today explains that it was definitely "not my intention" to inspire a Soviet invasion. Then Secretary of State Cyrus Vance's aide Marshall Shulman insists that the State Department worked hard to dissuade the Soviets from invading and would never have undertaken a program to encourage it, but admits he was unaware of the covert program at the time. Carter and Vance were hoodwinked—in a conspiracy against the US president. Does this sound like Rumsfeld vs. Powell in Iraq 2003 (this time a conspiracy by the US president)?

Is it fair to label Brzezinski et al as conspirators in 1979? I think so. Either way, it created the foundations for the greatest military build-up that the world has ever seen, as Reagan won a landslide election in 1980 on the promise to deposit the Soviet Union in history's trash heap.

The detentes of Khrushchev, even stodgy conservative Brezhnev, and most certainly Gorbachev were serious threats to the right wing agenda. The case of Gorbachev is particularly tragic. Rarely in history does the leader of a powerful nation honestly (and in retrospect, foolishly) propose disarmament, and reject any desire for world hegemony, as did Gorbachev.

But the US right could not countenance Gorbachev's betrayal of the rules of their game. US policy ruthlessly continued to undermine him, even while making loud noises in his praise. US funds and arms continued to flow into Afghanistan, even after Soviet troops had withdrawn, and Reagan/Bush Sr. refused to negotiate disarmament seriously with Gorbachev. Why show magnanimity when your opponent is down?

Lots of cui bono in Afghanistan in 1979, and this time there is lots of hard evidence. This conspiracy was the real thing and, what's shocking, is that we cheered it on at the time. As Bush famously said: "Fool me once, shame on you." But the perps have no sense of shame, and even bragged about it in their memoirs. They believed that their conspiracy was 'good', that they would win and be treated like heroes, their conspiracy forgiven and forgotten, like Pearl Harbor.

Turning point 5

Unfortunately for the right, Reagan's success had its downside. With the collapse of the Soviet Union the American war machine lost its raison d'etre and allowed a supposed disciple of JFK (Clinton, in case you fail to recognize the political legacy) to occupy the White House. Under eight years of Clinton, the US looked like it just might be coaxed towards a new era of internationalism comparable to that promised earlier by Pauling in his Nobel speech—nuclear disarmament, peace between the Palestinians and Israel, more reliance on international treaties, and greater authority for the UN.

Meanwhile, fears of global ecological disaster fueled the rise of a mass environmental movement, which demanded that the long-promised peace dividend be used to save the planet from a fate every bit as tragic as nuclear war. But the halting moves towards a saner world came crashing down with breathtaking acts of terrorism in the 1990s by Reagan's offspring in Afghanistan and elsewhere, culminating in a terrorist apotheosis on 9/11 (preceded by a cynical attempt to impeach Clinton and discredit his albeit problematic internationalist perspective).

Whether or not these tragic (or farcical events) were the active work of the CIA, etc, there is no doubt that in each case the events fit the needs of a US imperialism under attack.

Why gamble when it's a sure thing?

Imperialism, a systemic conspiracy, gets into gear when forces threaten, and history is bound to take its course with or without these dramatic footnotes. Bush's incompetence, his laissez-faire attitude once in office, his ignorance of international affairs, combined with his devotion to Saudi oil money,[365] caught up to him with a vengeance on 9/11.

Once it was clear the Taliban would not cave in to the offer of millions of dollars for a pipelines, and was every bit as anti-US as it was anti-Soviet, it became a matter of waiting for the appropriate terrorist pretext to be found to replace them. The Taliban were written off as a blip on the New World Order map, just as all anti-imperialist regimes are (see Bill Blum's *Killing Hope: U.S. Military and CIA Interventions Since World War II*).

And, come to think of it, if Brzezinski et al are bona fide conspirators, as argued above, then Bush certainly is one for invading Afghanistan and Iraq, if not Cheney (so far their conspiracy can't conceivably be labeled "good"). Lots of cui bono, but just as important, lots of hard evidence.

Is Cheney a Dr Strangelove? Sort of. But remember, Kubrick's film was a parody, a "what if?" For all Cheney's madness, he mercifully is gone from the scene and we are still alive. At least those who are not his "collateral damage."

If there is some element of active conspiracy of the "powers that be" in 9/11 itself, let's say the conspirators were at most hoping for a botched job that would serve as their pretext for steering the US economy more securely onto its warpath, away from international treaties and UN-sponsored policing of trouble spots. But no need to be too nefarious, especially with the worst president in US history;[366] lazy and stupid gets the job done without the nasty side effects of smoking guns. This is what is called LHOP (let it happen on purpose), which seems to me the most likely explanation of both the US and French 9/11s.

This analysis of geopolitical intrigues is grounded in Marx, who built his powerful critique of capitalism on the contradictions resulting from the difference between appearance and reality. Often what looks one way is in fact quite the opposite. A capitalist tries to beat his competition, say, by lowering his selling price, but instead something quite unpredictable happens. Perhaps his action induces a price war and he goes bankrupt, losing everything. Or perhaps his competition forms a cartel and conspires against him.

Often, these conspiracies are complex and change their appearance quickly, impossible to pinpoint precisely. On a political level, capitalism as a system generates—and then uses—such cataclysmic events as the Reichstag fire or 9/11 to wage war against the enemy of the day, whether or not there is any relationship between them, and regardless of who perpetrated them. It is a world of illusive paradox— the appearance of freedom and equality on the surface, and the reality of exploitation and inequality underneath. The best we can do as analysts is use Ockham's Razor and Marx to try to make sense of both appearance and reality. And a word of advice for would-be conspirators: make sure you win.

FALSE FLAG PARADIGM SHIFT:
A RESPONSE TO ATZMON AND WALBERG

Kevin Barrett

In the preceding two essays, Gilad Atzmon and Eric Walberg, both of whose work I generally admire, express discomfort with the outlook championed by this book as a whole, and by most of the other contributors. That new outlook amounts to a paradigm shift comparable to the Copernican revolution and other shifts in perspective discussed by Thomas Kuhn in *The Structure of Scientific Revolutions*. As Kuhn explains, it is normal for people educated in an era dominated by one paradigm to find it difficult or impossible to embrace a new paradigm, even when it is supported by logic and evidence.

To someone steeped in an old paradigm, proponents of a new paradigm seem to be making broad, sweeping, unsupported claims that clash with commonly-accepted knowledge and even common sense. Unable to understand the actual position of new-paradigm-proponents, defenders of conventional wisdom typically lapse into straw man arguments, among other fallacies. Atzmon, for example, suggests that those arguing for false flag interpretations "insist that there is a deeply concealed plot that may actually explain everything" and "designate as a 'false flag operation' every act that appears to be an Arab or Islamic related aggression," without offering any evidence that anyone has actually insisted or designated any such thing. (There have surely been hundreds of thousands or millions of acts of violence committed by or attributed to Arabs and Muslims during the past few decades, just as there have been even more millions committed against them; yet only a few such acts are suspected of being false flag operations, and nobody I have ever heard of thinks they are part of "a deeply concealed plot that may actually explain everything.")

Walberg, too, invents a straw man when, writing of 9/11, he claims:

> ...in my view, claims of such a conspiracy being MIHOP (made it happen on purpose) by **a secret cabal of hundreds of high level officials** *(my emphasis -KB)* are even more incredible than the conventional wisdom which accepts the inexplicable without bothering to get hard facts about what happened that day and who dunnit.

Who has ever posited "a secret cabal of hundreds of high level officials"? Covert operations specialists, the people who actually carry out political assassinations and false flag operations, are—as Webster Tarpley explains in *9/11 Synthetic Terror*—anonymous professional killers, not high level officials. John Perkins, who personally knows some of these professional killers or "asteroids," has explained that they typically carry out their mayhem on informal contract from the world's biggest financial institutions, extremely wealthy private individuals, and/or select members of intelligence agencies. There is no need for any cabal; false flag terror is just how things get done, just business as usual. Putting out a hit on an individual, or on the World Trade Center, is the same kind of deed; the latter job is just a bit bigger and more expensive than the former. Neocon strategist Patrick Clawson of the leading Middle East think tank WINEP admits as much in an interview in which he calls for the US to mount a false flag operation blamed on Iran in order to launch a war:

> I frankly think that crisis-initiation is really tough. And it's very hard for me to see how the United States President can get us to war with Iran. Which leads me to conclude that if compromise is not coming, that the traditional way that America gets to war is what is best for US interests. Some people might think that President Roosevelt wanted to get us into World War II; but he had to wait for Pearl Harbor. Some people might think Mr. Wilson wanted to get us into World War I; but you may recall he had to wait for the Lusitania episode. Some people might think that President Johnson wanted to send troops to Vietnam; you may recall that he had to wait for the Gulf of Tonkin episode. We didn't go to war with Spain until the *USS* — (here Clawson catches himself before saying *Liberty*)—until the *Maine* exploded. And may I point out that Mr. Lincoln didn't feel he could call out the federal army until Fort Sumpter was attacked; he did exactly that thing which the South Carolinians had said would cause an attack. So if in fact the Iranians aren't going to compromise, it would be best if "somebody else started the war."

Clawson was just openly expressing what everyone in high circles of power already knows: False flags are ubiquitous, they precede every war. (After all, wars are always begun by the more powerful party, for obvious reasons; yet they must be sold to citizens as "legitimate self-defense.") Clawson should have added that Mr. Bush, who like a mafia gangster ordered the Iraq invasion the moment he assumed office by ordered Cheney and Rumsfeld to "find me a way to get it done," had to wait until 9/11 before he could launch *his* pre-planned wars. And as former Italian President Cossiga has said:

"... all the [intelligence services] of America and Europe ... now know well that the disastrous attack (9/11) was planned and executed by the American CIA and the Mossad with the aid of the Zionist world in order to put under accusation the Arabic Countries and in order to induce the Western powers to take part ... in Iraq [and] Afghanistan."

Since these and so many other confessions make it plain that everyone close to decision-making circles understands precisely how these ubiquitous deep state gangland-style operations work, those who resist understanding such things must resort to such absurd straw man scenarios as "a secret cabal of thousands of high-level officials."

Straw man arguments are typical not only of relatively sophisticated anti-conspiratorial voices as Atzmon and Walberg; they are, in more noxious form, a staple of the mindless pro-official-story propaganda pumped out by the mainstream media controllers whenever they feel threatened by a possible public awakening. The CIA, for example, invented the straw man figure of the "conspiracy theorist" in the mid-1960s when it sent the notorious directive 1035-960 to its thousands of mainstream media assets, ordering them to insult and discredit researchers questioning the official story of the JFK assassination.[367] More recently, *The Guardian*, an MI-6 asset,[368] published an anti-conspiracy broadside quoting a "'recovering' conspiracy theorist":

"I remember reading about Final Fantasy VII, a movie I was really looking forward to. My initial reaction was disappointment that it was two years away—because by then we'd be under military control."[369]

Why did *The Guardian* choose a young, unsophisticated, seemingly unstable individual as a representative of "conspiracy theorists"—instead of, say, former UK Environment Minister Michael Meacher, a longtime 9/11 truth advocate, guest columnist for *The Guardian* itself, and close associate of Jeremy Corbyn? Perhaps one reason was that Meacher suddenly and without warning dropped dead a few months ago shortly after his friend Corbyn was elected Labor Party leader. Meacher's shockingly sudden death, which occurred just as he was preparing a Parliamentary inquiry seeking justice for the British victims of the 9/11 false flag operation, passed without a peep of protest or even curiosity from *The Guardian* and the rest of the corporate, intelligence-agency-infested mainstream and pseudo-alternative media.

Such logical lapses as the use of straw man pseudo-arguments are defense mechanisms that allow those uncomfortable with the new paradigm to pre-emptively dismiss it without considering actual arguments and evidence. Another, even more extreme logical lapse characteristic

of anti-conspiracy old-paradigm-defenders is the "it's not really important" ploy. Eric Walberg offers a beautiful example when he says,
speaking of the question of whether the JFK assassination was a coup
d'état by insiders:

> Was this a conspiracy? I don't know...It's not all that important if it
> was a personally orchestrated conspiracy by a few nasties. It was real-
> ly just part of the capitalist conspiracy holding us all hostage.

Really? It isn't important that the JFK murder was a coup d'etat that
crippled American democracy and led to the subsequent murders not
only of every decent American leader who mattered, from Malcolm X
to MLK to RFK to Paul Wellstone, but also to the murders of roughly
five million Vietnamese people along with millions of other Indone-
sians, Iraqis, Africans, and others?[370] Walberg is essentially saying that
nothing at all matters, because a nebulous "capitalist conspiracy holding
us all hostage" has somehow made everything else in the universe—
from what I choose to have for breakfast to the murders of tens of millions of people based on Big Lies—utterly irrelevant.

Such statements are sheer cant at best, lunacy at worst. Yet they are
all-too-characteristic of those shrinking away from the false flag paradigm shift. Noam Chomsky, for example, has famously insisted that it
doesn't really matter whether or not 9/11 was an inside job or if JFK's
killing was a coup d'état:

"What does it matter even if it was true? It wouldn't be significant." He then
refers back to the assassination of JFK in which he still insists that the assassin
was Oswald, but it doesn't really matter because "people get killed all the
time."[371]

What can Chomsky possibly mean by such statements? We know that
people faced by information of overwhelming importance that is emotionally threatening take refuge by saying "it isn't really important
anyway." The actual meaning, of course, is: "It is so incredibly important that I just can't deal with it."

Another fallacy typical of anti-conspiracy arguments is the resort to
uncertainty. By demanding an ever-higher standard of proof in cases of
alleged false flags, and endlessly raising the bar, it is possible to remain
in denial of the most obvious realities. Chomsky, for example, spent
years arguing that in the absence of publications in peer-reviewed professional journals, even the supremely obvious controlled demolition of
WTC-7, the nationally-televised confession of close Netanyahu friend
and insurance fraud suspect Larry Silverstein to demolishing his own
building, the films showing that officials anticipated the building was

"about to blow up," and so on, were meaningless. Then when articles on the 9/11 demolitions began appearing in scholarly and scientific journals, Chomsky simply raised the bar, going so far as to argue that even if the 9/11 truth movement proved that the World Trade Center had been demolished with explosives, that would simply mean that Bid Laden did it.[372] Clearly no amount of evidence could ever convince Chomsky that 9/11 was an inside job, and even if it did it wouldn't matter anyway. Likewise, Chomsky and other JFK deniers argued for decades that only confessions by the perpetrators would convince them. When confessions, including outright boasts, began to roll in from such perpetrators as David Sanchez Morales, Chauncy Holt, E. Howard Hunt, and (posthumously, by way of his mistress) even Lyndon Johnson, the anti-conspiracy crowd simply ignored them.

Walberg and Atzmon demand that in the cases of the most over-the-top State Crimes Against Democracy (SCADS)—the ones potentially the most disturbing to the citizenry—"we must unveil the truth by producing convincing evidence, the prototypical 'smoking gun'" as Atzmon writes, or "credible smoking guns" according to Walberg. But what criminal case in history has, prior to indictments, arrests, interrogations and prosecutions, ever featured a smoking gun on the scale of the demolition of WTC-7: repeatedly announced by authorities and mainstream media before it happened, confessed to by over-insured WTC landlord Silverstein, confidently attested-to by Europe's leading demolition expert Danny Jowenko shortly before his suspicious death, and analyzed to the last nanoparticle by independent architects and engineers? WTC-7 is the biggest smoking gun in the history of criminology; that anyone cannot see it as such attests to their blindness, which can only be accounted for by the powerful pathological processes analyzed by Fran Shure.[373] Many other smoking guns litter the crime scenes of all of the biggest, most media-hyped "terrorist attacks" since 9/11, plainly visible to anyone with eyes to see and ears to hear.

In arguing for "the primacy of the ear," Gilad Atzmon preposterously claims that those of us who have spent many thousands of hours studying these events, and have recognized the evidence that they are false flags, are somehow deaf to the message of the likes of "Jihadi John," an allegedly Muslim fan of the allegedly Islamic State a.k.a. Daesh. In fact, it is Gilad Atzmon, along with the majority of the citizenry of the West, who have stopped up their ears and refused to hear what Muslims are really saying. Polls show that Daesh's positive rating among Muslims hovers around 5% or less, which is, given the vagaries of polling, equivalent to zero. (The Devil himself could poll better than that.) And many polls since 9/11 show that a strong majority of Muslims has always rejected the official story. Additionally, polls show that Muslims, at a significantly higher rate than non-Muslims, reject terrorism (violence directed at civilians) yet support legitimate armed resistance to imperialism, colonialism and Zionism.[374]

Muslims have no difficulties identifying spectacular attacks on civilians—an utterly un-Islamic tactic, and one that only benefits the enemies of Islam—as obvious or likely false flags; while at the same time supporting legitimate armed resistance against occupation in Palestine, Afghanistan, Iraq, Somalia, Kashmir and elsewhere. This is the position of the vast majority of the Islamic world, and it is in line not only with "lesser jihad theory," the Islamic version of just war theory, but with Christian and secular just war theory as well.

I urge Gilad Atzmon, and everyone else confused by media-hyped "Islamic terrorism," to take their fingers out of their ears and actually listen to what Muslims are saying: Attacks on civilians are un-Islamic (as Bin Laden himself said in denying responsibility and deploring 9/11) and likely false flags; Daesh has nothing to do with Islam but is a band of US-Zionist mercenaries fighting for Greater Israel; and the war on terror is a complete hoax, a bogus excuse for anti-Islam genocide. For Gilad, and anyone else willing to listen to what Muslims really think, a good place to start is by reading the essays of the many Muslim contributors to this book.

Unfortunately, the mainstream media will not allow any Muslim who represents the mainstream, Muslim-majority view of these matters to express him- or herself to the Western public. Normally only "house Muslims," spineless cowards too timorous to even bring up WTC-7, are allowed on NPR, CBS-FOX-MSNBC. The public doesn't even have to stick its fingers in its ears, since the media is doing it for them.

The result is that the Western public thinks Daesh is Muslim; has no idea that most Muslims believe (for good reason) that the big terror stunts have been inside jobs; and is psychologically prepared to expel or mass-murder millions of Muslims, including all of those living in the West, after the next really big false flag. So please help continue the conversation begun by this book and its predecessor *We Are NOT Charlie Hebdo*. Contact the media and demand that real, representative Muslim views—like those offered in this book— be heard and heeded.

Youth for Truth:
A Generational Awakening?

TODAY, TERRORISM IS OUR COMMON WORRY:

A MESSAGE FROM THE AYATOLLAH SEYYED ALI KHAMENEI, LEADER OF THE ISLAMIC REPUBLIC OF IRAN, TO THE YOUTH OF EUROPE AND NORTH AMERICA

The bitter events brought about by blind terrorism in France have once again, moved me to speak to you young people.

In the Name of God, the Beneficent, the Merciful

To the Youth in Western Countries,

The bitter events brought about by blind terrorism in France have once again, moved me to speak to you young people. For me, it is unfortunate that such incidents would have to create the framework for a conversation; however the truth is that if painful matters do not create the grounds for finding solutions and mutual consultation, then the damage caused will be multiplied.

The pain of any human being anywhere in the world causes sorrow for a fellow human being. The sight of a child losing his life in the presence of his loved ones, a mother whose joy for her family turns into mourning, a husband who is rushing the lifeless body of his spouse to some place and the spectator who does not know whether he will be seeing the final scene of life—these are scenes that rouse the emotions and feelings of any human being. Anyone who has benefited from affection and humanity is affected and disturbed by witnessing these scenes—whether it occurs in France or in Palestine or Iraq or Lebanon or Syria.

I genuinely believe that it is only you youth who by learning the lessons of today's hardship, have the power to discover new means for building the future.

Without a doubt, the one-and-a-half billion Muslims also have these feelings and abhor and are revolted by the perpetrators and those responsible for these calamities. The issue, however, is that if today's pain is not used to build a better and safer future, then it will just turn into bitter and fruitless memories. I genuinely believe that it is only you youth who by learning the lessons of today's hardship, have the power to discover new means for building the future and who can be barriers in the misguided path that has brought the West to its current impasse.

Anyone who has benefited from affection and humanity is affected and disturbed by witnessing these scenes—whether they occur in France or in Palestine or Iraq or Lebanon or Syria.

It is correct that today terrorism is our common worry. However it is necessary for you to know that the insecurity and strain that you experienced during the recent events, differs from the pain that the people of Iraq, Yemen, Syria and Afghanistan have been experiencing for many years, in two significant ways. First, the Islamic world has been the victim of terror and brutality to a larger extent territorially, to greater amount quantitatively and for a longer period in terms of time. Second, that unfortunately this violence has been supported by certain great powers through various methods and effective means.

Today, there are very few people who are uninformed about the role of the United States of America in creating, nurturing and arming al-Qaeda, the Taliban and their inauspicious successors. Besides this direct support, the overt and well-known supporters of takfiri terrorism— despite having the most backward political systems—are standing arrayed as allies of the West while the most pioneering, brightest and most dynamic democrats in the region are suppressed mercilessly. The prejudiced response of the West to the awakening movement in the Islamic world is an illustrative example of the contradictory Western policies.

I genuinely believe that it is only you youth who, by learning the lessons of today's hardship, can be barriers in the misguided path that has brought the West to its current impasse.

The other side of these contradictory policies is seen in supporting the state terrorism of Israel. The oppressed people of Palestine have experienced the worst kind of terrorism for the last sixty years. If the people of Europe have now taken refuge in their homes for a few days and refrain from being present in busy places—it is decades that a Palestinian family is not secure even in its own home from the Zionist regime's death and destruction machinery. What kind of atrocious violence today is comparable to that of the settlement constructions of the Zionists regime?

This regime—without ever being seriously and significantly censured by its influential allies or even by the so-called independent international organizations—every day demolishes the homes of Palestinians and destroys their orchards and farms. This is done without even giving them time to gather their belongings or agricultural products; and usually it is done in front of the terrified and tear-filled eyes of women and children who witness the brutal beatings of their family members who in some cases are being dragged away to gruesome torture chambers. In today's world, do we know of any other violence on this scale and scope and for such an extended period of time?

Shooting down a woman in the middle of the street for the crime of protesting against a soldier who is armed to the teeth—if this is not terrorism, what is? This barbarism, because it is being done by the armed forces of an occupying government, should not be called extremism? Or maybe only because these scenes have been seen repeatedly on television screens for sixty years, they should no longer stir our consciences.

The military invasions of the Islamic world in recent years—with countless victims—are another example of the contradictory logic of the West. The assaulted countries, in addition to the human damage caused, have lost their economic and industrial infrastructure, their movement towards growth and development has been stopped or delayed and in some cases, has been thrown back decades. Despite all this, they are rudely being asked not to see themselves as oppressed. How can a country be turned into ruins, have its cities and towns covered in dust and then be told that it should please not view itself as oppressed? Instead of enticements to not understand and to not mention disasters, would not an honest apology be better? The pain that the Islamic world has suffered in these years from the hypocrisy and duplicity of the invaders is not less than the pain from the material damage.

Dear youth! I have the hope that you—now or in the future—can change this mentality corrupted by duplicity, a mentality whose highest skill is hiding long-term goals and adorning malevolent objectives.

Dear youth! I have the hope that you—now or in the future—can change this mentality corrupted by duplicity, a mentality whose highest skill is hiding long-term goals and adorning malevolent objectives. In my opinion, the first step in creating security and peace is reforming this violence-breeding mentality. As long as double-standards dominate Western policies, as long as terrorism—in the view of its powerful supporters – is divided into "good" and "bad" types, and as long as governmental interests are given precedence over human values and ethics, the roots of violence should not be searched for in other places.

Unfortunately, these roots have taken hold in the depths of Western political culture over the course of many years and they have caused a soft and silent invasion. Many countries of the world take pride in their local and national cultures, cultures which through development and regeneration have soundly nurtured human societies for centuries. The Islamic world is not an exception to this. However in the current era, the Western world with the use of advanced tools is insisting on the cloning and replication of its culture on a global scale. I consider the imposition of Western culture upon other peoples and the trivialization of independent cultures as a form of silent violence and extreme harmfulness.

Humiliating rich cultures and insulting the most honored parts of these, is occurring while the alternative culture being offered in no way has any qualification for being a replacement. For example, the two elements of "aggression" and "moral promiscuity" which unfortunately have become the main elements of Western culture, have even degraded the position and acceptability of its source region.

So now the question is: Are we "sinners" for not wanting an aggressive, vulgar and fatuous culture? Are we to be blamed for blocking the flood of impropriety that is directed towards our youth in the shape of various forms of quasi-art? I do not deny the importance and value of cultural interaction. Whenever these interactions are conducted in natural circumstances and with respect for the receiving culture, they result in growth, development and richness. On the contrary, inharmonious interactions have been unsuccessful and harmful impositions.

We have to state with full regret that vile groups such as Daesh are the spawn of such ill-fated pairings with imported cultures. If the matter was simply theological, we would have had to witness such phenomena before the colonialist era, yet history shows the contrary. Authoritative historical records clearly show how colonialist confluence of extremist and rejected thoughts in the heart of a Bedouin tribe planted the seed of extremism in this region. How then is it possible that such garbage as Daesh comes out of one of the most ethical and humane religious schools which as part of its inner core, includes the notion that taking the life of one human being is equivalent to killing the whole humanity?

One has to ask why people who are born in Europe and who have been intellectually and mentally nurtured in that environment are attracted to such groups? Can we really believe that people with only one or two trips to war zones, suddenly become so extreme that they can riddle the bodies of their compatriots with bullets? On this matter, we certainly cannot forget about the effects of a life nurtured in a pathologic culture in a corrupt environment borne out of violence. On this matter, we need complete analyses, analyses that see the hidden and apparent corruptions. Maybe a deep hate—planted in the years of economic and industrial growth and borne out of inequality and possibly legal and structural prejudice—created ideas that every few years appear in a sickening manner.

Any rushed and emotional reaction which would isolate, intimidate and create more anxiety for the Muslim communities living in Europe and America not only will not solve the problem but will increase the chasms and resentments.

In any case, you are the ones that have to uncover the apparent layers of your own society and untie and disentangle the knots and resentments. Fissures have to be sealed, not deepened. Hasty reaction is a major mistake when fighting terrorism; it only widens the chasms. Any rushed and emotional reaction which would isolate, intimidate and create more anxiety for the Muslim communities living in Europe and America—which are comprised of millions of active and responsible human beings—and which would deprive them of their basic rights more than has already happened and which would drive them away from society—not only will not solve the problem but will increase the chasms and resentments.

Superficial measures and reactions, especially if they take legal forms, will do nothing but increase the current polarizations, open the way for future crises and will result in nothing else. According to reports received, some countries in Europe have issued guidelines encouraging citizens to spy on Muslims. This behavior is unjust and we all know that pursuing injustice has the characteristic of unwanted reversibility. Besides, the Muslims do not deserve such ill-treatment. For centuries, the Western world has known Muslims well—the day that Westerners were guests in Islamic lands and were attracted to the riches of their hosts and on another day when they were hosts and benefitted from the efforts and thoughts of Muslims—they generally experienced nothing but kindness and forbearance.

Therefore I want you youth to lay the foundations for a correct and honorable interaction with the Islamic world based on correct understanding, deep insight and lessons learned from horrible experiences. In such a case and in the not too distant future, you will witness the edifice built on these firm foundations which creates a shade of confidence and trust which cools the crown of its architect, a warmth of security and peace that it bequeaths on them and a blaze of hope in a bright future which illuminates the canvass of the earth.

Sayyid Ali Khamenei
8th of Azar, 1394 - 29th of Nov, 2015

U.S. IMPERIALISM AND THE WAN-TON DESTRUCTION OF CULTURES: AN OPEN LETTER TO IRAN'S AYA-TOLLAH KHAMENEI

Anthony James Hall

To the Supreme Leader of the Islamic Republic of Iran,

Thank you for your second letter addressed To the Youth of Western Countries. The letter's title, "Today Terrorism Is Our Common Worry," suggests that the audience for your wise and inspired commentary is not constrained to any particular age because the universal nature of the divine truths you impart is ageless.

The meanings you convey transcend generational boundaries even as they also transcend religious, national, ethnic and ideological borders. To me it is clear you are addressing all of humanity in these times when the world is poised on the brink of global war.

At this moment of monumental crisis, when the forces of madness, division, and media engineered hatred are made to seem so pre-eminent, you have placed before us a blessed place of sanctuary. You have provided men, women and children of goodwill a literary space of contemplative reflection away from the psychological, militaristic, and economic storms all around us. Thank you for securing a refuge for moderation, reason, toleration and careful reflection in the midst of the mental and physical chaos that some of the most powerful cliques in the West are quite deliberately inculcating.

To me the terms "imperialism" and "colonization" are brought to the forefront by your observation that "the Western world is insisting on the cloning and replication of its culture on a global scale," that this process involves the "trivialization of independent cultures."

Terrorism and colonization in the Western Hemisphere

The Western world's efforts to replicate itself on one imperial frontier after the next began to gather momentum after 1492. That was the year when Christopher Columbus initiated a process whose true nature belongs at the forefront of contemporary questions about how North

Americans should best respond to the massive migrations of violently uprooted Islamic populations from the Middle East.

After 1492 the whole Western Hemisphere was remade as a frontier zone for the re-settlement of European migrants as well as for the forced and involuntary migration of Black Africans as slaves. In this process the "independent cultures" of the Indigenous peoples of the Western Hemisphere— those incorrectly described by Columbus as "Indians"— were indeed "trivialized" and worse, much worse.

The colonization of the First Nations of the Western Hemisphere extended over several centuries right up to the present day. Too often a shroud of amnesia is made to obscure this unbroken saga, a saga of theft and oppression extending even to genocide. In this terrible cycle of injustice, the so-called Indians of the Americas became true witnesses of the violent extremes of Western imperialism. As evidenced now by the violent uprooting of millions in the Levant, this wanton destruction of ancient and independent cultures becomes especially intense when the lust for ownership and control of new lands and resources is cloaked in the language of religion.

The founding of the United States as a white settler polity

The emergence of the United States as a settler polity on the frontiers of Western imperial expansion would have enormous consequences for the whole world. These days the rise of the most heavily militarized superpower the world has ever known is having especially grave consequences for the Indigenous peoples of Palestine, Syria, Iraq, Yemen and Lebanon. As you explain in your letter, the recent surge of violence in Paris needs to be seen in the context of the enormous suffering, disruption and homicidal insanity being rained down on countless innocent Muslim victims especially in the Middle East.

Although the founders of the United States invoked the language of universal human rights in their famous Manifesto of 1776, the Declaration of American Independence included racist provisions. The Black slaves amassed in the process of building up the tobacco and cotton plantations of the southern Anglo-American colonies were not to be included as rights-bearing citizens in the new republic. The Black slaves of America would remain the private property of the slave masters for most of the following century.

Moreover, The American Declaration of Independence included provisions whose effect was to racially profile and criminalize the Indigenous peoples then living on the lands that the United States was created to annex, control, incorporate and own in the forthcoming transcontinental expansion. This feature of the Declaration of Independence helps explain the psychology of the so-called Global War on Terror, a massive campaign of military and psychological warfare that can be said to originate on July 4, 1776, as much as on September 11, 2001.

Responding to the attempt by the UK's King George III to incorporate Indian lands into British North America through negotiation rather than conquest, Thomas Jefferson and the other drafters of the Declaration of 1776 accused the British monarch as follows:

> He has excited domestic insurrections amongst us, and has endeavoured to bring on the inhabitants of our frontiers, the merciless Indian savages, whose known rule of warfare, is undistinguished destruction of all ages, sexes and conditions.

Manufacturing enemies for the permanent war economy

It seems the United States has from its inception defined its real or imagined enemies in ways that help justify, define, and energize its imperial expansions. The Red Indians described in the Declaration of Independence as "merciless Indian savages" gave the nascent US war machine its original enemies. The Red Indians were subsequently replaced by the Red communists whose real, imagined or manufactured threat to the United States provided a justification to maintain and build up America's permanent war economy.

The real beneficiaries of this system of aggression and domination assert ownership and control over the lion's share of the tight corporate network of banking, military and media institutions currently vying for complete domination of the world's political economy. Since the demise of the Soviet Union in the late 1980s a new enemy was required to justify the continuing usurious, mental and military incursions into the diminishing realm of human health, freedom, dignity, self-determination and cultural independence.

The ongoing crusade to expand the frontiers of Western imperial powers extends to the contamination of our mental, spiritual and physical environments as well as to the pollution of life's sacred cycles of ecological renewal. With the events of 9/11, "Islamic terrorism" was cast as the new enemy of "the West." The role once assigned to the "merciless Indian savages" and then the Red communists was attached to the new all-purpose boogieman of Islamic "jihadism." After the Cold

War a new global enemy was required and a new global enemy was invented, armed, financed and set in motion to continue the hierarchical structure of a very corrupt pyramid of power.

The Global War on Terror maintained the same top-down regime of elitist oppression that coalesced in the dispossession of the Western Hemisphere's Indigenous peoples and in the building up of the so-called permanent war economy in the course of the Cold War.

False flag terrorism and Takfiri mercenary armies

Those who identify most with the expansionary schemes of the Jewish state of Israel have been leading architects of the so-called Global War on Terror. The concocted false flag events of 9/11 were instrumental in transforming the predominately Muslim and Arab peoples indigenous to the lands of so-called "Greater Israel" into the perceived global enemies of the so-called "West."

The very conception of the "West" is being re-engineered in the course of a gigantic psychological operation made to downplay the creative role of Islam. It is simply not true that the "West" emerged exclusively from Judeo-Christian roots and that Islam is an aberration recently imposed through newcomer immigration. We must not forget, for instance, that the genesis of the European Renaissance drew heavily on Islam as expressed, for instance, in the constructive interactions between Jews, Christians and Muslims that took place in the caliphate of Al-Andalus on the lands of present-day Spain.

This history has been documented and explained by Edward Said and other scholars who are expert in the overlap of Islam and Christendom. They have explained how the pluralism within Islam has from time to time been cynically manipulated and exploited to advance the interests of Western imperialism. After the Second World War the United States adopted this heritage from Hitlerian Germany in the quest to exploit Islam as an obstacle to the atheistic domination by the Soviet Union over parts of southern Eurasia.

The role in the 1980s of the CIA in creating, training, financing, and arming a Salafi proxy army to overthrow the Soviet backed government in Afghanistan is well known. One of the outgrowths of this project is al-Qaeda. The CIA's al-Qaeda became a kind of prototype of concocted Islamic terror. Al-Qaeda provided agents and patsies to be exploited in false flag terrorism such as that which took place on 9/11.

Al-Qaeda and its successors including al-Nusra and Daesh are best understood as Takfiri mercenary armies to be deployed in poisoning Western minds against Islam. These mercenaries also provide firepower as well as the ruse of an enemy to be defeated. Those engaged in such operations are made to seem in the Western media like independent entities motivated exclusively by religious fanaticism. The entities often financed and directed by Western intelligence agencies are, however, something quite different in reality.

The real aim of the invaders in the 9/11 wars is not to fight Islamic terror. It is rather to continue the process of toppling governments and whole societies slated for destruction by those vying for monopolistic domination. Those pushing forward the new incarnations of the Global War on Terror often project onto those they say they are fighting the very qualities that they themselves epitomize.

The new metropolis of an old empire

The cataclysmic outcome of this genre of malevolent intervention is on full display in the breakdown of civil order in Libya. Who can doubt that Syria has now become the frontier for the application of imperialism's updated formula for domination through divide-and-conquer? Who can doubt that beneath the deceptions of the Global War on Terror lie the politics of oil, pipelines and Israeli schemes for regional and global aggrandizement?

The Global War on Terror could better be described as the continuation of Western imperialism, with Israel as the new metropolis of an old empire with roots going back to the conquest of the Americas beginning in 1492. The continuation of this war agenda requires the creation of a constant flow of new terrorists as currently provided by Daesh, the proxy army whose sponsors prominently include Saudi Arabia, Qatar, Turkey and the United States as well as many of their corporate patrons and clients. Your letter, Supreme Leader, provides a very insightful account of the fevered mental environments that have become instrumental in advancing Daesh's recruitment strategies.

In conclusion let me quote your letter where you note, "The overt and well-known supporters of takfiri terrorism—despite having the most backward political systems—are standing arrayed as allies of the West while the most pioneering, brightest and dynamic democrats in the region are suppressed mercilessly."

Since my visit to Tehran last year I have had the pleasure and honor of meeting some of these pioneering, bright and dynamic democrats. Some of them, I have reason to believe, give you advice and suggestions from time to time. I am happy for the wealth of inspiration they must provide you through the grace of God.

Your comments about the Western powers' tendency to ally themselves with "the most backward political systems" have very important contemporary implications with many historical antecedents. Unfortunately a perennial characteristic of imperialism is its tendency to dominate peoples on the frontiers of empire. This oppression operates through the empowerment of puppet regimes engaged in systems of remote control domination by indirect rule.

It is the younger generation who can change these patterns of manipulation and control provided they receive proper and sound education from a variety of steadfast sources including those at the forefront of the Islamic Revolution in Iran.

Yours Sincerely,

Anthony James Hall
Professor of Globalization Studies,
University of Lethbridge

CONTRIBUTORS

Gilad Atzmon is a British jazz artist and author. He was born in Israel in 1963 and trained at the Rubin Academy of Music, Jerusalem (Composition and Jazz). A multi-instrumentalist he plays saxophones, clarinet and ethnic woodwind instruments. His album *Exile* was the BBC jazz album of the year in 2003. A member of the Blockheads, Gilad has also recorded and performed with Ian Dury, Robbie Williams, Sinead O'Connor and Paul McCartney. His books include The *Wandering Who?* and *A to Zion: The Definitive Israeli Lexicon.*

Rasheed al Ḥājj abū Muṭahhar is the author of *Sabīl Ibnis Sabīl Mā 'Indahu Sabīl, or the Way Of The Wayfarer Without A Way*, a multi-volume work of Qur'ānic exegesis cast in the form of narrative poetry. More information on this work can be found at www.mudlimbs.com.

Ajamu Baraka has taught political science at various universities. An Associate Fellow at the Institute for Policy Studies (IPS) and the Founding Executive Director of the US Human Rights Network (USHRN) from July 2004 until June 2011, he has provided human rights trainings for grassroots activists across the country, briefings on human rights to the U.S. Congress, and appeared before and provided statements to various United Nations agencies, including the UN Human Rights Commission (precursor to the current UN Human Rights Council).

Kevin Barrett, an American Muslim and PhD Arabist-Islamologist, is one of America's best-known critics of the War on Terror. He has authored and edited several books, appeared on Fox, CNN, PBS and other broadcast outlets, and inspired feature stories and op-eds in *the New York Times, the Christian Science Monitor, the Chicago Tribune*, and other mainstream publications. A former teacher of French, Arabic, Islamic Studies, and Humanities, he currently works as nonprofit organizer, editor at Veterans Today, radio host and pundit at Press TV and other international channels. His website is TruthJihad.com.

Ole Dammegard is a journalist who has authored six books, including the classic *Coup d'Etat in Slow Motion* on the murder of Swedish Prime Minister Olaf Palme. His website is LightOnConspiracies.com.

A.K. Dewdney is a Professor Emeritus of Computer Science at the University of Western Ontario. He has done advanced work in mathematics, environmental science, and mathematical biology, and has authored more than ten books on science and mathematics. He followed Martin Gardner and Douglas Hofstadter in authoring *Scientific American* magazine's recreational mathematics column. The founder of SPINE (Scientific Panel Investigating 9/11), his Project Achilles experiments proved the alleged cell phone calls from allegedly hijacked airliners could not have been placed from the air as claimed.

Philip Giraldi is a former CIA Case Officer and Army Intelligence Officer who spent twenty years overseas in Europe and the Middle East working terrorism cases. He holds a BA with honors from the University of Chicago and an MA and PhD in Modern History from the University of London. In addition to *The American Conservative* where he has been a contributing editor for nine years he writes regularly for Antiwar.com. He is currently Executive Director of the Council for the National Interest.

Anthony Hall is Professor of Globalization Studies at University of Lethbridge in Alberta Canada. His been a teacher in the Canadian university system since 1982. Dr. Hall has recently finished a big two-volume publishing project at McGill-Queen's University Press entitled *The Bowl with One Spoon*. The second volume, *Part II, Earth Into Property: Colonization, Decolonization and Capitalism* was selected by The Independent in the UK as one of the best books of 2010, and the Journal of the American Library Association called it "a scholarly tour de force." One of the book's features is to set 9/11 and the 9/11 Wars in the context of global history since 1492.

Zaid Hamid is a leading Pakistani defense analyst, journalist and television commentator. He is the founder of the defense consulting firm Brass Tacks, and author of several books including the classic memoir of the Afghan anti-Soviet resistance struggle *From Indus to Oxus*.

Imran N. Hosein was born in the Caribbean island of Trinidad in 1942 from parents whose ancestors had migrated as indentured laborers from India. He is a graduate of the Aleemiyah Institute in Karachi and has studied at several institutions of higher learning including the University of Karachi, the University of the West Indies, Al Azhar University and the Graduate Institute of International Relations in Switzerland. A former Director of Islamic Studies for the Joint Committee of Muslim Organizations of Greater New York, he is widely regarded as the world's leading Islamic eschatologist and has published many books including *Jerusalem in the Qur'an, Gog and Magog in the Modern Age,* and *The Prohibition of Ribah in the Qur'an and Sunnah.* His website is ImranHosein.org.

Mujahid Kamran is the Vice Chancellor of Punjab University, Lahore where he has been teaching physics since 1972. He was a Fulbright Fellow at University of Georgia USA during 1988–89 and professor of physics at King Saud University, Riyadh from 2001 to 2004. Kamran has won numerous awards including the Abdus Salam Prize (1985), the President's Pride of Performance Award (1999), the International Einstein Award for Scientific Achievement (2010) and the Sitara-e-Imtiaz (2015) for his outstanding contributions to research, teaching and popularization of science. His book *Jadeed Tabiyat Kay Bani* won the National Book Council award in 2000. His most recent books are *9/11 and the New World Order* and *The International Bankers, World Wars I, II, and Beyond.*

Ayatollah Seyyed Ali Khamenei is the Supreme Leader of the Islamic Republic of Iran.

Barry Kissin is an attorney and journalist based in Frederick MD, the home of Fort Detrick, the putative source of the 2001 anthrax letters. His investigative reports have shown that the 9/11 and anthrax attacks were a one-two punch orchestrated by the same high-level US government insiders.

Nick Kollerstrom holds a Ph.D. in History of Science. A former honorary research fellow in Science and Technology Studies at University College, London (UCL), and a former lunar gardening correspondent for the BBC, he is the author or co-author of a number of books, including *Gardening and Planting by the Moon* (an annual series beginning 1980), *Terror on the Tube* (2009), and *Breaking the Spell* (2014).

Stephen Lendman is a writer, syndicated columnist, activist, TV personality, and radio show host. He currently writes for Money News Now, Veterans Today, and Veterans News Now. He also hosts since 2007 a radio show at The Progressive Radio News Hour on The Progressive Radio Network. His latest book is *Flashpoint in Ukraine: How the US Drive for Hegemony Risks World War III.*

Henry Makow, is the author of *A Long Way to go for a Date, Cruel Hoax,* and *Illuminati I and II.* In 1984, he invented Scruples, a game of moral dilemmas which was translated into five languages and sold seven million copies worldwide. He received his Ph.D. in English Literature from the University of Toronto in 1982, waged a memorable academic freedom battle at the University of Winnepeg, and runs the popular website HenryMakow.com.

Brandon Martinez is an independent writer and journalist from Canada specializing in foreign policy issues, international affairs and 20th and 21st century history. His articles and analysis have appeared on Press TV, Veterans News Now, Media With Conscience News, Whatsupic, Intifada Palestine, Information Clearing House, What Really Happened, and other alternative media outlets. He co-founded Non-Aligned Media and the author of *Grand Deceptions: Zionist Intrigue in the 20th & 21st Centuries* and *The ISIS Conspiracy.*

Gearóid Ó Colmáin was born in Cork Ireland and is currently based in Paris. He is a former bilingual columnist with Metro Eireann. His interests include geopolitcs, globalisation, philosophy and the arts. He is a member of Pôle de renaissance communiste en France (PCRF) a political movement which advocates Marxism-Leninism and the formation of a revolutionary communist party in France. He appears as a commentator on Russia Today and other broadcast outlets.

Ken O'Keefe, a former United States Marine, is an Irish-Palestinian citizen, activist, and Gulf War veteran who attempted to renounce United States citizenship in 2001, and led the human shield effort in Iraq in 2003. In June 2010, O'Keefe was a passenger on board the MV Mavi Marmara. During the Gaza flotilla raid, O'Keefe clashed with the Israeli military on the ship, helping disarm two Israeli commandos. His subsequent verbal clashes with BBC's Hardfire hosts took mainstream TV to a whole new level.

James Petras is a Bartle Professor of Sociology at Binghamton University New York. He is the author of 64 books published in 29 languages and over 560 articles in professional journals including the American Sociological Review, British Journal of Sociology, Social Research, Journal of Contemporary Asia, and Journal of Peasant Studies. His latest book is *The Politics of Empire: The US, Israel and the Middle East.*

Paul Craig Roberts served as Assistant Secretary of the Treasury under President Reagan, and was later associate editor and columnist for the *Wall Street Journal.* He has held academic appointments at Virginia Tech, Tulane University, University of New Mexico, Stanford University where he was Senior Research Fellow in the Hoover Institution, George Mason University where he had a joint appointment as professor of economics and professor of business administration, and Georgetown University where he held the William E. Simon Chair in Political Economy in the Center for Strategic and International Studies. He is the author of many books including *How America Was Lost: from 9/11 to the Police/Warfare State* (2014).

Catherine Shakdam is a political analyst, writer and commentator for the Middle East with a special focus on radical movements and Yemen. Her writings are featured on RT, MintPress, Epic Times, Mehr News, The Foreign Policy Journal, The Age Of Reflection and many others. She hosts a weekly podcast: Breaking Point at Epic Times. The Director of Programs at the Shafaqna Institute for Middle Eastern Studies, Catherine is also the co-founder and director of Veritas Consulting, and the author of *Arabia's Rising—Under The Banner Of The First Imam*.

Alain Soral is politically-engaged philosopher, essayist, journalist, filmmaker and actor, and founder of the Egalité et Réconciliation (Equality and Reconciliation) political-cultural party, which advocates a "left for the workers, right for traditional values" position as a response to capitalist globalization. His books include *Comprendre l'Empire* (2011), *Chroniques d'avant-guerre* (2012) and *Dialogues désaccordés, combat de Blancs dans un tunnel* (interviews with Éric Naulleau) (2013).

Robert David Steele is a former CIA Clandestine Services Officer who is now a leading advocate of open source intelligence. He ran for President in the Reform Party in 2012. Steele is the pro bono Chief Executive Officer of Earth Intelligence Network a 501c3 devoted to teaching holistic analytics, true cost economics and open source everything engineering (OSEE).

James Tracy is a media scholar, educator and political analyst located in South Florida. He received his PhD from University of Iowa in 2002. His work on media history and politics has appeared in a wide variety of academic journals, edited volumes, and alternative news and opinion outlets including Global Research, Lew Rockwell, Activist Post, Information Clearing House, and Infowars. Tracy achieved national notoriety in 2013 for questioning the Sandy Hook Elementary School massacre and Boston Marathon bombing, and has since conducted extensive research on those events, much of which is available at memoryholeblog.

Eric Walberg, a graduate of University of Toronto and Cambridge in economics, has been writing on East-West relations since the 1980s. He has lived in both the Soviet Union and Russia, and then Uzbekistan, as a UN adviser, writer, translator and lecturer. A long-time writer for the foremost Cairo newspaper, *Al Ahram*, he is also a regular contributor to Counterpunch, Dissident Voice, Global Research, Al-Jazeerah and Turkish Weekly, and is a commentator on Voice of the Cape radio. His articles appear in Russian, German, Spanish and Arabic and are accessible at his website ericwalberg.com. His most recent books are *Postmodern Imperialism* and *From Postmodernism to Postsecularism*.

NOTES

1 http://www.veteranstoday.com/2015/11/13/charlie2/

2 The conclusion that Charlie Hebdo was a false flag emerges from the open-source intelligence project I edited, *We Are NOT Charlie Hebdo: Free Thinkers Question the French 9/11* (Madison, WI: Sifting and Winnowing, 2015).

3 Kevin Barrett, "Pre- and Post-9/11 False Flags: How Weapons of Mass Deception are Interdependent." In Barrett, ed. *We Are NOT Charlie Hebdo: Free Thinkers Question the French 9/11* (Madison, WI: Sifting and Winnowing, 2015).

4 My prediction came true. Someone, presumably the French authorities, pressured the organizers of the Islamophobia and Eroding Civil Society Conference, sponsored by the University of California-Berkeley, to informally but firmly exclude my presentation, despite the fact that it had been officially accepted by the Conference. So I flew to Paris anyway, attended the Conference, raised my concerns about false flags in the Q&A, and then with Professor Tony Hall (University of Lethbridge) organized and hosted an alternative Paris-based conference, the False Flag Islamophobia Conference, which may be viewed at http://noliesradio.org/archives/106841.

5 Thierry Meyssan, "The State Against the Republic: What Lies Behind the Anti 'Conspiracy Theorist Discourse.'" VoltaireNet, March 13, 2015. (http://www.voltairenet.org/article187030.html).

6 Fortunately, a courageous translator has been found, and the French edition of *We Are NOT Charlie Hebdo* is on track for publication in spring 2016.

7 Kevin Barrett, "French police target Charlie Hebdo witness: Is the Deep State trying to silence Mohamed Boutiche?" Veterans Today, Nov 9, 2015. (http://www.veteranstoday.com/2015/11/09/boutiche/).

8 Various contributors to *We Are NOT Charlie Hebdo* have documented the fact that Israeli Prime Minister Netanyahu repeatedly threatened that France would be hit with terrorism if it continued to side with the Palestinians or recognize a Palestinian state. In December 2014 France recognized Palestine; the Charlie Hebdo false flag happened one month later. Even right-wing pro-Zionist Israeli investigative journalist Barry Chamish has recognized that Netanyahu was likely behind the attacks.

9 Laurent Guyénot, "Prequel to Charlie Hebdo: The March 2012 Mohamed Merah Affair (A Joint Mossad-DCRI Co-production?)" and Ole Dammegard, "Copenhagen False Flag: Sequel to Charlie Hebdo?" In Barrett, ed., *We Are NOT Charlie Hebdo* (op.Cit.).

10 Ruth Styles, "EXCLUSIVE New riddle of San Bernardino massacre: Russian sisters married to shooters' 'terrorist' neighbor and brother have links to Israel—and murderer's brother was quizzed about domestic violence just before attacks." *Daily Mail*, Dec. 24, 2015. (http://www.dailymail.co.uk/news/article-3369393/EXCLUSIVE-New-riddle-San-Bernardino-massacre-Russian-sisters-married-shooters-terrorist-neighbor-brother-links-Israel-murderer-s-brother-quizzed-domestic-violence-just-attacks.html).

11 CNN, "Attorney for shooters' family: A lot of things don't add up." Dec. 4, 2015. (http://www.cnn.com/videos/us/2015/12/04/shooters-family-attorney-intv-cuomo-newday.cnn/video/playlists/san-bernardino-shooting/).

12 *Daily Mail*, "REVEALED: San Bernardino terrorist Syed Farook 'had contact with Syrian al Qaeda-affiliated group AND al Shabaab in Somalia'." Dec. 4 2015. (http://www.dailymail.co.uk/news/article-3346500/Pictured-handcuffed-body-San-Bernardino-terrorist-Pakistani-wife-pledged-allegiance-ISIS-Facebook-slaughter-14.html).

13 Thunderwood, "San Bernardino, Drills, 3rd Shooter and other weird stuff."

(http://www.daveandchad.com/2015/12/san-bernardino-drills-3rd-shooter-and-other-weird-stuff/). A compilation of multiple reports that the shootings were carried out by three gunmen, including detailed testimony by Inland Regional Center employee Sally Abdelmageed in a CBS interview with Scott Pelley, and additional corroboration from eyewitness Juan Hernandez, who confirmed Abdelmageed's account in an interview with the local NBC affiliate, saying the shooting was carried out by "three white men in military fatigues."

14 Paloma Esquivel, "San Bernardino shooting: Dramatic video shows police storming Inland Regional Center." *Los Angeles Times*, Dec. 2, 2015. (http://www.latimes.com/local/lanow/la-me-ln-san-bernardino-shooting-dramatic-video-shows-police-storming-inland-regional-center-20151202-story.html).

15 Webster Tarpley, "The Last Secret of 9/11 Truth: The 46 Drills, War Games, and Operations that Made It All Happen." (http://tarpley.net/2011/08/24/the-last-secret-of-911-truth/).

16 Prof Michel Chossudovsky, "Ten Years Ago: The London 7/7 Mock Terror Drill: What Relationship to the Real Time Terror Attacks? Fictional 7/7 scenario of multiple bomb attacks on London's subway." Global Research, July 7, 2015. (http://www.globalresearch.ca/7-7-mock-terror-drill-what-relationship-to-the-real-time-terror-attacks/821).

17 "Boston Bombing THIS IS A DRILL Announcement Heard Live." (https://www.youtube.com/watch?v=PaWCumjviWg).

18 Wire Buzz, "L'Exercice Pratique: Paris Terror Attack— The Road So Far." (http://21stcenturywire.com/2015/11/14/paris-terror-attack-the-road-so-far/).

19 Trevor Aaronson, *The Terror Factory: Inside the FBI's Manufactured War on Terrorism* (Brooklyn: Ig Publishing, 2013).

20 Wikispooks, "Operation Gladio B." (https://wikispooks.com/wiki/Operation_Gladio/B).

21 CBS News, "Witness Describes the San Bernardino Shooting." (http://www.cbsnews.com/videos/witness-describes-the-san-bernardino-shooting/).

22 Martin Hill, "Witness to San Bernardino Massacre Describes Shooters As Three White Men Dressed In Military Attire." (http://libertyfight.com/2015/witness_to_san_bernardino_massacre_describes_three_WHITE_MEN_shooters.html).

23 *Mirror*, "Paris attack witness says black Mercedes pulled up and shooters fired rifles from the hip." Nov. 14, 2015. (http://www.mirror.co.uk/news/uk-news/paris-attack-witness-says-black-6834503)

24 Dan Bloom, "Charlie Hebdo journalist reveals how she stared into killer's 'big, soft, troubled eyes' as he told her 'have no fear, we don't kill women' ." *Daily Mail*, January 13, 2015. (http://www.dailymail.co.uk/news/article-2909082/Spared-Charlie-Hebdo-journalist-reveals-stared-killer-s-big-soft-troubled-eyes-wouldn-t-spot-colleague-hiding-table.html).

25 Laurent Guyénot, Op. Cit.

26 Suskind, Ron, "Faith, Certainty and the Presidency of George W. Bush." *The New York Times Magazine*, Oct. 17, 2004. (http://www.nytimes.com/2004/10/17/magazine/faith-certainty-and-the-presidency-of-george-w-bush.html). The speaker, nameless in Suskind, is identifed as Rove in Mark Danner, "Words in a Time of War: On Rhetoric, Truth and Power." In Szántó, András, *What Orwell Didn't Know: Propaganda and the New Face of American Politics* (PublicAffairs, 2007). p. 17.

27 Pilots for 9/11 Truth, *9/11: Attack on the Pentagon*. (https://www.youtube.com/watch?v=JcMkIcdBzEk).

28   Arthur Naiman, Gregg Roberts and AE911Truth technical help, *9/11: The Simple Facts: Why the Official Story Can't Possibly Be True* (Soft Skull Press, 2011).

29   The name of my website and first 9/11-related book, *Truth Jihad: My Epic Struggle Against the 9/11 Big Lie* (Joshua Tree, CA: Progressive Press, 2007).

30   Kevin Barrett, *Questioning the War on Terror: A Primer for Obama Voters* (Madison, WI: Khadir Press, 2008).

31   RT, "German journo: European media writing pro-US stories under CIA pressure. Oct. 18, 2014. (https://www.rt.com/news/196984-german-journlaist-cia-pressure/).

32   LegitGov, "Before Paris Terrorist Attacks, CIA Director Brennan Met With French Intelligence DGSE Chief Bernard Bajolet: Report." Global Research, Nov. 13, 2015. (http://www.globalresearch.ca/before-paris-terrorist-attacks-cia-director-brennan-met-with-french-intelligence-ggse-chief-bernard-bajolet-report/5489143).

33   Sean Adl-Tabatabai, "'We Were Prepared': Counter-Terrorism Emergency Exercise on 'Multi-Site Attacks' Took Place On Same Day As Paris Terrorist Attacks." Global Research, Nov. 15, 2015. (http://www.globalresearch.ca/we-were-prepared-large-military-exercise-took-place-on-same-day-as-paris-terrorist-attacks/5489164).

34   21stcenturywire, "Magic Passports Redux: Syrian Passport Allegedly Discovered on Suicide Bomber." November 14, 2015. (http://21stcenturywire.com/2015/11/14/magic-passports-redux-syrian-passport-allegedly-discovered-on-suicide-bomber/) Tyler Durden, "The False Flag Link: Syrian Passport 'Found' Next To Suicide Bomber Was 'Definitely A Forgery'." (http://www.zerohedge.com/news/2015-11-15/false-flag-link-passport-found-next-suicide-bomber-was-fake-claim-us-french-sources).

35   Russia Today, "'Paris changes everything': Merkel's allies call for German refugee policy changes." Nov. 15, 2015. (https://www.rt.com/news/322208-paris-attacks-german-policy/).

36   Russia Today, "Political author Gearoid O Colmain discusses the Paris attacks with RT International." Nov. 14, 2015. (https://www.youtube.com/watch?v=L7GAbVhjTSw). See also his talk at the False Flag Islamophobia Conference in Paris, December 12, 2015. (http://noliesradio.org/archives/106841).

37   http://www.cnn.com/2015/11/16/politics/paris-attacks-isis-2016-reaction/index.html

38   Sputnik News, "In Bush's Footsteps: Paris Adopts Measures Similar to US Patriot Act." Nov. 17, 2015. (http://sptnkne.ws/af4R).

39   Sputnik News, "US Politicians Call for Invoking NATO Article 5 in Wake of Paris Attack." Nov. 18, 2015. (http://sptnkne.ws/aeUU).

40   Sputnik News, "Paris Attacks Make Possible Anti-ISIL Coalition Involving US, Russia." Nov. 18, 2015. (http://sptnkne.ws/avaZ).

41   Sputik News, "Deja Vu All Over Again: Senate Claims US Losing 'Media War' to RT, Sputnik. Nov. 18. 2015. (http://sptnkne.ws/aeVb).

42   Russia Today, "Paris shootout: 2 dead, incl. female suicide bomber, 7 arrested as police, army hunt suspects." Nov. 18, 2015. (https://www.rt.com/news/322507-gunfire-paris-night-police/).

43   The Millennium Report, "Paris Attack Reported on WIKIPEDIA and TWITTER before it happened." Nov. 16, 2015. (http://themillenniumreport.com/2015/11/paris-attack-reported-on-wikipedia-and-twitter-before-it-happened/).

44   Russ Winter, "Initial Impressions and Notes About the Paris Attacks." Winter Watch, Nov. 14, 2015. (http://winteractionables.com/?p=27146
Where are the eyewitness videos? http://winteractionables.com/?p=27202).

45   Russ Winter, "Paris Attacks Day 2: More Oddities, Lack of Substantive Eyewitness

Videos." Nov. 15, 2015. (http://winteractionables.com/?p=27202).

46 "France passes new surveillance law in wake of Charlie Hebdo attack ," The Guardian, May 5, 2015. http://www.theguardian.com/world/2015/may/05/france-passes-new-surveillance-law-in-wake-of-charlie-hebdo-attack

47 Ryan Gallagher, "FROM PARIS TO BOSTON, TERRORISTS WERE ALREADY KNOWN TO AUTHORITIES," The Intercept, Nov. 18, 2015. (https://theintercept.com/2015/11/18/terrorists-were-already-known-to-authorities/).

48 "Paris terror suspects: Everything we know about the ISIL attackers so far," The Telegraph, Nov. 14, 2015. (https://web.archive.org/web/20151114181826/http://www.telegraph.co.uk/news/worldnews/europe/france/11996120/Paris-attack-what-we-know-about-the-suspects.html).

49 "Molenbeek mayor received terror suspects list including on-the-run Salah Abdeslam one month before Paris attacks," The Telegraph, Nov. 26, 2015. (http://www.telegraph.co.uk/news/worldnews/europe/belgium/12011114/Brussels-Paris-attack-terror-alert-suspects-Salah-Abdeslam-manhunt-Monday-live.html?frame=3502253).

50 "Suspected Paris bomber Samy Amimour went to Syria two years ago: family," AFP/Yahoo News, Nov. 16, 2015. (http://news.yahoo.com/suspected-paris-bomber-samy-amimour-went-syria-two-102102741.html).

51 "Paris attacks: Bataclan suicide bomber Samy Amimour previously charged with terror offences," International Business Times, Nov. 16, 2015. (http://www.ibtimes.co.uk/paris-attacks-bataclan-suicide-bomber-samy-amimour-previously-charged-terror-offences-1528922).

52 Tony Cartalucci, "French Surveillance Law Amid Terror of Own Creation," New Eastern Outlook, May 15, 2015. (http://journal-neo.org/2015/05/14/french-surveillance-law-amid-terror-of-own-creation/).

53 "Overburdened French Dropped Surveillance of Brothers," Wall Street Journal, Jan. 9, 2015. (http://www.wsj.com/articles/kouachis-links-to-yemen-overlooked-by-french-intelligence-1420837677).

54 "Paris attacks: police raid apartment in Saint-Denis—as it happened," The Telegraph, Nov. 18, 2015. (http://www.telegraph.co.uk/news/worldnews/europe/france/12004669/Paris-attacks-police-raid-apartment-in-Saint-Denis-as-it-happened.html#update-20151118-2254).

55 Ibid.

56 "Paris attacks: Suspected ringleader Abdelhamid Abaaoud's life included petty crime, brother's kidnapping," CBC, Nov. 19, 2015. (http://www.cbc.ca/news/world/paris-attacks-abaaoud-timeline-1.3326787).

57 Ibid.

58 "Paris Attacks Suspect Was Monitored by Western Allies Seeking to Kill Him," Wall Street Journal, Nov. 17, 2015. (http://www.wsj.com/articles/french-authorities-raid-suspected-islamists-after-paris-attacks-1447661092).

59 "An ISIS Militant From Belgium Whose Own Family Wanted Him Dead," New York Times, Nov. 17, 2015. (http://www.nytimes.com/2015/11/18/world/europe/paris-attacks-abdelhamid-abaaoud-an-isis-militant-from-belgium-whose-own-family-wanted-him-dead.html).

60 "Paris Attacks Mastermind Brags About Escaping 'Crusader Intelligence'," Vocativ, Nov. 16, 2015. (http://www.vocativ.com/news/251207/paris-attacks-mastermind-brags-about-escaping-crusader-intelligence/).

61 "Paris 'Mastermind' Told ISIS Magazine that Bungling Police Officers Let Him

Escape," The Daily Beast, Nov. 16, 2015.
(http://www.thedailybeast.com/articles/2015/11/16/paris-mastermind-told-isis-magazine-that-bungling-police-officers-let-him-escape.html).

62 "Turkey Says It Warned France Twice About Paris Attacker," The Huffington Post, Nov. 16, 2015. (http://www.huffingtonpost.com/entry/turkey-warned-france-twice_5649c5ebe4b060377349be9c).

63 "Who is Paris attacker Ismael Omar Mostefai?" CNN, Nov. 16, 2015.)
(https://web.archive.org/web/20151117054808/http://www.cnn.com/2015/11/15/world/paris-attacker-mostefai/).

64 Ibid.

65 "Homegrown suicide bomber is identified after his FINGER was found among the Bataclan concert hall carnage," The Daily Mail, Nov. 15, 2015.
(http://www.dailymail.co.uk/news/article-3319127/First-Jihadi-suicide-bomber-Paris-terrorist-attacks-identified-finger.html).

66 "Profile: Omar Ismail Mostefai," BBC, Nov. 15, 2015.
(http://www.bbc.com/news/world-europe-34827541).

67 "Paris attacks: Bataclan gunman Ismail Mostefai was neighbour of Isis jihadi killed in Syria," International Business Times, Nov. 15, 2015.
(http://www.ibtimes.co.uk/paris-attacks-bataclan-gunman-ismail-mostefai-was-neighbour-isis-jihadi-killed-syria-1528860).

68 See note 18.

69 "'I have no explanation': Key suspect in Paris theatre attack was questioned – then released by police," Associated Press, Nov. 16, 2015.
(http://news.nationalpost.com/news/i-have-no-explanation-key-suspect-in-paris-theatre-attack-was-questioned-then-released-by-police).

70 Ibid.

71 "Suicide bomber's belt containing 'Mother of Satan' explosives is found dumped in a dustbin," Daily Mail, Nov. 23, 2015. (http://www.dailymail.co.uk/news/article-3330819/Suicide-bomber-s-explosive-belt-dumped-Paris-suburb-terrorist-fugitive-Salah-Abdeslam-escaped.html).

72 "Suspected Suicide Belt Found In Paris Dustbin," Sky News, Nov. 24, 2015.
(http://news.sky.com/story/1593074/suspected-suicide-belt-found-in-paris-dustbin).

73 See note 24.

74 Ibid.

75 "Arrested French jihadist 'instructed' to attack concert," France24, Sept. 18, 2015.
(http://www.france24.com/en/20150918-france-jihadist-arrested-terrorist-attack-plot-concert).

76 "Paris attacks: Belgian mayor 'had list of Isis terrorists including mastermind and gunmen' month before massacres," The Independent, Nov. 25, 2015.
(http://www.independent.co.uk/news/world/europe/paris-attacks-belgian-mayor-had-list-of-isis-terrorists-including-mastermind-and-gunmen-month-before-a6748661.html).

77 "French Soldiers Flood Streets Of Paris After Charlie Hebdo Attack, Jewish Community On Alert," International Business Times, Jan. 12, 2015.
(http://www.ibtimes.com/french-soldiers-flood-streets-paris-after-charlie-hebdo-attack-jewish-community-alert-1781058).

78 See note 1.

79 "Paris bomber Brahim Abdeslam 'smoked cannabis every day' but 'had no gripe with the West', says former wife," The Telegraph, Nov. 17, 2015.
(http://www.telegraph.co.uk/news/worldnews/europe/france/12002062/Paris-bomber-Ibrahim-Abdeslam-smoked-cannabis-every-day-but-had-no-gripe-with-the-

West-says-former-wife.html).

80   "The pot-smoking Paris suicide bomber: Ex-wife reveals 'blood brother' terrorist was a jobless layabout who spent his time taking drugs and sleeping... and never went to the mosque," *Daily Mail*, Nov. 17, 2015. (http://www.dailymail.co.uk/news/article-3322385/Ex-wife-Comptoir-Voltaire-caf-bomber-reveals-jobless-layabout-spent-day-bed-smoking-pot-French-say-blew-mistake-fiddling-suicide-vest.html).

81   "Paris attacks: Abdeslam brothers 'were manipulated, not radicalised,'" BBC, Nov. Nov. 22, 2015. (http://www.bbc.com/news/world-europe-34895294).

82   "ISIS jihadist and Paris attacks mastermind Abdelhamid Abaaoud seen 'drinking and smoking cannabis in Saint-Denis bar' after atrocities," The *Independent*, Nov. 20, 2015. (http://www.independent.co.uk/news/world/europe/paris-terror-mastermind-of-attacks-seen-drinking-outside-saint-denis-flat-after-atrocities-witnesses-a6741441.html).

83   "Paris terror attacks: Syrian and Egyptian passports found near bodies of suicide bombers at Stade de France," The *Independent*, Nov. 14, 2015. (http://www.independent.co.uk/news/world/europe/paris-terror-attacks-syrian-passport-found-on-body-of-suicide-bomber-at-stade-de-france-a6734491.html).

84   http://911research.wtc7.net/disinfo/deceptions/passport.html

85   http://www.takeourworldback.com/911/911passport.htm

86   "Syrian Passport by Stadium Stolen or Fake, A.F.P. Reports," *New York Times*, Nov. 17, 2015. (http://www.nytimes.com/live/paris-attacks-live-updates/syrian-passport-reportedly-was-stolen-or-fake/).

87   "Serbian police arrest man carrying Syrian passport with exact same details as document found on Paris bomber," The *Independent*, Nov. 17, 2015. (http://www.independent.co.uk/news/world/europe/serbian-police-arrest-man-carrying-syrian-passport-with-exact-same-details-as-document-found-on-a6736471.html)

88   Brandon Martinez, "Fox News Planted Fake Story Establishing ISIS Guilt Within Moments of Paris Attacks," Non-Aligned Media, Nov. 21, 2015. (http://nonalignedmedia.com/2015/11/fox-news-planted-fake-story-establishing-isis-guilt-within-moments-of-paris-attacks/).

89   https://www.youtube.com/watch?v=bN2MNqGj7ZY

90   "Suspect Arrested At Paris Concert Hall: 'I Am From ISIS'," Fox Nation, Nov. 13, 2015. (http://nation.foxnews.com/2015/11/13/suspect-arrested-paris-concert-hall-i-am-isis).

91   "Paris attacks kill more than 120 people – as it happened," The *Guardian*, Nov. 14, 2015. (http://www.theguardian.com/world/live/2015/nov/13/shootings-reported-in-eastern-paris-live#block-5646c062e4b091c2edb6cbab).

92   https://www.youtube.com/watch?v=m0sB49PwAZg

93   "Audio of shooting at Paris' Bataclan concert hall published online," Russia Today, Nov. 20, 2015. (https://www.rt.com/news/322903-bataclan-audio-paris-attacks/).

94   https://www.youtube.com/watch?v=H79hxpcf488

95   https://www.youtube.com/watch?v=KJUVqcNDZlk

96   https://www.youtube.com/watch?v=vaOOpiF3XcE

97   https://www.youtube.com/watch?v=U0xK9MLLdLU

98   "Hours Before the Terror Attacks, Paris Practiced for a Mass Shooting," *Bloomberg Business*, Nov. 17, 2015. http://www.bloomberg.com/news/articles/2015-11-17/hours-before-the-terror-attacks-paris-practiced-for-a-mass-shooting

99   https://www.youtube.com/watch?v=ATVPPSb3WrA

100 https://www.youtube.com/watch?v=iebVWcVn2PU

101 https://en.wikipedia.org/wiki/Patrick_Pelloux, accessed 12/13/2015.

102 "'I'm a medical soldier,' says doctor who treated victims at 2 Paris terror attacks," CBC, Nov. 17, 2015. (http://www.cbc.ca/news/world/nahlah-ayed-patrick-pelloux-paris-doctor-1.3321691).

103 http://www.imdb.com/name/nm1589892/

104 https://www.youtube.com/watch?v=ySu3dwrv04U

105 "Odigo Says Workers Were Warned of Attack," *Haaretz*, Sept. 26, 2001. (http://www.haaretz.com/print-edition/news/odigo-says-workers-were-warned-of-attack-1.70579).

106 "In France, defense experts 'see parallels to Israel'," *Times of Israel*, Nov. 14, 2015. (https://web.archive.org/web/20151116030750/http://www.timesofisrael.com/in-france-defense-experts-see-parallels-to-israel/).

107 https://twitter.com/DerorCurrency/status/666725201212604416

108 "Ex-owner of Bataclan: My Jewish, Israel ties had no link to attack," *Times of Israel*, Nov. 20, 2015. (http://www.timesofisrael.com/ex-owner-of-bataclan-my-jewish-israel-ties-had-no-link-to-attack/).

109 "Jewish owners recently sold Paris's Bataclan theater, where IS killed dozens," *Times of Israel*, Nov. 14, 2015. (http://www.timesofisrael.com/jewish-owners-recently-sold-pariss-bataclan-theater-where-is-killed-dozens/).

110 "Before terror, Paris' Bataclan theater threatened for pro-Israel events," *Jewish Telegraphic Agency*, Nov. 14, 2015. (http://www.jta.org/2015/11/14/news-opinion/world/before-bloodbath-paris-bataclan-theater-received-threats-over-pro-israel-events).

111 See note 62.

112 "Netanyahu responds to Paris terror: 'An attack on one of us is an attack on all of us'," *Jerusalem Post*, Nov. 14, 2015. (http://www.jpost.com/Israel-News/Netanyahu-responds-to-Paris-attack-An-attack-on-one-of-us-is-an-attack-on-all-of-us-433056).

113 "French Jews call for war on Jihadism as terror engulfs Paris," *Jerusalem Post*, Nov. 14, 2015. (http://www.jpost.com/Diaspora/French-Jews-call-for-war-on-Jihadism-as-terror-engulfs-Paris-433071).

114 "Outrage as France become first country in world to ban pro-Palestine demos," *Daily Mail*, July 18, 2014. (http://www.dailymail.co.uk/news/article-2697194/Outrage-France-country-world-ban-pro-Palestine-demos.html).

115 "Israel Controversy In France 2015: Pro-Palestine Protesters Punishment Upheld For Organizing BDS," *International Business Times*, Oct. 25, 2015. (http://www.ibtimes.com/israel-controversy-france-2015-pro-palestine-protesters-punishment-upheld-organizing-2155467).

116 "Report: French Jewish Defense League Stages Attacks on 'anti-Semites'," *Haaretz*, Dec. 25, 2013. (http://www.haaretz.com/jewish/news/1.565443).

117 "Sarkozy accused of working for Israeli intelligence," Global Research, Nov. 3, 2007. (http://www.globalresearch.ca/sarkozy-accused-of-working-for-israeli-intelligence/7245).

118 https://www.youtube.com/watch?v=825jBxhoYXA

119 "Analysis: Unpopular at home, Hollande appreciated in Israel," *Jerusalem Post*, Nov. 17, 2013. (http://www.jpost.com/Iranian-Threat/News/Hollande-receives-warm-welcome-in-Israel-as-Iran-deal-looms-large-331990).

120 "French president supports Israel's aggression against Gaza," Middle East Monitor, July 10, 2014. (https://www.middleeastmonitor.com/news/europe/12690-french-

president-supports-israels-aggression-against-gaza).

121 "New French prime minister "eternally tied" to Israel," Electronic Intifada, April 7, 2014. (https://electronicintifada.net/blogs/ali-abunimah/new-french-prime-minister-eternally-tied-israel).

122 "French PM 'under Jewish influence,' ex-minister charges," *Times of Israel*, Feb. 16, 2015. (http://www.timesofisrael.com/french-pm-is-under-jewish-influence-ex-minister-says/).

123 "France to Invest $107m in Fighting anti-Semitism, Racism," *Haaretz*, April 17, 2015. (http://www.haaretz.com/jewish/news/1.652353)

124 "France in a state or war with comedian Dieudonne," Veterans Today, Jan. 28, 2014. (http://www.veteranstoday.com/2014/01/28/france-in-a-state-or-war-with-comedian-dieudonne/).

125 "French authorities accused of double standards over hate speech crackdown," Russia Today, Jan. 15, 2015. (https://www.rt.com/news/222835-france-crackdown-hate-speech/).

126 https://www.youtube.com/watch?v=wtumOg0-9Ss

127 Brad Hoff, "2012 Defense Intelligence Agency document: West will facilitate rise of Islamic State 'in order to isolate the Syrian regime'," Levant Report, May 19, 2015. (http://levantreport.com/2015/05/19/2012-defense-intelligence-agency-document-west-will-facilitate-rise-of-islamic-state-in-order-to-isolate-the-syrian-regime/).

128 Nafeez Ahmed, "Pentagon report predicted West's support for Islamist rebels would create ISIS," Insurge Intelligence, May 22, 2015. (https://medium.com/insurge-intelligence/secret-pentagon-report-reveals-west-saw-isis-as-strategic-asset-b99ad7a29092).

129 Martin Chulov, "France funding Syrian rebels in new push to oust Assad," The *Guardian*, Dec. 7, 2012. (http://www.theguardian.com/world/2012/dec/07/france-funding-syrian-rebels).

130 Ibid.

131 "France delivered arms to Syrian rebels, Hollande confirms," France24, Aug. 21, 2014. (http://www.france24.com/en/20140821-france-arms-syria-rebels-hollande/).

132 Pierre Mabut, "France admits it directly supplied arms to Syrian 'rebels'," World Socialist Website, Aug. 27, 2014. (https://www.wsws.org/en/articles/2014/08/27/frsy-a27.html).

133 "'Israel wanted Assad gone since start of Syria civil war'," *Jerusalem Post*, Sept. 17, 2013. (http://www.jpost.com/Syria-Crisis/Oren-Jerusalem-has-wanted-Assad-ousted-since-the-outbreak-of-the-Syrian-civil-war-326328).

134 "Paris Attacks Suspect Was Monitored by Western Allies Seeking to Kill Him," *Wall Street Journal*, Nov. 17, 2015. (http://www.wsj.com/articles/french-authorities-raid-suspected-islamists-after-paris-attacks-1447661092).

135 "Paris attacks: François Hollande pushes for French state of emergency for three months," Sydney Morning Herald, Nov. 17, 2015. (http://www.smh.com.au/world/paris-attacks-François-hollande-extends-french-state-of-emergency-three-months-20151116-gl0hwk.html).

136 New police powers included the ability to keep people in their homes without trial, search the homes of people without a warrant from a judge, and the power to block any website that is deemed a problem.

137 Brandon Martinez, nonalignedmedia.com, "Decoding the Paris Attacks."

138 For discussion, see video, "The elusive Paris attack" by 'Professor Doom.' At 15 minutes, we are shown ambulances gathered together in central Paris in early evening for the drill.

139 www.challenges.fr/, 'Comment le Samus s'est préparé aux attentats simultanés de Paris', 15.11.15.

140 *Daily Mail*, 14 November: "Earlier on Friday, the German national football team had been evacuated from their hotel in Paris due to a bomb threat."

141 It was sold on 9/11 to the billionaire Arnaud Lagardère (Lagardere Group, Hechette, Larousse, France Telecom, Vuitton, Lazard, Vivendi Universal, etc). The largest Lagardère Group stockholder is the Emir of Qatar (a major ISIS sponsor), so the new owners may not feel had a very strong loyalty to France.

142 Matthew Drake and Dan Warburton, "Paris attack witness says black Mercedes pulled up and shooters fired rifles from the hip." *Mirror*, Nov. 14, 2015. (http://www.mirror.co.uk/news/uk-news/paris-attack-witness-says-black-6834503).

143 Oliver Wheaton, "Paris attacks: Details emerge of the three teams who killed 129 people." Metro, Nov. 14, 2015. (http://metro.co.uk/2015/11/14/paris-attacks-details-emerge-of-the-three-teams-who-killed-129-people-5502342/).

144 The *Observer*, 15th November.

145 His mother said he must have done it out of 'stress' (Daily Mail, 16 Nov.) which does not sound quite like a regular cannabis user.

146 Daniel Hopsicker, W*elcome to Terrorland: Mohamed Atta and the 9/11 Cover-up in Florida* (Eugene, OR: The MadCow Press, 2004).

147 Nick Kollerstrom, *Terror on the Tube: Behind the Veil of 7/7: An Investigation.* Joshua Tree, CA: Progressive Press, 2012.

148 Michel Chossudovsky, "The Paris Terrorist Attacks, '9/11 French-Style', 'Le 11 septembre à la française'." Global Research, November 14, 2015. (http://www.globalresearch.ca/the-paris-terrorist-attacks-911-french-style-le-11-septembre-a-la-francaise/5488896).

149 François Hollande, "Address to the Nation on the Terrorist Attacks in Paris." (http://americanrhetoric.com/speeches/Françoishollandeparisattackspeech.htm).

150 Tony Cartalucci, "Attack in France = State Sponsored Terror, But Which State?" Global Research, Nov. 14, 2015. (http://www.globalresearch.ca/attack-in-france-state-sponsored-terror-but-which-state/5488941).

151 Ibid.

152 See Spivey on absurdity of the given narrative: http://chrisspivey.org/qui-qui-poo-poo/

153 Peter Dale Scott, *The American Deep State: Wall Street, Big Oil, and the Attack on U.S. Democracy* (London, NY: Rowman & Littlefield, 2015).

154 "FBI Whistleblower: Pentagon, CIA, NATO and MI6 Were Masterminds Behind 9/11." George Washington's Blog, September 11, 2014. (http://www.washingtonsblog.com/2014/09/sibel-2.html).

155 Trevor Aaronson, *The Terror Factory: Inside the FBI's Manufactured War on Terrorism* (NY: Ig, 2013).

156 LiveLeak, "Terrorists shoot officer in Paris during terrorist attack at Charlie Hebdo." (http://www.liveleak.com/view?i=bc6_1420632668#IciYwUzHYF6lQTDJ.99).

157 See Architects and Engineers for 9/11 Truth. (http://www.ae911truth.org).

158 http://www.gatestoneinstitute.org/6677/david-miller-hilary-aked-kevin-macdonald.

159 http://www.islamophobiatoday.com/2014/04/16/latent-and-manifest-islamophobia-an-inception-of-ideas/ http://www.middleeasteye.net/columns/who-are-millionaires-behind-islamophobic-industry-america-1487378765 https://www.americanprogress.org/issues/religion/report/2015/02/11/106394/fear-inc-2-0/ http://www.islamophobiatoday.com/tag/islamophobia-industry/ http://www.ijan.org/wp-content/uploads/2015/04/IJAN-Business-of-Backlash-full-

report-web.pdf
160 http://www.frontpagemag.com/fpm/222457/terrorists-campus-ari-lieberman
161 http://www.lrb.co.uk/v37/n10/seymour-m-hersh/the-killing-of-osama-bin-laden
162 http://www.voltairenet.org/article189631.html
163 Aurélie Collas et Mattea Battaglia, "L'Etat islamique appelle à « tuer » des enseignants." *Le Monde*, Dec. 14, 2015. (http://www.lemonde.fr/attaques-a-paris/article/2015/12/04/l-etat-islamique-appelle-a-tuer-des-enseignants_4824384_4809495.html#4bHz1m73hgmi20Ox.99).
164 James Connolly, *In Praise of the Empire*. From *Workers' Republic*, October 9, 1915. Transcribed by The James Connolly Society in 1997. (https://www.marxists.org/archive/connolly/1915/10/prsempir.htm).
165 Martin Luther King, Jr., "Beyond Vietnam." April 4, 1967. (http://kingencyclopedia.stanford.edu/encyclopedia/documentsentry/doc_beyond_vi etnam/).
166 Associated Press, "Poland considering asking for access to nuclear weapons under Nato program." Dec. 6, 2015. (http://www.theguardian.com/world/2015/dec/06/poland-considering-asking-for-access-to-nuclear-weapons-under-nato-program).
167 *Washington Times*, "Hillary Clinton's 'WMD' moment: U.S. intelligence saw false narrative in Libya." Jan. 29, 2015. (http://www.washingtontimes.com/news/2015/jan/29/hillary-clinton-libya-war-genocide-narrative-rejec/print/).
168 *New York Times*, "Rebel Arms Flow Is Said to Benefit Jihadists in Syria." Oct. 14, 2012. (http://www.nytimes.com/2012/10/15/world/middleeast/jihadists-receiving-most-arms-sent-to-syrian-rebels.html?_r=0); Fars News Agency, "Terrorists Supported by America: U.S. Helicopter Delivering Weapons to the Islamic State (ISIS), Shot Down by Iraqi Popular Forces." March 1, 2015. (http://www.globalresearch.ca/u-s-helicopter-delivering-weapons-to-the-islamic-state-isis-shot-down-by-iraqi-popular-forces/5434230); *The Guardian*, "Now the truth emerges: how the US fuelled the rise of Isis in Syria and Iraq." June 3, 2015. (http://www.theguardian.com/commentisfree/2015/jun/03/us-isis-syria-iraq); *Washington Times*, "Rand Paul is right: Neocons created ISIS." June 9, 2015. (http://www.washingtontimes.com/news/2015/jun/9/bruce-fein-rand-paul-is-right-neocons-created-isis/?page=all); Ron Paul, "US Intelligence Confirms US Support for ISIS." Aug. 10, 2015. (http://www.informationclearinghouse.info/article42590.htm); *American Free Press*, "Is 'IS' a CIA-Mossad Creation?" Aug. 28, 2014. (http://americanfreepress.net/is-is-a-cia-mossad-creation/); Bill Van Auken, "General Petraeus Calls For Recruiting Al Qaeda." Sept. 16, 2015. (http://www.informationclearinghouse.info/article42874.htm); Moon of Alabama, "UK Accuses U.S. Of Supporting Terrorists But Sells Out To Saudi Arabia." Nov. 11, 2015. (http://www.informationclearinghouse.info/article43383.htm); *Washington Post,* "Iraqis think the U.S. is in cahoots with the Islamic State, and it is hurting the war." Dec. 1, 2015. (https://www.washingtonpost.com/world/middle_east/iraqis-think-the-us-is-in-cahoots-with-isis-and-it-is-hurting-the-war/2015/12/01/d00968ec-9243-11e5-befa-99ceebcbb272_story.html).
169 Consortium News, "The Saudi Connection to Terror." Nov. 20, 2015. (https://consortiumnews.com/2015/11/20/the-saudi-connection-to-terror/); Fars News Agency, "Iraq Arrests ISIL's US, Israeli Military Advisors in Mosul." March 7, 2015. (http://www.informationclearinghouse.info/article41158.htm); *Wall Street*

Journal, "Al Qaeda a Lesser Evil? Syria War Pulls U.S., Israel Apart." March 12, 2015. (http://www.wsj.com/articles/al-qaeda-a-lesser-evil-syria-war-pulls-u-s-israel-apart-1426169708); F. William Engdahl, "Israeli Colonel Caught with IS Pants Down." Nov. 26, 2015. (http://www.informationclearinghouse.info/article43544.htm); Washington's Blog, "Israeli Military Admits to Supporting Al Qaeda and ISIS in Syria." July 24, 2015. (http://www.globalresearch.ca/israeli-military-admits-to-supporting-al-qaeda-and-isis-in-syria/5464484); Associated Press, "Russia: Turkish president benefits from IS oil trade." Dec. 2, 2015. (http://www.nytimes.com/aponline/2015/12/02/world/europe/ap-eu-russia-turkey.html?_r=0); Tony Cartalucci, "Why the West Won't Hit ISIS Where it Hurts." Nov. 27, 2015. (http://www.opednews.com/articles/Why-the-West-Won-t-Hit-ISI-by-Tony-Cartalucci-Isis_NATO_Syria_Turkey-151127-8.html).

170 Barry Kissin, "The Truth about the Anthrax Attacks and its Cover-Up." Nov. 15, 2009. (http://www.informationclearinghouse.info/article23969.htm).

171 Graeme MacQueen, *The 2001 Anthrax Deception: The Case for a Domestic Conspiracy* (2014: Clarity Press), pp. 70-71.

172 *New York Times*, "U.S. Germ Warfare Research Pushes Treaty Limits." Sept. 4, 2001. (http://query.nytimes.com/gst/fullpage.html?res=9E02E1D71639F937A3575AC0A9679C8B63).

173 *Washington Post*, "Justice Dept. takes on itself in probe of 2001 anthrax attacks," Jan. 27, 2012 (http://articles.washingtonpost.com/2012-01-27/politics/35441863_1_bruce-e-ivins-anthrax-killer-anthrax-attacks)

174 Frontline, "New Evidence Adds Doubt to FBI's Case Against Anthrax Suspect." Oct. 10, 2011. (http://www.pbs.org/wgbh/frontline/article/new-evidence-adds-doubt-to-fbis-case-against-anthrax-suspect/); Frontline, ProPublica and McClatchy Newspapers, "The Anthrax Files." Oct.11, 2011. (http://video.pbs.org/video/2151158114/).

175 Barry Kissin, "Lessons from Amerithrax." June 4, 2011. (http://www.fredericknewspost.com/archive/lessons-from-amerithrax/article_0470699f-1938-58e8-97a1-623d2e5168a6.html) citing McClatchy Newspapers, "FBI lab reports on anthrax attacks suggest another miscue." May 19, 2011. (http://www.mcclatchydc.com/news/crime/article24635011.html).

176 MacQueen, *op. cit.,* pp. 72-85 and 106-120.

177 Ibid., p. 166.

178 Reuters, "California Massacre Shooter may be linked to Islamic State." Dec. 4, 2015. In preparing these footnotes, I have discovered that both Reuters and the Associated Press somehow modify their articles within days everywhere on the internet such that there are no longer links to the original version. The title of this article was changed to "FBI investigating California massacre as 'act of terrorism'" and replaced the verbiage I quoted as follows: "One startling disclosure came from social media network Facebook, which confirmed that comments praising Islamic State were posted around the time of the mass shooting to a Facebook account established under an alias by Malik. However, it was uncertain whether the comments were posted by Malik herself or someone with access to her page. A Facebook Inc spokesman said the profile in question was removed by the company on Thursday for violating its community standards barring promotion or praise for 'acts of terror.' He declined to elaborate on the material. But CNN and other news media outlets reported that Malik's Facebook posts included a pledge of allegiance

to Islamic State leader Abu Bakr al-Baghdadi." Link to modified article: http://www.reuters.com/article/us-california-shooting-isis-idUSKBN0TN1SR20151205.

179 Associated Press, "FBI: Shooters had been radicalized for a while." Dec. 8, 2015. See note 14. The verbiage I quoted was replaced as follows: "Newly released emergency radio transmissions from the fast-moving tragedy show that police identified Farook as a suspect almost immediately, even though witnesses reported that the attackers wore black ski masks. An unidentified police officer put out Farook's name because Farook had left the luncheon 'out of the blue' 20 minutes before the shooting, 'seemed nervous,' and matched the description of one of the attackers, according to audio recordings posted by The Press-Enterprise newspaper of Riverside." Link to modified article: http://bigstory.ap.org/article/402f6a52de45480eba3ade0aa0d1d880/woman-deadly-california-rampage-became-fervently-devout.

180 Martin Luther King, Jr., "The World House." Chapter in *Where Do We Go From Here: Chaos or Community?* (1967: Beacon Press).

181 Ibid.

182 Ibid.

183 *Los Angeles Times*, "San Bernardino shooting: Dramatic video shows police storming Inland Regional Center." Dec. 2, 2015. (http://www.latimes.com/local/lanow/la-me-ln-san-bernardino-shooting-dramatic-video-shows-police-storming-inland-regional-center-20151202-story.html).

184 Bloomberg Business, "Hours Before the Terror Attacks, Paris Practiced for a Mass Shooting." Nov. 17, 2015. (http://www.bloomberg.com/news/articles/2015-11-17/hours-before-the-terror-attacks-paris-practiced-for-a-mass-shooting).

185 "'Real-World or Exercise': Did the U.S. Military Mistake the 9/11 Attacks for a Training Scenario?" March 22, 2012. (http://911blogger.com/news/2012-03-22/real-world-or-exercise-did-us-military-mistake-911-attacks-training-scenario).

186 Webster Tarpley, "The 46 Drills, Operations, War Games, And Activities Of 9/11." ((http://thetruthnews.info/drills.html).

187 Ibid.

188 Michel Chossudovsky, "Ten Years Ago: The London 7/7 Mock Terror Drill: What Relationship to the Real Time Terror Attacks?" Aug. 8, 2005. (http://www.globalresearch.ca/7-7-mock-terror-drill-what-relationship-to-the-real-time-terror-attacks/821)

189 Public Intelligence, "Norwegian Police Conducted Drill for 'Almost Identical' Scenario Minutes Before Utoya Massacre," Aug. 30, 2011 (https://publicintelligence.net/norwegian-police-conducted-drill-for-almost-identical-scenario-minutes-before-utoya-massacre/)

190 Christopher Bollyn, ""The Terror Drills That Became Real." June 17, 2011. (http://www.bollyn.com/the-terror-drills-that-became-real).

191 Jon Rappoport, "Training Exercises Dovetail with Mass Shootings. What are the Odds?" Dec. 3, 2015. (http://www.globalresearch.ca/training-exercises-dovetail-with-mass-shootings-what-are-the-odds/5493110).

192 David Talbot, *The Devil's Chessboard: Allen Dulles, the CIA, and the Rise of America's Secret Government* (HarperCollins 2015), pp. 15-116.

193 Ibid., pp. 230-231.

194 Ibid., p. 232

195 Ibid., pp. 232-233

196 Ibid., p. 234

197 Ibid., p. 235

198 Ibid., pp. 236-240

199 Ibid., p. 239

200 Ibid., pp. 238-239

201 Ibid., pp. 375-389

202 Ibid., pp. 484-604

203 "Press Conference to Declassify the 28 Pages of 9/11 Joint Inquiry Report, Jan. 7, 2015." (https://larouchepac.com/20150108/press-conference-28-pages-sen-bob-graham).

204 Ibid.

205 Ibid.

206 Sputnik News, "The Saudi Connection? Congressmen Demand to Declassify Secret 9/11 Report." Sept.1, 2015. (http://sputniknews.com/us/20150108/1013438376.html#ixzz3tgCVfBoZ).

207 TheRealNews, "Investigating the Saudi Government's 9/11 Connection and the Path to Disillusionment —Sen. Graham on Reality Asserts Itself pt 1." Nov. 27, 2013. (http://therealnews.com/t2/index.php? option=com_content&task=view&id=31&Itemid=74&jumival=11103).

208 Sputnik News, op. cit.

209 Press Conference to Declassify the 28 Pages of 9/11 Joint Inquiry Report, op. cit.

210 Craig Unger, *House of Bush, House of Saud: The Secret Relationship between the World's Two Most Powerful Dynasties* (2004: Scribner); Consortium News, "The Saudi Connection to Terror," op. cit.

211 See the website http://hr14.org for an overview of the pending legislation. The text of S. 1471 is at http://hr14.org/s-b-1471/ .

212 Brian McGlinchey, "Obama's Unkept Promise to 9/11 Families: Releasing the 28 Pages." Aug. 18, 2014. (http://28pages.org/2014/08/18/obamas-unkept-promise-to-911-families-declassifying-28-pages/).

213 "Jon Gold Interviews Senator Bob Graham on the 28 Pages and More," March 25, 2015. (http://28pages.org/2015/03/25/jon-gold-interviews-senator-bob-graham-on-the-28-pages-and-more/).

214 PBS Video, "Intelligent Intelligence." Aug. 8, 2015. (http://video.pbs.org/video/2365541408/).

215 BBC News, "Profile: Prince Bandar." June 7, 2007. (http://news.bbc.co.uk/2/hi/middle_east/4635383.stm).

216 Philip Marshall, *The Big Bamboozle* (2012), p. 17; Philip Shenon, *The Commission: The Uncensored History of the 9/11 Investigation* (2008: Hachette Book Group), pp. 51-58.

217 The entire documentary *Fahrenheit 911* can be viewed at https://www.youtube.com/watch?v=HYPvsczdXTM. The entire script of the documentary is available at http://www.script-o-rama.com/movie_scripts/f/fahrenheit-911-script-transcript.html; Paul Sperry, "Inside the Saudi 9/11 Coverup." Dec. 15, 2013. (http://nypost.com/2013/12/15/inside-the-saudi-911-coverup/).

218 Vanity Fair News, "The Kingdom and the Towers." July 31, 2011. (http://www.vanityfair.com/news/2011/08/9-11-2011-201108).

219 Philip Marshall, op. cit.; Seymour Hersh, "The Redirection: Is the Administration's new policy benefitting our enemies in the war on terrorism?," March 5, 2007 (http://www.newyorker.com/magazine/2007/03/05/the-redirection)

220 Ibid.

221 "Senator Daniel Inouye warned of Shadow Government" (https://bunkerville.wordpress.com/2012/12/24/senator-daniel-inouye-warned-of-

shadow-government/)

222 Christof Lehmann, "Top US and Saudi Officials responsible for Chemical Weapons in Syria." Oct. 7, 2013. (http://nsnbc.me/2013/10/07/top-us-and-saudi-officials-responsible-for-chemical-weapons-in-syria/); Seymour Hersh, "Whose Sarin?" Dec. 19, 2013. (http://www.lrb.co.uk/v35/n24/seymour-m-hersh/whose-sarin); Seymour Hersh, "The Red Line and the Rat Line." April 17, 2014. (http://www.lrb.co.uk/v36/n08/seymour-m-hersh/the-red-line-and-the-rat-line).

223 See, for example, Cynthia McKinney's discussion of the Deep State in *We Are Not Charlie Hebdo* (2015: Sifting and Winnowing Books), pp. 159-170.

224 See: Daniel Ganser, *NATO's Secret Armies* (Routledge, 2005); Richard Cottrell, *Gladio: NATO's Dagger in the Heart of Europe—The Pentagon-Nazi-Mafia Axis* (Progressive Press, 2012); Paul L. Williams, *Operation Gladio: The Unholy Alliance between the Vatican, the CIA, and the Mafia* (Prometheus Books, 2015); Kevin J. Barrett (Ed.): *We Are NOT Charlie Hebdo: Free Thinkers Question The French 9/11*, (Sifting and Winnowing Books, 2015).

225 Cottrell, op. Cit.

226 Juri Lina, *Architects of Deception* (Referent Publishing 2004). Juri Lina had access to the records of numerous Masonic Lodges in many countries. He has stated that all international banking families are Masonic. He has also pointed out there are now Rothschild Lodges as well.

227 Zbigniew Brzezinski, *The Grand Chessboard: American Primacy and its Geostrategic Imperatives (*Basic Books, 1997).

228 Peter Dale Scott, *Systemic Destabilsation in Recent American History: 9/11, the JFK Assassination, and the Oklahoma City Bombing as Strategy of Tension* (http://www.informationclearinghouse.info/article32552.htm, http://www.japanfocus.org/-Peter_Dale-Scott/3835/article.html)

229 Cottrell, op. Cit., p 121.

230 See Nafeez Ahmed, "Anti-ISIS coalition knowingly sponsored violent extremists to 'isolate' Assad, rollback 'Shia expansion'." May 22, 2015. (https://medium.com/insurge-intelligence/secret-pentagon-report-reveals-west-saw-isis-as-strategic-asset-b99ad7a29092#.6rxemh430); *Washington Blog*, "Newly-Declassified U.S. Government Documents: The West Supported the Creation of ISIS." May 24, 2015. (http://www.washingtonsblog.com/2015/05/newly-declassified-u-s-government-documents-the-west-supported-the-creation-of-isis.html); *Washington Blog*, "U.S. Fighting On the Same Side as Three Terrorist Groups In Syria." Feb. 25, 2012. (http://www.washingtonsblog.com/2012/02/u-s-fighting-on-the-same-side-as-three-terrorist-groups-in-syria.html). Seumas Milne, "Now the truth emerges: how the US fuelled the rise of Isis in Syria and Iraq." *The Guardian,* June 3, 2015. (http://www.theguardian.com/commentisfree/2015/jun/03/us-isis-syria-iraq).

231 , M. Chossudovsky, "Why is a Hate Campaign being Waged Against Muslims?" *Global Research*, December 10, 2015. (http://www.globalresearch.ca/why-is-a-hate-campaign-being-waged-against-muslims/5494852).

232 See: Lyric R. Cabral and Felix David Sutcliffe, "The FBI Isn't Catching Terrorists — It's Creating Them." *Creative Time Reports*, 26 January 2015. (http://creativetimereports.org/2015/01/26/fbi-counterterrorism-lyric-cabral-david-felix-sutcliffe-sundance/); Trevor Aarnson, "How the FBI Created a Terrorist." The Intercept, March 16, 2015. (https://theintercept.com/2015/03/16/howthefbicreatedaterrorist/); Paul Szoldra, "The FBI Goes To Disturbing Lengths To Set Up Potential Terrorists." *Business Insider*, March 11, 2013. (http://www.businessinsider.com/the-fbi-hatched-some-

crazy-terror-plots-2013-3).

233 See: Richard Norton-Taylor, "Terror trial collapses after fears of deep embarrassment to security services." *The Guardian*, June 1, 2015. (http://www.theguardian.com/uk-news/2015/jun/01/trial-swedish-man-accused-terrorism-offences-collapse-bherlin-gildo); Duncan Gardham and Richard Spillett, "Suspected terrorist stopped at Heathrow with a guide to jihad walks free after intelligence services 'refuse to hand over evidence'." *Daily Mail*, June 1, 2015. (http://www.dailymail.co.uk/news/article-3105884/Terror-suspect-Bherlin-Gildo-freed-intelligence-services-refuse-hand-evidence.html).

234 GPD, "French ISIL Leader Mossad Agent —Simon Elliot, aka Al-Baghdadi, son of Jewish Parents, Mossad Agent." Veterans Today, August 4, 2014. (http://www.veteranstoday.com/2014/08/04/french-report-isil-leader-mossad/).

235 Anthony Hall, "Witch Hunt on Terrorism." In *We Are NOT Charlie Hebdo*, Op. Cit, p 83.

236 Barbara Honegger, "A Tale of Two Cities: Disturbing Parallels Between The New York and Paris 9/11s." In *We Are NOT Charlie Hebdo*, Op. Cit, p 67.

237 Alain Soral, "The Empire Strikes Back." In *We Are NOT Charlie Hebdo*, Op. Cit, p 113–114.

238 Ibid, p 115.

239 Syrian Free Press, "Bombshell: Russian Military Reveals Details of ISI-Daesh Funding, Turkey's Role in Supporting the Terrorists, Complete Transcript, Video Documents." December 3, 2015. (http://www.globalresearch.ca/bombshell-russian-military-reveals-details-of-isis-daesh-funding-turkeys-role-in-supporting-the-terrorists-complete-transcript-videos-documents/5493043).

240 Ibid

241 Urlich Rippert, "German Parliament Votes for Military Intervention in Syria." December 5 2015. (https://www.wsws.org/en/articles/2015/12/05/germ-d05.html).

242 Robert Stevens, "UK stages bombing raid on Syria hours after Parliamentary vote." December 4, 2015. (https://www.wsws.org/en/articles/2015/12/04/uksy-d04.html).

243 Jean Shaoul, "Israel's covert involvement in Syria to escalate." December 3, 2015. (https://www.wsws.org/en/articles/2015/12/03/isra-d03.html).

244 *New York Times*, December 15, 2015. "Three Hours of Terror in Paris, Moment by Moment." (http://www.nytimes.com/interactive/2015/11/13/world/europe/paris-shooting-attacks.html?_r=0).

245 M. Chossudovsky, "Why is a Hate Campaign being Waged Against Muslims?" December 10, 2015. (http://www.globalresearch.ca/why-is-a-hate-campaign-being-waged-against-muslims/5494852).

246 Ibid

247 Laurent Guyenot, "Prequel to Charlie Hebdo: The March 2012 Mohamed Merah Affair (A Mossad-DCRI Co-Production)." In *We are NOT Charlie Hebdo*.

248 Tom Heneghan, "Hollande says Paris attacks 'an act of war' by Islamic State." Reuters, November 14, 2015. (http://www.reuters.com/article/us-france-shooting-hollande-idUSKCN0T30JG20151114).

249 Laurent Guyenot, op cit, p 100.

250 Christoph Germann, "Paris Attacks: Western Intelligence's Vision Blinded by Allah?" November 17, 2015. (http://www.boilingfrogspost.com/2015/11/17/bfp-exclusive-paris-attacks-western-intelligences-vision-blinded-by-allah/).

251 Stephen Lendman, "Blowback or False Flag in Paris?" (http://sjlendman.blogspot.com/2015/11/blowback-or-false-flag-in-paris.html).

252 Peter Dale Scott, *The American Deep State: Wall Street, Big Oil, And The Attack On U.S. Democracy* (Rowman and Littlehead, 2015). p 38.

253 Also published in John-Paul Leonard, Ed. *ISIS is US* (2016: Progressive Press).

254 https://www.youtube.com/watch?v=_vmSHXF-vX8

255 In addition to classic studies on 9/11, see especially James Fetzer and Preston James, "Peeling the 9/11 Onion: Layers of Plots within Plots" (originally published 14 October 2014) and "9/11: Who was responsible and why" with Dennis Cimino, "The Real Deal Show #103" (11 September 2015) accessible on-line by a search using their titles.

256 Wesley Clark, Commonwealth Club of California, San Francisco (October 3, 2007), "US will attack 7 countries in 5 years" (YouTube).

257 Many commentators have observed that Russian intervention has turned the Zionist scheme into a nightmare. A nice case is "Russia destroys the Greater Israel Dream," platosguns.com (October 19, 2015).

258 See, for example, Justin Raimondo, "Transparent Hoax could lead to War." antiwar.com (August 26, 2013). The chemical weapons are widely believed to have been provided to the "rebels" by Prince Bandar of Saudi Arabia, to whom the Bush family refers as "Bandar Bush."

259 That, of course, reflects that the billions upon billions in benefits to private contractors, such as Halliburton, has come out of the pockets of American taxpayers and into the pockets of "no bid" contractors, as part of the plan envisioned by Dick Cheney and The Carlyle Group.

260 "Iraqi Army Downs 2 UK Planes Carrying Weaons for ISIL,"FARS (February 23, 2015). The enormity of the deception was not yet clear.

261 " Terrorists Supported by America: U.S. Helicopter Delivering Weapons to the Islamic State (ISIS), Shot Down by Iraqi Popular Forces." FARS (March 1, 2015), but ignored by the American press.

262 "US, Britian, France, Jordan refuse to name ISIL as separate terror group." PressTV (April 10, 2015). The reason would soon become clear.

263 Search "ISIS members sporting 'US Army tattoos'" on YouTube.

264 The DIA report states, "THE WEST, GULF COUNTRIES, AND TURKEY [WHO] SUPPORT THE [SYRIAN] OPPOSITION . . . [SUPPORT] ESTABLISHING A DECLARED OR UNDECLARED SALAFITST PRINCIPALITY IN EASTERN SYRIA . . . IN ORDER TO ISOLATE THE SYRIAN REGIME . . ." Even Judicial Watch does not appear to have appreciated the importance of this document, where its press release focused on the Benghazi attack. See judicialwatch.org (May 18, 2015).

265 As Nafeez Ahmed observed in medium.com (22 May 2015), "The revelations contradict the official line of Western governments on their policies in Syria and raise disturbing questions about secret Western support for violent extremists abroad, while using the burgeoning threat of terror to justify excessive mass surveillance and crackdowns on civil liberties at home"—which the US PATRIOT ACT exemplifies.

266 "US created ISIL for sake of Israel: Ex-CIA Contractor," published by PressTV (June 23, 2015), by IRNA (June 23, 2015), and elsewhere.

267 "Staged ISIS beheading video hacked from McCain Staffer," VeteransToday.com (July 11, 2015), in a great journalistic scoop.

268 In New Eastern Outlook (12 July 2015), journal-neo.org reported, "Late last year, Germany's broadcaster Deutsche Welle (DW) investigated what turned out to be hundreds of trucks a day carrying billions of dollars in supplied, flowing across the Turkish border into Syria and directly into the hands of the so-called 'Islamic State' (ISIS)."

269 He observed, "McCain accused us to striking out at US-trained insurgents . . .

However, since they have either run away or joint al-Qaeda, hitting them is a mission impossible . . . The US-led coalition spent a whole year pretending they were striking ISIL targets, but where are the results?" investmentwatchblog.com (October 4, 2015).

270 As anonhq.com explains, Putin told reporters that he had shared Russian intelligence on Islamic State financing with G-20 colleagues: "I provided examples based on our data on the financing of different Islamic State units by private individuals. This money, as we have established, comes from 40 countries and there are some G-20 members among them. This topic [the war on terror] was crucial. Especially after the Paris tragedy, we all understand that the means of financing terrorism [including illegal trade in oil] should be severed."

271 Some of these stories are making it half-way into the mainstream press. Freedomoutpost.com, "Obama Regime Ordered US Military to Warn ISIS fuel truck drivers before bombing their trucks," that even FOX News has reported, "We dropped leaflets, warning the drivers to scatter. . . . Next we strafed the area [with 30mm cannons] before dropping bombs," which is a clear sign of guilt on the part of Obama.

272 "Meet the man who funds ISIS: Bilal Erdogan, the son of Turkey's President," zerohedge.com (November 26, 2015). The personal and financial benefits derived by Turkey, its leader and his son, are no doubt major contributing factors to why ISIS has succeeded to date.

273 An excellent discussion of "amendment" of the Smith-Mundt Act to nullify the provisions excluding the use of propaganda and disinformation within the US has just appeared under the title, "Why did they pass a law that makes staged hoaxes and crisis-acted movies legal?"(YouTube). It was published on November 24, 2015.

274 "Try as He May, John McCain Can't Shake Falsehoods About Ties to ISIS." *The New York Times*, September 11, 2014. For good reason.

275 See Peter Koenig, "Is Turkey Starting a Proxi-War for NATO?" veteransnewsnow.com, November 25, 2015.

276 Finian Cunningham, "Turkey Shoots Down More Than Just a Russian Jet." strategic-culture.org (November 25, 2015).

277 Tom Parfitt, "ISIS claims Paris attacks as REVENGE for Syria airstrikes and insulting Islam's Prophet." express.co.uk (November 15, 2015).

278 For a history of the descent of America into a terrorist state, see Timothy M. Silver, "Lifting the Veil: An Investigative History of the United States Pathocracy." November 26, 2016. (wantoknow.info).

279 Editor's note: Another interpretation is that in many cases, such as that of the alleged 9/11 hijackers who got drunk and left an alcohol-soaked Qur'an at a bar the night before the attack—then later turned up alive— the people blamed for "jihadist" attacks are innocent patsies who have little or nothing to do with the crimes of which they have been accused. The alleged suicide bombers at the Stade de France, some of whom appear not to have blown themselves up but to have been blown up by remote control, are another possible example. But regardless of how many of these counter-examples we may find or suspect, M. Soral's larger point is well-taken.

280 Abdul-Kareem, "European colonialists conspired to destroy the Khilafah state", Khilafah.com, March 2007. (http://www.khilafah.com/index.php/the-khilafah/issues/84-european-colonialists-conspired-to-destroy-the-khilafah-state).

281 Wikipedia, "Decline of Ottoman Empire", http://en.wikipedia.org/wiki/Decline_of_the_Ottoman_Empire

282 Mark Zepezauer, "Boomerang:How our covert wars have created enemies across

the Middle East and brought terror to America.", Common Courage Press (November 1, 2002) , P. 110 (excerpt given at http://www.thirdworldtraveler.com/Zepezauer_Mark/SaudiArabia_Boomerang.html

283 Hussam S. Taimani, *Modern Intellectual Readings of the Kharijites* (Peter Lang Publishing, New York) p. 62.

284 Ibid p. 65

285 Mohammad Abbas, "Good Governance in Islam", Oct. 2010. (http://www.cssforum.com.pk/off-topic-section/islam/49239-caliph-al-farooq-hazrat-umar-ibn-al-khattab-ra-35.html).

286 Aisha Bewley, *Mu'awiya: Restorer of the Muslim Faith* (Dar al Taqwa, 2002). p. 13-14.

287 Waren Treadgold, *A History of the Byzantine State and Society* (Stanford University Press, Oct 1, 1997) p. 314.

288 Nahj ul Balagah, Letter #54.

289 25,000 were killed in Ali's forces while 45,000 were killed from Muawiyah's forces. For further details see. Gibbon, Edward, *The History of the Decline and Fall of the Roman Empire* (NY: Fred de Fau and Co. Publishers, 1906). Ch. L, p. 98; p.116

290 For detailed study of Battle of Naharwan, visit http://playandlearn.org/reader.asp? Type=History&fn=107

291 McCarthy, Kevin M. , "The Origin of Assassin." In *American Speech (*Duke UP*)* Volume 48, pp. 77–83.

292 Access the online version of *The History of the Assassins* at http://books.google.com.pk/books? id=q1sOAAAAQAAJ&printsec=frontcover&source=gbs_ge_summary_r&cad=0#v =onepage&q&f=false

293 EurActiv, "EU Gives Go-Ahead To States Sending Arms To Iraqi Kurds." *Eurasian Review*, Aug. 14, 2014. (http://www.eurasiareview.com/14082014-eu-gives-go-ahead-states-sending-arms-iraqi-kurds/).

294 Helene Cooper, "Obama Requests Money to Train 'Appropriately Vetted' Syrian Rebels." *New York Times*, June 26, 2014. (http://www.nytimes.com/2014/06/27/world/middleeast/obama-seeks-500-million-to-train-and-equip-syrian-opposition.html).

295 Charles Allen, *God's Terrorists: The Wahhabi Cult and the Hidden Roots of Modern Jihad* (Da Capo Press, 2006).

296 Francis Fukuyama, *Political Order and Political Decay: From the Industrial Revolution to the Globalisation of Democracy* (NY: Farrar, Strauss and Giroux, 2014).

297 Voltaire, *Toleration and Other Essays by Voltaire*. Tr. Joseph McCabe (NY: G.P. Putnam's Sons, 1912). December 24, 2015. (http://oll.libertyfund.org/titles/349>).

298 Ibid.

299 Bernard-Henri Lévy, *Left in Dark Times: A Stand Against the New Barbarism* (NY: Random House, 2009).

300 Eric Randolph, "France looks to enshrine emergency anti-terror laws in constitution." AFP (Yahoo News). Dec. 23, 2015. (http://news.yahoo.com/french-cabinet-backs-state-emergency-reforms-115006079.html).

301 Jon Henley and Ian Traynor, "Movements of ISIS extremist prior to Paris attack raise EU security questions." *The Guardian*, Nov. 19, 2015. (http://www.theguardian.com/world/2015/nov/19/movements-of-isis-extremist-prior-to-paris-attack-raises-eu-security-questions).

302 Christiane Timmerman, ed., *Faith-Based Radicalism: Christianity, Islam, and*

Judaism Between Constructive Activism and Destructive Fanaticism (Peter Lang International Academic Publishers, 2007).

303 Tariq Ramadan, "The governance of religious diversity, more or less secularism?" Lecture at Conference EUI, Oct. 26, 2015. (http://tariqramadan.com/english/2015/09/15/conference-eui-the-governance-of-religious-diversity-more-or-less-secularism-10062015/).

304 Francis J. Beckwith, Gregory Koukl, *Relativism: Feet Firmly Planted in Mid-Air* (Grand Rapids, MI: Baker Books, 1998).

305 Tony Steve Juge, *Racism in France: The Civilizing Mission of Whiteness* (UC-Riverside, 2008).

306 Matthew Drake and Dan Warburton, "Paris attack witness says black Mercedes pulled up and shooters fired rifles from the hip." The *Mirror*. (http://www.mirror.co.uk/news/uk-news/paris-attack-witness-says-black-6834503).

307 http://nodisinfo.com/dead-people-france-concert-theater-dummies-not-real-humans/

308 "Media news grill Emergency Services guy over drills." (https://www.youtube.com/watch?v=AUb721gXB5s).

309 USA Today, "Many in Islamic world doubt Arabs behind 9/11." (http://usatoday30.usatoday.com/news/sept11/2002/02/27/usat-poll.htm). World Public Opinion, "Muslims Believe US Seeks to Undermine Islam": "On average less than one in four (Muslims worldwide) believes al Qaeda was responsible for September 11th attacks." (http://www.worldpublicopinion.org/pipa/articles/brmiddleeastnafricara/346.php).

310 American Association of Newspaper Editors, "Statement of Principles." (http://asne.org/content.asp?pl=24&sl=171&contentid=171).

311 *New York Times*: Guidelines on Our Integrity." May 9, 1999. (http://asne.org/content.asp?pl=236&sl=317&contentid=317). See also Byron Calame, "The Guidelines on Our Integrity' from 1999 Are Worth a Look." *New York Times*, May 4, 2007. (http://publiceditor.blogs.nytimes.com/2007/05/04/the-guidelines-on-our-integrity-from-1999-are-worth-a-look/?_r=0).

312 "BBC: Editorial Guidelines: Accuracy." (http://www.bbc.co.uk/editorialguidelines/guidelines/accuracy/gathering-material).

313 "The Essentials of Reuters Sourcing." (http://handbook.reuters.com/index.php?title=The_Essentials_of_Reuters_sourcing#When_to_source).

314 Society of Professional Journalists, "Code of Ethics." (http://www.spj.org/ethicscode.asp).

315 "The *Washington Post* Standards and Ethics." (Available at http://asne.org/content.asp?pl=236&sl=19&contentid=335).

316 "The Essentials of Reuters Sourcing."

317 Rebecca Riffkin, "Americans' Trust in Media Remains at Historical Low." Gallup, September 28, 2015. (http://www.gallup.com/poll/185927/americans-trust-media-remains-historical-low.aspx?g_source=trust%20in%20media&g_medium=search&g_campaign=tiles).

318 "Paris—Bataclan November 13: was exactly repeated the same scenario on Friday morning—Pierre Carli." (https://www.youtube.com/watch?v=ct31yOROcuE). See also Anne-Laure Barret, "The Head of the SAMU Doctor: 'We Ordered a Dress Rehearsal Friday Morning," Le Journal du Dimanche, November 15, 2015. (http://www.lejdd.fr/Societe/Le-medecin-chef-du-Samu-Nous-avions-organise-une-repetition-generale-vendredi-matin-759863).

319 Luke Harding and Kim Willsher, "'Surgery of war': Paris hospital doctors reflect on 12 hours of mayhem." UK *Guardian*, November 19, 2015.

320 Martin Hirsch, Pierre Carli, Remy Nizard, Bruno Riou, et al., "The medical response to multisite terrorist attacks in Paris." *The Lancet*, November 24, 2015. (http://www.thelancet.com/pb/assets/raw/Lancet/pdfs/S0140673615010636.pdf).

321 "Patrick Pelloux," wikipedia.org. (https://en.wikipedia.org/wiki/Patrick_Pelloux). Patrick Pelloux LinkedIn Profile.

322 Nahlah Ayed, "I'm a medical soldier,' Says Doctor Who Treated Victims at Two Paris Terror Attacks." Canadian Broadcasting Corporation, November 17, 2015. (http://www.cbc.ca/news/world/nahlah-ayed-patrick-pelloux-paris-doctor-1.3321691).

323 Angelique Chrisafis, "Paris medic: 'We were treating war wounds made by war weapons'; Patrick Pelloux describes the impact of treating those injured in both Friday's atrocity and the Charlie Hebdo attack." UK *Guardian*, November 15, 2015. (http://www.theguardian.com/world/2015/nov/15/paris-attacks-medic-we-were-treating-war-wounds-made-by-war-weapons).

324 James F. Tracy, "Paris Attacks: 'Impromptu' Bataclan Footage Product of Professionals." Memory Hole Blog, November 24, 2015. (http://memoryholeblog.com/2015/11/24/paris-attacks-impromptu-bataclan-footage-product-of-professionals/).

325 "Video of Attack on Paris Concert Hall," *New York Times/Le Monde*, November 14, 2015. (http://www.nytimes.com/video/world/europe/100000004037762/video-from-behind-bataclan-concert-hall.html).

326 "'Then They Started Firing': Eyewitness Accounts in Wake of Paris Attacks." CTV News, November 13, 2015. (http://www.ctvnews.ca/world/then-they-started-firing-eyewitness-accounts-in-wake-of-paris-attacks-1.2658081).

327 Henry Samuel and Patrick Sawer, "I Survived 9/11 and the Bataclan Massacre," *Telegraph*, November 21, 2015. (http://www.telegraph.co.uk/news/worldnews/europe/france/12009520/Paris-attacks-I-survived-911-and-the-Bataclan-massacre.html).

328 Michael Schwirtz, "Out For Fun on a Friday Night, Victims are Mostly Young.'" *New York Times*, November 14, 2015. (http://www.nytimes.com/2015/11/15/nyregion/music-critic-lawyer-and-us-student-are-among-victims-in-paris-attacks.html?_r=0).

329 Adam Nossiter, Aurelien Breeden and Katrin Bennhold, "Manhunt Underway as Investigation Widens." *New York Times*, International Edition, November 16, 2015.

330 Vivienne Walt, "A sister rushes to Paris after attacks only to find out: 'I just lost a part of myself.'" *Time*, November 14, 2015. (http://time.com/4113347/paris-terror-attacks-bataclan-victim/).

331 Delphine LaCroix de Paretti LinkedIn Profile, accessed December 8, 2015; Floris Muller, "The Rothschilds' pressing Charlie Hebdo: 'We doubted whether we should buy the newspaper,'" *Quote*, January 9, 2015.

332 Crispian Balmer, "Partying on a Friday, many Paris victims were bright young things." Reuters. November 15, 2015. (http://in.reuters.com/article/france-shooting-victims-idINKCN0T40VW20151115).

333 Caroline Pallut LinkedIn Profile; (http://www.groupe-vianova.com).

334 "'Terrified' New Yorker hid under table inside Paris restaurant under siege by gun-toting terrorists." *New York Daily News*, November 15, 2015. (http://www.nydailynews.com/news/world/terrified-new-yorker-hid-paris-restaurant-siege-article-1.2434963).

335 Erin Allweiss LinkedIn Profile, accessed December 8, 2015; Caitlin Moscatello, "How to Quit Your Job and Launch Your Own Business." *Glamour*, January 29, 2015. (http://www.glamour.com/inspired/blogs/the-conversation/2015/01/launch-

your-own-business).

336 Monique Hore, "If I move, I am dead." *Herald Sun*, November 16, 2015. (http://www.pressreader.com/australia/herald-sun/20151116/).

337 Michael Safi, "Australian Emma Grace Parkinson Has Surgery After Being Shot in Paris Attacks." *UK Guardian*, November 14, 2015. (http://www.theguardian.com/world/2015/nov/15/australian-emma-grace-parkinson-has-surgery-after-being-shot-in-paris-attacks).

338 Safi, "Australian Emma Grace Parkinson has surgery."

339 Samantha Gunner LinkedIn Profile, accessed November 30, 2015.

340 "Paris Attacks: Melbourne Woman Narrowly Escapes Injury by Hiding and 'Pretending to be Dead'." Australian Broadcasting Corporation, November 14, 2015. (http://www.abc.net.au/news/2015-11-15/melbourne-woman-narrowly-escapes-injury-in-paris-attacks/6941730). Hore, "'If I move, I am dead.'"

341 Sophie Doran, LinkedIn Profile, accessed December 2, 2015.

342 "Paris Attacks: There were bodies everywhere, it was a bloodbath,' eyewitness says." Reuters/Australian Broadcasting Corporation, November 14, 2015. (http://www.abc.net.au/news/2015-11-14/paris-attacks-eyewitness-accounts/6941054).

343 Sam Davies LinkedIn Profile, accessed November 24, 2015.

344 Adam Nossiter and Andrew Higgins, "'Scene of Carnage' Inside Sold-Out Paris Concert Hall." *New York Times*, November 13, 2015. (http://www.nytimes.com/2015/11/14/world/europe/paris-attacks.html?_r=0).

345 Wolf Blitzer, "Terror in Paris." CNN, November 13, 2015. (http://transcripts.cnn.com/TRANSCRIPTS/1511/13/sitroom.02.html).

346 Patrick J. McDonnell, "Rampage Spotlights Europe's Vulnerability: Preventing Such Violence in a Free Society is a Daunting Security Challenge, Experts Caution." *Los Angeles Times*, November 15, 2015. (http://www.latimes.com/world/la-fg-paris-attacks-analysis-20151115-story.html).

347 "Paris Attacks: 'There were bodies everywhere, it was a bloodbath,' eyewitness says." Australian Broadcasting Corporation, November 13, 2015. (http://www.abc.net.au/news/2015-11-14/paris-attacks-eyewitness-accounts/6941054).

348 Webster Griffin Tarpley, *9/11 Synthetic Terror*, 5th Edition (Joshua Tree CA: Progressive Press, 2011).

349 Nicholas Kollerstrom, *Terror on the Tube*, Third Edition (Joshua Tree CA: Progressive Press, 2011).

350 Ole Dammegard: "The same 'traveling terror troupe' did Paris, San Bernardino, and other false flags." Truth Jihad Radio, Dec. 30, 2015. (http://noliesradio.org/archives/108369).

351 *Mirror*, "Paris attacks: Eagles Of Death Metal fans pictured beaming with joy moments before they were slaughtered by ISIS." Nov. 17, 2015. (http://www.mirror.co.uk/news/world-news/paris-attacks-eagles-death-metal-6842542).

352 "Eagles of Death Metal Were Vocally Anti-BDS; Concert Hall Probably Targeted Due to Jewish Owners, Pro-Israel Stance." (http://mahoundsparadise.blogspot.com/2015/11/band-playing-at-time-of-attack-was.html).

353 "Was 9/11 a ritual human sacrifice? Tom Breidenbach joins TJ radio." April 29, 2011. (http://noliesradio.org/archives/73852).

354 Dr. J. Landowsky, Tr. George Knupffer, *Red Symphony*. (Palmdale, CA: Christian Book Club of America, 1968, 2002). (http://mailstar.net/red-symphony.html).

355 For a detailed refutation of the claim that the Protocols are a plagiarized forgery, see Henry Makow, "Makow – Protocols Forgery Argument Is Flawed." (http://www.rense.com/general45/protodd.htm).

356 Matthew Drake and Dan Warburton, "Paris Attack Witness Says Black Mercedes Pulled Up and Shooters Fired Rifles from the Hip." *The Mirror.* (http://www.mirror.co.uk/news/uk-news/paris-attack-witness-says-black-6834503).

357 Gilad Atzmon and Kevin Barrett discuss this article at "Gilad Atzmon reflects on the false flag paradigm shift." Truth Jihad Radio, Jan. 6, 2016. (http://noliesradio.org/archives/108551).

358 Gilad Atzmon, "Amidst A Religious War in Europe Or Is It Just another False Flag Operation?" (http://www.gilad.co.uk/writings/2015/1/8/amidst-a-religious-war-in-europe-is-it-possibly-a-false-flag-operation).

359 "Syrian Passports Planted by Police At Scene of Paris Terror Attack Are Confirmed Fakes." (http://countercurrentnews.com/2015/11/syrian-passports-planted-police-at-paris-scene-confirmed-fakes/).

360 "Goyim were born only to serve us. Without that, they have no place in the world — only to serve the People of Israel." "Why are gentiles needed? They will work, they will plow, they will reap. We will sit like an effendi and eat... That is why gentiles were created." – Rabbi Ovadia Yosef Weekly Saturday night sermon, October 2010.

361 It didn't defeat the German patriotic spirit in Hamburg (1943), it didn't suppress Islamic resistance in Fallujah (2003), it didn't subdue Hamas's popularity in Gaza (2008) and, there is no reason to believe that it will achieve any military objective in Raqqa (2015).

362 http://www.dailyrecord.co.uk/news/scottish-news/im-back-ill-kill-brit-4155292

363 The US statistic is based on (40% approving the official version + 38% "some doubts"). According to a YouGov poll in 2013, 40% believe the official explanation, 38% have some doubts, 12% are unsure, and 10% do not believe it at all. In yet another poll, 11% of Americans believe it was actually the US government. See
http://www.worldpublicopinion.org/pipa/articles/brmiddleeastnafricara/346.php
http:// www.worldpublicopinion.org/pipa/articles/international_security_ bt/535.php
http://publicpolicypolling.com
For all muslims, belief in the official version on 9/11 varied from 3% in Pakistan and 11% in Jordan, to 35% in Morocco, 43% among Palestinians, and up to 71% in Nigeria (only 40% Muslim). I can't know from such polls, which are at best dubious, what the overall statistic is.

364 The most politic application of this principle was by Copernicus, who points out in his prefece to De revolutionibus orbium coelestium that the motions of the sun, moon and other solar system planets can be calculated using a geocentric model (the earth is at the center) or using a heliocentric model (the sun is at the center). Both work, but the geocentric system requires many more assumptions than the heliocentric system, which has only seven.

365 For buying out his bankrupt oil company back in 1984.

366 http://www.usnews.com/news/special-reports/the-worst-presidents/articles/2014/12/31/worst-presidents-george-w-bush-2001-2009

367 James Tracy, "CIA Document 1035-960: Foundation of a Weaponized Term." (http://memoryholeblog.com/2013/01/20/cia-document-1035-960-foundation-of-a-weaponized-term/).

368 Former US intelligence sources have told Veterans Today that the *Guardian* is "the left-wing voice of MI-6."

369 David Shariatmadari, "The truth is rushing out there: why conspiracy theories spread faster than ever." *The Guardian*, Dec. 26, 2015. (http://www.theguardian.com/world/2015/dec/26/the-truth-is-rushing-out-there-why-conspiracies-spread-faster-than-ever).

370 André Vltchek and Noam Chomsky cite the figure of 55 to 60 million people killed by US CIA and military interventions since World War II in *On Western Terrorism: From Hiroshima to Drone Warfare* (London: Pluto, 2013). JFK was moving to end all such interventions and engage in talks with Khrushchev leading to complete planetary disarmament, as documented by James Douglass in *JFK and the Unspeakable: Why He Died and Why It Matters* (Maryknoll, NY: Orbis, 2008).

371 http://rense.com/general74/cchom.htm

372 Kevin Barrett, "Guilty demeanor: The private 9/11 emails of Noam Chomsky." Veterans Today, Nov. 5, 2013. (http://www.veteranstoday.com/2013/11/05/chomsky-emails/).

373 Fran Shure, "Why Do Good People Become Silent—or Worse—About 9/11?" (http://www.ae911truth.org/news/211-news-media-events-fran-shure-part-15.html).

374 World Public Opinion, "Muslims Believe US Seeks to Undermine Islam." (http://www.worldpublicopinion.org/pipa/articles/brmiddleeastnafricara/346.php).

16733181R00186

Printed in Great Britain
by Amazon